Medicine, Health Care, & Ethics

CATHOLIC VOICES

EDITED BY John F. Morris

The Catholic University of America Press
Washington, D.C.

LIBRARY OF CONGRESS CATALOGING-IN-PUBLICATION DATA
Medicine, health care, and ethics : Catholic voices / edited by John F.
    Morris. — 1st ed.
        p. cm.
    Includes bibliographical references and index.
    ISBN-13: 978-0-8132-1483-2 (pbk. : alk. paper)
    ISBN-10: 0-8132-1483-1 (pbk. : alk. paper)
        1. Medical ethics—Religious aspects—Catholic Church.   2. Medicine
—Religious aspects—Catholic Church.   3. Christian ethics—Catholic
authors.   I. Morris, John F., 1967–   .
        [DNLM: 1. Ethics, Medical.   2. Catholicism.   3. Religion and Medicine.
4. Genetics, Medical—ethics.   5. Reproductive Medicine—ethics.
6. Health Care Reform—ethics.   W 50 M48983 2007]
    R725.56.M443 2007
        241′642—dc22   2006015189

For Carol

Contents

Acknowledgments   ix

Preface: Raising Our Voices   xiii

PART I. Why "Catholic" Health Care Ethics?   1

1. Wounded Humanity and Catholic Health Care   15
   JOHN KAVANAUGH, S.J.

2. What Counts as Respect?   28
   GREGORY R. BEABOUT

   SELECTED BIBLIOGRAPHY ON
   CATHOLIC BIOETHICS   43

PART II. Human Reproduction   45

3. New Reproductive Technologies and
   Catholic Teaching   59
   WILLIAM E. MAY

4. Contraception: Did *Humane Vitae* Contradict Itself?   89
   BENEDICT ASHLEY, O.P.

5. Abortion: A Catholic Moral Analysis   107
   JEANNE HEFFERNAN SCHINDLER

   SELECTED BIBLIOGRAPHY ON
   HUMAN REPRODUCTION   125

PART III. **Death and Dying**   127

6. Medically Assisted Nutrition and Hydration in
   Medicine and Moral Theology   143
   JOHN BERKMAN

7. Two Arguments against Euthanasia   173
   BRENDAN SWEETMAN

   SELECTED BIBLIOGRAPHY ON DEATH AND DYING   193

PART IV. **Genetics, Stem Cell Research, and Cloning**   195

8. Genetics and Ethics: Questions Raised by the
   Human Genome Project   211
   KEVIN D. O'ROURKE, O.P.

9. Genetic Enhancement as Freedom of Choice: The Myth   222
   CATHERINE GREEN

10. Stem Cells, Cloning, and the Human Person   252
    JOHN F. MORRIS

    SELECTED BIBLIOGRAPHY ON GENETICS, STEM CELLS,
    AND CLONING   299

PART V. **Health Care Reform**   301

11. Health Care Reform: Justice and the Common Good   309
    CLARKE E. COCHRAN

12. Health Care Reform and the "Consistent Ethic"   334
    MICHAEL D. PLACE

    SELECTED BIBLIOGRAPHY ON HEALTH CARE REFORM   349

General Bibliography   351

Contributors   357

Index   359

Acknowledgments

This book has been more than four years in the making, and I owe a great debt of thanks to the many people who helped me finally get it into your hands—without their support and encouragement I am not sure I could have seen this project through.

I would like to begin by thanking all of the people who sat with me for the six years that I was an ethicist on the Ethics and Human Values Committee for St. Joseph Health Center in Kansas City, Missouri. Not only did they take me as a fresh doctoral graduate and shower me with their wisdom and experience—but they also gave me the original impetus for this book. Special thanks go to my fellow committee member Paul Sokoloff, whose thoughtful questions and keen interest in understanding the thinking behind the moral and ethical teachings of the Catholic Church on medical issues brought me to see the value of a text that would present the wisdom of the Church's teaching in bioethics in a scholarly but accessible manner.

I am also deeply grateful to all of my many friends in the American Maritain Association who listened to my ideas for the book and who gave me much helpful advice. Their encouragement in the early stages gave me the confidence to take on this project—and their ongoing support has been appreciated.

I would also like to thank my fellow faculty members at Rockhurst University in Kansas City, Missouri. Rockhurst has the advantage of being a small, close-knit community, and I am thankful for the support that everyone has constantly provided. I especially want to thank Dr. Shelly Chabon of our Communication Sciences and Disorders program, with whom I have had the privilege to teach a course in ethics for the past several summers and collaborate on two articles on professional ethics. Any time I stopped by, Dr. Chabon would welcome me into her office and listen to my latest story involving the book—whether it was about a setback or a success—and would send me on my way with an encouraging word. Shelly's support and friendship was—and continues to be—deeply appreciated. I am also grateful to the financial assistance that the university formally provided me through a Presidential Grant that I received at the outset of the project, as well as release time to work on putting the book together in its later stages.

I am also very blessed to be part of what I would argue is one of the best academic departments anywhere in the country. My colleagues in the Department of Philosophy here at Rockhurst University are simply outstanding—both as scholars and as friends. Dr. Curtis Hancock was probably the first "fan" of this whole project, and helped me see that this was indeed a book that was needed and that could make a difference. His advice was always right on. Dr. Brendan Sweetman has also been a tremendous support throughout my work on the book. Not only was he gracious enough to write one of the chapters, but he shared with me what he had learned from his own experience in getting books published, which helped guide me much more smoothly through the process than if I had been going it alone. Curtis and Brendan were also the ones who encouraged me to send the book to the Catholic University of America Press—which, of course, was a truly excellent idea! I also want to thank Dr. Catherine Green, who wrote a chapter for the book, and who has been one of my biggest cheerleaders. Dr. Green came to philosophy after many years of working in health care as a nurse—she has enriched my own understanding of medical ethics through our many conversations, and provided many helpful ideas throughout the development of the book. I would also like to thank Fr. Wilfred LaCroix, S.J., Dr. Robert Vigliotti, and Dr. Teresa Reed for their many conversations—where would a philosopher be without interlocutors? I am also indebted to Fr. LaCroix's family; they have provided ongoing funds for scholarly work in the Philosophy Department here at Rockhurst University, which helped support part of my work on the book. And many thanks go out to Katie Hollenberg, our departmental work-study assistant for several years, who was invaluable in formatting the author's submissions for the book and in putting together its numerous bibliographies.

In helping to draw this project to a close, I am indebted to Gregory F. La-Nave, Ph.D., acquisitions editor at the Catholic University of America Press. Dr. LaNave was with me through the whole process—his patient efforts and support for the book were appreciated more than I can say. Thanks as well to the reviewers of the manuscript—their constructive comments and careful attention has definitely made this a far better book than it was when I sent in the first draft. I also want to thank the rest of the staff at CUA Press for their assistance in the final preparation of this volume.

Finally, I want to thank my sons, Michael and Kevin, for their love and support as their Dad does his "philosophy stuff." They have come to share my love of *Star Wars* and *Superheroes,* which helps to keep me grounded day to day in what really matters—love, truth, and goodness! And, of course, my biggest thanks go to my greatest support in life—my wife, Carol, to whom I have dedicated this book. Imagine the patience it takes to be married to a philosopher—I am truly blessed!

Preface: Raising Our Voices

I have been teaching medical ethics at Rockhurst University, and at Saint Louis University before that, for several years now. I have also served as an ethicist on the Ethics and Human Values Committee for St. Joseph Health Center in Kansas City, Missouri, for two consecutive three-year terms (1996–2002). In addition, I served two consecutive three-year terms as a public member of the American Occupational Therapy Association's Commission on Standards and Ethics (1998–2004). From my diverse experiences with both teaching and participating in discussions related to medical ethics, I have observed the need for texts that represent and explain the unique perspective of the Catholic tradition.

Of course, there is no shortage of textbooks in bioethics on the current market—I continue to receive new ones every semester for examination. The problem I have found with most bioethics textbooks is that they do not adequately represent the Catholic view in their anthologies—if it is represented at all. To be sure, some "classic" pieces continue to be anthologized. But a text that offers one or two essays from the Catholic perspective written in the 1970s set against essays from differing perspectives written in the late 1990s or early 2000s gives the impression that Catholic scholarship has nothing new to offer contemporary debates. I believe that this is the intent of some publishers, and yet that impression is simply not true. There are some very fine articles and essays being written by Catholic scholars at all levels. However, even though these can be found in specialized journals and on the Internet, they are not appearing in many textbooks.

The objective of my book is to correct this misimpression, and offer a collection of new essays to represent the Catholic perspective in today's pluralistic debates on bioethics.

My personal approach as a philosopher stresses applied philosophy. This is what drew me specifically to medical ethics—my belief that the theoretical aspects of philosophy offer concrete, practical guidance to society. I find this especially true in areas such as bioethics, which is evolving at a rapid pace with our developing technology. I emphasize the practical dimension of philosophy in all of my classes, from the obvious practical value of an ethical theory course, to the less obvious but valid applications one can draw from courses such as medieval philosophy. When I began to realize that in the majority of new textbooks being written in medical ethics the Catholic perspective was often missing or skewed, I saw a clear need for this book—one which draws on the theoretical background of Catholicism in an effort to solve practical problems in health care.

In this light, I believe this text offers a twofold benefit. First, it will provide an excellent supplemental text to any course in medical and health care ethics. I believe the text will have special appeal to faculty teaching such courses at Catholic institutions—although it would work well for any course attempting to take a genuinely pluralistic approach to bioethics. Further, the scope of this text is also broad enough to appeal to professors as a text for more general applied ethics courses.

The second benefit of this text will be for members of hospital ethics committees, and for anyone working in health care who deals with Catholic and Christian hospitals or health care networks. At St. Joseph Health Center, we had non-Christian members on the ethics committee who would come to me and ask where they could find books that might help explain the rationale behind many of the hospital's decisions. As a committee we would, of course, use the *Ethical and Religious Directives for Catholic Health Care Services* developed by the American bishops, but if you read these you will become aware that the directives are primarily a collection of statements— with very little by way of explanation. Once again, I could have copied sections of the *Catechism of the Catholic Church,* or gathered several articles off the Internet for my fellow committee members who approached me—but there really was no book that I could offer as a way to begin to understand the "scholarly view" of Catholicism and health care for them. These members of my committee led me to believe that such a text would be of great value for them, as they continue to make their living working within the Catholic health care system. I should add that this would also be true for Catholics and Christians who work within religious health care networks, who may not have time to keep up on contemporary bioethical debates, yet who still desire such knowledge.

The first, "introductory" part of the book focuses on the general approach of the Catholic tradition—especially the dignity of the human person and the fundamental role this plays in Catholic thought. The remainder of the text is organized around key topics of debate in contemporary medicine and health care: reproductive issues (abortion, contraception); death and dying (medically assisted nutrition and hydration, euthanasia); genetics and stem cells (human genome project, embryonic and adult stem cell research, cloning); and health care reform (focus on mission, care of the poor). Each part begins with an introduction that provides an overview of the Catholic perspective regarding the specific topic at hand. There are also selected bibliographies following each part of the book.

As noted earlier, part of my goal was to collect "contemporary" essays. Readers should note that all but four of the essays in this volume were written just for this text. The three essays by Kavanaugh, O'Rourke, and Place were originally published in *Health Progress*, the publication of the Catholic Health Association of the United States. The essay by John Berkman came from *The Thomist*. However, all of these essays are still relatively "new"— none older than 2000. The authors were told that they were free to draw upon the Catholic tradition openly, through textual references, personal views, etc.—but explicit references to the tradition or teachings of the Catholic Church were not required. Readers should also note that in selecting prospective authors for the volume, I purposely cut across disciplines and professions to collect a sampling of the very best scholars working within the Catholic tradition today. Some authors are names that will be easily recognized, while others are relatively new. But each offers a fresh perspective and a wealth of knowledge that will bring both greater understanding and deeper appreciation for the topics being addressed.

In today's culture of *pluralism* and *diversity*, we have both a *right* and a *duty* to present the Catholic perspective. I further believe that the Catholic tradition has much wisdom to contribute to our consideration of contemporary problems in medicine and health care. This collection of essays is offered in the spirit of open and honest dialogue for all those who are interested in seeking Truth.

PART I

Why "Catholic" Health Care Ethics?

F ROM ITS EARLIEST BEGINNINGS, the Catholic Church has
ministered to the sick and dying of the world. The Catholic involvement in health care is considered an important extension of the healing ministry of Jesus, to which all Christians are called. As the late John
Paul II explained in 1985 when he established the Pontifical Commission for
the Apostolate of Health Care Workers:

The deep interest which the Church has always demonstrated for the world of the suffering is well known. In this for that matter, she has done nothing more than follow
the very eloquent example of her Founder and Master. . . . In fact, over the course of
the centuries the Church has felt strongly that service to the sick and suffering is an
integral part of her mission, and not only has she encouraged among Christians the
blossoming of various works of mercy, but she has also established many religious
institutions within her with the specific aim to fostering, organizing, improving and
increasing help to the sick.[1]

The American bishops offered a nice overview of the Catholic mission in
health care in the General Introduction to the most recent edition of their
Ethical and Religious Directives for Catholic Health Care Services when they
wrote:

The Church has always sought to embody our Savior's concern for the sick. The gospel
accounts of Jesus' ministry draw special attention to his acts of healing: he cleansed
a man with leprosy (Mt 8:1–4; Mk 1:40–42); he gave sight to two people who were
blind (Mt 20:29–34; Mk 10:46–52); he enabled one who was mute to speak (Lk 11:14);
he cured a woman who was hemorrhaging (Mt 9:20–22; Mk 5:25–34); and he brought
a young girl back to life (Mt 9:18, 23–25; Mk 5:35–42). Indeed, the Gospels are replete

with examples of how the Lord cured every kind of ailment and disease (Mt 9:35). In the account of Matthew, Jesus' mission fulfilled the prophecy of Isaiah: "He took away our infirmities and bore our diseases" (Mt 8:17; cf. Is 53:4).

Jesus' healing mission went further than caring only for physical affliction. He touched people at the deepest level of their existence; he sought their physical, mental, and spiritual healing (Jn 6:35, 11:25–27). He "came so that they might have life and have it more abundantly" (Jn 10:10).

The mystery of Christ casts light on every facet of Catholic health care: to see Christian love as the animating principle of health care; to see healing and compassion as a continuation of Christ's mission; to see suffering as a participation in the redemptive power of Christ's passion, death, and resurrection; and to see death, transformed by the resurrection, as an opportunity for a final act of communion with Christ.[2]

Even today, as many hospitals and clinics close due to financial losses, or form bold, new partnerships in order to compete in today's health care market, the Catholic presence in health care remains strong. As a natural consequence, Catholic scholars have regularly addressed moral issues relating to health care, long before the term "bioethics" was coined. Certainly, the roots of a Catholic approach to bioethics can be found in the work of St. Thomas Aquinas in the thirteenth century. One could also point to the influential Spanish Dominican Francisco de Vitoria, who in the 1500s developed the work of Aquinas in regard to withholding and withdrawing medical treatment, and began to lay out the distinction between ordinary and extraordinary means of prolonging human life. Today this work is carried on in the United States by the American bishops, by groups such as the Catholic Health Association and the National Catholic Bioethics Center, as well as by ethics committees in local Catholic hospitals and Catholic women and men across the country.

However, under the current influences of secular humanism, fueled in part by the political notion of the "separation of Church and State," the views and arguments of Catholics appear less and less welcome in public discussions of health care ethics. Some question whether a specifically "Catholic" approach to health care ethics is legitimate. The larger concern here extends to anyone who follows a specific religious tradition. Certainly American society actively promotes religious tolerance, viewing religion as a personal and private choice. But does a religious person have a place in public discourse in this country, or must a person of faith live with a separated psyche—private religious beliefs and secularized public ideas?

At a time when America is recognizing the need to empower the disadvantaged in society, and to provide more open and public forums that recognize America's diversity, the religious voice is becoming marginalized in those very same forums. To be fair, the religious person is always "officially" welcome in the public forum as a "citizen"—no one is overtly denied the opportunity to voice opinions. But the unfortunate trend today is that the arguments of religious persons are often dismissed in the public arena and glossed over by the mainstream media *simply because they come from religious people!* Little attention is paid to whether the arguments themselves are based upon purely religious tenets, or on valid reasoning that happens to concur with a person's religious beliefs. Part of the problem here is that the difference between a "religious argument" and "an argument from a religious person" is being blurred. Because of this, religious voices are being neutralized within public discussions of health care and bioethics, as well as in other public policy debates in our society.

As an illustration, I can point to two specific examples within health care ethics that reflect this "marginalization" of the religious voice. First, consider the remarks of Justice Stevens in his dissenting opinion in *Webster v. Reproductive Health Services* (1989), one of the key pro-life legal victories following *Roe v. Wade* in 1973. The Supreme Court was considering the constitutionality of a Missouri law that would restrict access to abortion. In part, however, attention was drawn to this case because a preamble had been affixed to the law stating: "[that] life begins at conception and that unborn children have protectable interest in life, health, and well-being."[3] Note Justice Stevens' specific comments regarding this statement:

... the preamble, an unequivocal endorsement of a religious tenet of some but by no means all Christian faiths, serves no identifiable secular purpose. That fact alone compels a conclusion that the statute violates the Establishment Clause. ... Bolstering my conclusion that the preamble violates the First Amendment is the fact that the intensely divisive character of much of the national debate over the abortion issue reflects the deeply held religious convictions of many participants in the debate. The Missouri Legislature may not inject its endorsement of a particular religious tradition into this debate, for "[t]he Establishment Clause does not allow public bodies to foment such disagreement."[4]

Justice Stevens' argument that the preamble is "an unequivocal endorsement of a religious tenet" is curious, given that in the actual bill that was signed into law by the governor of Missouri in 1986, no specific religious arguments were included. That is, the statement in the preamble to which Justice Stevens reacts was never offered as a religious argument per se—but rather as a rational conclusion supported through empirical science. The suggestion that this statement was "religious" came from supporters for Reproductive Health Services. Obviously agreeing with these suggestions, Justice Stevens does not even consider the claim as a point worthy of consideration on its own merits. Regardless of the fact that numerous people would accept the statement that "life begins at conception" on purely scientific grounds, the idea of "life at conception" is being marginalized from the public discourse on abortion for its supposed "religious" connotations.

A second example can be found in the arguments of Timothy E. Quill, M.D., one of the leading supporters of physician-assisted suicide. In particular, Dr. Quill has argued against the principle of double effect, which is often employed in arguments against his view that assisted suicide is morally permissible. Double effect helps to explain why allowing a person to die under certain circumstances (i.e., when treatment is medically futile or there is the presence of a grave burden for a patient) may be permissible, when the intention is not to kill the person, but rather to act for some other important good. At the same time, double effect clearly shows that assisted suicide is impermissible, because the actual "assistance" here requires that one intend to kill the patient. Now, Quill has objected to this Principle at many levels in his written work in support of physician-assisted suicide. But in a 1997 "Sounding Board" article in the *New England Journal of Medicine,* note the first reason Quill offers for rejecting the principle of double effect:

The rule of double effect has many shortcomings as an ethical guide for either clinical practice or public policy. First, the rule originated in the context of a particular religious tradition. American society incorporates multiple religious, ethical, and professional traditions, so medicine must accommodate various approaches to assessing the morality of end-of-life practices.[5]

Although Dr. Quill presents other arguments in his article, what is striking is that his very *first* claim against double effect is that it comes from a "particular religious tradition," which he notes earlier as the Roman Catholic tradition. However, in current applications of double effect no religious or theological arguments are asserted in its defense by those who employ the principle. It is offered as a reasonable guideline in its own right. Yet, Dr. Quill and others would marginalize its application because of its "religious" association.

Many other examples could be offered in further support of the marginalization of the religious voice in public debates on issues in bioethics. Even the very identity of religious health care facilities as "religious" and "denominational" is coming under fire in the public arena. There is increased government and public pressure on religious medical facilities to perform treatments that secular society deems necessary and important, yet which conflict with these hospitals' religious missions. When the conflicts are pointed out to the media, the religious objections are generally viewed unfavorably and are cast as attempts to "force" religious views upon others. Religious hospitals and health care facilities are charged with being unresponsive to the needs of the community, and—what seems worse to many in the public forum—intolerant of others. This has been increasingly noticeable in recent years regarding reproductive rights and women's health issues, HIV and AIDS, and issues related to the so-called "right to die." The reasons for not providing certain treatments, drugs, and services are characterized as "Catholic reasons"—not just "reasons." How can Catholic health care institutions and other faith-based medical facilities respond if the "religious" voice is marginalized in the public debate of these important health care issues?

The first line of response to this marginalization of the religious voice is grounded in justice. The presence and participation of religious believers in public discourse must be allowed in the name of justice. Easy catchphrases such as "separation of Church and State" are still too vague to provide much concrete guidance, as the continued debate over the meaning and implications of the Establishment Clause illustrates. To clarify this point, I would argue that there is a distinction between the *political* arena of public policy making and what I take to be the much broader realm of *public* debate and discourse. My contention is that contemporary *political* debate has been setting the tone for *public* discourse—but the two are not co-equal. What may not be appropriate for the State to do is not necessarily inappropriate for society—especially a society that claims to be genuinely pluralistic and diverse. Thus, to achieve justice at the *political* level of public policy making, where specific religious, theological, or scriptural arguments would not seem appropriate, there must be a correlating openness to a plurality of views at the broader *public* level, within the norms of civil discourse. We can achieve the common good only when all parties are allowed a meaningful presence at the discussion table. This in no way implies that we have to meet all the interests that come forth in our society—*political* policies will have to "discriminate" in some sense. But to achieve fairness in a pluralistic society, the *pub-*

lic forum needs to be genuinely open. To marginalize people of traditional religious backgrounds is a violation of justice. And so, recognizing the limitations of our *political* system regarding "official" endorsements of religion does not mean that we must accept the marginalization of the religious voice *and* the religious person that is occurring in contemporary *public* discourse.

The same concerns were reflected in an article written by Drs. Sulmasy and Pellegrino in response to Quill's arguments against double effect, which I referred to in my earlier illustration. In their rebuttal essay, titled "The Rule of Double Effect: Clearing Up the Double Talk," these authors address the claim that the religious association of double effect is a hindrance to its effectiveness as an ethical principle:

> The religious origins of a moral principle or rule should not preclude its discussion in civil society. Nor should the congruence between a moral argument's conclusions and the teachings of a religion undermine the validity of the argument. An exhortation to exclude such rules and principles in the name of tolerance seems itself highly intolerant.[6]

As noted before, whereas the principle of double effect was developed by religious people, no specific theological or scriptural arguments are asserted in its defense.[7] However, in addition to arguing that double effect needs to be considered on its own merits, the authors go further and call Quill to task for this inappropriate attack:

> To raise the question of the origins of the rule as a reason to discredit it is a form of the logical fallacy of the ad hominem argument—to claim to discredit an argument because of who states it. . . . The argument that it should be rejected out of hand simply because it originated with a particular religious tradition is completely unwarranted.[8]

I believe that we must continue to challenge such ad hominem attacks raised against the arguments of religious persons, and call for serious consideration and discussion in their place. This is the only way we can hope to reach Truth. Whatever *political* concerns our country may have regarding religion and public policy decisions, I do not believe there is a corresponding need for such a strong secularization of ideas in *public* discourse. Our country has come such a long way in recognizing the dangers and injustices of exclusion, with women and minorities for example, that it seems a shame to forget what has been learned. The marginalization of ideas that come from religious persons, without regard for the merit or truth of those ideas, is a tendency that must be reversed.

But the question still remains, Why insist on a specifically "Catholic" approach to health care ethics? Is there really a need to make such an explicit identification? Would it not be more effective to voluntarily secularize the "Catholic" approach so that the ideas would be more acceptable? I find this line of thought troubling for Catholic scholars and Catholic institutions. I believe that such an attitude accepts the ad hominem attacks that are made within public discourse as legitimate criticisms of the ideas of religious persons, rather than recognizing such attacks as fallacious and unjust attempts to neutralize legitimate ethical criticism.

Instead, I want to suggest two specific reasons why there is, indeed, a need for a "Catholic" approach to bioethics within contemporary American society, which in turn clarify why I believe a text like this present volume is necessary. First, I would insist that the Catholic approach brings to the table a unique perspective that is founded on a carefully thought-out understanding of the human person—an understanding that is lacking within the general arena of bioethical discussion. Second, I believe that developing a specifically "Catholic" approach to bioethics is appropriate for Catholic scholars as part of fulfilling their temporal mission as Christians.

In regard to the first point, we must note that while one may speak at times of "Catholic bioethics," the Church, as noted consistently in official documents and teaching, cannot have an authoritative bioethics properly speaking. Bioethics is an applied field of philosophy, and as John Paul II reminded us in *Fides et Ratio,* there is no "official philosophy of the Church, since the faith as such is not a philosophy."[9] Now, this does not mean that the Church is unable to speak on medical-moral issues—far from it. The Church today continues its long tradition of authoritative teaching on all issues that involve the dignity of human persons. As John Paul II explained so eloquently, yet so forcefully, in his introduction to *The Gospel of Life:*

Today there exists a great multitude of weak and defenseless human beings, unborn children in particular, whose fundamental right to life is being trampled upon. If, at the end of the last century, the Church could not be silent about the injustices of those times, still less can she be silent today, when the social injustices of the past, unfortunately not yet overcome, are being compounded in many regions of the world by still more grievous forms of injustice and oppression, even if these are being presented as elements of progress in view of a new world order.[10]

This continued development of Catholic teaching and moral theology is one of the great works within the Church, and is especially prominent in the areas of health care, medicine, and scientific research upon human sub-jects, about which the Church continues to have much to offer contempo-rary society.

However, one can also identify a specific ethic that flows out of the wis-dom of the Catholic tradition, but which is also compatible with other world traditions because it flows out of natural human reason. At the center of this ethic is the human person. One of the significant failings of modern phi-losophies, and the ethical systems that flow from them, has been their im-poverished views of human nature—specifically the tendency to focus only upon one aspect of humanity such as our materiality, even to the point of denying the existence of a soul or psyche in human beings, or the other ex-treme of focusing only on our spiritual or immaterial dimension with no regard for the reality of human embodiment. The wisdom of the Catho-lic tradition offers a deeply nuanced, holistic understanding of the human person. With this notion of the human person as their foundation, Catho-lic scholars have been able to develop a person-centered ethic that is under-standable and defensible on rational grounds, yet which is in harmony with the teachings and doctrine of the Church. (That is why, as readers will see in this volume, Catholic scholars often cite and make reference to Catho-lic teaching and official documents, in order to show their connectedness with the Catholic tradition even while offering arguments that appeal to our common human reason.) In short, we must remember that Catholic schol-ars are not two people, but one. And as one person, it is certainly possible to develop oneself as a scholar and be true to the demands of one's discipline, without at the same time offending one's fundamental religious beliefs. In fact, the unity of Truth demands this harmony of faith and reason.

Nor is any of this discussion meant to imply that Catholic moral theol-ogy has no value in the public sphere. As the American bishops noted in their *Ethical and Religious Directives,* "Throughout the centuries, with the aid of other sciences, a body of moral principles has emerged that expresses the Church's teaching on medical and moral matters and has proven to be pertinent and applicable to the ever-changing circumstances of health care and its delivery."[11] The development of the moral theology of the Church is itself a rational endeavor—guided by faith—that seeks to unfold the truths of God's revelation, and those truths ought to be allowed a voice in society. However, this specific text is not offered as a work of moral theology per se; rather—with its focus on health care and medicine—it reflects an authen-tic bioethic that flows from, and is in keeping with, the Catholic tradition.

In support of this, one can see that in terms of the philosophical dimension of Catholic scholarship, John Paul II noted in his encyclical letter *Fides et Ratio* that there can be a genuine, "Christian way of philosophizing, a philosophical speculation conceived in dynamic union with faith."[12] Given his own philosophical background, the late Holy Father was not naïve about the demands of philosophy, which require it to be independent and autonomous. However, he expressed in his letter the Catholic view that philosophy and Christianity are compatible: "philosophy must obey its own rules and be based upon its own principles; truth, however, can only be one. The content of Revelation can never debase the discoveries and legitimate autonomy of reason."[13] Again, we see the influence of the unity of Truth and its foundational role in Catholic scholarship.

In regard to the specific role of philosophy in Catholic scholarship, John Paul II went on to note in *Fides et Ratio:*

Philosophical thought is often the only ground for understanding and dialogue with those who do not share our faith. . . . Such a ground for understanding and dialogue is all the more vital nowadays, since the most pressing issues facing humanity—ecology, peace, and the co-existence of different races and cultures, for instance—may possibly find a solution if there is a clear and honest collaboration between Christians and the followers of other religions and all those who, while not sharing a religious belief, have at heart the renewal of humanity.[14]

I believe that these insights apply to Catholic scholarship as a whole. The work of Catholic scholars throughout the various disciplines of inquiry and research help establish a common ground from which Catholics can both reach out to, and draw from, non-Catholics of all types, and work toward those common goals shared with all of humanity.

What, then, does the Catholic teacher, nurse, philosopher, doctor, theologian, psychologist, etc., bring to the "real world" of public discourse regarding issues in bioethics? First and foremost is the focus on the human person that is inherent within the philosophical and theological traditions of the Church, and the primacy of the person over the community. This focus on the human person is crucial in today's public discussions of health care ethics, especially in the growing field of medical research and technological development. One must not mistake the current favoritism for "autonomy" in American bioethics for a genuine respect for the person. Abortion, euthanasia, assisted suicide, genetic manipulation, cloning, and embryonic stem cell research are often justified in the name of autonomy and individual choice, yet all pose serious threats to vulnerable, human persons. The affront to the dignity of human persons is due, in part, to the lack of a clear understanding of human nature in the contemporary arena, especially within scientific discourse. For example, with developments in the Human Genome Project we may be on the verge of changing what we think it means to be human, yet few in the scientific community seem concerned. They simply do not understand the seriousness of what we are doing because they lack a critical understanding of what they are working upon. Under the contemporary influence of secular humanism, biology, neurology, psychology, sociology, and genetics have become the "tools" for *public* discourse, yet none of these provide a complete understanding of human nature on their own. Nor have the various philosophies of modernism and postmodernism offered anything to help our understanding. In sum, the secularized and largely scientific attitudes that dominate *public* discourse simply do not address all the questions relevant to human society. Thus, I believe that the Church and Catholic scholars working in the field of bioethics both have an important duty to continue to call attention to and protect the dignity of human persons. In particular, the rational insights of Catholic scholars who are drawn to health care ethics because of their faith background are indeed relevant for our society as we consider where we are heading in this new millennium. The Catholic tradition has much wisdom to offer all members of our society.

The second reason I noted above for developing a specifically "Catholic" approach to bioethics related to the temporal mission of all Christians. Although Christianity directs the believer toward God and a life beyond this physical world, that does not imply that Christians are to separate themselves from the world. Christians must not seek worldly things over God, yet all believers have a calling in our life on earth to work toward the transformation of our world and all living in it for the greater glory of God. This notion of "a calling" was also raised in *Fides et Ratio*, when John Paul II issued a challenge to Catholic philosophers—which he admitted was daunting—to help people "come to a unified and organic vision of knowledge."[15] This challenge was summarized in the conclusion of the letter:

I appeal also to *philosophers*, and to all *teachers of philosophy*, asking them to have the courage to recover, in the flow of an enduringly valid philosophical tradition, the range of authentic wisdom and truth—metaphysical truth included—which is proper to philosophical enquiry. They should be open to the impelling questions which arise from the word of God and they should be strong enough to shape their thought and discussion in response to that challenge. Let them always strive for truth, alert to the good which truth contains. Then they will be able to formulate the genuine ethics which humanity needs so urgently at this particular time.[16]

I believe that this call from the late Holy Father for Catholic philosophers to work for the betterment of humanity, which clearly applies to all Catholic scholars as well, serves as the ultimate foundation for a specifically "Catholic" approach in the fields of health care and bioethics.

And so, we return to our question, why a specifically "Catholic" approach to health care ethics? The "need" here comes from several factors. First, the unique perspective that the Catholic Church has on the primacy and dignity of the human person needs to be continually asserted within *public* debates on bioethical issues. Related to this is the need to revitalize contemporary thinking in regard to human nature with the philosophical wisdom embodied in the Catholic tradition. And finally, the "need" is seen as one manner in which to fulfill the temporal mission of Catholics in the world today—a mission encouraged by John Paul II's encyclical *Fides et Ratio*.

To further illuminate these reflections, this "introductory" part of the book includes two essays that highlight the philosophical foundations of the Catholic Church's focus upon the dignity of the human person. In his piece, "Wounded Humanity and Catholic Health Care," John Kavanaugh, S.J., offers an eloquent expression of the Catholic tradition's core belief in the inalienable value and dignity of every human being. Kavanaugh argues that it is the fear of our own frailty and vulnerability that drives many to marginalize the weak and wounded members of our society, for the very reason that they so vividly remind us of the aforementioned deeply held fears. But he warns us, "In refusing to attend to the wounded and marginal, however, we reject our own humanity." In the end, Kavanaugh paints a beautiful image of the prophetic role that Catholic health care ministry can play in contemporary society.

The second essay by Gregory Beabout delves deeper into the Catholic position on the dignity of the human person by asking the question, "What Counts as Respect?" In addressing this question, Beabout explores the subtle nuances in the concept of autonomy. He explains how a carefully developed notion of what he calls "ordered autonomy" is compatible with the Catholic tradition's focus on respect for persons, while clarifying why the more contemporary understanding of "radical autonomy" is not compatible. Within this discussion, Beabout argues that a genuine understanding of treating others with respect, ". . . means that *for the entire range of persons, one should treat every person in a manner that gives due recognition to the other as one endowed with the capacity to make self-determining choices in accord with the objective moral order.*"

Readers will find that these first two essays complement each other in many ways. Further, by explaining the foundations upon which Catholic health care ethics rest, Kavanaugh and Beabout help prepare the reader for the later chapters, which explore specific topics within bioethics. In close, I believe that Catholic scholars today have inherited a tremendous gift from the tradition they work within, as well as an important opportunity to foster the living presence of Christ and the search for Truth within the world today. Perhaps the greatest strength we have to stand on is that the Catholic tradition integrates faith and reason—this is the heritage left to us by the great Church fathers and doctors. Not that we will ever know the mysteries of this life fully, but there is reason and wisdom here to be shared with the entire human community which, as John Paul II reminded us in *The Gospel of Life,* all who seek truth will be able to recognize and accept:

Even in the midst of difficulties and uncertainties, every person sincerely open to truth and goodness can, by the light of reason and the hidden action of grace, come to recognize in the natural law written in the heart (cf. Rom 2:14–15) the sacred value of human life from its very beginning until its end, and can affirm the right of every human being to have this primary good respected to the highest degree. Upon the recognition of this right, every human community and the political community itself are founded.[17]

NOTES

1. John Paul II, *Dolentium Hominum,* no. 1.

2. United States Conference of Catholic Bishops, *Ethical and Religious Directives for Catholic Health Care Services,* 4th ed. (Washington, D.C.: USCCB, 2001), p. 4.

3. Missouri Senate Committee Substitute for House Bill No. 1596 (1986), preamble.

4. Justice John Paul Stevens, dissenting opinion, *Webster v. Reproductive Health Services,* 492 U.S. 490 (1989).

5. Timothy E. Quill, M.D., et al., "The Rule of Double Effect—A Critique of Its Role in End-of-Life Decision Making," *New England Journal of Medicine* 337, no. 24 (December 11, 1997): 1770.

6. Daniel P. Sulmasy, O.F.M., M.D., and Edmund Pellegrino, M.D., "The Rule of Double Effect: Clearing Up the Double Talk," *Archives of Internal Medicine* 159, no. 6 (March 22, 1999): 545–50. See especially p. 548.

7. Ibid., pp. 548–49.

8. Ibid., p. 549.

9. John Paul II, *Fides et Ratio,* no. 76. For a fuller statement of this same point, see no. 49:

The Church has no philosophy of her own nor does she canonize any one particular philosophy in preference to others. The underlying reason for this reluctance is that, even when it engages theology, philosophy must remain faithful to its own principles and methods. Otherwise there would be no guarantee that it would remain oriented to truth and that it was moving towards truth by way of a process governed by reason. A philosophy which did not proceed in the light of reason according to its own principles and methods would serve little purpose. At the deepest level, the autonomy which philosophy enjoys is rooted in the fact that reason is by its nature oriented to truth and is equipped moreover with the means necessary to arrive at truth. A philosophy conscious of this as its "constitutive status" cannot but respect the demands and the data of revealed truth.

10. John Paul II, *Evangelium Vitae,* no. 5.
11. United States Conference of Catholic Bishops, p. 1.
12. John Paul II, *Fides et Ratio,* no. 76.
13. Ibid., no. 79.
14. Ibid., no. 104.
15. Ibid., no. 85.
16. Ibid., no. 106.
17. John Paul II, *Evangelium Vitae,* no. 2.

CHAPTER I

Wounded Humanity and Catholic Health Care

JOHN KAVANAUGH, S.J.

Catholic health care today is engaged in a massive ideological struggle with an increasingly powerful school of thought. A leading theorist of this school is Peter Singer, who teaches ethics at Princeton University. In 1994 Singer announced—in his book *Rethinking Life and Death* (a text used in university ethics courses throughout the nation)—that the 2,000-year-old Western ethic governing decisions about life and death has collapsed. Hardly anyone believes any longer that all human life is sacred, Singer says.

This collapse applies, he argues, not just to the belief that it is wrong to intentionally end the life of an innocent human being, but even to our understanding of who counts—or does not count—as a member of the community of human persons. "The traditional ethic is defended by bishops and conservative bioethicists who speak in reverent tones about the intrinsic value of all human life, irrespective of its nature or quality," Singer writes. "[But] readers will already know that I do not speak in hushed tones when I refer to the traditional ethics of the sanctity of human life."[1] We Catholics should note that if Singer is correct in his prognosis, and if his opinion wins out, everything we stand for, as articulated in every medical code—and especially in the mission statements of every Catholic Health Association

This article originally appeared in *Health Progress* (September–October 2000): 12–18. Copyright © 2000 by the Catholic Health Association. Reprinted with permission.

(CHA) member—is, if not in shambles, at least quite near disintegration.

Singer is a leading member of a group of theorists who—although willing to give "personal" status to great apes and possibly also whales, dolphins, dogs, and pigs—suggest that unborn, profoundly handicapped, and brain-damaged humans do *not* qualify for it.[2] His argument is similar to that offered by, for example, Evelyn Pluhar. Both believe that "persons" are only those who have "full personhood"—who possess, on one hand, the ability to act to fulfill conscious desires and, on the other, the self-knowledge and sense of responsibility that mark adult humans as moral agents. This of course excludes all people who, for one reason or another, cannot exercise their capacities.

As Pluhar puts it in *Beyond Prejudice: The Moral Significance of Human and Nonhuman Animals,* healthy animals perform as a rule much more effectively than marginal humans, and so should be given at least the same consideration, protection, and respect as is given to infants or brain-damaged humans, who—because of their limitations—are not "full-fledged persons."[3] "Even primates considerably less well endowed mentally than [chimpanzees] have demonstrated capacities beyond the abilities of some humans," Pluhar writes. "Birds can carry out acts that appear to require considerable planning, cooperation. . . . Unfortunately there are many humans who could never equal any of these feats."[4]

This argument is interesting—and malicious. For indeed a spider *can* do much more than a human fetus. A rat performs more impressively than a three-day-old baby does—which is why some theorists do not want to give human babies personal status. They suggest that we wait a year or so before pronouncing babies members of the human community. Mary Ann Warren goes so far as to argue that infanticide is not the killing of a person. Infants are, in their lack of experience, more like fetuses than "full" persons, she writes.[5]

This depersonalizing tactic can be seen in the political world as well. At present, our courts and legislatures are debating a procedure called "partial-birth abortion."[6] But it is indubitable that, even in the second trimester, a fetus is a living being; it has a beating heart, an active brain, and is responsive to its environment. Even if one will not admit that a fetus is human, one must at least agree that it is an *animal.* And yet contemporary society refuses to give a second trimester human animal the protection it gives to laboratory rats. Such is our insensitivity to the most vulnerable at the margins of personal existence.

In December 1999, *Life* magazine published a powerful rebuke to the court's denial of human status to an unborn human being. The article, "Born Twice," was accompanied by a splendid full-page photograph of a swollen womb—but one taken from *outside* the body of the pregnant mother. Seen reaching through an incision in the uterus is a tiny human hand, grasping the giant-like finger of a physician who is trying to peer inside the womb.[7]

The evidence is inescapable. This, we see, is a human hand, not a mouse's paw or even the hand of a great ape. This is a human *patient's* hand—the hand of Sara Marie Switzer, who was born a few weeks after the photo was taken. Our judiciary is currently debating whether it is more appropriate to dismember fetuses like her inside or outside the womb. But they are human. To kill them is homicide, whether one thinks it justifiable or not.

I know that some readers will be discomfited by this discussion; I apologize for my lack of propriety. But nothing short of impropriety will do in a society that rips apart its young without constraint. If we can be tolerant of that, we can be tolerant of anything. And if we are tolerant of everything, we will find that we truly love nothing.

The End of Human Dignity

This debate is not new. In *Twilight of the Gods* (1889), Friedrich Nietzsche declared (in a chapter called "A Moral for Doctors"):

The sick man is a parasite of society. In certain cases, it is indecent to go on living. To continue to vegetate in a state of cowardly dependence . . . once the meaning of life, the right to life has been lost, ought to be regarded with the greatest contempt by society. Doctors, for their part, should be agents for imparting this contempt. They should no longer prepare prescription, but should every day administer a fresh dose of disgust to their patients. A new responsibility should be created, that of the doctor—the responsibility of ruthlessly suppressing and eliminating degenerate life.[8]

Will Nietzsche's ominous prophecy become a standard for health care in our new century? One certainly hears a Nietzschean echo in the 1996 decision, written for a federal appellate court majority by Judge Stephen Reinhardt, striking down the state of Washington's law against assisted suicide: "A competent, terminally ill adult, having lived nearly the full measure of life, has a strong liberty interest in choosing a dignified and humane death, rather than being reduced at the end of his existence, to a childlike state of helplessness, diapered, sedated, incontinent."[9]

Wherein lies the dignity or value of a human being? We increasingly answer such questions by referring either to a subjective state of mind ("I have dignity if I feel I have it") or to the results of some extrinsic standard of measurement ("I have value or dignity because I got a raise or because I am not incontinent"). But when human worth is reduced to mere subjective attitude or external performance, no one is valued any longer for his or her own sake. If Reinhardt is right, then none of us has *intrinsic* dignity.

This odd forgetfulness, this repression of our inherent, inalienable value as persons, is a complete break with the Judeo-Christian tradition (as well as with Islamic law)—and especially with the very vocation of Catholic health care. But then the Judeo-Christian tradition is precisely what Singer is talking about when he says it should be abandoned and replaced by the values of utility.

Consider end-of-life decisions, for example. To believe in the inherent dignity of a dying—and thus profoundly wounded—person is not to presume that all therapies must be undertaken in his or her behalf, or that none may be withdrawn. Ironically enough, it is the very fear of *woundedness* that often drives people to prolong their own or others' dying. What the dying need most is neither prolongation of their suffering nor even an end to it, but rather acceptance of themselves as persons, because this acceptance is *healing*.

What the dying do not need is "physician-assisted suicide." The deliberate killing of a patient—even with his or her consent—carries with it a deeper wound than that borne by the sufferer. It is a cutting into the heart of ethics itself, an assertion that human vulnerability, our very condition as embodied persons, is degrading and undignified. A community that truly values the intrinsic dignity of persons does not kill its sufferers. Instead, it alleviates the suffering and affirms the sufferer's goodness. As far as we in Catholic health care are concerned, no patient can have an illness so severe or so "degenerate" as to be robbed by it of his or her intrinsic value. And we reject the deliberate killing of damaged persons because it betrays that value.

The Meaning of Being Human

Underlying the debate about dignity, value, and performance is an old question: Who gets to define what a human person is? History is replete with the attempts of one group of people to bar others from "full" personhood. The poor, the uneducated, the racially different, the "enemy," the "unclean"—all at different times have qualified for noninclusion. Today human fetuses are described as "blobs of protoplasm" or "tissue"; criminals are "vermin"; profoundly damaged patients are "vegetables." The ancient habit of stripping certain people of their humanity continues.

But the truth is that any human person is an unfolding, developing, organic reality—a historical life, in which special endowments make possible the emergence of certain activities, among which are learning and loving. Many do not fulfill their potential, perhaps because of a lack of maturation or opportunity. Many others can no longer fulfill their potential because of trauma or simple aging. But they are still persons, even though unfulfilled or injured. Theorists like Singer fail to see this because they make a fundamental mistake. They identify personal reality with the performance of activities. Our actions, however, only reveal our personal nature. They do not constitute it.

Human beings are *not* their mental states, performances, achievements, or activities—not even their expressive behavior or communication with others. These do indeed *fulfill* us as persons, but they do not *make* us persons. Our performances are possible because we are embodied persons who can act in quite wonderful ways. We are beings who, possessing certain latent endowments that make us persons, are capable of informed consent and autonomous choice. It is only because there are persons in the world that there is autonomy, or ethics, at all.

We are personal lives, from the moment our lives begin. At that moment, we are not "potential" persons, but persons with potential. If we fail to perform well—because of lack of development, education, or opportunity—we are then unfulfilled persons, but persons nonetheless. If we happen to be afflicted with Alzheimer's disease, we are not for that reason "marginal persons" but wounded ones, unable to express our personhood, unable to perform as others might.

Chimpanzees, for example, can perform more impressively than can babies or adults who are comatose. Chimps are non-personal animals expressing their endowments, often on splendid array. Babies and comatose adults, however, have personal endowments, albeit unrealized and unexpressed. We humans are always much more than any particular stage of our development, than any achievement or any loss. We are living, developing beings, open always to more life, open always to death.

Four-year-old Helen Keller, both blind and deaf, "performed" more poorly than most pets. Presumably destined to spend her life in institutions, she was saved by the intervention of Annie Sullivan and the language of touch. But even before she met Sullivan, Keller was a human being with personal capacities, not a potential person. Sullivan's healing powers did not bestow on Keller the endowments of personhood. The therapist *recognized* and *unlocked* the inherent dignity that had, until then, gone unseen.

Human beings are indeed—as Singer, Pluhar, and others insist—animals. But we are animals with unique endowments. Singer and Pluhar, denying our special powers, equate us with animals. Other thinkers, denying our essential animality, find our dignity as persons incompatible with our fleshy and temporal frailty. I believe that disgust at our very animality is, oddly enough, at the root of our willingness to disassociate ourselves from our earliest stages of development, and also from the most diminished, dependent aspects of our dying.

The Wound of Humanity

People today have a great ambivalence about themselves as *embodied* persons. We tend to fear and reject our animality—our bodies, our developmental lives, our dependence on each other and the Earth—because that reminds us we are imperfect creatures who ultimately die. This tendency can be seen in a number of apparently disparate phenomena.

Undesirable Down Syndrome

In 1990, Joycelyn Elders, then Arkansas's health director, told a congressional committee that the legalization of abortion was good because it had reduced the number of children born with severe defects. "The number of Down's Syndrome infants in Washington state in 1976 was 64 percent lower than it would have been without legal abortion," she said.[10] A 1990 study of 22,000 Canadian women who had received a prenatal diagnosis revealed that 88 percent of those pregnant with a Down syndrome fetus aborted the pregnancy.[11]

The aborting of such pregnancies is clearly, no matter what the motives, the elimination of damaged or incomplete human beings—a choice that an increasing number of ethicists, scientists, and philosophers recommend, even after birth.

Down syndrome itself is a genetic anomaly that may some day be corrected before fetal life even begins. Most of us would celebrate such an advance. But are we sure that the world would be better without Down syndrome people? I am not.

Desirable DNA

Earlier this year, an advertisement in Ivy League newspapers offered $50,000 for donor ova for "assisted reproduction." The donor, the ad said, must be blonde and 5 foot 9 inches tall and have an IQ of 140. Of course, men and women have for centuries tried interbreeding, in hope of producing children with certain positive traits. Today, however, with the availability of genetic testing, we are more likely to seek the elimination of negative ones: a proclivity for violence, for example, or alcohol addiction, colorblindness, Down syndrome, or depression.

But how can we be sure that such traits are in fact negative? I happen to be colorblind, for instance; I also have pretty good pitch. Could there be a connection between the two traits, one "positive" and one "negative"? And who, after all, is to define positive and negative? Might not some apparent disability turn out to be of use to the world?

Bothersome Bodies

Medical science can now reconstruct the bodies we were born with. In fact, it is quite a lucrative enterprise. In a 1998 *Frontline* program on the Public Broadcasting Service (PBS), a surgeon confessed that he had ceased performing reconstructive surgery on children with birth defects because he could make more money doing liposuctions, face-lifts, and breast augmentations on adults.[12] Here again we are dealing with presumably embarrassing human traits. But what, ultimately, is the trait we would *most* love to alter. Is it not the body itself? Is it not our mortality?

We are entering a century during which we may change the very meaning of what we are as personal animals, as embodied spiritual beings. Bill Joy, the founder and guru of Sun Microsystems, predicted in the April issue of *Wired* magazine that advancements in genetics, molecular technology, and micro-robotics will make possible not only the refashioning but the *casting off* of our woundable bodies.[13]

Why not trade our flesh and bones for silicon, if that enables us to live for 200 years? Some philosophers imagine "downloading" the entire content of human experience into a computer that will never wound or scar. As machines we could avoid suffering the fate of our shameful animality. We would not have to endure the disfigurement of our bodies or bear the cross of our incarnate, fleshy spirit, which—though we be like gods in intellect—reminds us that we must die.

I am not a Luddite in these matters. I am grateful for the gains that genetic therapy, genetic diagnosis, and even molecular electronics offer us. Even so, I am forced to ask: What is behind it all?

The Fright of Our Fragility

It is, I suspect, our fear of death that both drives us irrationally and impersonally to prolong dying and, at the same time, to control it, so as to avoid experiencing our own dependency and need for others.

Christianity invites us to take our bodies seriously. We Christians celebrate conceptions, births, marriages, and, yes, our woundedness and our deaths as well. We are fully aware that once we were fetuses and will, on another day, be dying bodies. Our relationship to our bodies is problematic, and the difficulty lies in our animality. Both birth and death signal our ultimate lack of control over our existence, and so we seek to control or to deny both events. "I never was a dependent, needy fetus or an infant that needed to be fed or cleaned," we try to tell ourselves. "I never will be a dependent, needy old person, relying on others to nurture me, to clean me." This is our terrible fear, the fear of our mortality.

The protagonist of Tolstoy's *The Death of Ivan Ilyich* is the perfect exemplar of our fear of death. Ilyich can comprehend the death of other people, but not his own. In unguarded moments, however, death creeps unavoidably into his thoughts.

He could not understand it; and he endeavored to put away this thought as false, unjust, unwholesome, and to supplant it with other thoughts true and wholesome. But this thought, not merely as a thought, but, as it were, a reality, kept recurring and taking form before him. . . . And he summoned in place of this thought other thoughts, one after the other, in the hope of finding succor in them. He strove to return to his former course of reasoning, which hid from him of old the thought of death.[14]

Fear of death drives what Daniel Callahan calls the "troubled dream of life," wherein we attempt to deny the reality of death, clinging instead to illusions of control and mastery.[15] This fear drives the decisions so many of us make—encouraged to do so by the availability of ever more astonishing technology—to prolong our dying rather than accept it and enter it with care and hope. The fear drives our anxieties about helplessness and dependency.

We are haunted by our animality. We would prefer to be wholly identified with our brains, with the brain's "higher" state and its more elegant and controlled expressions. But we human persons are more than mind. We are incarnate, fleshy beings. Our brains themselves, so marvelous in operation, look like embarrassing mounds of meat.

Sooner or later, our animality forces us to embrace our creaturehood, our needs and neediness. The shock of our enfleshed condition jolts us, like Ilyich, into self-confrontation. Rather than induce panic or self-rejection, however, such moments of recognition beckon us to *accept* our truth, love ourselves as we really are, and finally be healed.

What, then, is it that *needs* healing? What is it that is sick, diseased, dying? Is it not the way we try to deal with our woundedness? Is it not our very disgust with our creatureliness that needs healing? And might it be only the wounded who—because their frailty cannot fit the American dream of control, performance, and success; because their frailty reminds us of our own—can heal us?

There is great resistance to this question. A 1993 PBS broadcast of *The Health Quarterly* concerned legal euthanasia in Holland. In one case, a man afflicted with AIDS has decided he wishes to die. The decision discomfits the treating physician, and the patient notes his reaction, asking, "Is this difficult for you?" "No," the doctor replies, "I've had three others." But when talking to colleagues, the physician admits that he does indeed have great difficulty controlling his anguish in performing euthanasia. In a second case, a retired professor apparently in the early stages of Alzheimer's is asked whether he wants to die. "No," he says, "but I see no reason to go on living."[16]

Watching such exchanges is excruciating. In the first instance, the doctor cannot admit even to himself that assisting in suicide is personally painful for him. In the second, a lonely old man is clearly seeking a bit of human warmth from his physician, whose "professionalism" will not allow him to respond in a warm way. The two patients are studies in depression. Both obviously hunger for someone who cares enough to urge them to go on living. Such is the harrowing reality of authentic relationship. Such is our fear of anything beyond our control, especially death.

In an essay called "Hospice: A Prophetic Moment," the physician Sheila

Cassidy recounts with uncommon honesty her own transition from "professionalism" to the care and comforting of people whom Nietzsche would have described as "degenerate life":

It is difficult to explain the love-hate relationships we have with those specters at the feast of life, gaunt figures with their tissues and their vomit bowls, oblivious to the appalling stench from their foul necrotic tumors. We are not immune to the smell of decaying flesh, and, like anyone, we long to escape to where the air is pure. And yet, cohabiting peacefully with our distaste, is a real love for these broken people. People mutter: "How awful! If it were a dog, you'd have it put down." But then, [the patient] is not a dog, but a man with cancer in his mouth, who is living out his last precarious days, loved and cherished in a way that he has never known before. It is in this lavishing of love on patients that the hospice movement stands in a prophetic relationship to society at large, for it affirms the value of the brain-damaged, the mutilated and the old to a world which values the clever, the physically beautiful and the athletic.[17]

It is what Cassidy calls the "love-hate" quality of such relationships that makes them so poignant. The sight of a broken body reminds us of the shame we feel concerning our own bodies—because they are woundable, subject to infirmity, powerless before time. That reminder is capable of generating the most profound of hates and fears, such as Nietzsche's. But it is also capable of evoking our strongest courage and deepest love.

Authentic Healing of the Person

What needs to be healed—both in ourselves as individuals and in our national culture—is our terrible sense of shame over our vulnerability, our wounded sense of personal dignity. "Marginal" people, whom so many would like to eliminate (or at least forget), remind us of who and what we are. The physically, psychologically, and economically afflicted invade our comfort, and we want to flee from them. In refusing to attend to the wounded and marginal, however, we reject our own humanity.

This brings us, at last, to the prophetic role of the Catholic health ministry, which, as I understand it, has two, inextricably connected aspects:

- To act as a voice for the voiceless, the marginal, Nietzsche's "degenerate humanity."
- To provide true healing for all the wounded.

Catholic health care providers sometimes feel themselves to be on the defensive, primarily because of their opposition to abortion and assisted suicide. The forces favoring both measures are increasingly strong in our culture—so strong that I can imagine a future in which Catholic facilities are known as "places where they don't kill you just because you are unwanted." That could well occur if the thinking represented by Peter Singer and his sympathizers becomes culturally dominant.

But health care of that sort could provide only *false healing*. It would, as Leon Kass, M.D., suggests, amount to trying to eliminate the source of our wounds by eliminating the wounded among us.[18] It would deprive the dying patient of the only experience that can heal even death itself, God's love as expressed through human contact, affection, and care.

True healing is the healing mission of Jesus, the word made flesh. Through it, God enters our humanity so as to transform our wounds. When we flee from the wounds of our brothers and sisters, from the fact of woundedness, we reject our very humanity. The Canadian philosopher Charles Taylor gently chides some contemporary philosophers (whom he calls "naturalist humanists") for their shortsightedness:

Is the naturalist affirmation conditional on a vision of human nature in the fullness of its health and strength? Does it move us to extend help to the irremediably broken, such as the mentally handicapped, those dying without dignity, fetuses with genetic defects? Perhaps one might judge that it doesn't and that this is a point in their favor; perhaps effort shouldn't be wasted on these unpromising cases. But the careers of Mother Teresa or Jean Vanier seem to point to a different pattern, emerging from a Christian spirituality. I am obviously not neutral in posing these questions. . . . I do think naturalist humanism defective in these respects.[19]

Taylor suggests that if we expose our hearts and intellects to "the damaged," "the handicapped," and "the defective," they may reveal to us the deepest truths of our being. For what is defective in them serves to remind us of the contingency that is one with our frail embodiment as persons. What we lose by ignoring them may be nothing less than the power of our humanity to call forth and bestow love.

In the Manner of Jesus

A discussion of this kind can seem abstract. But it certainly is not. Talk about healing always reminds me of my late friend Sr. Ann Manganaro, S.L., M.D.

Sr. Ann, a physician, teacher, and the founder of several small health care organizations in Central America, died in St. Louis at age 47. Bereft of her great skill and her lovely appearance, she was reduced in her last days to receiving care from others.

"I finally understand the wounds," Sr. Ann told a friend at that time.

"Your wounds?" the friend asked, for Sr. Ann had undergone a mastectomy when she was first found to have cancer. "No," she replied.

"The wounds of El Salvador?" the friend persisted. Sr. Ann had often performed emergency surgery in that country during its civil war.

"No," she answered. "I mean the wounds of humanity, the wounds of us all."

Ann Manganaro was a woman of the Gospels. As we know from the resurrection narratives, St. Thomas was scandalized by the terrible reality of Jesus' wounds—they blocked his faith and his hope. It was for that reason that, when the risen Lord came to him, Jesus said only, "Enter the wounds."

Like St. Thomas, we are all called to acknowledge not only the wounds of the Lord but also the wounds of our own humanity. We must not repress the memory of what we truly are. We must love our wounds. If we love them, they will never disgrace or degrade us. They will be our glory.

As a teaching resident physician, Sr. Ann had spent a good deal of her time in the neonatal intensive care unit with Tamika, a tiny, family-less girl who had been born prematurely. When Tamika died, six weeks after she was born, only Sr. Ann, the funeral director, and I attended the wake. I was desolated and angry. "This poor baby," I complained. "She had no family, no real funeral; she never had a day unplugged from tubes and shunts, never a day of breathing on her own; her life was meaningless."

But Ann disagreed. "You are forgetting that Tamika had the power to evoke my love."

And so, when Ann herself came to die, just a few years later, she finally came to share with little Tamika only the power to evoke our love, nothing else. In her dying as in her living, she learned, as we all must, that the wound of our humanity is never repressed or denied. But it can be transformed and made into something of glory.[20]

NOTES

1. Peter Singer, *Rethinking Life and Death: The Collapse of our Traditional Ethics* (New York: St. Martins, 1994), p. 4.

2. Ibid., p. 182.

3. Evelyn Pluhar, *Beyond Prejudice: The Moral Significance of Human and Nonhuman Animals* (Durham, NC: Duke University Press, 1985), pp. 77–81.

4. Ibid., p. 83.

5. Mary Ann Warren, "Postscript on Infanticide," in *Life and Death,* ed. Louis Pojman (Boston: Jones and Bartlett Publishers, 1993), pp. 311–12.

6. On June 28, 2000, the U.S. Supreme Court, by a 5-4 vote, struck down a Nebraska law forbidding the procedure. But the debate goes on.

7. Skip Hollandsworth, "Born Twice," *Life,* December 1999, p. 114.

8. Friedrich Nietzsche, *The Philosophy of Nietzsche,* ed. Geoffrey Clive (New York: Mentor, 1965), p. 425.

9. *Compassion in Dying v. State of Washington,* 79 F. 3d 790, Ninth Circuit Court (1996).

10. Quoted in Tucker Carlson, "Eugenics, American Style," *Weekly Standard,* December 2, 1996, p. 20.

11. Ibid.

12. "The High Price of Health," produced by Rachel Dretzin, *Frontline,* April 14, 1998.

13. Bill Joy, "Why the Future Doesn't Need Us," *Wired,* electronic edition (www.wired.com), April 2000.

14. Leo Tolstoy, *The Death of Ivan Ilyich and Other Stories,* trans. Almayer Maude (New York: New American Library, 1960), pp. 132–33.

15. Daniel Callahan, *The Troubled Dream of Life* (New York: Simon & Schuster, 1993).

16. "Choosing Death," *Health Quarterly,* March 23, 1993.

17. Sheila Cassidy, "Hospice: A Prophetic Moment," in *Spiritual Journeys,* ed. Stanislaus Kennedy (Dublin, Ireland: Veritas, 1997), p. 163.

18. An extended, if somewhat early, version of Kass's humane vision of medicine can be found in *Toward a More Natural Science* (New York: Free Press, 1985). See especially chapter 8, "Thinking about the Body."

19. Charles Taylor, *Sources of the Self* (Cambridge, MA: Harvard University Press, 1989), p. 518.

20. The anecdotes about Sr. Ann, as well as some of the ideas, themes, and examples used in this article, have previously appeared in different form in the "Ethics Notebook" column of *America* magazine. Fuller discussions of "intrinsic human value" and acceptance of vulnerability will be found in two chapters of my book *Who Count as Persons? Human Identity and the Ethics of Killing* (Georgetown University Press, 2001).

CHAPTER 2

What Counts as Respect?

GREGORY R. BEABOUT

Almost all health care institutions and personnel are, in some sense, committed to the principle of respect for persons. The mission statements of countless hospitals and health care institutions begin with some formulation of respect for persons, as do the codes of ethics of almost every group of health care professionals. Despite the near universal concern in health care to treat people with respect, there are many cases and instances in which there is significant disagreement about what it means to treat a person with respect.

One area in which there is significant disagreement centers around the question "Who counts as a person?" For example, many of the controversies surrounding the topic of abortion center on this question. In Catholicism, the traditional answer is that every living human being, from the moment of conception until natural death, is a person. Of course, there are a growing number of people who answer the question in a different way, arguing that personhood is a state entered at a subsequent point in human development. In a similar way, some of the debates about the removal of artificial nutrition and hydration center on disagreements about the end of human personhood.

My colleague John Kavanaugh has devoted himself to a detailed study of this question.[1] I would like to complement his project by turning to another debate that arises among those committed to the principle of respect for persons. In particular, my aim is to show that in contemporary culture, there is significant disagreement about what counts as respect. In this essay, I argue that part of this disagreement about the meaning of respect centers on subtle differences in the meaning of autonomy. After distinguishing between two kinds of autonomy, "radical" and "ordered," I show that ordered autonomy is compatible with Catholic moral theology. Finally, I present a series of arguments against radical autonomy along with arguments that ordered autonomy is a better way to understand what it means to treat someone with respect as a person.

Respect and Autonomy

In determining what counts as respect, we quickly come to the concept of autonomy. For example, suppose we ask why it is wrong to hold a person in slavery. There seems to be a well-developed intuition among most contemporary people that slavery is absolutely wrong. In attempting to articulate that intuition, we tend to say that slavery is wrong because it fails to treat the enslaved human as a person, or that slavery fails to respect the inherent dignity and worth of the person. When we press further, to articulate more clearly what it means to respect someone as a person, we find that part of the reason slavery is reprehensible is that it fails to respect the person's capacity to make self-determining choices. In other words, slavery is wrong because holding a person in slavery fails to respect the enslaved person as an autonomous agent.

In seeking to clarify what it means to treat someone "as an autonomous agent," it is worth pausing for a moment to reflect on several various senses in which we use the phrase "as a . . . ." For example, one might say, "As a professional quarterback, you should practice throwing accurate passes." In this sentence, the phrase "as a . . ." could be used to refer to range, manner, justification, or a combination of these.[2] First, the prescription "you should practice throwing accurate passes" could be seen as being qualified in range or scope by the phrase "as a professional quarterback." All who fit in the range should follow the prescription. Second, it may specify the manner in which the command should be followed. How should you practice? You should practice the way a professional quarterback would, rather than using the approach of a high school player. In other words, in this case it might refer to the intensity and focus that characterize the habits of a professional. Third, it may be seen as justifying the command. Why should you practice throwing accurate passes? Because you are a professional quarterback. Finally, the phrase "as a . . ." could serve all three functions.

In saying we should treat someone with respect "as a person," we seem to mean all three of these things. When we say that slavery is wrong because it fails to respect the enslaved individual "as a person," we mean that (1) for the entire *range* of persons, slavery is wrong; (2) the *manner* in which we should treat others is "as" persons; and (3) it is wrong to enslave someone *because* the individual is a person. So, slavery is immoral because it fails to treat someone with respect as a person in terms of range, manner, and justification.

If we probe the justification aspect more deeply, we might ask why being a person counts as a reason for forbidding slavery. The case of slavery is helpful in this regard, because our intuitions run very deep with regard to the wrongfulness of slavery. For example, we recognize that it is perfectly permissible to sit on a chair, using it as a piece of furniture. Yet, if someone were to capture a human being and force the captive to kneel down with all four limbs on the ground so that one could sit on the captive's back as a chair, we would recognize that there is something deeply dehumanizing about this case. Why is it wrong forcibly to use a person as a chair? If we are to avoid circularity (simply saying "because that individual is a person"), we seem to come to the concept of autonomy. We reason that as a person, the captive is endowed with a capacity for self-determination, and using the person as a chair fails to respect this endowment.

Autonomy: Ordered or Radical?

What does it mean to say that we should respect someone as an autonomous agent? There is a deep but rather subtle difference between two ways of understanding autonomy. I will call these ordered autonomy and radical autonomy.

By "radical autonomy" I mean *the freedom both to makes one's own choices and to define for oneself one's own conception of the good.* From this conception of autonomy, it follows that each one can choose for oneself anything one wants, so long as it does not violate the autonomy of others. Radical autonomy does not include the freedom to define the good of other persons, but only of oneself. Each one is free to conceive of the ultimate ends, aims, and values of one's life however one sees fit, provided that doing so does not violate the autonomy of others. This way of understanding autonomy is widespread (though often implicit) in various versions of contemporary individualism.

The notion of ordered autonomy is older than its modern counterpart. Because its origins are more distant from us, it may strike us, in some ways, as foreign; nonetheless, the basic notion of ordered autonomy continues to resonate with deep elements of contemporary culture. According to this notion, each person is free to make self-determining choices subject to the moral law. This way of thinking recognizes that there is an objective moral order discoverable in part by every person. Each person is sovereign in a limited sense. Because human institutions are sometimes distorted with regard to this objective moral order, each person has the responsibility to evaluate the habits and practices of various social institutions, including those of one's own culture. Hence, "ordered autonomy" is *the freedom to use one's power of self-determination in a responsible manner in accord with the objective moral order.* The moral order is objective in the sense that it stands over against human perception and exists independent of individual apprehension. This moral order is discoverable in part by each human being. Given the frailties and incompleteness of human knowledge, no individual or human institution has a grasp of the moral order in its fullness. Further, the moral order is disclosed dialectically, so that individuals who challenge or critique social institutions on moral grounds may be sharpening our perception of the moral order.

Both radical autonomy and ordered autonomy are present in elements of contemporary culture as alternative ways of understanding the meaning of autonomy. One of the most explicit articulations of radical autonomy can be found in the Supreme Court's majority decision in *Planned Parenthood v. Casey* (1992): "At the heart of liberty is the right to define one's own concept of existence, of meaning, of the universe, and of the mystery of human life."[3] According to this way of understanding liberty and autonomy, each one is free to do whatever one wants, so long as one does not impose one's own ideas or meanings on others.

But there is an older way of understanding autonomy in American life. The Declaration of Independence understands autonomy and independence as self-governance in accord with the "Laws of Nature and of Nature's God," where liberty is to be exercised in accord with an objective moral order of human rights endowed by our creator. Abraham Lincoln appealed to this objective moral order in his Gettysburg Address when he articulated the American ideal of liberty, declaring that "this nation, under God, shall have a new birth of freedom." Likewise, in "America, the Beautiful," we sing, "confirm thy soul in self-control, thy liberty in law." In this tradition of ordered liberty, autonomy is the power of self-determination to make responsible choices in accord with the objective moral order.

In many instances, there is virtually no difference between these two ways of understanding autonomy at the level of application. For example, in the case of enslaving someone, both those who hold for radical autonomy and those who hold for ordered autonomy find slavery morally repugnant. Those who hold for radical autonomy might reason as follows. It is wrong to enslave a person because it involves imposing one's own conception of what is good for another person against their will. Since each person ought to be free to make their own choices and to define their own conception of the good, forcing someone to do something that runs counter to their own conception of the good for them is a failure to respect their autonomy.

Those who hold for ordered autonomy might come to the same conclusion using a slightly different line of reasoning. A proponent of ordered autonomy would likely argue that since each person should be accorded the freedom to use one's power of self-determination in a responsible manner in accord with the moral order, it is wrong to enslave a person. This kind of enslavement is wrong on several counts. First, it fails to respect the captive as a person with the power of self-determination. Second, in treating the captive merely as an object to be used, it fails to respect the objective value of the person that is part of the moral order.

The subtle difference between these two ways of understanding autonomy can have significant differences when it comes to various topics in contemporary health care. For example, in considering the topic of euthanasia, a profound difference arises when these two competing notions of autonomy are applied. Those who hold for radical autonomy usually end up supporting efforts to make active euthanasia available. They reason that each person is autonomous in the sense that each one should be free to make one's own choices and to define for oneself one's own conception of the good. From this conception of radical autonomy, it follows that one's conception of the good may include terminating one's life.

In contrast, for those who hold a conception of ordered autonomy, there is a different response to someone who expresses a desire to terminate their own life. The power to make self-determined choices is a power that ought to be used in a responsible manner in accord with the moral order. Further, the power of self-determination is a power that can be misused, especially in moments of weakness. Just as one should intervene when a friend is abusing alcohol, so too one should intervene when an aged or ill person requests to actively end their life.

In a consumer culture such as ours, it is very easy, even for health care professionals, to think that treating a person with respect means honoring the freedom of each person to choose for themselves what they want, including their own conception of the good. Yet many health care professionals are drawn to their vocation of caring because of a recognition that there is an objective good in providing care for others. In other words, many health care professionals find themselves influenced (and perhaps frustrated) by consumer culture in adopting a notion of radical autonomy, while also drawn to the goods intrinsic to health care, including a notion of ordered autonomy.

Respect for the Person in the Catholic Tradition

So far, I have shown that there are two competing ways to understand what it means to treat a person with respect. I take it as uncontroversial to recognize that there is a strong tendency in contemporary secular culture to understand respect for the person as implying respect for radical autonomy. Without trying to trace the intellectual origins of this tendency, I will turn instead to the notion of respect for persons in the Catholic tradition.

In the Catholic tradition and its approach to questions about the morality of actions, perhaps the central concept is the notion of human dignity. For example, in almost every difficult issue in bioethics and health care ethics, the tradition of Catholic thought makes appeal to the principle of the dignity of the human person. In almost all of the difficult moral issues that arise in health care ethics—abortion, euthanasia, stem cell research, removal of hydration and nutrition, allocation of scarce resources—the Catholic moral tradition is distinctive in its insistence on human dignity.

Consider the approach used in the 1994 statement by the National Conference of Catholic Bishops *Ethical and Religious Directives for Catholic Health Care Services*. The bishops articulate the goal of their statement in these terms:

The purpose of these *Ethical and Religious Directives* then is twofold: first, to reaffirm the ethical standards of behavior in health care that flow from the Church's teaching about the dignity of the human person; second, to provide authoritative guidance on certain moral issues that face Catholic health care today.[4]

This emphasis on the dignity of the human person is a constant theme in the teaching of the bishops and the popes. Consider the words of Pope John XXIII:

Any human society, if it is to be well-ordered and productive, must lay down as a foundation this principle, namely, that every human being is a person, that is, his nature is endowed with intelligence and free will. Indeed, precisely because he is a person he has rights and obligations flowing directly and simultaneously from his very nature.[5]

The Second Vatican Council also emphasized this theme:

This Council lays stress on reverence for the human person; everyone must consider one's every neighbor without exception as another self, taking into account first of all life and the means necessary to living it with dignity.[6]

In the American bishops' pastoral letter on the economy, human dignity is of central importance:

Human personhood must be respected with a reverence that is religious. When we deal with each other, we should do so with the sense of awe that arises in the presence of something holy and sacred. For that is what human beings are: we are created in the image of God (Gn 1:27).[7]

Likewise, the moral teaching of Pope John Paul II has placed a strong emphasis on the dignity of the human person. As John Paul II has stated, "The deepest element of God's commandment to protect human life is the requirement to show reverence and love for every person and the life of every person."[8] Further, this emphasis on the dignity of the human person is summarized in the moral teaching of the *Catechism of the Catholic Church:*[9]

Respect for the human person considers the other "another self." It presupposes respect for the fundamental rights that flow from the dignity intrinsic of the person. The equality of men concerns their dignity as persons and the rights that flow from it.[10]

In the statements of Catholic leaders who write on moral matters there are many similar passages that place a strong emphasis on the dignity of the human person. Suffice it to say, the principle of the dignity of the human person is central in Catholic morality generally, and especially in moral issues in the areas of health care and bioethics.

While the principle of respect for the dignity of the human person is central in Catholic morality, this principle is not based on a notion of radical autonomy. While the human person is understood as created in God's image and endowed with a capacity for intelligence and free will, the person's will is free to choose from among various means, with the recognition that many means available are destructive and contrary to the moral order.

There are a range of theological arguments that could be presented to show that the Catholic understanding of respect for the dignity of the human person includes respect for ordered autonomy, not radical autonomy. In the tradition of Catholic moral thought, the emphasis on human dignity as a central moral principle is understood as having two complementary sources. In addition to the teaching of the scriptures, especially the teaching that every human being is created in God's image,[11] Catholicism teaches that human reason can ascertain basic moral precepts. This emphasis on the human ability to gain moral knowledge flows from St. Paul's claim that the moral law is written on our hearts.[12] St. Thomas Aquinas extends this teaching when he claims that the light of natural reason, whereby we discern what is good and what is evil, is imprinted on every human being.[13] Without taking up these issues in detail, I want to turn to the notion of radical autonomy and identify two of its philosophical deficiencies.

Problems with Radical Autonomy

So far, I have shown that, although there may be wide agreement in contemporary society that we should treat people with respect, there is a deep division on certain issues that can be traced in part to competing understandings of autonomy. While the notion of treating a person with respect seems to include a respect for personal autonomy of some sort, there is a significant difference between radical autonomy and ordered autonomy. Further, I have shown that the Catholic tradition of ethics places a strong emphasis on respect for the person, while intimating that this includes respect for ordered autonomy rather than radical autonomy. Next, I would like to outline two problems that arise for those who adopt an understanding of radical autonomy.

In order to understand an action as autonomous, it will help to begin with an understanding of the basic components of a human action. To say that an action is autonomous means, at the very least, that the action flows from the individual's self-determination. Here, it helps to rule out two kinds of factors that could violate autonomy. On the one had, if there is an external physical factor that produces human movement (e.g., a strong wind blows while a person is walking, forcing the person to fall), then the movement obviously is not autonomous. However, there are more complicated cases in which an external object may cause a human being to move by provoking a desire. This could range from a piece of dust that enters a person's nose, causing a twitch and then a sneeze, to the appearance of aromatic food that induces a sense of hunger. In the case of the sneeze, it seems clear that the movement, though originating in the person in some sense, is not an autonomous action. A person's response to food is more complicated. In that case, we can distinguish between the person's desire and the person's choice to act on that desire.

Harry Frankfurt has drawn attention to this distinction, calling the one a "first order desire," and the other a "second order desire."[14] A first order desire is immediate and unreflective, while a second order desire is the result of reflection, a rational decision to pursue a certain course of action.

Given this distinction between first and second order desires, we can distinguish between two aspects of freedom. On the one hand, a non-human animal may be free in the sense that a first order desire is unrestrained. For example, suppose a lion sees and smells its prey. There is nothing keeping the lion from its prey, so it attacks and then devours it. Were the lion locked in a cage with its prey on the other side, the lion would not have the same freedom to act on its desire. This kind of freedom, often called "negative freedom," is merely the *freedom from* external restraints.

Given the distinction between first and second order desires, we can identify another aspect of freedom. Suppose I have a strong desire for the food that appears before me. As I reflect on that desire, I reflectively evaluate whether I should eat it. Am I on a special diet? Is it healthy? Will it spoil my dinner plans? Upon reflection, I make a self-determined choice to eat the food. In this case, I am free not simply in the sense that I am unrestrained. There is another aspect of freedom involved. As one in possession of my faculties and capable of governing my life, with a control of my desires, I choose this course of action. This is a "positive freedom." It is not simply freedom from restraint. This freedom of self-determination is *freedom for* something.

In many instances, the freedom of self-determination is most obvious when one makes a choice to restrain oneself from acting on a desire. For example, I have a desire for the food that appears before me, but I make a self-determined choice to abstain from it. Perhaps I am on a special diet, or for moral reasons I don't eat this kind of food, or I am on a religious fast. Whatever the case, it takes a special kind of determination to maintain this self-discipline. One who can control oneself in the presence of immediate gratification possesses a habit of auto-determination.

One deficiency with the notion of radical autonomy is that it does not seem to have the internal resources to distinguish between these two aspects of freedom. Radical autonomy, with its emphasis on one's being free to choose whatever one wants so long as one does not violate the autonomy of another, seems unable to distinguish between negative freedom (e.g., the freedom of a beast or a wanton who is able to satisfy unreflective, immediate gratification) and positive freedom (the self-determined freedom of a person who reflectively chooses the desires upon which to act).

To summarize the first problem with the notion of radical autonomy, notice that those who emphasize radical autonomy rely on the concept of self-determination to gain moral credibility for their position. However, instead of emphasizing the responsibilities of self-determination, the stress in radical autonomy is on the *freedom from* restraint. While emphasizing "freedom from," there is a neglect for the question of what freedom is for.

A second problem arises when we turn to examine more carefully the question of what the freedom of self-determination is for. Those who emphasize radical autonomy hold that the freedom of self-determination is for one to choose according to one's own standards. However, notice that in describing the positive freedom of self-determination and the reflection that is involved in making self-determined choices, it is necessary to describe the appeal to other criteria that transcend the deliberative process. In reflecting on whether I should act on my desire to eat, I reflect on my desire in light of various criteria. Is it healthy? Will it spoil my dinner plans? In order to make a self-determined choice, I must appeal to some criterion that transcends me. For example, health is a good that transcends me. Likewise, the good of eating dinner together with my family is a good that transcends me.

No matter what self-determined choice I make, I have to make that choice according to some criterion. There are two points that I want to make about the criteria that are used in making a self-determined choice. The first of these is the most subtle and difficult to articulate.

In order to make a self-determined choice, that is, a reflective, rational choice for which one is personally responsible, one must appeal to a criterion of goodness that transcends oneself. My first piece of evidence for this is simply experiential. By examining one's own choices, one sees that a specific course of action is chosen because it is good in some respect, and the goodness involved is a value that transcends the one doing the choosing.

For example, I choose to eat the food because it is good for my health and it will taste good. The action then draws me out of myself, beyond my current state to a good that lies beyond me, in this case, the goods of health and enjoyable taste.

Someone who holds for radical autonomy might respond, "But I have chosen the goods of health and enjoyable taste as well." They might reason, "I have chosen to eat the food because I think it will promote health, and I am also the one who has chosen that health is a value for me."

This raises the question "Why have you chosen health as a value?" The answer will eventually lead to some good beyond oneself. If it continues on to infinity (I chose *a* for the sake of *b,* and *b* for the sake of *c,* etc., but each was my choice), then one is left ultimately without any reflective criteria for making a choice. In that case, there would be no substantive difference between the wanton (who cravenly acts on desires) and the one who makes reflective, self-determined choices. In other words, there is an internal contradiction in holding both that the self can make responsible choices and that the self chooses the criterion by which choices are made.

The force of this argument is to show that anyone who accepts Frankfurt's distinction between first and second order desires and then privileges the positive freedom of self-determination is also committed to the claim that there is a criterion, or as Charles Taylor calls it, a horizon of goodness, against which we make self-determined choices.[15] Self-determined choices are only possible within a backdrop of an objective moral order, dim though its perception may be.

The task then becomes the quest to articulate the horizon of goodness against which we make responsible, self-determining choices. But that task is social in character.

That leads us to a third problem with the notion of radical autonomy. The first two problems were at the level of justification. Radical autonomy is a flawed justification for treating a person with respect. The third problem is at the level of manner. Treating someone as if the other were a radically autonomous agent is the wrong manner to treat someone, for it falsifies the self's relation to others. Treating people as radically autonomous agents falsifies our reliance on others, including our relation to social mores, traditions, narratives, moral authorities, and representative models of the good life in our quest to gain insight into the objective moral order. The notion of radical autonomy paints a false picture of the self's ability to define for itself its own conception of the good. When the person is conceived of as a radically autonomous agent, there is a disregard for the way in which the person's ability to be self-reflective and self-determining arose in a concrete social nexus, within a language and a specific historical tradition, influenced by specific others and existing social traditions.

When applied to the area of health care, the social deficiencies in the notion of radical autonomy have at least two negative implications at the level of the manner of treatment. First, by focusing on patient autonomy as if the patient's choice were the highest good, there is a potential to disregard the social implications of the patient's decision. Second, the notion of radical autonomy leads to a tendency to disregard the patient's ability to engage in critical dialogue and reflection on the good life. By a perverse logic, the desire to allow each person to have their own conception of the good leads to an indifference about the insights of others about the good life. The result is that instead of treating others with respect by engaging them in a critical dialogue about the good life, one ends up treating others with indifference: to each his own. In sum, the notion of radical autonomy rests on an inaccurate assumption about the relation between the individual and society.

What Counts as Respect

So far, I have argued that there are a number of severe deficiencies in the notion of radical autonomy. It emphasizes freedom from restraint without adequately answering what freedom should be used for. Further, the claim that the individual is free to make choices and free to choose the criterion used to make choices (in an ultimate sense) rests on an internal contradiction. Finally, radical autonomy ends up falsifying the relation between the individual and society and leading to a flawed manner of relations.

Given that radical autonomy is a severely problematical notion, it follows that it should be abandoned as a way to understand what it means to treat someone with respect.

So, with regard to autonomy, what does it mean to treat others with the respect befitting a person? It means that *for the entire range of persons, one should treat every person in a manner that gives due recognition to the other as one endowed with the capacity to make self-determining choices in accord with the objective moral order.*

Let me try to respond to two objections to this way of understanding what it means to treat a person with respect.

First, it might be objected that this is a flawed way of understanding what it means to treat someone with respect since it assumes that we have knowledge of the objective moral order, even though in many cases it is very difficult to determine how the objective moral order applies to one's concrete situation.

To respond to this objection, it helps to draw a distinction between two claims about the difficulties of knowing the moral order. There is a difference between the claims that (1) human knowledge of the moral order is incomplete, so applying the moral order is sometimes very difficult; and (2) human knowledge of the moral order is nonexistent, so applying the moral order is impossible. The main force of the objection rests on the important insight that human knowledge of the moral order is incomplete, especially at the level of application. Because there are situations that contain many contingencies and particularities involving individuals and novel situations, it is sometimes very difficult to know how someone seeking to live in accord with the moral order should act in a given situation. Given the limited character of our knowledge of the objective moral order, there are many circumstances in which we should be careful about drawing hasty moral conclusions or in which we should be careful about overestimating our full grasp of the demands of the objective moral order. However, it does not follow from this recognition of the limits of human knowledge that it is impossible to know anything at all about the objective moral order. Respecting a person entails recognizing the person's legitimate responsibility to make their own self-determining choices in accord with the moral order to the degree that it is known. In most cases, this opens up a very wide range of permissible moral actions. However, just because knowledge of the moral order is at times difficult to attain and incomplete at the level of application, it does not follow that the moral order is so nebulous that every choice is permissible. In sum, the objection falsely presupposes that we have no knowledge of the objective moral order.

Here is a second objection. Someone might counter that the above account of respect as ordered autonomy is flawed because it involves imposing one's own conception of the good on others in a paternalistic manner.

To respond to this objection, it is worth noting that the objection rests on a deep insight about the meaning of respect, an insight that is shared in the notion of ordered autonomy. The deep insight is that it is inappropriate to impose one's own choices upon another in a coercive manner, and this is especially egregious when the person being coerced is capable of making self-determining choices.

With that having been said, it should also be acknowledged that there are stages in life in which a person's ability to make self-determining choices is in the process of development. For example, there are developmentally appropriate interventions that differ for a three-year-old child compared to a ten-year-old or a fifteen-year-old. In dealing with children, there are times when the appropriate way to treat a child with respect as a person may involve elements of paternalism, properly understood. So one part of the response to this objection is to point out that paternalism, properly understood, does not violate the notion of treating a person with respect, provided that the person being treated paternalistically is developing the capacity to make self-determining choices. In addition, it should be acknowledged that there are many cases in which reasonable people could disagree about the kind of paternalism that would be appropriate. For example, it may be difficult to know the amount of paternalism that should be exercised with a seventeen-year-old, or with an adult who suffers from a mental disability associated with a tendency to inflict severe harm on oneself. Such cases may prove difficult for those who hold for ordered autonomy in the sense that it may be difficult to know who should intervene, or in what way, or to what extent. Admittedly, there may be some instances of intervention, done in the name of "respecting the person," that are coercive. But that does not mean that every intervention is coercive.

Further, the objection contains a warning against imposing one's own conception of the good on others. But the principle of respect, as articulated above, does not immediately entail a coercive imposition of a narrow conception of the good. In respecting the ordered autonomy of others, there is room for a wide range of choices. In some cases, those choices might legitimately include challenging another person to rethink the moral responsibilities of a proposed course of action. In other cases, it may be morally legitimate to enact the power of the law to limit certain choices that egregiously violate human dignity.

In sum, the second objection is flawed because it disregards several key truths of human social relations: (1) there are stages in life in which a person's ability to make self-determining choices is in the process of development, (2) there are times when it is legitimate to challenge another person to rethink the moral responsibilities of a proposed course of action, and (3) it may be morally legitimate to enact the power of the law to limit certain choices.

Conclusion

In conclusion, I have tried to show that, despite widespread agreement in name about the principle of respect for persons, there is actually a significant difference between two competing ways of understanding what it means to treat someone with respect as a person. (Based on my experience with health care students and professionals, I fear that some people who study and work in Catholic settings are committed to the principle of respect for persons, but in fact end up interpreting the principle to mean respect for radical autonomy.) I have tried to show that there is a significant difference between ordered autonomy and radical autonomy. Further, I have argued that ordered autonomy is compatible with Catholic moral theology, while radical autonomy is not. I outlined a number of deficiencies in understanding respect for persons in terms of radical autonomy. Finally, I tried to show that, with regard to autonomy, treating a person with respect means giving due recognition to others as persons endowed with the capacity to make self-determining choices in accord with the objective moral order.

NOTES

1. John Kavanaugh, *Who Count as Persons?* (Washington, DC: Georgetown University Press, 2001).

2. This distinction comes from Thomas Hill, "Donagan's Kant," *Ethics* 104 (1993): 38.

3. *Planned Parenthood v. Casey,* 112 S. Ct. 2791 (1992).

4. National Conference of Catholic Bishops, *Ethical and Religious Directives for Catholic Health Care Services* (1994), preamble.

5. Pope John XXIII, *Pacem in Terris* (April 11, 1963), no. 9.

6. *Gaudium et Spes* (December 7, 1965), no. 27.

7. U.S. Catholic Bishops, *Economic Justice for All* (1986), no. 28.

8. Pope John Paul II, *Evangelium Vitae* (March 25, 1995), no. 43.

9. *Catechism of the Catholic Church,* see especially part 3, chapter 1, article 1, sections 1700ff.

10. Ibid., 1944–45.

11. See the National Conference of Catholic Bishops, *Ethical and Religious Directives,* part 2: "The primary justification for the emphasis on human dignity comes from the scriptures. The dignity of human life flows from creation in the image of God (Gn 1:26), from redemption by Jesus Christ (Eph 1:10; 1 Tm 2:4–6), and from our common destiny to share a life with God beyond all corruption (1 Cor 15:42–57)."

12. Romans 2:15.

13. St. Thomas Aquinas, *Summa theologiae* I-II, q. 91, a. 2.

14. Harry Frankfurt, "Freedom of the Will and the Concept of the Person," in *The Importance of What We Care About: Philosophical Essays* (New York: Cambridge University Press, 1988), p. 16.

15. See Charles Taylor, *Sources of the Self* (Cambridge, MA: Harvard University Press, 1989).

SELECTED BIBLIOGRAPHY ON CATHOLIC BIOETHICS

Ashley, Benedict, O.P., and Kevin D. O'Rourke, O.P. *Ethics of Health Care: An Introductory Textbook*. 3rd ed. Washington, DC: Georgetown University Press, 2002.

Boyle, Philip, and Kevin D. O'Rourke, O.P. "Medical Ethics: Sources of Catholic Teachings." *Health Progress* 81, no. 3 (2000).

Brodeur, Dennis. "Catholic Health Care: Rationale for Ministry." *Christian Bioethics* 5, no. 1 (April 1999): 5–25.

Cataldo, Peter J., and Albert S. Moraczewski, O.P. *Catholic Healthcare Ethics: A Manual for Ethics Committees*. Boston: National Catholic Bioethics Center, 2002.

Devine, Richard J. *Good Care, Painful Choices: Medical Ethics for Ordinary People*. 2nd ed. Boston: Paulist Press, 2000.

Diamond, Eugene F. *A Catholic Guide to Medical Ethics*. Rockford, IL: Tan Books and Publishers, 2003.

Dort, Veronica M., and Edward J. Furton. *Ethical Principle in Catholic Health Care*. Boston: National Catholic Bioethics Center, 1999.

Gomez-Lobo, Alfonso. *Morality and the Human Goods: An Introduction to Natural Law Ethics*. Washington, DC: Georgetown University Press, 2002.

Gormally, Luke, ed. *Issues for a Catholic Bioethic*. Chicago: University of Chicago Press, 2001.

Guinan, Patrick, and Ted Jagielo, eds. *Catholic Medical Ethics: Core Reading*. Bloomington, IN: Authorhouse, 1999.

Hamel, Ron. "Of What Good Is the 'Common Good'?" *Health Progress* 80, no. 3 (1999): 45–47.

Hehir, J. Bryan. "Policy Arguments in a Public Church: Catholic Social Ethics and Bioethics." *Journal of Medicine and Philosophy* 17, no. 3 (1992): 347–64.

Kavanaugh, John F. *Who Count As Persons?: Human Identity and the Ethics of Killing*. Washington, DC: Georgetown University Press, 2001.

McInerny, Ralph M. *The Question of Christian Ethics*. Washington, DC: Catholic University of America Press, 1993.

Overberg, Kenneth R., S.J. *Creating a Culture of Life*. Allen, TX: Thomas More Publishing, 2002.

Pinckaers, Servais, O.P. *The Sources of Christian Ethics*. Washington, DC: Catholic University of America Press, 1995.

Schockenhoff, Eberhard. *Natural Law and Human Dignity: Universal Ethics in an Historical World*. Translated by Brian McNeil. Washington, DC: Catholic University of America Press, 2003.

Tropman, John E. *The Catholic Ethic and the Spirit of the Community*. Washington, DC: Georgetown University Press, 2002.

PART II

Human Reproduction

T HE GENERAL CHRISTIAN PERSPECTIVE on human reproduction is rooted in the faith conviction that human beings are created in the image and likeness of God. As explained in the *Catechism
of the Catholic Church:* "'God created man in his own image, in the image
of God he created him, male and female he created them.' Man occupies a
unique place in creation: (I) he is 'in the image of God'; (II) in his own nature he unites the spiritual and material worlds; (III) he is created 'male and
female'; (IV) God established him in his friendship."[1] From this core belief
flows a rich view of human life in which the dignity of each member of the
human family is recognized. As expressed a few lines later in the *Catechism:*
"Being in the image of God the human individual possesses the dignity of
a person, who is not just something, but someone. He is capable of self-
knowledge, of self-possession and of freely giving himself and entering into
communion with other persons. And he is called by grace to a covenant
with his Creator, to offer him a response of faith and love that no other creature can give in his stead."[2]

With this acknowledgment of "human dignity" comes a specific responsibility to protect and promote human life, and to treat all human beings
with the utmost respect—a responsibility that falls upon both the individual and society as a whole. As John Paul II explained in his encyclical letter
The Gospel of Life:

The Gospel of life is for the whole of human society. To be actively pro-life is to contribute to the renewal of society through the promotion of the common good. It is
impossible to further the common good without acknowledging and defending the

right to life, upon which all the other inalienable rights of individuals are founded and from which they develop. A society lacks solid foundations when, on the one hand, it asserts values such as the dignity of the person, justice and peace, but then, on the other hand, radically acts to the contrary by allowing or tolerating a variety of ways in which human life is devalued and violated, especially where it is weak or marginalized. Only respect for life can be the foundation and guarantee of the most precious and essential goods of society, such as democracy and peace.[3]

This obligation to treat humanity with respect is clearly expressed throughout sacred scripture, from the Ten Commandments through the letters of St. Paul. Within the context of the Bible, many Christians believe that God has given specific rules and guidelines for the faithful to follow. And yet, the Bible does not explicitly speak about many of the most troubling issues Christians are facing today. Regarding human reproduction, there is no direct mention of abortion, contraception, artificial reproduction, cloning, etc. It is at this point that the conscientious Christian must call upon the gift of reason to help form his or her conscience regarding the ethical nature of various aspects of human reproduction, and to help answer what is perhaps the most important ethical question regarding human reproduction as a whole, "When does human life begin?"

Of course, the Bible does provide some guidance on the question of when life begins. For example, Jeremiah 1:5 proclaims: "Before I formed you in the womb I knew you, before you were born I dedicated you, a prophet to the nations I appointed you"; and Psalm 139:13–14 says: "You formed my inmost being; you knit me in my mother's womb. I praise you, so wonderfully you made me; wonderful are your works! My very self you knew. . . ." For many Christians, these scripture passages reinforce the belief that God creates each unique human soul at the moment of our conception, which in turn clarifies the immoral nature of abortion. However, that being said, opposition to abortion need not be viewed solely as a religious argument. As Frs. Ashley and O'Rourke point out regarding abortion in their text *Health Care Ethics: A Theological Analysis:*

Officially the Catholic Church has never based its opposition to direct abortion on the claim that the human soul is created at conception. *The Declaration on Procured Abortion* (CDF, 1974), while affirming that from the time of conception direct abortion is always a grave sin, appended a note #19 saying, "This declaration expressly leaves aside the question of the moment when the spiritual soul is infused. There is not a unanimous tradition on this point and authors are as yet in disagreement."[4]

Nevertheless, Ashley and O'Rourke go on to point out that advances in contemporary embryology—while not definitive—clearly support the belief that ensoulment occurs at conception. Thus, the Congregation for the Doctrine of the Faith noted in the 1987 *Instruction on Respect for Human Life in Its Origin and on the Dignity of Creation (Donum Vitae):*

> Certainly no experimental datum can be in itself sufficient to bring us to the recognition of a spiritual soul; nevertheless, the conclusions of science regarding the human embryo provide a valuable indication for discerning by the use of reason a personal presence at the moment of this first appearance of a human life: How could a human individual not be a human person? . . . Thus the fruit of human generation from the first moment of its existence, that is to say, from the moment the zygote has formed, demands the unconditional respect that is morally due to the human being in his bodily and spiritual totality. The human being is to be respected and treated as a person from the moment of conception and therefore from that same moment its rights as a person must be recognized, among which in the first place is the inviolable right of every innocent human being to life.[5]

Note that the conclusions drawn in this passage from *Donum Vitae* are based upon the science of embryology. And what does embryology tell us? While obviously not discussing ensoulment, embryology is clear as to the question of when human life begins. Consider what Jan Langman wrote in *Medical Embryology* from 1975: "The development of a human being begins with fertilization, a process by which two highly specialized cells, the spermatozoon from the male and the oocyte from the female, unite to give rise to a new organism, the zygote."[6] Or, as noted in *Van Nostrand's Scientific Encyclopedia* published in 1976: "At the moment the sperm cell of the human male meets the ovum of the female and the union results in a fertilized ovum (zygote), a new life has begun. . . ."[7] Also, from 1988, Keith Moore explained in *Essentials of Human Embryology*: "Fertilization is a sequence of events that begins with the contact of a *sperm* (spermatozoon) with a *secondary oocyte* (ovum) and ends with the fusion of their *pronuclei* (the haploid nuclei of the sperm and ovum) and the mingling of their chromosomes to form a new cell. This fertilized ovum, known as a *zygote,* is a large diploid cell that is the beginning, or *primordium, of a human being.*"[8] More recent textbooks continue to add to the evidence regarding when human life begins. For example, in 1996 O'Rahilly and Müller wrote in *Human Embryology & Teratology:* "Although life is a continuous process, fertilization is a critical landmark because, under ordinary circumstances, a new, genetically distinct human organism is thereby formed. . . . The combination of 23 chromosomes present in each pronucleus results in 46 chromosomes in the *zygote*. Thus the diploid number is restored and the embryonic genome is formed. The embryo now exists as a genetic unity."[9] Most of the above quotes (many more of which could be provided) reference the specific act of fertilization, when the sperm actually enters the ovum, and this is sometimes confused with the idea of conception. For the purposes of this discussion, the two terms can be used in concert, with the general understanding being that conception refers more specifically to the completion of the fusion of chromosomes. Thus, the Catholic position that life begins at conception does not run counter to modern science, but rather faith and reason are in harmony here.[10]

Further, contemporary embryology provides a solid, rational basis upon which to rest the ethical conclusion that human life deserves respect and must be protected from the very moment it begins. In his book *Who Count as Persons?*, Fr. John Kavanaugh, S.J., provides an excellent account of the support that modern science gives to the Catholic tradition's view of the respect owed to human beings from the moment of conception:

Humans begin their lives when the process of conception is completed. That is when the "life" begins.... The strongest evidence for this position is genetic. Something radically new takes place when a human ovum is united with a human sperm. A complete and unique genotype with its own internal principle of self-development is created. It has its inherent system of information for the elaboration and development of its own capacities and endowments. The career of a human person is launched—a person with potentials, not a potential person.[11]

So, while the conclusions Kavanaugh and others reach that respect is owed to all human beings from the moment of our conception on accords with the faith tradition and teachings of the Catholic Church, such conclusions are also supported through reason and thus can be discussed in the *public* forum as well, regardless of unsettled questions over ensoulment. John Paul II summed up this line of reasoning in *The Gospel of Life,* noting that:

Furthermore, what is at stake is so important that, from the standpoint of moral obligation, the mere probability that a human person is involved would suffice to justify an absolutely clear prohibition of any intervention aimed at killing a human embryo. Precisely for this reason, over and above all scientific debates and those philosophical affirmations to which the Magisterium has not expressly committed itself, the Church has always taught and continues to teach that the result of human procreation, from the first moment of its existence, must be guaranteed that unconditional respect which is morally due to the human being in his or her totality and unity as body and spirit....[12]

I would add that beyond the scientific evidence helping to support that human life begins at conception, there is another, deeper, metaphysical point that is also crucial to acknowledge in understanding the Catholic Church's overall position regarding human reproduction. Metaphysically speaking, no human being actually gives "existence" to another human being. It is true that human intercourse provides for the biological development of a new member of the human species, providing the chromosomes and material endowments of the new being through the sperm and the ovum. However, what happens once the sperm and ovum are joined in the act of fertilization moves beyond the activity of the woman and man. And while it is true that we have an influence on the development of this new being throughout her or his life, an influence that can be either positive or negative, we do not have the power to give "existence"—this is simply beyond our ability. Why? Because we do not possess our own "existence" in such a way that we can take from it and give "existence" to another being. This is a subtle metaphysical point to grasp, but it is important nonetheless. Consider a mother holding her dying child in her arms. She cannot keep the life—the very "existence" that is flowing out of her child—from slipping away. If we possessed the power to give "existence," then the tragic death of a child could always be prevented. Nor can we give "existence" to inanimate objects—thus, the story of Pinocchio becoming a real boy is but a fairytale. This is why, at best, humans are called co-creators with God in terms of reproduction—we do set the process in motion, but God completes the creation of the new being. Why is God able to do this when we, as human beings, cannot? Because God is *Pure Esse—Pure Existence*. This argument can be found formulated more fully in the short work of St. Thomas Aquinas, *On Being and Essence.* And, although the argument itself is subtle and difficult to follow, it is important for rounding out the Catholic position, for if one fails to recognize that human "existence" does not come solely from the efforts of human beings, one will not understand the Catholic view that life is a *gift*.

And so, from the above discussion that began with the faith conviction that each human being is created in the image and likeness of God, a further metaphysical conclusion is reached that tells us the life of each human being is given as a free gift from God.

Now, while the conviction that we are made in God's image is theological, the conclusion that our very life and existence is a gift that each of us receives through no action or merit of our own is drawn from reason and human experience. Some are tempted to call life an "accident" rather than a "gift," not wanting to acknowledge any sort of Creator or plan in the universe. However, even if some dispute the origins of life, and the belief in creation and our dependence upon God for our very existence, there is still a common ground to be found here that is recognized by reason and supported by contemporary science: a new, unique human life begins at the moment of human conception. Thus, the Catholic position is still in harmony with natural reason. John Paul II reminded us of this very point in *The Gospel of Life* when he argued:

The Gospel of life is not for believers alone: it is for everyone. The issue of life and its defence and promotion is not a concern of Christians alone. Although faith provides special light and strength, this question arises in every human conscience which seeks the truth and which cares about the future of humanity. Life certainly has a sacred and religious value, but in no way is that value a concern only of believers. The value at stake is one which every human being can grasp by the light of reason; thus it necessarily concerns everyone.[13]

Our common task, then, is to determine what our obligations are toward a human being from his or her very beginning.

The primary obligation that reason recognizes here is to treat all human life with respect. Since the act of human fertilization results in a new, unique human individual (an individual that is a gift that we did not "create"), the Catholic Church recognizes that parents do not own their children. Children are not things, they are not property—this is perhaps one of the most mistaken and dangerous notions contemporary society could have regarding human reproduction. While acknowledging the suffering caused by infertility within marriage, the Congregation for the Doctrine of the Faith argued in *The Instruction on Respect for Human Life* that:

On the part of the spouses, the desire for a child is natural: it expresses the vocation to fatherhood and motherhood inscribed in conjugal love. This desire can be even stronger if the couple is affected by sterility which appears incurable. Nevertheless, marriage does not confer upon the spouses the right to have a child, but only the right to perform those natural acts which are *per se* ordered to procreation. (57) *A true and proper right to a child would be contrary to the child's dignity and nature. The child is not an object to which one has a right, nor can he be considered as an object of ownership: rather, a child is a gift, "the supreme gift" (58) and the most gratuitous gift of marriage, and is a living testimony of the mutual giving of his parents. For this reason, the child has the right, as already mentioned, to be the fruit of the specific act of the conjugal love of his parents; and he also has the right to be respected as a person from the moment of his conception.*[14]

And so, each child is a unique being bearing the likeness of God and deserving the utmost respect. In this light, the Catholic understanding of parenting is one of stewardship. We are to act toward all of creation, including the new lives of which we are co-creators, as stewards.

This point, unfortunately, does not seem to be widely recognized in society today. As we discussed in the first part of this book, our culture is one in which many groups of people are marginalized—children often seem to be among those groups. Some recent legal decisions have attempted to give more power to children, for example by letting them divorce their parents. However, children tend to be treated more like property with regard to divorce, abortion, and artificial reproduction. Certainly when one hears of the 400,000 embryos[15] held in frozen stasis in the United States—sadly often called "leftovers" from in vitro fertilization—one will realize that not all human life is treated with respect today and undeveloped children in the womb seem merely the biological products of their parents. But a careful, reasonable consideration of the freezing of human life for the convenience of science and parents should tell us that this is simply wrong. We really have no defensible right to treat these human beings in this manner—rather, the unborn have been marginalized in this country. Stewardship demands that we respect all human life—even at the embryonic stage of development—and protect such embryos, and the unborn in general, from neglect or harm.

Now many people tend to agree with the above reasoning when discussing children, or at least fetuses past the point of viability. But they wonder why the Catholic perspective has come to insist specifically that life begins at the moment of conception—especially since there is no agreement among Christians on the issue of ensoulment, as noted earlier. If there is no soul, then is there really a human being present? And, if we are unsure whether or not there is a human being present, can we not consider other factors as more important—at least until we are sure that the new life is actually a unique human being, or a person? And for those who do not believe in the existence of "souls," and see human reproduction solely as a biological process, the case is even harder to make. After all, they will say, an embryo or a fetus is certainly not like a human that has already been born. So why give the embryo or fetus the same respect—especially if one has needs and concerns deemed more pressing than that of the unborn?

The pro-choice lobby has played upon this uncertainty for many years now. Consider the following excerpts from the 1989 *Webster v. Reproductive*

Health Services case, which came before the United States Supreme Court. In his oral argument for Reproductive Health Services, Frank Susman was insisting for the pro-choice side that abortion was a "fundamental right" of a woman. Susman partly argued that the Constitution supported a woman's right to an abortion. But Susman also recognized the lack of scientific certitude in determining the humanity of the unborn. Since no one knew for sure, a woman should be the sole person to decide when a fetus was a human or not. Justice Scalia objected to this line of reasoning. The record of the discussion between Scalia and Susman portrays the striking divergence of opinion that arises over the uncertainty of the status of the unborn:

Justice Scalia: Let me inquire—I can see deriving a fundamental right from either a long tradition that this, the right to abort, has always been protected—I don't see that tradition, but I suppose you could also derive a fundamental right just simply from the text of the Constitution, plus the logic of the matter or whatever.

How can—can you derive it that way here without making a determination as to whether the fetus is a human life or not? It is very hard to say it just is a matter of basic principle that it must be a fundamental right unless you make the determination that the organism that is destroyed is not a human life. Can you as a matter of logic or principle make that determination otherwise?

Mr. Susman: I think the basic question—and, of course, it goes to one of the specific provisions of the statute as to whether this is a human life or whether human life begins at conception—is not something that is verifiable as a fact. It is a question verifiable only by reliance upon faith.

It is a question of labels. Neither side in this issue and debate would ever disagree on the physiological facts. Both sides would agree as to when a heartbeat can first be detected. Both sides would agree to when brain waves can first be detected. But when you come to try to place the emotional labels on what you call that collection of physiological facts, that is where people part company.

Justice Scalia: I agree with you entirely, but what conclusion does that lead you to? That, therefore, there must be a fundamental right on the part of the woman to destroy this thing that we don't know what it is or, rather, that whether there is or isn't is a matter that you vote upon; since we don't know the answer, people have to make up their minds the best they can.

Mr. Susman: The conclusion to which it leads me is that, when you have an issue that is so divisive and so emotional and so personal and so intimate, it must be left as a fundamental right to the individual to make that choice under her then attendant circumstances, her religious beliefs, her moral beliefs, and in consultation with her physician.[16]

The uncertainty regarding the humanity of the unborn is openly admitted by both parties in this discussion. How should a moral agent act regarding abortion in the face of such uncertainty? Susman indicates that the very presence of uncertainty on this issue secures the right of the woman as the only one who can make the decision to terminate a fetus. But is this the most appropriate way for human moral agents to act? What we have to ask is whether or not it is reasonable to base a strong, positive right to control one's body to the extent that certain people can determine the humanity of the unborn upon their personal belief and be both legally and morally justified, all upon an uncertainty—a lack of knowledge? Or, is it reasonable to protect the fetus as human life, regardless of whether it ever achieves its full potential? A woman contemplating an abortion, or a doctor contemplating doing such a procedure, cannot simply say they do not know for sure what we are doing. We need to examine those facts that we do know and follow the strongest evidence at hand.

In this regard, John T. Noonan offered the following argument against abortion:

If a fetus is destroyed, one destroys a being already possessed of the genetic code, organs, and sensitivity to pain, and one which had an 80 percent chance of developing further into a baby outside the womb, who, in time, would reason. . . . It is this genetic information which determines his characteristics, which is the biological carrier of the possibility of human wisdom, which makes him a self-evolving being. A being with a human genetic code is man.[17]

Noonan first advanced this argument in 1970—well before the *Roe v. Wade* decision. The boom in genetic research and the Human Genome Project, however, have clearly added to the strength of this argument today. An appeal to genetic evidence—as Kavanaugh noted earlier—reveals that an embryo from conception on has all that he or she will ever need to develop as a human being. How, then, can we see this embryo as anything less than human? Yet, the 1975 argument of the prominent ethicist Baruch Brody, which had objected that the genetic argument was still inconclusive from a scientific perspective, continues to reign (as we read with Frank Susman and pro-choice advocates). Brody's point was that the mere presence of human genetic information does not "prove" that human "life" is present. And so he pursues other avenues for arguing against abortion.[18] Today, the debate has spread to the issue of human embryonic stem cell research. The arguments continue to be raised that a few cells are not a "human person," while the issue of genetic identity is rarely brought into the debate. But in the absence of complete "scientific" certitude, one must consider the evidence that *is* available. What Noonan indicates is that every fertilized human egg by possessing its genetic information has the potentiality of full human life. This is an important point. No one denies that once conceived a fetus will become nothing but human if nurtured. However, this is often glossed over as a trivial point. *But this is evidence!* The "collection of physiological facts" that Susman mentions, facts such as a complete human genome in a unique, self-developing entity, represent evidence that a human agent must recognize before making a moral decision. Human reason recognizes that the fertilized egg from the very moment of conception contains the full potentiality of a human being—a potentiality that is, and will continue to be, developing. All of the possibilities of that human being in all of her or his uniqueness are present in that first cell.

In the end, the Catholic understanding of human life as beginning at conception, far from being at odds with modern science or standing in the way of progress and civil rights, is actually focused upon the betterment of human life in society. As John Paul II argued in *The Gospel of Life:* "When the Church declares that unconditional respect for the right to life of every innocent person—from conception to natural death—is one of the pillars on which every civil society stands, she 'wants simply to promote a human State. A State which recognizes the defence of the fundamental rights of the human person, especially of the weakest, as its primary duty.'"[19] Contemporary embryology and genetics provide evidence that confirms the Catholic Church's view that all human life deserves respect, while also providing a common ground to guide our public policy decision making in society as a whole. This evidence can provide the moral certitude in our public debates to recognize that unborn life is indeed human life and deserves protection.

The conclusion that all human life deserves respect and protection from conception on then leads to other conclusions regarding artificial reproduction, cloning, the freezing of embryos, etc. There are also implications here for contraception and family planning, in that the nature of human sexuality through which we become co-creators of life with God demands that sexual activity be treated with respect both for the individuals who engage in such intimate and life-giving actions, as well as for the new lives engendered. The essays in this second part of the book show how the basic Catholic tenets laid out here and in the introductory essays can be applied to various issues in human reproduction.

The first essay, by William E. May, is "The New Reproductive Technologies and Catholic Teaching." To begin with, May offers a thorough discussion of current reproductive technologies. In his presentation, he clarifies the difference between *artificial* and *assisted* reproduction and explores the specific problems raised by heterologous versus homologous procedures. Then May goes on to give an equally thorough review of the Catholic Church's official teachings regarding human reproduction and technology. Readers will appreciate the breadth and depth of May's research, which provides a crucial background for understanding the Catholic position. Special attention is given to the process of GIFT. May is candid and forthright regarding current discussions of this procedure among Catholic theologians and scholars, especially those drawing upon proportionalist moral thinking, and he offers his own insightful critique. At the heart of his own position is May's argument that: ". . . husbands and wives have no *right* to have a child. They have no right to have a child because a child is not a thing, not a pet, not a toy, but a person of inviolable dignity. . . . Their desire to bear and raise children is noble and legitimate, but this desire does not justify any and every means to see its fulfillment." May's open and honest discussion of the new reproductive technologies helps reveal that the Catholic position is not a static, rigid view, but rather embodies the true dynamism of a living tradition with much wisdom to offer contemporary society.

The second essay in this part moves on to the controversial yet increasingly relevant topic of contraception. This is a difficult topic to address these days because for many, using contraception is part and parcel of living in the modern world. Thus the Catholic position is viewed as completely unreasonable—and even worse, inconsistent, since the Church approves of Natural Family Planning. In his essay, "Contraception: A Hard Saying," Benedict Ashley, O.P., meets these charges head on. Ashley's response presents a clear, precise, and frank discussion of the key issues behind the contraception debate. He carefully explores the subtle nuances of human sexuality that underlie contraceptive practices, and reveals the broader connections to marriage and family that flow out of our common nature as sexual beings. Of particular benefit is Ashley's argument regarding the relation between the unitive and procreative aspects of the marital act, which is itself the fundamental basis of the Catholic tradition's teachings on contraception. Throughout the essay, Ashley openly recognizes that many Catholics struggle with the issue of contraception, due probably in no small part to the relativistic influences of contemporary American society. This is one of those "issues" where the Catholic Church is clearly "countercultural." Nevertheless, Ashley notes that for critics of the Church to be fair, they must realize that ". . . only when viewed in the context of the total Catholic worldview and value system is the Church's teaching on the particular question of contraception revealed as consistent, reasonable, and life-affirming."

The final essay in this part is by Jeanne Heffernan Schindler, and addresses the crucial issue of abortion. There are many, many people who say they are tired of talking about the abortion issue—but it is simply not going away, nor should it. As Heffernan Schindler notes, there is increasing pressure within the public arena to force Catholic hospitals to perform abortions, or at least, following mergers with non-Catholic facilities, to allow them, as well as growing pressure upon Catholic medical schools to provide abortion training. She notes: "These bold attempts to change the climate of American medical practice pose a serious challenge to opponents of abortion. Now, perhaps more than ever over the last thirty years, the burden is upon them to articulate a case against abortion that is publicly intelligible. . . . Fortunately, there is a compelling case to be made against abortion. The Catholic Church has been making it for two thousand years. . . ." In this vein, Heffernan Schindler lays out the Catholic tradition's opposition to abortion. She begins with the historical development of the Church's stance, from its roots in sacred scripture, through the witness of the early Christians, into the official teaching of the Church and canon law. As a result, Heffernan Schindler highlights the remarkable consistency of the Catholic tradition's position. Heffernan Schindler then explains the rationale behind the Church's teaching on abortion by presenting the moral case against abortion, which she points out is a position that is intelligible for both Catholics and non-Catholics alike. Her discussion is thorough, taking into account contemporary science and embryology, as well as the common ethical arguments used in support of abortion—including the "personhood" argument. Readers will find Heffernan Schindler's essay a clearly articulated explanation of the wisdom that grounds the Catholic position on the sanctity of life and the immorality of abortion.

NOTES

1. *Catechism of the Catholic Church,* English Translation for the United States of America (New York: Catholic Book Publishing Company, 1994), no. 355, p. 91.
    2. Ibid.
    3. John Paul II, *Evangelium Vitae,* no. 101.

4. Benedict M. Ashley, O.P., and Kevin D. O'Rourke, O.P., *Health Care Ethics: A Theological Analysis,* 4th ed. (Washington, DC: Georgetown University Press, 1997), pp. 228–29.

5. Congregation for the Doctrine of the Faith, *Donum Vitae,* 1987, part I, no. 1.

6. Jan Langman, *Medical Embryology,* 3rd ed. (Baltimore: Williams and Wilkins, 1975), p. 3.

7. *Van Nostrand's Scientific Encyclopedia,* ed. Douglas Considine, 5th ed. (New York: Van Nostrand Reinhold Company, 1976), p. 943.

8. Keith L. Moore, *Essentials of Human Embryology* (Toronto: B. C. Decker, 1988), p. 2.

9. Ronan O'Rahilly and Fabiola Müller, *Human Embryology & Teratology,* 2nd ed. (New York: Wiley-Liss, 1996), pp. 8, 29.

10. For an excellent overview and discussion of the Catholic debate regarding when human life begins, see Ashley and O'Rourke, *Health Care Ethics,* pp. 227–40.

11. John F. Kavanaugh, S.J., *Who Count as Persons? Human Identity and the Ethics of Killing* (Washington, DC: Georgetown University Press, 2001), p. 131.

12. *Evangelium Vitae,* no. 60.

13. Ibid., no. 101.

14. *Donum Vitae,* part II, no. 8.

15. David Hoffman et al., "Cryopreserved Embryos in the United States and Their Availability for Research," *Fertility and Sterility* 79, no. 5 (May 2003): 1063–69.

16. From "Oral Argument of Frank Susman on Behalf of the Appellees," *Webster v. Reproductive Health Services* (1989), in *Landmark Briefs and Arguments of the Supreme Court of the United States: Constitutional Law,* ed. Philip B. Kurland and Gerhard Casper (Frederick, MD: University Publications of America, 1990), pp. 944–45.

17. John T. Noonan, Jr., "An Almost Absolute Value in History," in *The Morality of Abortion,* ed. John T. Noonan, Jr. (Cambridge, MA: Harvard University Press, 1970), p. 57.

18. Baruch Brody, *Abortion and the Sanctity of Human Life* (Cambridge, MA: MIT Press, 1975), p. 91.

19. *Evangelium Vitae,* no. 101.

CHAPTER 3

New Reproductive Technologies and Catholic Teaching

WILLIAM E. MAY

This paper examines "new reproductive technologies," i.e., ways of generating human life that dispense with the need for coital union between a man and woman, whether marital or not. In it I will defend the teaching of the Church that God, in his wise and loving plan for human existence, wills that human life be given—"begotten"—*only* through the marital embrace, i.e., through a procreative marital act, and that, consequently, it is always wrong to generate human life through procedures that substitute for the marital act.

I will first describe the new reproductive technologies; second, summarize relevant teaching of the Church; third, provide reasoned arguments to support the truth of the Church's teaching. As we will see, the magisterium of the Church distinguishes between *artificial* insemination (a technological procedure which substitutes for the marital act) and *assisted* insemination (a technological procedure that enables a marital act to be crowned with the gift of life), declaring the first intrinsically immoral and the second morally permissible. Thus, a final part of this paper will consider the question of "assisted insemination," and in particular the procedure known as

Much of the material in this essay is taken from "Generating Human Life: Marriage and the New Reproductive Technologies," chapter 3 of my book *Catholic Bioethics and the Gift of Human Life* (Huntington, IN: Our Sunday Visitor, 2000), pp. 65–118.

GIFT, or gamete intrafallopian tube transfer, which some Catholic theologians defend as "assisting" the marital act and others reject as "substituting" for the marital act.

The New Reproductive Technologies

The new reproductive technologies can be divided into two broad categories: (1) artificial fertilization, which embraces (a) artificial insemination and (b) in vitro fertilization and embryo transfer; and (2) agametic reproduction or cloning.

1. Artificial Fertilization

Artificial fertilization occurs when male sperm are united with the female ovum not through coition but by other means. In artificial insemination male sperm are introduced into the female reproductive tract by the use of a cannula or other instruments, and fertilization occurs when one of the sperm fuses with the woman's ovum. Fertilization occurs within the woman's body. In in vitro fertilization male sperm and female ova are placed in a petri dish and fusion of sperm and ovum and fertilization occur outside the woman's body. Subsequently, the developing embryo can be implanted in the womb of a woman, who can be either the one whose ovum was fertilized or some other person.

Both these forms of artificial fertilization can be either *homologous*, when the gametic cells used are provided by a married couple, or *heterologous*, which uses gametic cells of persons who are not married to one another (although one or both of the parties whose gametic cells are used may be married to another person).[1]

A. Artificial Insemination

i. Homologous artificial insemination, or AIH Homologous artificial insemination, or artificial insemination by the husband (AIH), introduces the husband's sperm into his wife's body by the use of a cannula or other instruments. Ordinarily, the husband's sperm are obtained by masturbation, although an alternative is intercourse using a perforated condom, or, in cases of obstruction of the vas deferens, which serves as the conduit for spermatozoa, the surgical removal of sperm from the epididymis, where the sperm are stored.[2]

ii. Heterologous artificial insemination, or AID   Heterologous artificial insemination is usually referred to by the acronym AID, signifying "artificial insemination by a donor." But, as Walter Wadlington correctly observes, "the term 'sperm donor' is a misnomer because compensation of persons supplying semen has been a long-standing practice."[3] It is thus more accurate to designate this form of artificial insemination as "artificial insemination by a *vendor*."

Traditionally, heterologous artificial insemination was used by married couples to allow the wife to bear a child genetically her own when her husband is infertile or in cases of "genetic incompatibility" between the couple, i.e., when the couple are bearers of a recessive genetic defect and there is thus the likelihood that any child they conceive may be actually affected by this genetic impairment. Today, however, artificial insemination is also used by single women who want to bear a child and who, as Walter Wadlington puts it, "do not have a marital or other stable heterosexual partner or by a woman in a life partnership with another woman."[4] It is also used in implementing surrogacy agreements under which a woman will conceive and bear a child who will then be turned over to the sperm "vendor" or other parties after birth.

B. In Vitro Fertilization and Embryo Transfer

In the late 1970s Patrick Steptoe and Robert Edwards succeeded in bringing to birth a child conceived in vitro and transferred a few days after conception to her mother's womb. Thus, with the birth of Louise Brown on July 25, 1978, a new mode of human reproduction became a reality, in vitro fertilization.[5]

In vitro fertilization makes it possible for human life to be conceived outside the body of the (genetic) mother, but it is still a form of generating human life that is gametic, i.e., it is possible only by fusing a male gametic cell, the sperm, with a female gametic cell, the ovum. The new human life is conceived in a petri dish using sperm provided by a man and ova provided by a woman. Approximately two days after the fertilization process has been completed the embryo, which by then has developed to the four-to-eight-cell stage, is ready for transfer into the uterus, where it can implant and, if implantation is successful, continue intrauterine development until birth.

IVF-ET was carried out initially by obtaining a single egg (ovum) from a woman through a laparoscopy, a procedure requiring general anesthesia.

When a laparoscopy is performed, the physician aspirates the woman's egg through a hollow needle inserted into the abdomen and guided by a narrow optical instrument called a laparoscope. Today, it is standard procedure to overstimulate the ovaries with ovulatory drugs so that the woman will produce several oocytes for retrieval and subsequent fertilization. Current practice is to retrieve the oocytes (ova) she produces, not by laparoscopy with its attendant requirement of a general anesthesia, but by ultrasound-guided transvaginal aspiration, which can be done without general anesthesia. This, of course, greatly simplifies the procedure. It is also standard practice today to fertilize many eggs, mixing them in the petri dish with sperm (usually collected by masturbation) that have been "washed" in order to make them more apt to succeed in the fertilization process. This is done so that several new human zygotes can be generated and allowed to grow to the early embryo stage. Of these very early embryos, it is now customary to transfer two to four to the womb to increase the probability of implantation and subsequent gestation and birth, and to freeze and store the others so that they can be used for implantation purposes in the event that the initial attempts at embryo transfer, gestation, and birth are unsuccessful. The "spare" frozen embryos may also be "donated" for research purposes. Eventually, if not claimed by the persons responsible for their manufacture or used in research, the frozen embryos will be destroyed.[6]

i. Homologous IVF and embryo transfer   Initially homologous IVF and embryo transfer was used almost exclusively in women with damaged fallopian tubes, to enable them and their husbands to have children of their own. But indications for homologous IVF and embryo transfer have now been extended to include male factor infertility (oligospermia, for instance) and other cases in which no precise cause for the infertility of the couple has been determined.[7] Since it is now possible to separate male sperm carrying y chromosomes (that produce male children) from those carrying x chromosomes (that produce female children), this procedure can now be used to avoid generating a child with hemophilia (always a male) for couples at risk of having a hemophiliac child. Undoubtedly, with advances in identifying chromosomal causes of genetically induced pathologies, the use of in vitro and embryo transfer to avoid the generation of children afflicted by such pathologies will increase in the future.

ii. Heterologous IVF and embryo transfer   Obviously, IVF and embryo transfer make it possible for the gametic cells (ova and sperm) of individuals who are not married to each other to be used to generate new human life in the laboratory. Heterologous in vitro fertilization is thus sometimes used instead of artificial insemination by a donor/vendor in instances when there is genetic incompatibility between the spouses. It is also used when the wife lacks ovaries and does not therefore produce ova. Ova can be "donated" by another woman, fertilized in vitro with sperm provided by her husband, and the embryo implanted in his wife's womb. Embryos, too, can be "donated." In fact, sperm and embryo "donation" is easier to manage than egg donation inasmuch as the latter is complicated by the need to synchronize the menstrual cycles of the donor and the woman in whom the resulting embryo conceived in vitro will be implanted. Both homologous and heterologous IVF can involve transferring the embryo into the womb of a woman other than the one who supplied the ovum, a so-called surrogate mother.[8]

As can be seen from the above, many permutations and combinations of generating human life are now technically feasible as a result of in vitro fertilization, among them such procedures as ZIFT (zygote intrafallopian tube transfer), which occurs when the zygote resulting from IVF is inserted into the fallopian tube, rather than having the embryo transferred to the uterus; and PROST (pronuclear-stage tubal transfer), which transfers the very early embryo by use of a laparoscope into the fallopian tube.[9] Other combinations are possible and undoubtedly more will be developed in the future.

C. Alternative Technologies Making Use of Male and Female Gametic Cells

Certain contemporary techniques are not, strictly speaking, variants of in vitro fertilization inasmuch as fertilization takes place within the mother's body and not outside of it in a petri dish. Thus they are technically more closely related to artificial insemination than to in vitro fertilization as methods of artificial fertilization, but their development was stimulated by research into in vitro fertilization and embryo transfer. Nor, in these procedures, is sexual coition necessary in order to unite the male and female gametic cells.

One such technique is called SIFT, or sperm intrafallopian tube transfer. This is sometimes used as an option for infertile couples who have not conceived following AIH. In this procedure the woman's ovaries are hyperstimulated; hyperstimulation is coupled with a laparoscopy under a general anesthesia to inject a "washed" or prepared concentrate of the husband's sperm (or that of a "donor" if necessary) into the fallopian tubes so that conception can occur there.[10]

Another procedure of special interest is GIFT, or gamete intrafallopian tube transfer. This is similar to IVF in that the woman's ovaries are hyperstimulated to produce multiple eggs. The eggs are retrieved either by laparoscopy or ultrasound-guided transvaginal procedures. An egg (or eggs) is placed into a catheter with sperm (provided either by masturbation or by the use of a perforated condom during coition) that have been treated and "capacitated," with an air bubble separating ova from sperm so that fertilization cannot occur outside the woman's body. The catheter is then inserted into the woman's womb, the ovum(a) and sperm are released from the catheter and fertilization/conception can then occur within the body of the woman (who can, of course, be the wife of the man whose sperm are used).[11]

2. *Cloning, or Agametic Reproduction*

The February 27, 1997, issue of the journal *Nature* carried the news of the birth of the sheep "Dolly" through the work of Scottish researchers Jan Vilmut and K. H. S. Campbell and their associates at Edinburgh's Roslin Institute. They succeeded in generating a new sheep by a process called "cloning," or more technically, "somatic-cell nuclear transfer."[12] What they did was to produce Dolly by fusing the nucleus of a somatic (body) cell of an adult sheep with an oocyte whose nucleus had been removed, that is, an oocyte deprived of the maternal genome. The genetic identity of the new individual sheep, Dolly, was derived from only one source, namely, the adult sheep whose somatic cell nucleus was transferred into the denucleated oocyte to "trigger" development into a new individual of the species. This procedure can, in principle, be used to generate new human beings, and toward the end of 1998 a team of scientists in Korea claimed to have succeeded in generating a new human life through cloning. Cloning is a mode of generating life through a procedure that is asexual or agametic in nature. Thus, even from a biological perspective, cloning is a far more radical mode of reproduction than artificial insemination or in vitro fertilization and embryo transfer. It represents, as the Pontifical Academy for Life has noted, "a radical manipulation of the constitutive relationality and complementarity which is at the origin of human procreation. . . . It tends to make bisexuality a purely functional leftover, given that an ovum must be used without its nucleus in order to make room for the clone-embryo."[13]

Church Teaching on Reproductive Technologies

The principal sources for the teaching of the magisterium of the Church on these new reproductive technologies are found in four addresses by Pope Pius XII and in the *Instruction on Respect for Human Life in Its Origin and on the Dignity of Procreation* (*Donum Vitae* in Latin) issued by the Congregation for the Doctrine of the Faith in February 1987. The *Catechism of the Catholic Church* in essence summarizes the teaching of the *Instruction* (cf. *Catechism,* nos. 2375–78). Another magisterial document, important because it takes up the question of cloning, not considered by Pius XII and noted (and rejected) only briefly by *Donum Vitae,* is the Pontifical Academy for Life's *Reflections on Cloning,* released toward the end of June 1997.

Here I will provide an overview of the teaching of Pope Pius XII, a more detailed account of the *Instruction on Respect for Human Life* (hereafter referred to by its Latin title, *Donum Vitae*), and conclude by considering the document from the Pontifical Academy for Life.

1. The Teaching of Pope Pius XII (d. 1958)

In four of his addresses Pius XII considered the morality of artificial insemination, although this was not the central topic with which he was concerned, and in one of these four he also addressed the morality of in vitro fertilization, which, at the time of his address, was proposed as a way of reproducing humans, although it was not then realistically possible.[14]

Pius' teaching is quite clear. Artificial insemination, whether by a third party or by the husband, is intrinsically immoral. Pius summarized matters in the following passage. "The Church," he wrote,

has ... rejected the ... attitude which pretended to separate in procreation the biological activity from the personal relations of husband and wife. The child is the fruit of the marriage union, when it finds full expression by the placing in action of the functional organs, of the sensible emotions thereto related, and of the spiritual and disinterested love which animates such a union; it is in the unity of this human act that there must be considered the biological condition of procreation. *Never is it permitted to separate these different aspects to the point of excluding positively either the intention of procreation or the conjugal relation.*[15]

Here Pius articulates the principle of the inseparability, willed by God and not lawful for man to break on his own initiative, between the unitive and procreative meanings of the marital act.

Specifically with reference to artificial insemination by the husband, the following remarks from his 1951 address to Italian midwives are most pertinent:

To reduce the common life of a husband and wife and the conjugal act to a mere organic function for the transmission of seed would be but to convert the domestic hearth, the family sanctuary, into a biological laboratory. Therefore, in our allocution of September 29, 1949, to the International Congress of Catholic Doctors, We expressly excluded artificial insemination in marriage. The conjugal act in its natural structure is a personal action, a simultaneous and immediate cooperation of husband and wife, which by the very nature of the agents and the propriety of the act, is an expression of the reciprocal gift, which, according to Holy Writ, effects the union "in one flesh." That is much more than the union of two genes, which can be effected even by artificial means, that is, without the natural action of the husband and wife. The conjugal act, ordained and designed by nature, is a personal cooperation, to which husband and wife, when contracting marriage, exchange the right.[16]

In one of his addresses Pius XII explicitly condemned in vitro fertilization, at that time only a possibility and not a reality. Addressing this matter, he declared in no uncertain terms: "As regards experiments of human artificial fecundation 'in vitro,' let it be sufficient to observe that they must be rejected as immoral and absolutely unlawful."[17] Pius did not, however, attempt to provide arguments to show why in vitro fertilization is absolutely immoral.

Although he condemned *artificial insemination* by a husband as intrinsically immoral, Pius XII declared that "this does not necessarily proscribe the use of certain artificial means destined solely to facilitate the marital act, or to assure the accomplishment of the end of the natural act normally performed."[18] He distinguished, in other words, between technological procedures *substituting* for the marital act (artificial insemination, whether homologous or heterologous) and procedures *assisting* the marital act to be crowned with the gift of human life. This distinction, as we shall now see, is central to the teaching of *Donum Vitae.*

2. The Teaching of Donum Vitae

This lengthy document contains an introduction, three major sections, and a conclusion. The first major section deals with the respect due to human embryos; the second treats explicitly of the new reproductive technologies; and the third deals with the values and moral obligations that must be respected by civil law.

The basic norm *Donum Vitae* provides for morally evaluating reproductive technologies is the following:

[F]ertilization is licitly sought when it is the result of a "conjugal act which is *per se* suitable for the generation of children to which marriage is ordered by its nature and by which the spouses become one flesh." But from the moral point of view procreation is deprived of its proper perfection when it is not desired as the fruit of the conjugal act, that is to say, of the specific act of the spouses' union.[19]

By a conjugal act "*per se* suitable for the generation of children" the document means the sort or kind of act through which new human life can be given if the persons engaging in it are fertile and the conditions for conception favorable.

Donum Vitae then draws a conclusion from this normative premise, namely, that a reproductive technology for effecting fertilization "cannot be admitted except for those cases in which *the technical means is not a substitute for the conjugal act but serves to facilitate and help* so that the act attains its natural purpose."[20]

The instruction here incorporates the teaching of Pope Pius XII: the basic principle for morally evaluating a reproductive technology is whether it assists or replaces the conjugal act. If it replaces the marital act it is absolutely immoral; if it assists the act, i.e., if it helps the marital act itself attain its natural end and be crowned with the gift of life, then it can be morally permissible.

The distinction made by Pius XII and *Donum Vitae* between technological procedures substituting for the marital act and those "assisting" it to procreate human life was later reaffirmed by Pope John Paul II in a message to fellow bishops who gathered to study the issues raised by new technologies in the light of *Donum Vitae*. In his message the Holy Father said, after citing a relevant passage from the instruction, that it "is important to distinguish artificial fertilization . . . from therapeutic techniques which aim at remedying deficiencies of nature."[21]

Donum Vitae then takes up in some detail first heterologous artificial fertilization and then homologous artificial fertilization. It repudiates heterologous fertilization as immoral because it violates the unity of marriage, the dignity of the spouses, and the right of the child to be conceived and brought into the world in marriage and from marriage. Moreover, the fertilization of a woman who is unmarried or widowed can never be justified, no matter who the donor might be.[22]

It then addresses the issue of homologous artificial fertilization, i.e., the fertilization of the wife either by artificially inseminating her with her own husband's sperm or by removing eggs from her body and fertilizing them in vitro with her husband's sperm. The key moral principle invoked to show why homologous artificial insemination is immoral is the one already noted and rooted in the intimate bond between procreation and the marital act: the procreation of a new human person must be "the fruit and sign of the mutual self-giving of the spouses."[23]

The document then develops three lines of argument to support its teaching on the grave immorality of homologous fertilization. The first (1) is based on the inseparable connection, willed by God and unlawful for man to break on his own initiative, between the unitive and procreative meanings of the conjugal act; the second (2), on the dignity of the child conceived, who ought not to be treated as if he were a product; the third (3), on the "language of the body."[24]

The first line of argument, on the inseparable bond between the unitive and procreative meanings of the conjugal act, was, as *Donum Vitae* notes, the reason given by Pius XII for repudiating artificial insemination by a husband. Reaffirming this inseparable connection, *Donum Vitae* then declares: "[h]omologous artificial fertilization, in seeking a procreation which is not the fruit of a specific act of conjugal union, objectively effects . . . a separation between the goods and meanings of marriage."[25]

The second line of argument holds that the dignity of the child as a person is violated by artificial fertilization, even if this is homologous and not heterologous. The child's dignity is violated because the child is treated as if he were a product and not as a person equal in dignity to his parents. As *Donum Vitae* puts it, "The one conceived must be the fruit of his parents' love. He cannot be desired or conceived as the product of an intervention of medical or biological techniques; that would be equivalent to reducing him to an object of scientific technology. No one may subject the coming of a child into the world to conditions of technical efficiency, which are to be evaluated according to standards of control and dominion."[26]

In introducing the third line of argument, the Vatican instruction refers to the teaching of Pope John Paul II,[27] who has written and spoken at length on the truth that spouses express their unique love for one another in the "language of the body." Summarizing his thought, *Donum Vitae* puts matters as follows:

The conjugal act by which the couple mutually express their self-gift at the same time expresses openness to the gift of life. It is an act that is inseparably corporal and spiritual. It is in their bodies and through their bodies that the spouses consummate their marriage and are able to become father and mother. In order to respect the language of their bodies and their natural generosity, the conjugal union must take place with respect for its openness to procreation; and the procreation of a person must be the fruit and the result of married love. The origin of the human being thus follows from a procreation that is "linked to the union, not only biological but also spiritual, of the parents, made one by the bond of marriage."[28]

3. "Reflections on Cloning"

This paper of the Pontifical Academy for Life was issued in late June 1997, after the success of the Vilmut team in cloning "Dolly." It is the only magisterial document to deal explicitly with cloning as a reproductive technology. After noting that cloning "represents a radical manipulation of the constitutive relationality and complementarity which is at the origin of human procreation in both its biological and strictly personal aspects," it declares: "All the moral reasons which led to the condemnation of in vitro fertilization as such and to the radical censure of in vitro fertilization for merely experimental purposes must also be applied to human cloning."[29]

An Ethical and Theological Evaluation of New Reproductive Technologies

Here I will first offer reasons of an ethical/philosophical nature to show the truth of the Church's teaching that it is morally permissible to generate human life *only* in and through the marital act and that consequently new reproductive technologies which *substitute* for the marital act, whether heterologous or homologous, are intrinsically immoral. I will then offer a consideration, rooted in a theological understanding of human existence, to support this teaching. In my presentation I will focus attention on *homologous insemination* and *in vitro fertilization,* i.e., procedures in which the gametic cells used to achieve fertilization come from husband and wife. I do so because if it can be shown that homologous insemination/fertilization is always immoral, it follows a fortiori that *heterologous* insemination/fertilization is always wrong.

1. Ethical/Philosophical Reasons Why Nonmarital Modes of Generating Human Life Are Immoral

As we saw earlier, *Donum Vitae* provides three lines of reasoning to support the conclusion that it is always immoral to generate human life outside the marital act. Here I will develop the second line of reasoning sketched in *Donum Vitae,* namely, that generating human life by procedures that substitute for the marital act violate the child's dignity insofar as the child is treated as if he or she were a product, thus changing an act of *procreation* to one of *reproduction.* I do so because I believe that this line of reasoning provides the most direct and cogent argument in support of the claim that generating human life outside the marital act is always wrong. But before doing so I will provide some brief reflections regarding the first and third lines of argumentation. These two lines of reasoning illumine the wider issues concerning human existence raised by the new reproductive technologies. But to appreciate them it is necessary to probe the meaning of marriage and the bonds uniting marriage and the marital act, as well as the relationship between marriage, the marital act, and the generation of human life.

Marital Rights and Capabilities, the Marital Act, and the Generation of Human Life

The central truth undergirding the first line of reasoning based on the inseparability of the unitive and procreative meanings of the marital act is that husbands and wives, precisely because they have given themselves irrevocably to one another in marriage, have *capacitated* themselves—made themselves *fit*—to do what married couples are supposed to do, namely, to give one another a special kind of love, spousal or conjugal love, to express that love in the marital act, and to welcome the gift of new human life and give it the home where it can take root and grow. In sharp contrast to the genital act of fornicators and adulterers, which in no way unites two irreplaceable and nonsubstitutable spouses but simply joins two individuals who are in principle replaceable, substitutable, disposable, the marital act of husbands and wives unites two persons who have, by their own free and irrevocable choice, made each other utterly irreplaceable and nonsubstitutable. Precisely because they have done this, husbands and wives have rendered themselves fit to engage in the marital act and, in and through it, to welcome the gift of human life lovingly, to nourish it humanely, and to educate it in the love and service of God and neighbor.[30] They have, in other words, given themselves the capacity to be parents, mothers and fathers, of new human persons. Indeed, as Pope Paul VI said, the marital act "makes them *capable* (the Latin text says *eos idoneos* [literally 'fit'] *facit*) of bringing forth new life according to laws inscribed in their very being as husband and wife."[31] The marital act, in other words, is not merely a sexual act between persons who simply happen to be married. It is, rather, by its own inner nature and dynamism, love-giving (unitive) and life-giving (procreative); it is an act, in short, participating in the "goods" or "blessings" of marriage. The bond, therefore, that unites the two meanings of the marital act is the marriage itself. But "what God has joined together, let no man put asunder." It is for this reason, I believe, that there is an inseparable connection, willed by God and not lawful for man to break on his own initiative, between the unitive and procreative meanings of the conjugal act.

The marital act, moreover, as the third line of reasoning maintains, is an act that speaks the "language of the body," beautifully embodying the personal, bodily integrity and unity of the spouses. It does so because in the marital act, husband and wife are freely choosing and realizing real goods in the world—their own marital union, and the gift of life to which their union is open—and their own bodily activity, "the language of their body," is a constitutive subject of what they do: their bodily gift of themselves to one another makes them to be "one flesh," the common subject of the same act, and their cooperation is not only appropriate but absolutely essential and necessary. To see what this means, it is worth pondering the following observations of John Finnis concerning personal, bodily integrity:

> . . . personal integrity involves . . . that one be reaching out with one's will, that is, freely choosing, real goods, and that one's efforts to realize these goods involves, where appropriate, one's bodily activity, so that that activity is as much the constitutive subject of what one does as one's act of choosing is. That one really be realizing real goods in the world; that one be doing so by one's free and aware choice; that that choice be carried into effect by one's own bodily action, including, where appropriate, bodily acts of communication and cooperation with other real people—these are the fundamental aspects of personal integrity.[32]

In the marital act, a husband and wife are indeed freely choosing and realizing real goods in the world—their own marital union and new human life; their bodily activity—the "language of the body"—is a constitutive subject of what they do; and cooperation with another is not only appropriate but absolutely essential. This is the truth undergirding the third line of reasoning employed by *Donum Vitae*.

Procreation versus Reproduction

I believe that the second argument advanced in *Donum Vitae* to support its teaching that it is always immoral to generate human life outside the marital act requires us first to consider the central distinction between two forms of human action, "doing" and "making." The marital act is not an act of "making," either babies or love. Love is not a product that one makes; it is a gift that one gives—the gift of self. Similarly, a baby is not a product inferior to its producers; it is, rather, a person equal in dignity to its parents. The marital act is surely something that husbands and wives "do"; it is not something that they "make." But what is the difference between "making" and "doing," and what bearing does this have on the issue of artificial insemination and homologous in vitro fertilization?

In "making," the action proceeds from an agent or agents to something in the external world, to a product. Autoworkers, for instance, produce cars, cooks make meals, bakers bake cakes, and so on. Such action is transitive in nature because it passes from the acting subject(s) to an object fashioned by him (or them) and external to them. In making, which is governed by the rules of art, interest centers on the product made—and ordinarily products that do not measure up to standards are discarded; they are at any rate regarded as "defective." Those who produce the product in question may be morally good or morally bad, but our interest in making is in the product and most of us would rather have delicious pies made by a morally bad cook than indigestible ones made by a saint.

In "doing," the action abides in the acting subject(s). The action is immanent and governed by the requirements of a moral virtue, prudence. If the act done is good, it perfects the agent; if bad, it degrades and dehumanizes him. It must be noted, moreover, that every act of making is also a doing insofar as it is freely chosen, for the choice to make something is something that we "do," and this choice, as self-determining, abides in us. There are, moreover, some things we ought *not* choose to make, e.g., pornographic films.[33]

When human life comes to be in and through the marital act, it comes, even when ardently desired, as a "gift" crowning the act itself. When husband and wife engage in the marital act, they are "doing" something, that is, engaging in an act open to the communication and fostering of their unique conjugal love (its "unitive" meaning) and open also to receive the gift of new human life from God should the conditions for receiving this gift be present. When they engage in the marital act, husbands and wives are not "making" anything: they are not "making" love, because love is not a product but is rather the sincere gift of self. Nor, should human life come as a gift crowning their personal union, do they "make" the baby. The new human life that crowns the marital act of husband and wife is surely not treated as if it were a product. The life they beget is not the product of their art but, as the Catholic bishops of England accurately noted, is a "gift supervening on and giving permanent embodiment to" the marital act itself.[34] When human life comes to be through the marital act, we can truly say that the spouses are "begetting" or "procreating" new human life. They are not "making" anything. The life they receive is "begotten, not made."

But when new human life comes to be as a result of artificial homologous insemination or by homologous in vitro fertilization, it is the end product of a series of actions, transitive in nature, undertaken by different persons in order to make a particular product, a human baby. The spouses "produce" the gametic materials which others then use in order to make the final product, the child. In such a procedure, the child "comes into existence, not as a gift supervening on an act expressive of the marital union . . . but rather in the manner of a product of making (and, typically, as the end product of a process managed and carried out by persons other than his parents)."[35] The new human life is "made," not "begotten."

Precisely because homologous artificial insemination/fertilization—like heterologous artificial insemination/fertilization—is an act of "making," it is standard procedure to overstimulate the woman's ovaries so that several ova can be retrieved and then fertilized with sperm (usually obtained through masturbation), with the result that several new human beings (zygotes at this stage of development) are brought into existence. Some of these new human beings are usually then frozen and kept on reserve should initial efforts to achieve implantation and gestation to birth fail. Moreover, it is not uncommon for several embryos to be implanted in the womb to enhance the probability of successful implantation and, should too large a number of embryos successfully implant, to discard the "excess" number of human lives through a procedure some euphemistically call "pregnancy reduction." Moreover, it is common, in practicing in vitro fertilization, to monitor the development of the new human life both while it is still outside the womb and afterwards to determine whether or not it suffers from any "defects." Should serious defects be discovered, then it is not uncommon for abortion to be recommended. As a form of "making" or "producing," artificial insemination/fertilization, whether homologous or heterologous, leads to the use of these methods, for they simply carry out the logic of manufacturing commodities: one should use the most efficient, time-saving methods available to deliver the desired product, and quality controls ought to be put in place to assure that the resulting "product" is in no way "defective."

One readily sees how dehumanizing such "production" of human babies is. Human babies are not to be treated as products inferior to their producers and subject to quality controls; they are persons equal in dignity to their parents.

But some persons, including some Catholic theologians, note, correctly, that homologous insemination/fertilization does not *require* hyperovulating the woman, creating a number of new human beings in the petri dish, freezing some, implanting others, monitoring development with a view to abortion should "defects" be discovered, etc. According to them, if these features commonly associated with homologous insemination/fertilization are rejected, then a limited resort by married couples to artificial insemination/fertilization does not necessarily transform the generation of human life from an act of procreation to an act of reproducing.

A leading representative of this school of thought, Richard A. McCormick, S.J., argues that spouses who resort to homologous in vitro fertilization do not perceive this as the "'manufacture' of a 'product.' Fertilization *happens* when sperm and egg are brought together in a petri dish," but "the technician's 'intervention' is a condition for its happening; it is not a cause."[36] Moreover, he continues, "the attitudes of the parents and the technicians can be every bit as reverential and respectful as they would be in the face of human life naturally conceived."[37] In fact, in McCormick's view, and in that of some other writers as well, for instance, Thomas A. Shannon, Lisa Sowle Cahill, and Jean Porter,[38] homologous in vitro fertilization can be considered as an "extension" of marital intercourse, so that the child generated can still be regarded as the "fruit" of the spouses' love. While it is preferable, if possible, to generate the baby through the marital act, it is, in the cases of concern to us, impossible to do this, and hence their marital act— so these writers claim—can be, as it were, "extended" to embrace in vitro fertilization.

Given the concrete situation, any disadvantages inherent in the generation of human lives apart from the marital act, so these authors reason, are clearly counterbalanced by the great good of new human lives and the fulfillment of the desire for children of couples who otherwise would not be able to have them. In such conditions, the argument runs, it is not unrealistic to say that in vitro fertilization and embryo transfer is simply a way of "extending" the marital act.

This justification of homologous fertilization is rooted in the proportionalist method of making moral judgments. It claims that one can rightly intend so-called "premoral" or "nonmoral" or "ontic" evils (the "disadvantages" referred to above) in order to attain a proportionately greater good, in this case, helping the couple have a child of their own. But this method of making moral judgments is very flawed and was explicitly repudiated by Pope John Paul II in *Veritatis Splendor*. It comes down to the claim that one can never judge any human action morally evil because of the object freely chosen, but that one can judge an act to be morally good or morally bad only by taking into account its "object," the circumstances in which it is done, and above all the "end" for whose sake it is done. If the end for whose sake it is done is a "proportionately greater good," then the evil one does by choosing this object (e.g., making a baby in a petri dish, intentionally killing an innocent person) can be morally justifiable.[39]

In addition, it seems to me that the reasoning advanced by McCormick and others is rhetorical and not realistic. Obviously, those who choose to produce a baby make that choice as a means to an ulterior end. They may well "intend"—in the sense of their "further" intention—that the baby be received into an authentic child-parent relationship, in which he or she will live in a communion of persons which befits those who share personal dignity. If realized, this intended end for whose sake the choice is made to produce the baby will be good for the baby as well as for the parents. But, even so, and despite McCormick's claim to the contrary, their "present intention," i.e., the choice they are here and now freely making, is precisely "to make a baby"; the baby's initial status is the status of a product. In in vitro fertilization the technician does not simply *assist* the marital act (that would be licit) but, as Benedict Ashley, O.P., rightly notes, "*substitutes* for that act of personal relationship and communication one which is like a chemist making a compound or gardener planting a seed. The technician has thus become the principal cause of generation, acting through the instrumental forms of sperm and ovum."[40]

Moreover, the claim that in vitro fertilization is an "extension" of the marital act and not a substitution for it is simply contrary to fact. "What is extended," as Ashley also notes, "is not the act of intercourse, but the intention: from an intention to beget a child naturally to getting it by IVF, by artificial insemination, or by help of a surrogate mother."[41] Since the child's initial status is thus, in these procedures, that of a product, its status is subpersonal. Thus, the choice to produce a baby is inevitably the choice to enter into a relationship with the baby, not as an equal, but as a product inferior to its producers. But this initial relationship of those who choose to produce babies with the babies they produce is inconsistent with and so impedes the communion of persons endowed with equal dignity that is appropriate for any interpersonal relationship. It is the choice of a bad means to a good end. Moreover, in producing babies, if the product is defective, a new person comes to be as *unwanted*. Thus, those who choose to produce babies not only choose life for some, but—and can this be realistically doubted?—at times quietly dispose at least some of those who are not developing normally.[42]

In my opinion, the reasons advanced here to show that it is not morally right to generate new human life outside the marital act can be summarized in the form of a syllogism, which I offer for consideration. It is the following:

Any act of generating human life that is nonmarital is irresponsible and violates the respect due to human life in its generation.

But artificial insemination, in vitro fertilization, and other forms of the laboratory generation of human life, including cloning, are nonmarital.

Therefore, these modes of generating human life are irresponsible and violate the respect due to human life in its generation.

I believe that the minor premise of this syllogism does not require extensive discussion. However, McCormick, commenting on an earlier essay of mine in which I advanced this syllogism, claims that my use of the term "nonmarital" in the minor premise is "impenetrable," because the meaning of a "nonmarital" action is not at all clear.[43] This objection, however, fails to take into account all that I had said in that essay regarding the *marital act*, which is not simply a *genital* act between persons who happen to be married, but is the "one-flesh," bodily, sexual union of husband and wife (an act of coition) participating in or open to the *goods of marriage.*[44]

It is obvious, I believe, that heterologous insemination or fertilization and cloning are "nonmarital." But "nonmarital" too, are homologous artificial insemination/fertilization. Even though married persons have collaborated in them, these procedures nonetheless remain nonmarital because the marital status of the man and woman participating in them is accidental and not essential. Not only are the procedures ones that can in principle be carried out by nonmarried individuals, they are also procedures in which the marital character of those participating in them is, as such, completely irrelevant. What makes husband and wife capable of participating in homologous insemination/fertilization is definitely *not* their marital union and the act (the marital act) which participates in their marital union and is made possible only by virtue of it. To the contrary, they are able to take part in these procedures simply because, like nonmarried men and women, they are producers of gametic cells that other individuals can then use to fabricate new human life. Just as spouses do not generate human life *maritally* when this life (which is *always* good and precious, no matter how engendered) is initiated through an act of spousal abuse, so they do not generate new human life maritally when they simply provide other persons with gametic cells that can be united by those persons' transitive acts.

The foregoing reflections should suffice to clarify the meaning of the minor premise of the syllogism and to establish its truth.

The truth of the major premise is supported by everything that I have said about the intimate bonds uniting marriage, the marital act, and the generation of human life. Those bonds are the indispensable and necessary means for properly respecting human life. They safeguard respect for the irreplaceable goodness of the marital union and for new human life, which needs a home where it can take root and grow—a "home" prepared for it by the unique love of the spouses.

2. The Basic Theological Reason Why Human Life Ought to Be Given Only in the Marital Act

There is, in my opinion, a very profound theological reason that offers ultimate support for the truth, set forth in the Church's teaching, that new human life ought to be given *only* in and through the marital act—the act proper to and unique to spouses—and not generated by acts of fornication, adultery, spousal abuse, or new "reproductive" technologies.

The reason is this: human life ought to be "begotten, not made." Human life is the life of a human person, a being, inescapably male or female, made in the image and likeness of the all-holy God. A human person, who comes to be when new human life comes into existence, is, as it were, an icon or "word" of God. Human beings are, as it were, the "created words" that the Father's Uncreated Word became and is,[45] precisely to show us how deeply God loves us and to enable us to be, like him, children of the Father and members of the divine family.

But the Uncreated Word, whose brothers and sisters human persons are called to be, was "begotten, not made." These words were chosen by the Fathers of the Council of Nicea in A.D. 325 to express unequivocally their belief that the eternal and uncreated Word of God the Father is indeed, like the Father, true God. This Word, who personally became true man in Jesus Christ while remaining true God, was not inferior to his Father; he was not a product of the Father's will, a being made by the Father and subordinate in dignity to him. Rather, the Word was one in being with the Father and was hence, like the Father, true God. The Word, the Father's Son, was begotten by an immanent act of personal love.

Similarly, human persons, the "created words" of God, ought, like the Uncreated Word, be "begotten, not made." Like the Uncreated Word, they are one in nature with their parents and are not products inferior to their producers. Their personal dignity is equal to that of their parents, just as the Uncreated Word's personal dignity is equal to the personal dignity of his Father. That dignity is respected when their life is "begotten" in an act of spousal love. It is not respected when that life is "made," that is, is the end product of a series of transitive actions on the part of different people.

"Assisted" Insemination/Fertilization

The Church's magisterium, as we have seen, distinguishes between technological procedures, such as artificial insemination and in vitro fertilization, whether homologous or heterologous, which *substitute for or replace the marital act,* and procedures which *assist* the marital act in being crowned with the gift of human life. Although married couples ought never use techniques which replace the marital act, they can legitimately use those that assist it in generating new human life. As Pope John Paul II has said, "infertile couples . . . have a right to whatever legitimate therapies may be available to remedy their infertility."[46]

But there is serious controversy, even among Catholics who defend the truth of the Church's teaching on the generation of human life, regarding the kinds of procedures which assist rather than replace the marital act. After presenting basic criteria to help distinguish procedures that "assist" the conjugal act from those replacing it, I will then examine some specific techniques. We will find that there is a consensus among Catholic theologians regarding some of these procedures, whereas over others there is controversy.

Basic Criteria

The basic principle operative here is accurately formulated in the following text from *Donum Vitae:*

The human person must be accepted in his parents' act of union and love; the generation of a child must therefore be the fruit of that mutual giving which is realized in the conjugal act wherein the spouses cooperate as servants and not as masters in the work of the Creator who is love.[47]

If the child is to be the "fruit" of the marital act, the marital act must be directly related (have a direct causal relationship) to the origin of new human life. The marital act, in other words, must be the "principal" cause of the conception of the child. It is so because the marital act not only unites husband and wife in an intimate "one-flesh" unity but also directly and personally introduces into the wife's body the sperm of her husband which then actively seek an ovum in order to fertilize it and cause the conception of the child. Given that the marital or conjugal act is and must be the principal cause of the child's conception if the dignity of human life in its origin is to be respected, then what basic criteria will enable us to determine whether a technological intervention "assists" the marital act rather than "replaces" it or "substitutes" for it?

In an excellent study of this issue,[48] John Doerfler offers a thorough review of relevant literature, offering perceptive critiques of several essays and judging one of the most helpful an insightful (but neglected) essay by Josef Seifert.[49] Doerfler proposes that the marital act is and remains the principal cause of conception if the technical procedure only enables it to be performed either by removing obstacles preventing the conjugal act from being effective or enabling it to be performed by providing active condition(s) for it to exercise its own principal causality (technical procedures of this type will be illustrated below). But the conjugal act is not or does not remain the principal cause of conception if the natural causal process initiated by the marital act and leading to conception is interrupted by the technical means, and it is so interrupted if the technical means terminate or stop the natural causal process, if these means require the husband's sperm to be removed from the wife's body after the marital act has taken place, if conception occurs outside the wife's body, or if the technical means initiate the process anew once it has been stopped. Obviously, too, the conjugal act is not the principal cause of conception if it merely serves as a means for obtaining sperm. These are the major criteria developed by Doerfler[50] (I have in some measure simplified them for presentation here), and in my opinion these are very helpful in enabling us to determine whether a given technical intervention assists or replaces the conjugal act.

From this it follows, I believe, that a procedure assists the marital act if and only if a marital act takes place and the procedure in question either circumvents obstacles preventing the specific marital act from being fruitful or supplies condition(s) needed for it to become effective in causing conception.

With these criteria in mind I will now examine some specific procedures claimed by Catholic theologians to be licit examples of techniques that "assist" rather than "replace" the conjugal act. As will be seen, there is sharp disagreement among these theologians over some of the procedures to be examined. I will begin with techniques which all commentators, so far as I know, regard as instances of "assisted" insemination or fertilization, and then take up techniques over which controversy exists, offering my own assessment, guided by the criteria developed by Doerfler in his comprehensive study.

Acknowledged Instances of Assisted Insemination or Fertilization

1. Use of Perforated Condom to Circumvent Hypospadias

Hypospadias is an anomaly of the male penis in which the urethra does not open at the distal end of the penis but on its underside, close to the man's body. This frequently prevents the husband from ejaculating sperm into his wife's vagina during the marital act. The use of a perforated condom would prevent the husband's sperm from being emitted outside his wife's body and facilitate their entrance into her vagina. This would thus be an instance of a technical means that would *remove an obstacle* to the fruitfulness of the conjugal act; all Catholic theologians who have discussed this procedure agree that it assists and does not replace the marital act and that, consequently, it is morally licit. It surely meets the criteria developed by Doerfler.[51]

2. Low Tubal Ovum Transfer (LTOT)

This procedure, originally designed for women whose infertility was caused by blocked, damaged, or diseased fallopian tubes, relocates her ovum, bypassing and circumventing the area of tubal pathology in order to place the ovum into the fallopian tube below the point of damage, disease, or blockage so that her own husband's sperm, introduced into her body by the marital act, can then effect fertilization. It is called "*low* tubal ovum transfer" because ordinarily the ovum is relocated in the lower part of the fallopian tube (or at times in the uterus itself).

This procedure evidently "removes an obstacle" preventing conception from occurring after the marital act has taken place or provides the conditions necessary if the marital act is to be fruitful. All the procedure does is to relocate the wife's ovum within her body prior to the marital act. The sperm that fertilize the ovum are introduced into her body-person directly as a result of the marital act. This technique clearly meets the criteria set forth by Doerfler.

All Catholic theologians who have addressed this technique agree that LTOT is a morally legitimate way of assisting the marital act.[52]

3. Moving Sperm Deposited in the Vagina into the
Uterus and Fallopian Tubes

Apparently the fruitfulness of some marital acts is impeded because the husband's sperm do not migrate far enough or rapidly enough into the reproductive tract of his wife, but linger in the vagina or at most migrate only very slowly to those portions of the wife's reproductive tract where conception is most likely to occur, with the result that most of the sperm die before they are able to unite with an ovum and fertilize it.

This obstacle to the fruitfulness of the marital act is removed and the conditions favorable for it to bear fruit can be fulfilled if the physician, after husband and wife have completed the marital act, uses some instruments to propel the sperm deposited in the vagina into the uterus and fallopian tubes. If this is the way the technical intervention occurs, then it seems evident that it merely removes an obstacle preventing the marital act from being fruitful, supplying condition(s) necessary for it to be effective. It thus meets the criteria we have noted before and can rightly be said to assist and not replace the marital act.[53]

Controverted Techniques

1. Temporal Removal of Sperm to "Wash" and "Capacitate" or of Ovum

The procedure just discussed, namely, moving and relocating within the wife's body sperm deposited by her husband during the marital act may be modified somewhat, requiring the sperm to be removed temporarily from the wife's body or perhaps having her ovum temporarily removed and treated for some pathological condition, and then relocating one or both elements to the fallopian tube where they can unite. Many Catholic theologians who have discussed this procedure believe that it too can be regarded as legitimate assistance of the marital act.[54] This procedure, too, so it seems to them, assists the marital act by removing an obstacle to its fruitfulness or by supplying the conditions under which it can be effective.

Despite my respect for this opinion, I believe that the procedure in question does not truly assist the marital act but rather substitutes for it. One of the criteria developed by Doerfler in his well-reasoned study and supported by the analysis given by Seifert is that a technical means which stops or terminates the natural causal process initiated by the marital act and then initiates the process anew after its termination can hardly be designated as assisting the conjugal act or the causal process initiated by it.[55] It seems to me quite clear that distinct human acts, specified by their objects, are being chosen and done, and that one of them definitely *stops* or *terminates* a causal process initiated by the other. One of the acts is the marital act; the other is the technical intervention of removing and treating either the sperm introduced into the wife's body by the marital act or the ovum present within her body when the marital act occurred, treating them in some fashion. This act is not marital, nor does it assist the causal process initiated by the marital act to be fruitful. It does not assist because it terminates the act in order to do something else, i.e., to treat sperm or ova. A third human act is then required to initiate the causal process that leads to conception, since a new human choice is needed for the reintroduction of sperm and/or ovum into the wife's body. It thus seems clear to me that this procedure substitutes for the marital act and does not assist it.

2. Accumulating Sperm from a Series of Marital Acts and Introducing Them into the Wife's Vagina in Conjunction with a Marital Act

In order to cope with infertility caused by oligospermia (a condition causing relatively low sperm production by the husband), some theologians propose that the physician collect amounts of sperm from the husband's ejaculate (by morally permissible means, such as use of a perforated condom), conserve and centrifuge such accumulated sperm, and then place this concentrate into the wife's generative tract in association with a marital act (usually prior to one) in order to mix with and fortify the husband's ejaculate during the marital act.

Although some Catholic theologians who accept the teaching of *Donum*

Vitae think that this procedure assists the marital act,[56] I believe that a proper assessment of what is going on shows that this technique replaces the marital act and does not assist it.

First of all, in this procedure one does not know whether the sperm that fertilize the ovum are sperm introduced into the wife's body by the husband during the marital act or sperm contained in the concentrate obtained by collecting sperm into a perforated condom during previous marital acts. But if the sperm that fertilize the ovum derive from that concentrate, then they simply *cannot* and *must not* be considered as part of the marital act. They cannot and must not be so considered precisely because they have been *intentionally withheld* from prior marital acts in order to procure sperm in a nonmasturbatory way. The marital act merely serves as an instrument for obtaining sperm. And since one cannot say whether fertilization is caused by sperm introduced into the wife's body by the specific marital act in question or by sperm contained in the concentrate resulting from *deliberately withholding sperm* from prior marital acts, one cannot truly say that the procedure "assists" the specific marital act in question. This procedure clearly violates one of the criteria developed by Doerfler.[57]

3. Gamete Intrafallopian Tube Transfer (GIFT) and Tubal Ovum Transfer with Sperm (TOTS)

GIFT has already been described: the wife's eggs are removed by laparoscopy or ultrasound-guided transvaginal procedures. An egg (or eggs) is placed in a catheter with sperm (provided either by masturbation or by using a perforated condom during previous marital acts) that have been treated and "capacitated," with an air bubble separating ovum (ova) from sperm in the catheter while outside the wife's body. Thus fertilization does not take place outside the wife's body. The catheter is then inserted into the wife's womb (and this can be done either prior to or immediately following a marital act), the ovum and sperm are released from the catheter and fertilization and conception can then take place within the wife's body, caused by the concentrate of sperm placed in the catheter and released after its insertion into the wife's body or perhaps by sperm released into her body by the marital act in association with which the catheter is inserted.

Several Catholic theologians—among them, Donald McCarthy, Orville Griese, Peter Cataldo, and John W. Carlson—strongly defend GIFT as a procedure that assists the marital act in being fruitful.[58]

With many others I disagree completely with this approval of GIFT. First of all, the procedure was originally developed as an offshoot of IVF and the husband's sperm was collected by masturbation. Informed that the Catholic Church condemns masturbation, even as a way of obtaining a husband's sperm, the doctors who used the method suggested that sperm be obtained by using a perforated condom during the marital act. This shows definitely that with GIFT the marital act is merely incidental to the entire procedure, used only as a way of obtaining sperm in a nonmasturbatory way. These sperm, since they have been *deliberately, intentionally withheld from a marital act or series of marital acts,* can then not be said truly to be integral to the marital act when the catheter containing these sperm and the wife's ovum are inserted into her body. Although subsequent fertilization of her ovum *may* be caused by sperm introduced into her body during the accompanying marital act, such fertilization would be *per accidens* and not *per se.* Thus with many others, including Doerfler, Seifert, DeMarco, Tonti-Filippini, Grisez, and Ashley and O'Rourke, I believe that GIFT definitely substitutes for or replaces the marital act and does not assist it; and that, therefore, it is immoral to make use of it.[59]

TOTS is similar to GIFT. In this procedure sperm are procured from the husband either by masturbation or use of a perforated condom. Sperm are then placed in a catheter along with the wife's ovum (ova) and separated by an air bubble, and the catheter is then inserted into the fallopian tube (hence the name tubal ovum transfer with sperm), where ovum (ova) and sperm are released and fertilization can then occur. As can be seen, TOTS is quite similar to GIFT and not similar to LTOT, or low tubal ovum transfer. Like GIFT it substitutes for the marital act and does not assist it since the marital act is only incidental to retrieval of sperm and sperm so retrieved are intentionally withheld from a marital act and hence cannot be regarded as part of a marital act.

Someone might say that, with respect to procedures where reputable Catholic theologians disagree, and since there is no specific magisterial teaching on them, Catholics are at liberty to follow whatever view they prefer as a "probable opinion." This way of looking at the issue is quite legalistic in my opinion. What one ought to do is examine the arguments and reasons given by theologians to support their claims to see which is true and takes into account the realities involved.

Conclusion

Some may think that the position taken here in support of the teaching of the Church is cruel and heartless, unconcerned with the anguish experienced by married couples who ardently and legitimately long for a child of their own and must suffer disappointment because of some pathological condition.

I do not believe that this position is cruel, heartless, and unconcerned with the suffering of many married couples. We must bear two things in mind before looking at some possible alternatives made possible by modern medicine. The first is that husbands and wives have no *right* to have a child. They have no right to have a child because a child is not a thing, not a pet, not a toy, but a person of inviolable dignity. Husbands and wives have the right to engage in the sort of action inwardly fit to receive new human life—the marital act. But they do not have a right to a child. Their desire to bear and raise children is noble and legitimate, but this desire does not justify any and every means to see to its fulfillment.

The second point to keep in mind is that we must be realistic and recognize that for some reasons it will not be possible for some married couples to beget a child in and through their marital act. If this is the case, then it is necessary to recognize that we must all carry our cross. But we must remember that Jesus is our Simon of Cyrene, and that he will help us bear any cross he may give us.

NOTES

1. Here it is instructive to note that in his article on artificial insemination in the prestigious *Encyclopedia of Bioethics*, Luigi Mastroianni includes under "homologous" fertilization procedures "utilizing the semen of the husband *or designated sexual partner*" (emphasis added) ("Reproductive Technologies, Introduction," in *Encyclopedia of Bioethics*, ed. Warren T. Reich, 2nd rev. ed. [New York: McGraw-Hill, 1995], p. 2207). Inasmuch as this edition of the *Encyclopedia of Bioethics* now includes an essay entitled "Marriage and *Other Domestic Partnerships*" (emphasis added) by Barbara Hilkert Anderson (pp. 1397–1402), Mastroianni's apparent equation of husbands with "designated partners" is not too surprising. It is, sadly, an indication of contemporary Western attitudes.

2. See Mastroianni, "Reproductive Technologies, Introduction."

3. Walter Wadlington, "Reproductive Technologies, Artificial Insemination," in *Encyclopedia of Bioethics*, p. 2220.

4. Ibid., p. 2217.

5. It is ironic to note that Louise was born on the tenth anniversary of Pope Paul VI's encyclical *Humanae Vitae*, in which he affirmed the "inseparable connection, willed by God and unlawful for man to break on his own initiative, between the unitive and procreative meanings of the conjugal act."

6. On all this see Mastroianni, "Reproductive Technologies, Introduction," pp. 2209–10; Andrea L. Bonnicksen, "Reproductive Technologies, In Vitro Fertilization and Embryo Transfer," pp. 2221–24; and McLaughlin, "A Scientific Introduction to Reproductive Technologies," pp. 58–59, all in *Encyclopedia of Bioethics*.

7. Mastroianni, "Reproductive Technologies, Introduction," p. 2211.

8. Bonnicksen, "Reproductive Technologies, In Vitro Fertilization and Embryo Transfer," p. 2222.

9. On these and other procedures see McLaughlin, "A Scientific Introduction to Reproductive Technologies," pp. 60–62.

10. Ibid.

11. Ibid. See also Mastroianni, "Reproductive Technologies, Introduction," pp. 2211–12.

12. "Somatic cell nuclear transfer" is the expression used to describe mammalian cloning by the National Bioethics Advisory Commission in its document, released in June 1997, "Cloning Human Beings: The Report and Recommendations of the National Bioethics Advisory Commission." A summary of this report is printed in *Hastings Center Report* (September–October 1997): 7–9.

13. Pontifical Academy for Life, *Reflections on Cloning* (Vatican City: Libreria Editrice Vaticana, 1997), pp. 10–11.

14. The four addresses are the following: (1) Allocution to the Fourth International Conference of Catholic Doctors, September 29, 1949; text in *Papal Teachings on Matrimony*, ed. The Benedictine Monks of Solemnes, trans. Michael J. Byrnes (Boston: St. Paul Editions, 1963), pp. 381–85; (2) Allocution to Italian Catholic Midwives, October 29, 1951; text in *Papal Teachings*, pp. 405–34; (3) Allocution to the Second World Congress on Fertility and Human Sterility, May 19, 1956; text in *Papal Teachings*, pp. 482–92; and (4) Allocution to the Seventh Hematological Congress, September 12, 1958; text in *Papal Teachings*, pp. 513–25. He took up artificial insemination, whether by a "donor" or a husband, in all four of these addresses, and in no. 3 he explicitly considered the issue of in vitro fertilization.

15. Pope Pius XII, Allocution to the Second World Congress on Fertility and Human Sterility, p. 485. Emphasis added.

16. Pope Pius XII, Allocution to Italian Catholic Midwives, pp. 427–28.

17. Pope Pius XII, Allocution to the Second World Congress on Fertility and Human Sterility, p. 470.

18. Pope Pius XII, Allocution to the Fourth International Congress of Catholic Doctors, p. 559.

19. Congregation for the Doctrine of the Faith, *Donum Vitae*, II, B, no. 4. The internal citation is to the *Code of Canon Law*, c. 1061.

20. *Donum Vitae*, II, B, no. 6; emphasis added.

21. Pope John Paul II, "To my brother bishops from North and Central America and the Caribbean assembled in Dallas, Texas," in *Reproductive Technologies, Marriage and the Church* (Braintree, MA: The Pope John Center, 1988), p. xv.

22. *Donum Vitae*, II, A, no. 2.

23. Ibid., II, A, no. 1.

24. Ibid., B, no. 4.

25. Ibid.

26. Ibid.

27. In footnote 43, *Donum Vitae* refers to John Paul II's General Audience on January 16, 1980. This audience was but one in a series of Wednesday audiences on "the theology of the body" over a span of several years, from September 5, 1979, to November 28, 1984. These audiences are now available in a one-volume edition, John Paul II, *Man and Woman He Created Them: A Theology of the Body* (Boston: Pauline Books and Media, 2006).

28. *Donum Vitae*, II, B, no. 4. The internal citation is to John Paul II, Discourse to those taking part in the 35th General Assembly of the World Medical Association, October 29, 1983.

29. Pontifical Academy for Life, *Reflections on Cloning*, pp. 10, 14.

30. St. Augustine expressed this truth beautifully centuries ago in his *De genesi ad literam,* 9, 7 (PL 34, 397).

31. Pope Paul VI, *Humanae Vitae,* no. 12.

32. John Finnis, "Personal Integrity, Sexual Morality, and Responsible Parenthood," *Anthropos* (now *Anthropotes*) 1, no.1 (1981): 46.

33. Classic sources on the distinction between making and doing are Aristotle, *Metaphysics,* Bk. 9, c. 8, 1050a23–1050b1; St. Thomas Aquinas, *In IX Metaphysicorum,* lect. 8, no. 1865; *Summa theologiae,* 1, 4, 2, ad 2; 1, 14, 5, ad 1; 1, 181, 1.

34. Catholic Bishops of England, Committee on Bioethical Issues, *In Vitro Fertilization: Morality and Public Policy* (London: Catholic Information Services, 1983), no. 23.

35. Ibid., no. 24.

36. Richard McCormick, S.J., *The Critical Calling: Reflections on Moral Dilemmas Since Vatican II* (Washington, DC: Georgetown University Press, 1989), p. 337. The internal citation is from William Daniel, S.J., "*In Vitro* Fertilization: Two Problem Areas," *Australasian Catholic Record* 63 (1986): 27.

37. Richard McCormick, *The Critical Calling,* p. 337.

38. See Thomas A. Shannon and Lisa Sowle Cahill, *Religion and Artificial Reproduction: An Inquiry into the Vatican "Instruction on Respect for Human Life"* (New York: Crossroads, 1988), p. 138; Jean Porter, "Human Need and Natural Law," in *Infertility: A Crossroad of Faith, Medicine, and Technology,* ed. Kevin Wm. Wildes, S.J. (Dordrecht/Boston/London: Kluwer Academic Publishers, 1997), pp. 103–5. It should be noted that Shannon and Cahill, employing an argument proportionalistic in nature—that is, that it can be morally permissible to intend a so-called nonmoral evil (e.g., heterologous generation of human life) should a sufficiently greater nonmoral good be possible (e.g., providing a couple otherwise childless with a child of their own), insinuate that, if the spouses consent, recourse to third parties for gametes or even to surrogate mothers might not truly violate spousal dignity or unity. See *Religion and Artificial Reproduction,* p. 115.

39. As noted in the text, Pope John Paul II repudiates (and rightly so) this proportionalist method of making moral judgments in his encyclical *Veritatis Splendor.* For a critique of proportionalism see my *An Introduction to Moral Theology,* 2nd ed. (Huntington, IN: Our Sunday Visitor, 2003), chapter 3.

40. Benedict Ashley, O.P., "The Chill Factor in Moral Theology," *Linacre Quarterly* 57, no. 4 (1990): 71.

41. Ibid., 72.

42. The argument advanced in the previous paragraphs was set forth originally in an earlier essay I wrote on the laboratory generation of human life, "*Donum Vitae:* Catholic Teaching on Homologous *In Vitro* Fertilization," in *Infertility: A Crossroad of Faith, Medicine, and Technology,* pp. 73–92, esp. pp. 81–87, making use, too, of material developed by Germain Grisez, John Finnis, Joseph Boyle, and William E. May in "'Every Marital Act Ought to Be Open to New Life': Toward a Clearer Understanding," *The Thomist* 52 (1988): 365–426.

43. Richard A. McCormick, "Notes on Moral Theology," *Theological Studies* 45 (1984): 102.

44. In her essay "Human Needs and Natural Law" (cf. endnote 38), Jean Porter claims that my argument in support of the teaching of *Donum Vitae* is based on a "Kantian" sexual ethic, one that "gives pride of place to autonomy" (pp. 100–101). She even claims that I "dissent" from Catholic teaching in my analysis of the marital act because of my emphasis on the role played by intention in determining the moral significance of human action. Porter fails to recognize that my analysis, far from being Kantian, is rooted in the Catholic tradition which stresses the self-determining character of human actions. My analysis, I believe, is rooted also in the understanding of human sexuality and human action set forth by John Paul II.

45. Here it most important to stress that Christian faith proclaims that the Word Incarnate is still a human being. Christian faith rejects docetism, the doctrine that the Uncreated Word only seemed to become human and ceased appearing human after the resurrection.

46. Pope John Paul II, "To my brother bishops from North and Central America and the

Caribbean assembled in Dallas, Texas," in *Reproductive Technologies, Marriage and the Church*, p. xv.

47. *Donum Vitae*, II, B, 4, no. 7.

48. Rev. John Doerfler, "Assisting or Replacing the Conjugal Act: Criteria for a Moral Evaluation of Reproductive Techniques," unpublished 1999 S.T.L. dissertation on file at the John Paul II Institute for Studies on Marriage and Family, Washington, D.C. A substantive summary was published in *Linacre Quarterly* 67 (2000), 22–66.

49. Josef Seifert, "Substitution of the Conjugal Act or Assistance to It? IVF, GIFT and Some Other Medical Interventions. Philosophical Reflections on the Vatican Declaration 'Donum Vitae,'" *Anthropotes: Rivista di Studi sulla Persona e Famiglia* 4 (1988): 273–86.

50. See Doerfler, "Assisting or Replacing the Conjugal Act," pp. 89–90.

51. See, for example, Thomas J. O'Donnell, S.J., *Medicine and Christian Morality*, 2nd rev. ed. (New York: Alba House, 1991), p. 238.

52. See, for instance, the following: Donald T. DeMarco, "Catholic Moral Teaching and TOT/GIFT," in *Reproductive Technologies, Marriage and the Church*, pp. 122–39; Nicholas Tonti-Filippini, "'Donum Vitae' and Gamete Intra-Fallopian Tube Transfer," *Linacre Quarterly* 572 (May 1989): 68–79; Benedict Ashley, O.P., and Kevin O'Rourke, O.P., *Health Care Ethics: A Theological Analysis*, 4th ed. (Washington, DC: Georgetown University Press, 1997), pp. 242–47; Germain Grisez, *Difficult Moral Questions*, vol. 3 of *The Way of the Lord Jesus* (Quincy, IL: Franciscan Press, 1997), pp. 244–49.

53. See Grisez, *Difficult Moral Questions*, p. 248; Orville N. Griese, *Catholic Identity in Health Care: Principles and Practice* (Braintree, MA: The Pope John XXIII Medical Moral Center, 1987), pp. 443–44; John W. Carlson, "Interventions Upon Gametes in Assisting the Conjugal Act Toward Fertilization," in *Infertility: A Crossroad of Faith, Medicine, and Technology*, pp. 110–11; Tonti-Filippini, "'Donum Vitae' and Gamete Intra-Fallopian Tube Transfer," p. 70.

54. This seems to me to be the position of Grisez, Griese, and Carlson (see preceding note for bibliographical details).

55. On this see Doerfler, "Assisting or Replacing the Conjugal Act," pp. 89ff.

56. Two Catholic theologians explicitly accepting this procedure are O'Donnell, *Medicine and Christian Morality*, p. 238; Griese, *Catholic Identity in Health Care*, p. 6.

57. Good critiques of this procedure are provided by Grisez, *Difficult Moral Questions*, pp. 247–249; Tonti-Filippini, "'Donum Vitae' and Gamete Intra-Fallopian Tube Transfer."

58. The most extensive and initially plausible defense of GIFT is given by Peter J. Cataldo. His most detailed effort to justify it is found in his essay "The Newest Reproductive Technologies: Applying Catholic Teaching," in *The Gospel of Life and the Vision of Health Care*, ed. Russell Smith (Braintree, MA: The Pope John XXIII Medical Moral Center, 1996), pp. 61–94. A briefer presentation of his argument is given in "Reproductive Technologies," *Ethics & Medics* 21, no.1 (January 1996): 1–3. See also Donald McCarthy, "Infertility Bypass," *Ethics & Medics* 8, no.10 (October 1983): 1–2; McCarthy, "Catholic Moral Teaching and TOT/GIFT: A Response to Donald T. DeMarco," in *Reproductive Technologies, Marriage and the Church*, pp. 140–45; Griese, *Catholic Identity in Health Care*, pp. 47–49.

59. For Doerfler, in addition to the study referred to in note 48, see his "Is GIFT Compatible with the Teaching of *Donum Vitae*?" *Linacre Quarterly* 64, no.1 (February 1997): 41–47. See also Grisez, *Difficult Moral Questions*, pp. 246–48; Tonti-Filippini, "'Donum Vitae' and Gamete Intra-Fallopian Tube Transfer," pp. 68–89; DeMarco, "Catholic Moral Teaching and TOT/GIFT," in *Reproductive Technologies, Marriage and the Church*, pp. 122–40; Ashley and O'Rourke, *Health Care Ethics*, pp. 246–47; Seifert, "Substitution of the Conjugal Act or Assistance to It?"

CHAPTER 4

Contraception

Did *Humane Vitae* Contradict Itself?

BENEDICT ASHLEY, O.P.

For many Catholics the teaching of *Humanae Vitae* against contraception seems absurdly contradictory and hence an abuse of Church authority that can be in good conscience ignored. Certain well-known Catholic moral theologians have supported them in this opinion.[1] Is it not contradictory to approve the practice of Natural Family Planning (abstinence in the woman's fertile period) in order to prevent pregnancy while condemning the use of contraception for the same purpose? Since the moral purpose or intention and the effect is the same in both cases how can NFP be moral but contraception immoral?[2]

Humanae Vitae, however, does not declare contraception to be immoral because the end or goal intended is to prevent pregnancy, but because of the *means* used to achieve this end. The encyclical abides by the traditional axiom that "the end does not always justify the means." Thus the question is whether there is in fact a moral difference in the two means (abstinence in the fertile period or the use of contraception) used for this end that in itself (at least in some circumstances) can be a good, moral goal. According to the encyclical the morally significant difference between these two means is that *those who perform the marital act contraceptively intend to render a naturally fertile act of sexual intercourse infertile,* while those who use sex only in the infertile period have *no such intention.* Thus what *Humanae Vitae* teaches is that because contraception violates the "principle of the inseparability of the unitive from the procreative meanings of the marital act" it is *intrinsically* (that is, in every circumstance and even for every good intention) morally wrong. It therefore declares that any fertile marital act that is deliberately rendered infertile by whatever method — a condom, diaphragm, IUD, anti-ovulant drugs, withdrawal, sterilization by tying the fallopian tubes of the woman or vasectomy for the man, etc. — is contraceptive and an intrinsically immoral means, no matter how good the end it is used to achieve.[3]

Therefore the real question about *Humanae Vitae*'s teaching is whether those who contracept, even in marriage and for good intentions such as health or economic reasons or to strengthen their marriage, are using an intrinsically immoral means even when this is for a good end because this means renders a naturally fertile act infertile. Certainly it cannot be denied that there are some such immoral means that are chosen for the sake of an otherwise good end. For example, a husband cannot really express his love for his wife by sexual intercourse against her consent, since the nature of such an act is a means that intrinsically contradicts its good intention. What *Humanae Vitae* asserts is that a contraceptive act, although mutually intended as an act of marital love, is in respect to that end a self-contradictory and therefore self-defeating means. It can no more express marital love than can a forced act of marital intercourse. Although even this conclusion seems absurd to many today, whether it is true or not is the real question that must be explored if justice is to be done to the Church's teaching.

How Can a Sexual Act Be Intrinsically Evil?

To explore this question it is first of all necessary to understand how in general an act can be "intrinsically evil" as a means when performed for a good end. What makes a choice morally good or bad is not primarily that it obeys or violates some "law" or "norm." Moral laws and norms are themselves binding or void depending on whether or not they rest on the basic needs of human nature. The goal of human action is "happiness," but not everything that people think will make them happy can do so. Human persons can attain happiness only if they make choices that will satisfy the basic needs of human nature and in the right hierarchical order of importance.[4] Consequently if they make choices that do not objectively lead toward true happiness or that block the way to it, they act immorally even if their choice is a mistaken one performed in good will. Such mistakes excuse the agent from moral guilt, but they do not make the action objectively good. Moreover the agent, though morally guiltless, will ordinarily suffer the unhappy consequences of her or his mistaken act. Those who eat what is objectively too much will get fat, even if they think they are not overeating.

Yet if they do what is objectively wrong through mistaken views that they could not correct, or without full freedom of choice, they do not by such an objectively bad act make themselves bad persons. Only choices that are knowingly and deliberately moral or immoral change the character of a person. It is by our free and deliberate acts that we make ourselves good or bad persons. This is because acts form virtues (skills in choosing means that will really lead to happiness) or vices (skills in choices that lead to misery). As acquiring skill in a sport or an art makes what at first was difficult and inconsistently effective to become spontaneous, easy, and consistently effective, so virtue makes the journey to happiness easier and easier, while vice causes the person to bog down into addiction and self-destruction.[5]

Thus "consequentialism" is an inadequate method of moral judgment. *Before* an act has "consequences," by its own intrinsic morality or immorality it changes the one performing it and affects their ability to make future decisions. Even if his lie deceives no one, he who lies becomes a liar and by beginning to cope with life problems in the wrong way begins to acquire a vice that will, until he admits his dishonesty and starts over again, make telling the truth ever more difficult. The first act of *excessive* drinking is the beginning of alcoholic addiction. Thus to say that contraception is "intrinsically evil" means that the contraceptive act initiates a sexual *vice* that makes good sexual living more and more difficult and ultimately ends by blocking true happiness.

But how can we judge whether a sexual act is an effective means to true happiness or a false step that leads away from it? To answer this question we must inquire as to the place of sexuality among the needs intrinsic to the human person: what is its function in the striving for true happiness, and how important is the satisfaction of this need in relation to other intrinsic needs? The question is not with regard to "needs" that have been acquired either unknowingly or by free choice, since it is all too obvious that the fulfillment of such needs presupposes more basic, natural needs. The need I have acquired for coffee is not innate but an acquired modification of my natural need for water. These acquired needs are modifications of intrinsic, natural needs, either modifications that serve these needs or that seem to do so but in fact conflict with their real satisfaction. Thus our acquired need for a prescription drug may serve some natural need such as a normal blood pressure, but an addiction to alcohol conflicts with our natural need for a healthy drink. Thus in regard to sexual "needs" moral judgment must be based on natural needs, not merely on a person's sexual habits or preferences. A sexual addict is fulfilling his acquired need for constant physical pleasure, but this is an obsessive, not a natural, need.

Why Are We Sexual?

Why then are human persons sexual? Some, in our culture all too many, answer that the purpose of sexual intercourse is pleasure, "good sex." This is like saying that the purpose of eating is pleasure. Those who think that way usually get too fat. It does not take a great deal of experience to realize that if physical pleasure is made an end in itself it soon becomes an acquired addictive and self-destructive need that exceeds and corrupts some natural need. Physical pleasure is a natural support of the basic human activities necessary for happiness, but it cannot alone make us happy.[6] If eating and drinking were not physically pleasant, we could not endure the daily boredom of it all and our race would not have survived.

Moreover, the human body needs pleasure as a kind of "recreation" or rest from the wear and tear of activities and the restoration of the body that pleasure provides. When, however, physical pleasure becomes an end in itself, rather than a support for other goods that are more important elements of human happiness, it begins to block human happiness and takes on a morbid character, as we see in eating addictions. To be happy a human being must subordinate physical pleasures to more specifically human activities by acquiring the virtue of moderation *(temperantia)*. On the other hand, to be unable to enjoy physical pleasure, as in the case of the anorexic or sexually frigid person, is also a disorder, though a much less common one.

Thus, if sex did not have a more basic function than mere recreation, it is unlikely that evolution would have retained it as part of our intrinsic human makeup. In fact venereal diseases and the many disorders to which our sexual organs are liable (breast and ovarian cancer, prostate cancer, etc.) are among the chief threats to human survival. Hence it might seem that some asexual mode of reproduction would have been of greater evolutionary advantage. Science has given us a partial answer to this question by showing why animals reproduce sexually rather than asexually, as do one-celled organisms and many plants. Sexual reproduction makes for biodiversity within the species and hence a fuller realization of its potentialities than does asexual reproduction (cloning). Thus the human species in its material community with other animals is divided into male and female and its growth in membership and survival as a species is made possible by sexual copulation.

Yet it is conceivable that the human species, in making such an advance in intelligence, freedom, and ability to control its own destiny, might have also evolved a mode of reproduction less clumsy and dangerous than that of brute animals. This possibility is already realized in artificial reproduction. Present procedures still involve the perils of pregnancy but the invention of artificial wombs may soon eliminate this limitation on reproductive technology. Would sex then still be necessary for the sake of its recreative pleasures? Drug addicts prefer their pleasures to sex and there is no reason to doubt that eventually a drug "high" can be produced without its present physiological damage and yet more pleasurable than orgasm. Moreover some prefer masturbation as a similar and safer and less complicating way of sexual release than personal sexual relations. Such considerations make it evident that something much more important for happiness than physical pleasure is involved in sex, namely, the personal relationship of man and woman, that sexual pleasure only encourages and supports, as our pleasure in eating and drinking is greatly enhanced by companionship at the table or at a party.

Thus human sex, in marked differentiation from animal sex, is intensely "personal," and when sex is depersonalized, as in masturbation, it does not truly meet human needs. This has always been a part of Church teaching; the words of Genesis 2:18–24, "It is not good for man to be alone," recalled by Jesus (Mk 10:1–12), clearly apply to union that is more than physical. It is a union that overcomes the loneliness of the person as a mere individual. To be a member of the human species, a "person," is to have intelligence and freedom and this means that, to a degree, the human person transcends the material order; that the person is a "spiritual" being.

It is difficult indeed for modern science to understand what it means to say we are "spiritual beings." We moderns or postmoderns place a high value on human *freedom*. Yet, though modern science has come to admit both determinism and chance in nature, it cannot account for the freedom by which we transcend both determinism and chance and thus can understand and control the material world. A sound ethics must seek to enhance human freedom, not to reduce us to robots or addicts enslaved by physical urges for pleasure.

Because spiritual beings have intelligence and free will they are also open to know and freely love other persons, to form a *community*. Christians believe that God is a perfect community of Three Persons who so totally share one life and one being that they are truly one God. Finite persons cannot achieve such perfect community, yet our happiness requires us to strive for as total a communion as is possible. The human person, however, is not a pure spirit. We have intelligence and free will, but these also in this life depend on a material body to function. Material things are much more closed in upon themselves than spiritual beings, since they have quantity, "parts outside of parts," that communicate with each other only upon superficial contact or through some material medium. It is to transcend such limits that we have more and more freely through science and technology created means of communication across space and time, ever striving to bring the human race closer together in personal community.

Thus human persons, although primarily spiritual, cannot communicate except when spatially present to each other, perhaps by actual physical contact, or through some kind of language, itself made of material signs. Moreover, the possibilities of the human spirit cannot be entirely realized in any individual. Individuals have unique bodies and these bodies are mortal. Hence, while pure spirits can each have a unique form and constitute a perfect hierarchy from highest to lowest, human souls occupy physical bodies and are all essentially of one species. Thus we are a community made up of essentially equal persons having equal rights.

Evolution may be able to explain the material origin of our human body with its great brain that like a supercomputer serves as an instrument of spiritual thought and freedom, but it has not explained how this body thinks abstractly and consequently is free. Yet it is human "intelligence" that makes science and a creative technology based on science possible.[7] The best explanation of this undeniable fact of our unique intelligence and freedom is that an all-powerful God has used evolutionary forces as instruments to produce our specifically human bodies yet completes each human person by a soul he directly creates. Such an explanation grounds the dignity of every human person, gives them inalienable human rights, and requires respect for their own freedom. Yet our human soul is the least of spirits since it needs a material body to operate. Science has shown us that the whole human species has also been prepared from the matter of the universe through a long cosmic and biological evolution. Through evolution God has guided the development of the universe up to production of the human species and he finishes this work by creating a spiritual soul for each human body when it is sufficiently prepared at the fertilization of a human ovum by a human sperm through the sexual intercourse of its human parents.[8]

Why Is Human Reproduction Procreative?

It is specific to the human community, in accordance with the spirituality by which it transcends other animal species, that the human person has a very large and complex brain as the instrument of intelligence and free will. Consequently, human persons require a long embryological development and then a very long period of care and education by their parents. These parents transmit to the next generation an elaborate culture, including a true language that, unlike the language of lower animals, can both express abstract truth and convey spiritual meaning. Thus, essential to the survival and well-being of the human species is not only sexual reproduction, but the permanent family in which both man and wife perform complementary roles.

Feminists emphasize that throughout human history difference of gender has led to a perpetual "war of the sexes" that imperils a good family milieu for the offspring. Hence the personal gender complementarity of husband and wife in the family must be of great value if it is to compensate for these bitter struggles. It must be sufficient to outweigh in evolutionary advantage not only the physiological risks of sexual reproduction but also the risks of the relational conflicts caused by gender differences. Thus, for the human species evolution must eminently have favored sexual reproduction because of its support of the family as the basic social unit in which children are socialized, that is, in which they begin to acquire the virtues necessary for communal living.

Families are not sufficient, however, for a fully formed human culture in which the achievement of all the virtues needed for true human fulfillment is possible. Persons also need a wider human community, an extended family, a tribe, a nation, a state, and the human community as a global whole if human happiness is to be adequately achieved. Good families are the basis of society, but reciprocally a good society is necessary for good families to realize their full potential.

Human relationships in family and society must protect basic human rights and they must all seek both the production and distribution of material goods that justly enable each person to achieve happiness. Material goods, like human bodies, are primarily private because they must be divided among those who use them. But spiritual goods can be shared, since I lose nothing of truth by sharing it with you, but rather by our mutual sharing our possession of truth is enhanced. Thus, the spiritual elements of culture are the principal elements of the common good, while the material elements produced and distributed justly among the members are best left to private ownership.[9]

Is the Sexual Relationship a Friendship?

Therefore the perfection of human sharing is to be found in the mutual communication of spiritual goods and this is called "friendship" or a relation of "love."[10] This involves not only a will to seek the other's happiness, but also to share this happiness with them in common. Love always seeks union or the sharing of life among those who love each other. Because of our material limitations, however, there must be an order of sharing *(ordo amoris)*.[11] We first love those closest to us physically and culturally and then in lessening degrees those more remote. Hence, the family, in which there is a physical sharing through sexual union and reproduction as well as domestic life, is "the school of love." Without such a family the citizens of the state are ill prepared to form a wider community based on a union of love that is less emotionally intense yet to which more intimate friendships must be subordinated.[12] Human virtues are perfected only in adulthood but they are initiated in childhood and adolescence in the virtuous family.

It is in view of this account of the human person that it becomes possible to attain a realistic view of human sexual morality, that is, what uses of sex best promote true human happiness and what abuses of sex are injurious to it and hence are intrinsically immoral. Yet there are two perspectives from which this question can be viewed: that of the *origin* of the human person, and that of the *perfection* of the human person, true happiness or fulfillment in the common good. From the viewpoint of the origins of each person it should be obvious that a child once in existence has a right to love, proper care, and education. In Church documents this is called "procreation," so as to indicate it is not mere biological reproduction but cultural education as well. The best insurance for this is that the parents have acquired the virtues necessary for marriage and have committed themselves to a permanent marriage based on a genuine love that implies both a physical and a spiritual sharing. This requires that the parents truly share one life. They must communicate with each other, because spiritual union requires communication.

It is in this context that the full moral value of physical sexual union becomes evident. Human communication by living together and talking together and having common possessions is not sufficient for such a familial friendship. Evolution has also provided a physical union, the marital act, both as the cause of reproduction or origin of the child, but also as a natural language by which the mutual commitment of marriage that makes the child's origin, care, and education possible is expressed. Human friendships require expression: first of all simply by presence, by eating meals together, by conversation in the language of the culture, but at least by a handshake or embrace or simply a smile that are natural physical signs found in all cultures, though with modifications. Sexual union in the act of intercourse is for the human race a profoundly natural language of love and union. Not only does the male body partially penetrate the female body, but ejaculation of semen in the vagina is, so to speak, the "melting" of one body into the other. Moreover in this act both the physical and psychological characteristics of masculinity and femininity, the different ways of imagining and feeling of the two sexes, are joined in a complementary way.[13]

It is important to the child in its growing up to realize that it is the product not only of its parents' bodies but of their act of union. To be formed from the matter of the parents' bodies is important—"bone of my bone, flesh of my flesh" as Adam in Genesis 2:23 expresses physical bonding—but it is even more important that this physical bond result from the spiritual, free, and mutual act of the parents. This is evidenced by the great curiosity adopted children have about their biological parents. Nor is this intimate bonding adequately supplied by artificial reproduction, since in that case a third person is introduced as the direct agent who produces the child out of material from the parents' bodies and thus the child's identity becomes painfully vague. A painting is not a Raphael just because an assistant used Raphael's paints.

While the sexual intercourse of our parents is veiled in mystery, this mystery must be answered for each of us, as must the further mystery of our origin in God, if we are to gain our full personal identity as we grow up. To lack a satisfactory answer to this question is a profound deprivation for children that will cause difficulties in their coming to understand and control their own sexuality. Thus from the perspective of human origins, a child has a fundamental right to be produced by the natural sexual act as an expression of the loving commitment of its parents to each other and to the child.

The second perspective from which the marital union must be viewed is that of the perfection of the husband and wife. For a human person to be completely fulfilled it is necessary first of all that they attain self-knowledge and virtue. An important element in this is to understand their masculine or feminine gender and to prepare themselves for future marriage. They must, therefore, understand the requirements of genuine love for a member of the opposite sex and be able to express themselves as persons in the sexual union. An important prerequisite for this is the model of marital love provided for them by their parents. Whatever the probably complex causes of same-sex orientation may be, it is certainly a "disorder," that is, an incapacity for a normal and satisfactory heterosexual marriage.[14] To suppose homosexuality is simply a normal variation of human personality is without empirical evidence, and in view of why the human species is sexual can only be regarded as a developmental failure or aberration. It can also be a learned condition resulting from seduction or immoral experimentation. The normal desire for marriage implies a natural desire for children. The physical mortality of the human race also makes it natural that people want to live and survive in their children.

Yet at the beginning of "falling in love" the desire for children is not always manifest. The natural course of events is romantic, simply the desire of union with another. This desire, however, is not merely a physical urge for sensual pleasure. The boy or girl who wants nothing but sexual pleasure out of a partner is not someone in whom the virtues have begun to be formed in a good family. It is true that masturbation, particularly in boys, and bad example from their peers, often produces in boys (and in girls, too) a purely animal attitude toward persons of the other sex, who are treated simply as objects, not persons. But a first romance normally already has a marked spiritual character, as the poetry of the world proclaims. The two sexes find in each other not only physically but psychologically a deep complementarity. The boy or girl who has normally learned how to be a good friend to another person of his or her own sex now finds that friendship with a person of the opposite sex is more deeply fulfilling. This natural desire for fulfillment in a friendship that fulfills one's gender through its complement and looks forward to a life like one's parents should lead to a permanent marital commitment. It is a gradual process of realization of one's own needs and those of the other that continues in the marital state as this sexual friendship deepens.

Why Are Sexual Union and Procreation Ethically Inseparable?

We are now ready to ask why the two meanings of the marital act, union and procreation, are "inseparable" according to *Humanae Vitae*. I would answer this question by saying that human persons by nature tend to intimate friendships of love that have a complementary physical and spiritual character. The most intimate of these is the love relation or friendship between a man and a woman in which they complete the incompleteness of each gender in a realization of the full potentiality of human nature, the "image of God." Yet because of the physical mortality and limitations of human spiritual embodiment, this always implies the procreation and education of a wider and future human community.

Since sexual pleasure is not an end in itself, anymore than pleasure in eating is an end in itself, but is the natural support for the proper use of sex, sexual activity even in its recreative use promotes human persons to happiness only when subordinated to more important goals. When the recreative use of sex becomes dominant it leads to all sorts of foolish and vicious behavior. Consequently, the virtue of chastity is essential for true human happiness. This means that no one is prepared for marriage who has not acquired control over sexual appetites, so as to be able to abstain when the pursuit of greater goods requires it, and who cannot truly enjoy sex and give this enjoyment to the partner without, however, viewing the partner as a person one loves merely as an object of pleasure or possessive domination.

From this it follows that extramarital sex not only cannot fulfill human sexual needs but instead tends to form a vicious character that becomes more and more incapable of true marital love. Only the person who has acquired at least the beginning of the virtue of chastity can live in a satisfactory marriage. Thus for such a person to practice periodic abstinence when there is good reason for this is not impossible nor does it weaken the marriage, but strengthens it. On the contrary it should be clear that to make pleasure the dominant feature of the marriage relation depersonalizes the marital act and tends to block true union. Similarly a selfish desire not to have children yet enjoy the physical pleasure of intercourse is injurious to personal character, to the marriage partner, and to any children. Thus the question reduces to the problem situation in which a married couple believe that they have good reasons to avoid pregnancy but also believe that the practice of Natural Family Planning is impractical for them.

Before directly attacking this question, I want to return to the question of the morality of artificial reproduction, because some have accused Church teaching of self-contradiction in deploring contraception to prevent reproduction while also deploring artificial means to promote reproduction. Since, however, the issue is not the intention to reproduce or not to reproduce, but the means used to effect these intentions, there is nothing contradictory about saying that both contraception and artificial reproduction are intrinsically immoral means, although intended for different ends. When a child is produced by introducing the husband's sperm into the wife without intercourse, or the sperm of a donor is so inserted, or a child is produced in vitro by a technician combining the ovum and sperm of the couple, a child is produced with the aid of God's creation of a human soul. Yet this is done in a manner in which the couple's act of intercourse is not the effective cause of reproduction. It is of course for the good of the child that it comes into existence but it comes into existence deprived of its natural link to the parents. It is also good for an illegitimate child to exist, but its illegitimacy deprives it of its rights to a stable family composed of both its own parents. It is in this sense that artificial reproduction separates the two meanings of marriage by separating the good of procreation from that of the parental union and is intrinsically wrong because it deliberately produces a deprived child.

Moreover, these various modes of artificial reproduction in one way or another are intrinsically evil because they weaken the character of the pretended parents. Their sterility is not necessarily their fault, but their love for each other requires of them not to let infertility weaken or break their love for each other but to strengthen it in mutual support. On the other hand, to agree to satisfy their desire for a child by deliberately producing a deprived child cannot be justified. Too often it is the woman's anxiety that she will lose her husband's love because of her infertility, or the man's that he will be exposed as sterile, that motivates such procedures.

To return to the question of contraception, and in view of what has already been said, it becomes possible to state exactly what the relation between the unitive and the procreative meaning of the marital act is, a point *Humanae Vitae* leaves unsaid. The *genus* of the moral act is that of an intimate friendship essential to true human fulfillment, but this friendship is *specified* by its sexual character as the complementary physical union of persons of opposite sex and psychology, supported by great physical pleasure, procreative of a family of children, and suited for their development toward happiness. In brief, marriage is a union, a friendship of a special procreative or familial kind. These two meanings cannot be separated because a species always presupposes its genus as fundamental to its very essence. On the other hand, although a genus can be abstracted in thought from any of its species it cannot exist except in some concrete specified realization. Thus virtuous and intimate human relationship, friendship, can have many forms, but marital and parental friendship by its physical, psychological, and moral intimacy and by its procreative necessity for the existence of the whole human community is unique.

The marital act that consummates and expresses this union ought, therefore, retain its natural, God-given significance. To attempt to perform it while deliberately changing its meaning is contrary to the natural function of human sexuality and cannot be a valid means to true human happiness. Indeed it perverts it, initiates the formation of sexual vice, and hence is intrinsically and seriously immoral. As an immoral means it cannot be made moral by any circumstance, not even by good but mistaken intentions of the couple. If they engage in it through an erroneous conscience, misled perhaps by dissenting theological opinions, they will still suffer its harmful consequences and the weakening of their marriage.

Why Isn't Voluntary Celibacy Immoral?

For every human person a good family is essential for happiness, but it is not of absolute necessity that every human person reproduce or marry. The social order needs families but it does not need every one of its members to reproduce for it to grow or survive. Single persons can also achieve sufficient friendships for happiness and perhaps may contribute more to society by remaining single. Thus, celibacy chosen for good reasons is not contrary to the search for human happiness, and can by its example encourage other married persons to acquire a virtuous control over their legitimate use of sex.

When men and women manage to achieve healthy heterosexual maturity and have acquired the virtues necessary for a stable marriage and the proper care of children, they are able without excessive difficulty to subordinate their need for sexual pleasure to the requirements of their marriage bond and responsibilities. This subordination is similar to that required for a healthy diet and exercise. Good health does not take away pleasure in food and drink but relates it to other even more important elements that make up true human happiness. Similarly the use of sex in marriage for physical pleasure has to be subordinated to other important elements in family life.

Strangely today people are ready to regulate sexual pleasure so as not to interfere with their job, money making, and other career aims, sometimes accepting considerable sexual discipline, yet are unwilling to do this for the sake of family stability. They blame the Church for requiring the practice of Natural Family Planning rather than contraception, instead of recognizing that the injustices of the social order are the main reason that today it is so difficult for couples to have more than one or two children. Social injustice, however, cannot justify actions that aggravate social disorder rather than aim to correct it. In a society that insured a family wage, contraception would seem much less necessary.

What Does Christian Faith Add to This Argument?

The foregoing argument rests purely on reason. For the most part it is supported by modern evolutionary theory about the origin and survival of the human species. Yet to explain human freedom and the spirituality of the human person it is necessary to go beyond the materialistic reductionism of current science to speak *philosophically,* and thus remain within the limits and terms of human reason regarding truths about human spirituality and of God as creator of the human person. Christian faith and theology support this argument and add to it an even greater certitude. God has revealed to us the true meaning of human sexuality and its right use, not to restrict human freedom but to enhance it by enabling us to seek human happiness in a true and effective way. In particular the Gospel has shown us that the obvious difficulties humanity has in freeing itself from sexual abuses are not due to a defect of human nature as God created it. It is humanity's sinful history that has made it ever more difficult for humans coming into this fallen world to find their way to happiness.

The Good News is that the grace of Christ can free us from the mess the human race has made of itself and its world. Christ has elevated the meaning of marriage to a *sacrament* so that for the baptized the family becomes not only the natural school of early love but also the sign of the eternal love of Christ for his Church and for each of its members, God's children. The husband is to love his wife as Christ loved the Church in total sacrifice (Eph 5: 21–32). Thus one of the chief reasons for family failure in a fallen world, the male oppression of women, their treatment of women not as persons but as sexual objects, is destroyed. Reciprocally, the wife's love of her husband, like the Church's love of Christ, becomes fruitful of a good future for humanity.

Their mutual and sacramental love in the family and its perpetuation in their children thus is the basis both of the Church community and of a just society.

Since certain theologians have successfully refuted the various arguments first made against *Humanae Vitae,* many Catholic theologians who dissent from it have come to rely on the specious argument that since so many Catholics ignore its teaching it has not been "received" by the *sensus fidelium.* They argue that this non-reception is a sign that the Holy Spirit does not approve this teaching. Therefore, they hopefully prophesy that eventually in the course of the development of doctrine the Church will have to rescind the teaching of *Humanae Vitae* along with that of the many similar papal declarations that preceded it. Some cite the historic changes in papal moral teaching with regard to the morality of taking interest on a loan, on the rights of religious conscience, on capital punishment, etc., etc., to show that the Church has frequently been forced to rescind its moral condemnations.[15] Yet the history of the Church also shows that to argue in this way from the *sensus fidelium* overlooks the fact that throughout the history of the Church there has also been widespread acceptance by the faithful of practices, such as slavery, torture, and anti-Semitism, that contradicted the Gospel. The Church has never infallibly accepted these abuses and in the course of the development of doctrine has more forcibly condemned them.

The *sensus fidelium* is not popular Catholic opinion or practice but the consistent witness to the faith *(sensus fidei)* by truly faithful Catholics. I doubt that a polling of informed and practicing Catholics would show that they believe that God has revealed that contraception has his approval, or that it is a matter of faith that *Humanae Vitae* is mistaken. Whether it is consistent with God's revelation cannot be settled by popular vote by Catholics, many of whom unfortunately are badly instructed or merely nominally Christian. It always remains the responsibility of the teaching authorities of the Church to discern the work of the Holy Spirit in the faithful as distinct from the influences of our worldly culture on their opinions and lives. It must also discern what in the speculations of theologians is consistent, according to the *analogia fidei,* with the major creedal teachings of the Gospel.

Moral judgments take place in the context of a value system and every value system implies a worldview, that is, certain convictions about human persons and the world in which they live. Today the split between Church teaching and popular opinion in the Church is not just the result of a debate over one restricted moral question. Rather, it is strong evidence that Catholics are deeply influenced by the predominant worldview and value system of current American culture that stands in stark opposition to the whole worldview and value system of the Church. Only when viewed in the context of the total Catholic worldview and value system is the Church's teaching on the particular question of contraception revealed as consistent, reasonable, and life-affirming. No doubt there will be future development in the Church of doctrine on the ethics of human sexuality, but it will have to be in accordance with the hard sayings of Jesus, who said to the rabbis who inquired about what reasons would permit a man to divorce his wife,

Because of the hardness of your hearts he [Moses] wrote you this commandment. But from the beginning of creation God made them male and female. For this reason a man shall leave his father and mother and be joined to his wife and the two shall become one flesh. So they are no longer two but one flesh. Therefore what God has joined together, no human being must separate ... Whoever divorces his wife and marries another commits adultery against her; and if she divorces her husband and marries another, she commits adultery (Mk 10:4b–12).

I doubt that the majority of those who call themselves Catholics in the United States are convinced that divorce and remarriage are always wrong! Some dissenting theologians may even argue that this means the Holy Spirit is revising Jesus' own interpretation of the Scriptures! Nevertheless, though the development of doctrine can confirm and clarify certain elements of the Gospel tradition, it cannot contradict the Gospel preached from the beginning. St. Paul says, "If anyone preaches to you a gospel other than the one you received, let that one be anathema!" (Gal 1:9).

NOTES

1. William H. Shannon, *The Lively Debate: Response to Humanae Vitae* (New York: Sheed and Ward, 1970).

2. "Two days later, on August 1 [1968, after the issuance of *Humanae Vitae*] two members of the Birth Control Commission, Dr. André Hellegers and Thomas Burch, along with John T. Noonan Jr., who had been the commission's expert on the history of contraception, appeared at a news conference in Washington. Noonan, speaking for all three, said that the encyclical suffers from 'internal inconsistency' since the central teaching that every marriage must remain 'open to the transmission of life' contradicts the encyclical's parallel teaching that 'the rhythm system of contraception may be used for appropriate reasons.' Also, said Noonan, 'it is, to say the least, surprising that what is alleged to be the design of God could only be discovered in the utmost secrecy of a military character and without subjecting the statement of the alleged design of God to the scrutiny of moral theologians ... or the comment of the faithful.'" Robert McClory, *Turning Point: The Inside Story of the Papal Birth Control Commission, and How Humanae Vitae Changed the Life of Patty Crowley and the Future of the Church* (New York: Crossroad, 1995), a work based on the views of Ms. Crowley, a lay member of the commission who voted for the "Majority Report," whose conclusion Paul VI rejected. McClory made also much

use of the polemical work of Robert Blair Kaiser, *The Politics of Sex and Religion* (Kansas City, MO: Leaven Press, 1985), and blames Paul VI's decision on the efforts of Cardinal Ottaviani, one of the bishops of the commission. Paul VI, however, had to make up his own mind as to whose arguments of these consultant groups were the better in the light of the Church's tradition. There is no reason to doubt that he did so not only to maintain papal authority, as some claim, but in the light of the arguments of both sides and the *analogia fidei*. The "Majority Report" on the question of whether contraception was intrinsically evil had nine bishops voting no, three yes and three abstaining. It is noteworthy that perhaps the most prominent of the theologians producing this report was Josef Fuchs, S.J., who soon published the fundamental statement of the theory of "proportionalism" as a general method of moral judgment, later condemned by John Paul II in *Veritatis Splendor*. The "Minority Report" was produced by five other authors, led by John Ford, S.J., supported by Ottaviani. These documents that had only a consultative status were never officially published by the Vatican but were made public in the *National Catholic Reporter*, April 1967.

3. Note that most moralists admit that a woman who is in imminent danger of rape can use anti-ovulants to prevent a possible pregnancy, since rape is not a marital act. Extramarital sexual acts are, on the part of those who perform them, also intrinsically immoral, but it could be argued that it is a lesser evil, though still a serious evil, for such couples to use contraceptives to avoid an illegitimate birth. Could it be argued that a woman for good reasons could use anti-ovulants if her husband refuses to practice abstinence during her fertile period? In my opinion she could not, because the marriage covenant gives each spouse the right to ask for intercourse even if that entails its possible and natural result of pregnancy. These and other such questions deserve a fuller treatment than can be given here.

4. Unfortunately moral theologians who support *Humanae Vitae* differ somewhat on how these needs or goods necessary for happiness are to be defined or if they are to be ranked hierarchically. Germain Grisez leads those moralists who revise St. Thomas Aquinas' moral theology to make it independent of his anthropology and of his unification of moral life by a single ultimate goal that measures all lesser goals. They contend that "integral human fulfillment" is achieved by a balancing of certain "incommensurable" goods, one of which is that of human sexuality. Thus contraception is intrinsically evil because it violates this incommensurable life good. It seems that Grisez's *Contraception and the Natural Law* (Milwaukee: Bruce, 1964) and his article "A New Formulation of a Natural Law Argument against Contraception," *The Thomist* 30 (1966): 343–61, may have, through John Ford, S.J., one of the writers of the so-called "Minority Report," had some influence on Paul VI's decision. In my opinion, however, Aquinas, by grounding ethics in anthropology and by subordinating the good of human sexuality to a commitment to a single ultimate end, provides a stronger answer to the present question. For my criticism of Grisez's theory see my article "What Is the End of the Human Person: The Vision of God and Integral Human Fulfillment," in *Moral Truth and Moral Tradition: Essays in Honour of Peter Geach and Elizabeth Anscombe*, ed. Luke Gormally (Dublin and Portland, OR: Four Courts Press, 1994), pp. 68–96. For a detailed criticism of Grisez's arguments against contraception, see Janet E. Smith, *Humanae Vitae: A Generation Later* (Washington, DC: Catholic University of America Press, 1991), appendix 4: "A Critique of the Work of Germain Grisez, Joseph Boyle, John Finnis, and William May," pp. 340–70. Smith's is the best and most thorough study of this whole question and her translation of *Humanae Vitae*, appendix 1, pp. 169–295, is recommended.

5. Aquinas, *Summa theologiae* I-II, q. 63, a. 1–2. For the harmony between biblical morality and Aristotelian "virtue theory," see my *Living the Truth in Love: A Biblical Introduction to Moral Theology* (Staten Island, NY: Alba House, 1996), pp. 24–40. For the importance of "virtue theory" in ethics (minimized by the Grisez school as not leading to specific moral arguments), see Jean Porter, *The Recovery of Virtue: The Relevance of Aquinas for Christian Ethics* (Louisville, KY: Westminister/Know, 1990).

6. On pleasure, see Aristotle, *Nicomachean Ethics*, Bk. X, cc. 1–5, with Aquinas' commentary available in English, trans. C. T. Litzinger, O.P., 2 vols., reprint (Notre Dame, IN: Dumb Ox

Books, 1993). Also *Summa theologiae* I-II, q. 34, a. 4c. Aquinas is not a "puritan"; he holds that physical pleasure is necessary for human beings, I-II, q. 34, a. 1c; II-II, and that before the fall sexual pleasure was even greater than now, I, q. 99, a. 2 ad 3.

7. See the noted physicist Roger Penrose, *The Emperor's New Mind: Concerning Computers, Minds, and the Laws of Physics* (New York: Oxford University Press, 1989), on this limitation of a reductionist science. From a philosophical point of view see Richard Swinburne, *The Evolution of the Soul* (Oxford: Clarendon Press, 1986), pp. 7–16.

8. The direct creation of the human soul was confirmed by Pius XII in *Humani Generis* and this is repeated in the *Catechism of the Catholic Church,* 2nd ed. (Rome: Libreria Editrici Vaticana, 1997), # 366, 1703; DS 1440. On the question of modern embryology and "ensoulment," see my article "When Does a Human Person Begin to Exist?" in *The Ashley Reader: Redeeming Reason* (Naples, FL: Sapientia and Ave Maria University Press, 2006), chap. 20.

9. For an extended treatment of Aquinas' view of community and the common good see Charles De Koninck, *De la primauté du bien commun contre les personalistes* (Québec: University of Laval, 1943), and "In Defense of S. Thomas," *Laval Théologique et Philosophique* 1, no. 2 (1945): 1–103.

10. The classic treatment of friendship is Aristotle's *Nicomachean Ethics,* Bks. VIII–IX, with Aquinas' commentary (note 6 above) and *Summa theologiae* II-II, q. 23. Christian love is the graced form of friendship.

11. Ibid., II-II, q. 26. Note that for Aquinas (a. 4) we must first love ourselves rightly in order to be able to love others because our happiness consists primarily in participating in the common good in true friendship.

12. Ibid., a. 8.

13. This understanding of sexual union as a language was beautifully explained by Paul Quay, S.J., in an article written even before *Humanae Vitae:* "Contraception and Conjugal Love," in *Why Was Humane Vitae Right: A Reader,* ed. Janet E. Smith (San Francisco: Ignatius Press, 1993), pp. 17–46.

14. Some have complained that the use of the term "disorder" for homosexuality by the Congregation for the Doctrine of the Faith is "insensitive," yet they speak of "eating disorders." If the teleology of sex is procreative, as seems obvious, then a psychological condition by which a person cannot happily enter marriage stands in the way of attaining this end and is not rightly ordered.

15. John T. Noonan Jr., in *Contraception: A History of Its Treatment by the Catholic Theologians and Canonists,* enlarged ed. (Cambridge, MA: Harvard University Press, 1986), argued for such changes of doctrine regarding that area of sexual morality but submits to Church teaching.

CHAPTER 5

Abortion

A Catholic Moral Analysis

JEANNE HEFFERNAN SCHINDLER

In the spring of 2002 New York City made national headlines when it became the first American city to require abortion training for obstetrics and gynecology residents in its public hospitals.[1] Supporters and critics alike recognized the significance of the policy, as New York remains an influential player in the nation's medical establishment—New York State trains one in every seven doctors nationwide, while New York City runs the country's largest public hospital system. If the policy succeeds, its supporters hope to duplicate it across the country in order to reverse a reported decline in the number of physicians performing abortions. Just as the state was a forerunner in the liberalization of abortion laws, what happens to public medicine in New York may well be a harbinger of things to come.

Other developments in recent years have likewise attempted to render abortion a mainstream element of medical training across the country. In 1996 the Accreditation Council for Graduate Medical Education, for instance, demanded that residency programs in obstetrics and gynecology seeking accreditation provide instruction in abortion techniques.[2] While initially an absolute requirement, the revised ACGME mandate included an exemption for individuals and institutions that oppose abortion; but it nevertheless required these institutions to allow their students to be trained in abortion procedures at another site. In effect, the mandate forces Catholic medical programs to compromise their principles by allowing students to violate deeply held convictions that define the identity of the institution. As Dr. Henry Clever incisively observed, "To require of religious institutions such culpability in an act that they abhor shows either incredible ignorance or contempt for the moral and religious principles these institutions uphold."[3]

The aggressive measures taken by New York City and the ACGME deliberately normalize what is still a highly morally contentious undertaking.[4] The fact that the American public remains deeply divided over the issue of abortion indicates just how radical these measures are; they do not emerge out of a consensus. They also place the burden of resistance upon those who oppose the practice—a dramatic change in policy, as abortion training was formerly considered an elective. Now, however, residents in New York who object to abortion training, for instance, must file a petition for exemption. While there is no formal penalty for non-participation, it is probable that there will be informal liabilities for opting out. Beyond the likely occurrence of peer pressure and stigmatization, residents who resist the training may be at a competitive disadvantage for hiring. On the front end, applicants for New York City residency programs may be screened out on account of their unwillingness to undertake what has now been deemed "integral" to good medical training. Given the intention of the New York and ACGME measures to render abortion a standard element of medical care, it is conceivable that individuals and institutions refusing abortion training will be categorized as medically irresponsible.

These bold attempts to change the climate of American medical practice pose a serious challenge to opponents of abortion. Now, perhaps more than ever over the last thirty years, the burden is upon them to articulate a case against abortion that is publicly intelligible. This burden is candidly acknowledged by an editorial in the *New England Journal of Medicine* that insists: "Residents who wish to opt out of abortion training should be required to explain why in a way that satisfies stringent and explicit criteria."[5]

Fortunately, there is a compelling case to be made against abortion. The Catholic Church has been making it for 2,000 years, and while its teaching is informed by theological reflection, it bears relevance to the debate in the wider culture. As John Noonan has put it: "The moral teaching of a religious body may also embody insights, protect perceptions, [and] exemplify values which concern humanity."[6]

Catholic Opposition to Abortion: The Historical Record

Insofar as the Catholic Church has been the leading critic of abortion in this country for the past thirty years, most Americans know of its stance. Yet few Americans, even Catholics, know how central, consistent, and long-standing this opposition has been in Catholic moral thinking. Moreover, few understand the deep rationale behind such opposition. Most people do not know that the Church's pro-life position is a deeply thoughtful one, which finds support in biblical, theological, philosophical, and scientific sources.

Scriptural Support for Church Teaching

One finds little explicit reference to abortion in either the Old or New Testaments. The only direct mention of abortion in the Hebrew scriptures appears in Exodus 21:22–24, which treats the subject in the context of accidental injury to a pregnant woman. The Jewish penal code in this instance imposes a fine on any such offender who causes miscarriage, which indicates a certain valuation of fetal life; yet, insofar as the code imposes a heavier penalty for injury to the mother, it suggests "the fetus did not have the same status as the mother in Hebrew law."[7]

Notably, the Septuagint version of the Old Testament—the third-century B.C. Greek translation of the Hebrew scriptures—translates the Exodus passage differently. Whereas the Hebrew text distinguishes between the fetus and the pregnant woman and accords different penalties for injuries to each, the Greek text distinguishes between an "unformed" and a "formed" fetus, imposing a fine for causing the death of the first and capital punishment for the second. Some have argued that the Septuagint version involves a critical mistranslation of Hebrew terms and that it imposes on the Jewish text a foreign conceptual framework, likely of Greek origin.[8] Indeed, the appeal to "formation" appears to be a distinctly Aristotelian understanding according to which the fetus becomes a human being, that is, possesses a human soul, at a certain point in its intrauterine development (forty days for males; ninety for females).[9] As we shall see, the conceptual framework employed by the Septuagint text exercised considerable influence over the discussion of abortion in the Catholic Church for centuries.

Talmudic commentary corroborates the Hebrew version of the Exodus passage, rather than the Greek, as it makes no developmental distinctions in prenatal life and identifies the fetus as part of the mother until birth; hence, according to Talmudic tradition, the unborn child did not enjoy distinct legal personhood under Mosaic law. This disparity in status did not yield a "right" to abortion, however.[10] Indeed, the only instance in which the Talmud sanctions the taking of unborn life is in the extreme case where the life of the mother is imperiled. Why should there have been only one such exception? And why should the Torah and Talmud have addressed the subject of abortion so minimally? Does the paucity of attention to the issue indicate acceptance of the practice? John Connery, S.J., contends that more likely:

[T]he thought of intentionally causing an abortion was so foreign to the mind of the Jewish woman that there was no felt need for penal legislation against it. There were actually many indications that the idea of abortion was totally alien to the Jewish mentality. The attitude of the Jews toward barrenness as a curse, the regard for fertility as one of God's greatest blessings, the mandate to increase and multiply, the hope of the Jewish maiden that she might bear the Messiah, all militated against any easy attitude toward self-induced abortion, or even any deliberate abortion.[11]

The moral sense held by the Jews, especially the Alexandrian Jews, on this question informed the reckoning of the early Church. Despite the lack of explicit textual references to abortion in the New Testament, one finds, nevertheless, what Richard Hays suggestively calls a "symbolic world" within which the early Christians moved.[12] Informed by their Jewish heritage, in which abortion would have been "unthinkable or unintelligible," their moral sensibilities were shaped by the Hebrew scripture's poetic celebration of unborn life, and they perceived children to be a great gift.[13] As Hays underscores, "The normal response to pregnancy, within the Bible's symbolic world, is one of rejoicing for God's gift—even when that gift comes unexpectedly."[14] The young Virgin Mary's initially fearful, yet ultimately joyful, response is paradigmatic here.

The Consistent Pro-Life Witness of the Early Church

That the symbolic world of the New Testament Church would have included opposition to abortion finds strong confirmation in early Christian writings. The *Didache,* or *Teachings of the Apostles,* composed in the first century, explicitly condemned abortion. A teaching manual used to instruct Gentile converts, the *Didache* marks out the distinctive principles by which Christians live. In its description of "The Way of Life," as opposed to "The Way of Death," the text declares: "You shall not murder a child by abortion, nor shall you kill one who has been born."[15] Similarly, an early-second-century teaching document, the *Epistle of Barnabas,* commands the Christian: "You shall love your neighbor more than your own life. You shall not slay the child by abortions. You shall not kill what is generated."[16] The act of abortion violates both the sovereign creativity of God—the unborn are his handiwork—and the commandment to love one's neighbor.[17] These convictions, echoed in other contemporary texts, constitute "simple, clear condemnations of abortion without any attempt to distinguish or classify."[18]

The attempt to distinguish among different types of abortion, that is, abortion performed at different points in fetal development, came later. Recall that the Septuagint version of Exodus 21:22–24 made a distinction between the "formed" and "unformed" fetus, the latter being considered a full human being whose destruction was punishable by death. While the documents of the early Church mentioned above do not entertain such a distinction, later theologians, Church councils, and canon law attempt to reckon with the possible theological, moral, and canonical significance of fetal development, often employing the category of "formation" found in the Septuagint. The issue of formation was coupled with that of "animation"—the former referring to a stage in the physical development of the unborn, the latter to the time of its ensoulment (i.e., when God infused the living being with a distinctively human, immortal soul).

Over the centuries these categories were debated intensely. Some theologians held that the fetus did not become fully human until it matured to a certain point physically (usually forty days after conception), whereupon it received a human soul; others held that the embryo was animated immediately, the presence of the human soul directing its growth. These speculations depended heavily upon the scientific knowledge of the period in question. While Church teaching on these matters cannot be identified with the thinking of any one theologian or any one period, it did officially recognize the distinction between the unformed and formed fetus for several centuries. This played a role in determining canonical penalties for the sin of abortion; it did not determine the morality of abortion per se.[19] While the abortion of a formed fetus—formation being understood as coincident with animation—was considered a more serious sin, requiring a more severe and lengthier penance, abortion at any time after conception was deemed gravely sinful.[20] Thus, after a comprehensive survey of Church teaching over time, John Connery, S.J., can assert:

Whatever one would want to hold about the time of animation, or when the fetus became a human being in the strict sense of the term, abortion from the time of conception was considered wrong, and the time of animation was never looked on as a moral dividing line between permissible and immoral abortion. As long as what was aborted was destined to be a human being, it made no difference whether the abortion was induced before or after it became so. The final result was the same: a child was not born.[21]

Over time, with advances in medical knowledge, the theory of immediate animation gained ground; though it had been held by some since the early Church, it became by the nineteenth century the common opinion among Catholic moralists. It was also adopted in Church practice with Pius IX's 1869 removal of the distinction between the formed and unformed fetus from canon law penalties. Henceforth, every direct abortion from conception to birth would incur the same penalty of excommunication.[22]

The development of official Church teaching on this question parallels the developments in canon law. Thus, the Church, speaking in council at Vatican II, eschews any distinctions concerning stages of fetal life and declares simply:

God, the Lord of life, has entrusted to men the noble mission of safeguarding life, and men must carry it out in a manner worthy of themselves. Life must be protected with the utmost care from the moment of conception: abortion and infanticide are abominable crimes.[23]

This basic framework, one that upholds the Church's ancient and consistent opposition to abortion at any stage of prenatal development, finds further confirmation in the universal *Catechism*. In discussing the believer's new life in Christ, the *Catechism* affirms that the covenant of Christ fulfills, not destroys, the law and the prophets. Thus the Christian, far from exempt from the Decalogue, carries out the spirit and the letter of its commands with the supernatural assistance of grace. In this vein, the follower of Jesus strains to observe the Fifth Commandment's prohibition on killing by, among other things, not procuring or in any way assisting an abortion, for:

Human life must be respected and protected absolutely from the moment of conception. From the first moment of his existence, a human being must be recognized as having the rights of a person—among which is the inviolable right of every innocent being to life ... Direct abortion, that is to say, abortion willed either as an end or a means, is [thus] gravely contrary to the moral law.[24]

Such an unqualified regard for unborn human life is strongly reaffirmed by Pope John Paul II in his 1995 encyclical *The Gospel of Life (Evangelium Vitae),* wherein he declares: "[B]y the authority which Christ conferred upon Peter and his Successors, and in communion with the bishops of the Catholic Church, *I confirm that the direct and voluntary killing of an innocent human being is always gravely immoral.*"[25] Thus, after acknowledging the long history of Christian opposition to abortion, the pope concludes that procured abortion—the killing of an innocent human being—can never be justified either as an end or as a means.

The Moral Case against Abortion

In surveying Church teaching against abortion one finds a remarkable consistency over the course of two millennia, with the proscription of abortion achieving more precision and careful articulation over the centuries. This is especially true of Pope John Paul II's pontificate. Yet, this is to describe Church teaching; it does not elaborate upon the rationale behind the teaching. It is important to do this, however, since the issue of abortion is not one that concerns religious believers alone. The Church's position is meant as a norm for all, not just for Catholics. But how is this position intelligible to those who do not accept the teaching authority of the Catholic Church? It is intelligible because of the nature of the teaching, that is to say, the teaching is grounded in moral principles that are intelligible to believers and non-believers alike; they do not depend upon Revelation in the way that doctrinal matters, like the Trinity or Incarnation, do.

The current work of pro-life scholars, both religious and non-religious, makes this plain. Whether they be physicians, philosophers, political scientists, or moral theologians, these scholars offer cogent and compelling arguments against abortion that rest centrally upon philosophical, scientific, and ethical grounds. While their cases are buttressed by religious insights, they do not require them. Abortion is treated as a question of basic human rights, not a topic of arcane theological speculation. Thus, the best arguments in favor of a pro-life position not only square with the deep theological rationale behind Church teaching on abortion, they also merit consideration on their own terms by the widest audience.

The basic argument against abortion can be summarized, as Patrick Lee has done, in a straightforward syllogism:

Intentionally killing an innocent person always is morally wrong.
Abortion is the intentional killing of an innocent person.
Therefore, abortion is always morally wrong.[26]

Yet, public debate over the morality of abortion exists because there is disagreement over the first and, especially, the second premises. There are many and varied pro-choice arguments, but most of them hinge upon a denial that abortion kills an innocent person. Even those defenders of abortion rights who candidly admit that abortion takes a human life, argue that abortion is "justifiable homicide,"[27] since the human life in question does not constitute a rights-bearing *person*. Thus for many abortion advocates, the crux of the matter is the distinction between "human beings" and "persons." They argue, in the main, that while conception issues in a new human organism, this organism does not attain the status of a person until some point later in its development; hence, it does not merit protection from abortion from conception onward but only at the moment when it becomes a person, enjoys a moral status, and thus merits legal recognition.

Notably, the U.S. Supreme Court employed such a distinction in its reasoning in the landmark abortion-rights case of *Roe v. Wade* (1973). After claiming that the law concerning abortion could not hinge upon the question of when life begins—a hopelessly disputed question that, Justice Blackmun insisted, entered the taboo precincts of religion—it effectively proposed its own view of when life begins, that is, of when life begins to be valuable and worthy of legal protection. This it did in its famous "trimester" framework, whereby the Court arbitrarily divided up pregnancy into three trimesters, holding that fetal life did not merit legal consideration until "viability," or until it was capable of life outside the womb (which, given the state of prenatal medicine in 1973, meant some point early in the third trimester).[28] At that point, according to the Court, the state did have a compelling interest in protecting fetal life, except in cases where the "health" of the mother was at stake. Importantly, "health" was defined in *Roe*'s companion case, *Doe v. Bolton,* in the broadest terms, including "all factors . . . relevant to the well-being of the patient."[29] This expansive conception of "health" has largely nullified restrictions on abortion throughout pregnancy and even during the birth process (the Court has struck down legislation banning partial-birth abortion on these "health" grounds).[30] As a result, observes Harvard law professor Mary Ann Glendon, "Today, abortion is subject to less regulation in the United States than in any other country in the Western world."[31]

To change the legal status of abortion in America requires one to challenge the legal and moral reasoning upon which the right to abortion was constructed, and since the legal reasoning establishing the abortion right presupposes a certain view of the moral issues at stake, an examination of the latter is in order first. At the heart of the matter is the moral status of the unborn child—scores of implications radiate from this issue—which rests, in turn, upon the question of when life begins.

If one argues from science, it is undeniable that a new human life begins at conception or "syngamy"—the process by which the twenty-three chromosomes of the sperm and egg unite to produce "a nucleus containing a full complement of forty-six human chromosomes, the first cell of a unique new living human being with its own entirely distinct chromosomal pattern."[32] Possessed of the full human genetic code, this new human being, unlike the gametes from which it arose, has "the active capacity or potency to develop itself into a human embryo, fetus, infant, child, adolescent, and adult."[33] And this it does, directing its own growth from one stage of life to another, retaining a substantial identity over time. The womb affords a hospitable environment within which to grow. But whether *in utero* or *ex utero*, at no point from conception until death does the human being change fundamentally, that is, change its nature. It does not skip from being pre-human to being human at any point in its development: an individual at the two-cell stage is the same individual at the two-month stage, two-year stage, etc.

This is not to say that human life only comes about through sexual reproduction. Human clones and monozygotic twins result from asexual reproduction; yet each is human. These phenomena, some would argue, cast doubt upon the pro-life case. The fact of cloning, they contend, renders an embryo the moral equivalent of a somatic cell. This overlooks a critical fact, however: the somatic cell used in cloning undergoes a fundamental change, a change in its nature, which transforms it from, say, a skin cell or hair cell, into an embryo. The somatic cell of its own nature cannot develop into a human being; rather, like a gamete, "[t]he somatic cell is something from which (together with other causes) a new organism can be generated." As Robert George describes,

When the nucleus of an ovum is removed and a somatic cell is inserted into the remainder of the ovum and given an electric stimulus, this does far more than merely place the somatic cell in an environment hospitable to its continuing maturation and development. Indeed, it generates a wholly distinct, self-integrating, entirely new organism—indeed, it generates an embryo. The entity—the embryo—brought into being by this process is quite radically different from the constituents that entered into its generation.[34]

Similarly, the fact that twinning occurs does not undermine the claim that conception yields a distinct, self-organizing individual human being. The fact that until a certain point of development (before the emergence of the "primitive streak" at around fourteen days) and under certain circumstances a cell splits off from the original human organism and develops into a distinct embryo does not suggest that there was no original human organism to begin with. Before this cleavage, the "totipotent"[35] cell—which, when isolated, forms a new embryo—functions as a part of a whole, united organism, not merely as one among a mass of undifferentiated cells.[36] Indeed, embryological evidence indicates that even at the two-, three-, and four-cell stages, there is a substantial unity present, with the cells functioning in distinct, related ways. In other words, a unified multi-cellular organism exists that directs its own growth according to the sequence that is specific to the human species.

From a pro-life perspective, the substantial identity of the human being over time compels us to accord moral status to the embryo, fetus, infant, toddler, and adult. There is no qualitative change that would mark the individual in one stage as a rights-bearing person, as distinct from a mere human being. All human beings at whatever stage of development must be treated as persons. As Jay Budziszewski observes, "[O]ne is either a person or not, just as one is either a human or not. Unborn human beings are not 'potential' persons, but *actual* persons loaded with inbuilt potentialities."[37] There is no such thing as a potential person, only *persons with potential.*

Now, as mentioned above, abortion rights advocates will sometimes acknowledge that human life begins at conception, while insisting that the "person" comes into being later on. In the words of pro-choice philosopher Ronald Dworkin, human life "in the biological sense" differs from human life "in the moral sense."[38] In Dworkin's line of argument, the critical difference concerns consciousness, which depends upon a certain level of cognitive development. In other pro-choice positions the defining marks of personhood differ, including: self-awareness, sensitivity to pain, viability, birth, the capacity to relate to others, and even the mother's acceptance of the child.[39] Each of these criteria is highly problematic.

Take cognitive development, for instance. It is true that human beings are distinguished as a species for their intellectual capacity. What makes human beings distinctive is their unique ability to engage in higher-order mental functions, but this capacity doesn't become actualized until well after birth. Hence, to embrace actual cognitive development as the standard for personhood forces us to deny the personhood not only of unborn children, but also of newborns and infants (whose cerebral cortex is only partly developed) and severely mentally retarded adults. The most candid among pro-choice writers concede the point: the argument for abortion justifies more than abortion.[40]

Take another criterion, viability. As noted above, the Supreme Court used viability, or the capacity of a fetus to live outside the womb, as the benchmark for legal protection. Yet, it provided no compelling rationale for such a distinction. It did not say what *moral* relevance the capacity to live outside the womb yields. Perhaps it was reticent on the question because the standard of viability may be convenient, but it is unreasonable. First, the standard loads the distinctive location of the womb with a moral significance it does not have. The womb is a hospitable setting within which the human being grows; it provides warmth, protection, and nutrition to the developing baby. But these things are exactly what a "viable" fetus requires outside the womb—without warmth, protection, and nutrition, the "viable" fetus in the neo-natal unit will die. The helplessness of the child within or outside the womb is not qualitatively different. The pre-viable and viable fetus alike require exquisite care; they are both utterly dependent, fragile human beings. Infants and the infirm elderly are in a similar state of total dependence.

A second reason that the viability standard fails is that it is contingent upon technological development. In 1973 the earliest age at which an unborn child could live outside the womb was twenty-eight weeks. With improvements in neo-natology, that age has been pushed back significantly. According to the logic of *Roe v. Wade*, then, a whole class of unborn human beings would now merit legal protection but would not have merited it then.[41] But this is to rest a life and death decision upon the contingencies of science—hardly a morally compelling standard. Given the rapid advances in neo-natal technology, including the possible development of an artificial womb, the unreasonableness of the viability benchmark becomes painfully clear. As renowned fertility specialist Dr. Landrum Shettles observed:

An abortion law truly based on "viability" would require constant redefinition. What was not considered protectable human life last year might be this year. If we were to take the Court at its word, we would find ourselves with a law that makes last year's "abortions" this year's homicides in some cases.[42]

Viability, in short, is not a morally plausible basis upon which to say who can or cannot be killed. The moral status of a human being ought not depend upon such contingencies as age, location, or state of dependence.

Each of the other criteria for personhood proposed by abortion advocates likewise fails. While the pro-choice arguments differ regarding the specific quality that confers moral status on the unborn, they share a critically important feature: each of them separates personhood from the biological life of the human being and relies upon a functionalist conception of human value. An individual human life gains or loses its value based upon what it can do. These arguments thus rest upon philosophical, not scientific, judgments. As Robert George observes:

[T]he pro-choice position collapses if the issue is to be settled purely on the basis of scientific inquiry into the question of when a new member of Homo sapiens comes into existence as a self-integrating organism whose unity, distinctiveness, and identity remain intact as it develops without substantial change from the point of its beginning through the various stages of its development and into adulthood.[43]

Pro-choice writers make value judgments about what characteristics confer moral worth; this is what the debate about "personhood" is about.[44] Ronald Dworkin, Jeffrey Reiman, Mary Anne Warren, Peter Singer, and Judith Jarvis Thomson, among others, each locate the beginning of personhood in a different place, and the criterion that each proposes is, as Patrick Lee suggests, "an arbitrarily selected degree of development of a capacity that all human beings possess, from conception on through until their death as physical organisms."[45] If one affixes personhood to the present ability to reason or communicate or to exhibit self-awareness, as these prominent abortion advocates do, then, as Jay Budziszewski points out, "It isn't hard to see that if unborn babies may be killed because they fall short of these capacities, then a great many other individuals may be killed for the same reasons—for example the asleep, unconscious, demented, addicted, and very young, not to mention sundry others . . ."[46]

A pro-life position, by contrast, protects against the devaluation of all human beings, since it recognizes the personhood of every individual, irrespective of his present ability to perform certain functions. It argues that conception is *the* non-arbitrary beginning of human life and recognizes a continuity of personhood over time, regardless of stages of development.

"A human . . . is a person because of what he *is,* not what he does."[47] And by virtue of the simple fact that an individual human being is human, a pro-life position demands that he receive basic moral regard and legal protection throughout the life cycle, that is, from conception to natural death.

Conclusion

As noted at the start of the chapter, abortion advocates won an important victory when New York City recently required abortion training in their residency programs. The decision has potentially far-reaching effects—which are not lost on abortion rights supporters. Emboldened by the New York victory, such groups as NARAL Pro-Choice America and Planned Parenthood have called for similar changes in other public health systems. Such a striking departure from traditional medical protocol represents a bold attempt to normalize the abortion procedure, stripping it of its moral gravity and jeopardizing the professional status of those who object to its use.

This is merely one current example of the enduring challenge pro-life people face in American culture. It is a serious one, and it needs to be addressed. Fortunately, those who oppose abortion have the strongest arguments on their side. Catholics, in particular, should be well equipped to make these arguments in light of the profound and longstanding pro-life witness of the Catholic Church.

The Church has for 2,000 years consistently affirmed the value of prenatal life and has, in turn, consistently condemned abortion. Its position has been shaped over time by rich theological resources. Drawing upon the high regard for fetal life in the Jewish tradition, the early Church explicitly condemned abortion as the killing of the innocent. Abortion was regarded as an offense against God, the author of life, and against our neighbor. The Church has never wavered from the straightforward condemnation of abortion found in the texts of the early Church. What has varied over time has been the thinking of individual theologians and Church councils concerning the penalties imposed for having an abortion. As we have seen, these complicated debates involved scientific as well as theological dimensions. Ultimately the Church dispensed with gradations of penalties for abortion depending upon the development of the fetus, voicing a general condemnation of abortion per se—whenever it occurs during the pregnancy.

Philosophically and scientifically this makes good sense. As we have noted, the human being undergoes no substantial change, that is, a change of its nature, from the embryonic to the fetal to the neo-natal stage. It is the same living being in every phase of its life; it does not earn the right to life based upon what it can do; it has the right to life because of what it is. From the Catholic perspective, this living being is a creation of God, endowed with dignity and "a supernatural destiny." Life in the womb, like life in the nursery, deserves care, nurture, and protection. It is sacred.

While the Church's understanding of the sanctity of unborn life is grounded in its basic theological conviction that God is the author of life, its conviction that the unborn are human beings and should be given protection is not an exclusively Catholic or even religious argument. It is shared by many—believers and non-believers alike. In light of the range of resources available to them, Catholics have a unique opportunity before them. They can enter the public square and respectfully attempt to persuade their fellow citizens of the profound philosophical and scientific logic of the pro-life position, and they can likewise speak to fellow Christians about the duty of disciples to protect God's handiwork in the womb. In short, whether in schools or courtrooms or church halls, Catholics have been given the responsibility and the resources to build what John Paul II describes as a "culture of life."

NOTES

1. Sara Kugler, "Abortion Training to Become Core Requirement for Obstetrics Residents This Summer," *Associated Press State and Local Wire*, April 4, 2002; Linda Villarosa, "Newest Skill for Future Ob-Gyns: Abortion Training," *New York Times*, June 11, 2002, p. 6; Evan Osnos, "NYC Leads New Effort to Train MDs in Abortions," *Chicago Tribune*, July 4, 2002, p. 1.

2. So dramatic was this move by the ACGME that it prompted national lawmakers to intervene. Recognizing that a loss of accreditation could jeopardize federal aid to medical programs that refused abortion training, as well as the licensure of their graduates, Rep. Peter Hoekstra (R-MI) and Sen. Dan Coats (R-IN) proposed the Medical Training Nondiscrimination Act of 1995, a measure subsequently adopted as part of the United States Code (Title 42, Section 238n). According to this provision, neither the federal government nor any state or local government body receiving federal aid can discriminate for purposes of aid or licensure against an institution whose accreditation was forfeited on account of its refusal to provide or refer for abortion training.

3. "Abortion Training Violates Conscience," *St. Louis Post-Dispatch*, July 24, 1995, p. 7B. See also Dr. Glenn P. Dewberry Jr., "Accreditation Council Wrong to Require Abortion Training," *Daily Oklahoman*, August 9, 1995, p. 6.

4. In the words of Dr. Pamela Smith, ob-gyn training director at Chicago's Mount Sinai Medical Center, "This [ACGME] mandate has the clear purpose of 'mainstreaming' abortion practice within the medical community and presenting to the American public the totally false impression that all physicians believe that abortion is just another medical procedure, when clearly it is not" (Rod Dreher, "House Members Try to Change Rule on Abortion Training," *Washington Times*, June 15, 1995, p. A10). Dr. Kevin J. Murrell, then-president of the National Federation of Catholic Physicians Guild (today's Catholic Medical Association), concurred, ar-

guing that the ACGME action strains to make "abortion a routine and expected norm for medical practice, a direction . . . that places the killing of patients on the same moral plane as curing them. This denies the explicit and implicit foundation of medicine as a healing profession" (Tommy Denton, "Will All Ob-Gyns Be Abortionists?" *Plain Dealer,* June 26, 1995, p. 9B).

5. *New England Journal of Medicine,* Guest Editorial, February 23, 1995, p. 532.

6. John T. Noonan, "An Almost Absolute Value in History," in *The Morality of Abortion: Legal and Historical Perspectives,* ed. John T. Noonan (Cambridge, MA: Harvard University Press, 1970), p. 3.

7. John Connery, S.J., *Abortion: The Development of the Roman Catholic Perspective* (Chicago: Loyola University Press, 1977), p. 11.

8. Donald DeMarco, for instance, contends that "through a mistranslation by Hebrew scholars who were conversant with Greek thought, the distinction between the 'formed' and 'unformed' or 'preformed' fetus was given moral significance and Biblical authority . . . The Septuagint mistranslation of the Exodus passage," he continues, "had allowed Greek thinking in biological matters to gain a theological respectability it did not deserve" ("The Roman Catholic Church and Abortion: An Historical Perspective—Part I," *Homiletic and Pastoral Review* [July 1984]: 59–66). Connery notes that the Septuagint rendering of the Exodus passage held sway with the Alexandrian Jews, among whom was the influential philosopher Philo (25 B.C.– c. 41 A.D.). In articulating a case against infanticide, Philo explicitly appeals to the capital penalty imposed by the Mosaic law for causing the death of the formed fetus; from this, Philo extrapolates a prohibition on exposure (*Abortion,* pp. 18–20).

9. Connery, *Abortion,* p. 18.

10. Interestingly, Josephus Flavius, a renowned Jewish historian of the first century A.D., condemns infanticide and abortion as murder, despite his reliance upon the Hebrew version of Exodus 21:22–24 (Connery, *Abortion,* p. 20).

11. Connery, *Abortion,* p. 14. Although he does not hold the full Catholic position on abortion, Methodist scripture scholar Richard Hays' discussion of the "symbolic world" of the Jews, in which "children are a great blessing from God, and childlessness a terrible affliction," is instructive here. Hays, *The Moral Vision of the New Testament* (San Francisco: Harper, 1996), p. 449.

12. There is scholarly disagreement as to whether Paul might have had abortion in mind in his epistle to the Galatians when he condemns "sorcery" *(pharmakeia)* among the "works of the flesh" (Gal 5:19–20). According to John Noonan, sorcery would likely have connoted "the employment of drugs with occult properties for a variety of purposes, including, in particular, contraception or abortion" ("An Almost Absolute Value," pp. 8–9). While Noonan acknowledges that Paul's use of the term can't be restricted to abortifacient drugs, he contends that it probably included them, a probability confirmed by the association of sorcery with sexual sins and homicide that appears not only in Galatians but also in John's Apocalypse and extra-biblical writings, such as the *Didache.* John Connery, S.J., and, especially, Richard Hays take issue with this interpretation.

13. See Pope John Paul II's reflections on such passages from Jeremiah, Job, and the Psalms in *Evangelium Vitae,* no. 44.

14. Hays, pp. 449–450. See also *Evangelium Vitae,* no. 44.

15. *Didache* 2:2, cited in Connery, p. 36; Noonan, pp. 9–10; and Hays, p. 453.

16. *Epistle of Barnabas* 19:5, cited in Noonan, p. 10, and Connery, p. 36.

17. Thus, as Connery notes, "In spite of the silence of the New Testament, the incompatibility of abortion, as well as infanticide, with the Christian message came through quite clearly" (*Abortion,* p. 35). He further explains that if one attends to context, the apparent asymmetry between the New Testament and other Christian sources on this question dissolves. The New Testament's lack of explicit attention to abortion makes sense in light of its largely Jewish audience—a people for whom abortion and infanticide were forbidden. The clear condemnation of the practice found in other early Christian sources, like the *Didache* and the *Epistle,* likewise makes sense, he maintains, given that they were addressed to Gentiles in whose culture abortion and infanticide were widely practiced. According to Connery, there is a strong case to be

made that the opposition of the early Christians to abortion seems continuous with the Jewish view. Without such continuity, the attitude of the primitive church is difficult to explain; the surrounding pagan culture didn't provide it, nor did the Christian scriptures provide explicit guidance.

18. Connery, *Abortion*, p. 34. One finds similar condemnations in the canonical legislation of the Councils of Elvira (305 A.D.) and Ancyra (314 A.D.), as well as in the writings of Church Fathers, East and West, from Athenagoras and Clement of Alexandria to St. Cyprian and Lactantius. In short, the early Church spoke with one mind in presenting an "unequivocal condemnation of abortion" (Connery, p. 45).

19. Donald DeMarco notes, "The first time the distinction between the formed and unformed fetus became legally operative in Church history is in Gratian's *Decretum* of 1140" ("The Roman Catholic Church and Abortion," p. 64). The distinction was officially removed from canon law in 1869 by Pope Pius IX.

20. Roger Huser in *The Crime of Abortion in Canon Law* (Washington, DC: Catholic University of America Press, 1942), explains, "The Church has always held in regard to the morality of abortion that it is a serious sin to destroy a foetus at any stage of development. However, as a *juridical norm* in the determination of penalties against abortion, the Church at various times did accept the distinction between a *formed* and a *non-formed*, an *animated* and a *non-animated* foetus" (Preliminary note).

21. Connery, *Abortion*, p. 304. While Connery surveys the development of Catholic teaching on the subject of abortion, one should note that there are parallel expressions of moral censure found within other Christian traditions. Dietrich Bonhoeffer, for instance, represents a strong line of Protestant ethical reflection on the question when he writes: "Destruction of the embryo in the mother's womb is a violation of the right to live which God has bestowed upon this nascent life. To raise the question whether we are here concerned already with a human being or not is merely to confuse the issue. The simple fact is that God certainly intended to create a human being and that this nascent human being has been deliberately deprived of his life. And this is nothing but murder." Bonhoeffer, *Ethics* (London: N. H. Smith, 1955), p. 149, cited in Michael Banner, *Christian Ethics and Contemporary Moral Problems* (Cambridge: Cambridge University Press, 1999), p. 86. It is in light of the long tradition of Christian (Catholic and Protestant) opposition to abortion that Richard Hays observes, "The recent shift in some branches of liberal Protestantism to advocacy for abortion rights is a major departure from the church's historic teaching" (*The Moral Vision of the New Testament*, p. 453).

22. As the *Catechism of the Catholic Church* makes clear, excommunication is the most severe penalty in canon law; by committing certain gravely sinful actions, an individual effectively separates himself—breaks communion with—the body of Christ and hence cannot receive the sacraments. Absolution in these cases must be granted by the pope, the bishop, or a priest authorized by them (except in danger of death, when any ordained priest can absolve the penitent from excommunication) (*Catechism* 1463). In highlighting the pastoral, rather than punitive, function of the penalty, the *Catechism* stresses, "The Church does not thereby intend to restrict the scope of mercy. Rather she makes clear the gravity of the crime committed, the irreparable harm done to the innocent who is put to death, as well as to the parents and the whole of society" (2272).

23. *Gaudium et Spes*, no. 51.

24. *Catechism* 2270–71. It should be noted that the Church uses the qualifiers "direct" or "procured" before the noun "abortion" advisedly. This is to distinguish the intentional killing of an unborn human being from the unintended and indirect death of an unborn human being that results from medical interventions aimed at saving the mother's life. The two acts have a fundamentally different moral character. In a life-threatening emergency, the Church counsels the physician to do everything in his or her power to save both mother and child, while at the same time permitting him or her to use maternal life-saving means—licit in and of themselves—that may place the child's life at risk.

25. *Evangelium Vitae*, no. 57.

26. Patrick Lee, *Abortion and Unborn Human Life* (Washington, DC: Catholic University of America Press, 1996), p. 1.

27. See Naomi Wolfe, "Our Bodies, Our Souls," *New Republic,* October 16, 1995, pp. 26–31; Judith Jarvis Thomson, "A Defense of Abortion," in Marshall Cohen, ed., *The Rights and Wrongs of Abortion* (Princeton, NJ: Princeton University Press, 1974); and Peggy Loonan, "Don't Compromise on Abortion," *New York Times,* January 15, 2003, p. A21.

28. Several justices have since admitted the faulty framework of *Roe,* declaring, "It is clear that the trimester approach violates the fundamental aspiration of judicial decision-making through the application of neutral principles 'sufficiently absolute to give them roots throughout the community and continuity over significant periods of time. . . .' A. Cox, *The Role of the Supreme Court in American Government* 114 (1976). The *Roe* framework is inherently tied to the state of medical technology that exists whenever particular litigation ensues . . . Even assuming that there is a fundamental right to terminate pregnancy in some situations, there is no justification in law or logic for the trimester framework adopted in *Roe* and employed by the Court today on the basis of stare decisis. For the reasons stated above, that framework is clearly an unworkable means of balancing the fundamental right and the compelling state interests that are indisputably implicated" *Akron v. Akron Center for Reproductive Health, Inc.,* 462 U.S. 416, 467 [1983].

29. *Doe v. Bolton,* 410 U.S. 179, 192 (1973).

30. *Stenberg v. Carhart,* 120 S.Ct. 2597, 68 USLW 4702 (2000).

31. *Abortion and Divorce in Western Law: American Failures, European Challenges* (Cambridge, MA: Harvard University Press, 1987), p. 112.

32. John Collins Harvey, M.D., "Distinctly Human: The When, Where, and How of Life's Beginnings," *Commonweal,* February 8, 2002. p. 12.

33. Robert George, *Clash of Orthodoxies: Law, Religion, and Morality in Crisis* (Wilmington, DE: ISI Books, 2001), p. 70.

34. Robert George, "The Ethics of Embryonic Stem Cell Research and Human Cloning," in *Building a Culture of Life 30 Years After Roe v. Wade,* ed. William L. Saunders and Brian C. Robertson (Washington, DC: Family Research Council, 2002), p. 27.

35. As Patrick Lee explains, "'Totipotency' refers to the ability of a cell, when isolated from other cells, to develop into a whole, mature organism" (*Abortion and Unborn Human Life,* p. 94).

36. The "proximate potency of the parts to become a separate whole upon physical division is in no way incompatible with the present substantial unity of the whole" (Lee, pp. 94–95).

37. Jay Budziszewski, "Thou Shalt Not Kill . . . Whom? The Meaning of the Person," paper delivered at the American Political Science Association convention, August 2002, p. 6. One can find an elaboration of Budziszewski's thesis in *What We Can't Not Know: A Guide* (Spence, 2003), chap. 3.

38. Cited in George, *Clash of Orthodoxies,* p. 68.

39. Abortionist James McMahon candidly admitted such a stance saying, "I've always been a classic liberal. I believe in freedom in the broadest sense . . . I frankly think the soul or personage comes in when the fetus is accepted by the mother." "The Abortions of Last Resort: The Question of Ending Pregnancy in its Later Stages May Be the Most Anguishing of the Entire Abortion Debate," *Los Angeles Times Magazine,* February 7, 1990. McMahon's position finds philosophical defense in the work of Mary Anne Warren. Upon admitting that her argument for abortion justifies infanticide, she proposes a criterion that would render infanticide impermissible, namely, the fact that the infant is *wanted:* "[Infanticide] would be wrong . . . because even if its parents do not want it and would not suffer from its destruction, there are other people who would like to have it, and would, in all probability, be deprived of a great deal of pleasure by its destruction. Thus, infanticide is wrong for reasons analogous to those which make it wrong to wantonly destroy natural resources, or great works of art." She continues, "[M]ost people value infants and would much prefer that they be preserved . . . So long as there are people who want an infant preserved, and who are willing and able to provide the means

of caring for it, under reasonably humane conditions, it is, *ceteris paribus*, wrong to destroy it." Cited in Budziszewski, "Thou Shalt Not Kill ... Whom?," p. 9. Commenting upon Warren's logic, Jay Budziszewski notes, "Whereas in the traditional view, the helpless and unwanted have the greatest claim on our protection, Warren finds that it is precisely the helpless and unwanted who have no claim."

40. See Peter Singer's *Practical Ethics*, 2nd ed. (Cambridge: Cambridge University Press, 1993), pp. 181–91, and Peter Singer and Helga Kuhse, *Should the Baby Live? The Problem of Handicapped Infants* (Oxford: Oxford University Press, 1988), pp. 194–97.

41. Bear in mind, however, the fact that the "health" exception in *Doe* has rendered the legal protection of the unborn after viability non-existent. Any discussion of actual protection of the unborn within the viability framework is speculative.

42. Cited in Randy Alcorn, *ProLife Answers to ProChoice Arguments* (Sisters, OR: Multnomah Publishers, Inc., 2000), p. 86. Even Justice Sandra Day O'Connor conceded, "The *Roe* framework is clearly on a collision course with itself. As the medical risks of various abortion procedures decrease, the point at which the state may regulate for reasons of maternal health is moved further forward to actual childbirth. As medical science becomes better able to provide for the separate existence of the fetus, the point of viability is moved further back toward conception. . . . The *Roe* framework is inherently tied to the state of medical technology that exists whenever particular litigation ensues." *Akron v. Akron Center for Reproductive Health, Inc.* 462 U.S. 416, 467 (1983).

43. George, p. 68.

44. This is ironic, in light of the predilection of abortion advocates—including Supreme Court justices—for bracketing philosophical and religious concerns in favor of empirical fact.

45. Patrick Lee, "The Pro-Life Argument from Substantial Identity: A Defense," *Bioethics* 18, no. 3 (2004): 249–64. The arbitrariness of pro-choice markers of personhood was not lost on Supreme Court Justice Byron White, who observed in his dissenting opinion in the *Thornburgh* case, "there is no non-arbitrary line separating a fetus from a child."

46. Budziszewski, p. 8.

47. Ibid.

SELECTED BIBLIOGRAPHY ON
HUMAN REPRODUCTION

Burke, Theresa Karminski, and Barbara Cullen. *Rachel's Vineyard: A Psychological and Spiritual Journey of Post-Abortion Healing: A Model for Groups.* New York: Alba House, 1995.

Cataldo, Peter J. "Reproductive Technologies." *Ethics and Medics* 21 (1996): 1–3.

Cioffi, Alfred, S.T.D. *Fetus as Medical Patient: Moral Dilemmas in Prenatal Diagnosis.* Lanham, MD: University Press of America, 1995.

DeBlois, Jean, C.S.J., and Kevin D. O'Rourke, O.P. "Care for the Beginning of Life." *Health Progress* 76, no. 7 (1995).

Grady, John. Abortion: *Yes or No?* Rockford, IL: Tan Books and Publishers, 1993.

Hahn, Kimberly Kirk. *Life Giving Love: Embracing God's Beautiful Design for Marriage.* Ann Arbor, MI: Servant Publications, 2002.

Heaney, Stephen J., ed. *Abortion: A New Generation of Catholic Responses.* Boston: National Catholic Bioethics Center, 1992.

Hilgers, Thomas W. "The Natural Methods for the Regulation of Fertility: The Authentic Alternative." *Linacre Quarterly* 62 (1995): 52–59.

Lee, Patrick. *Abortion and Unborn Human Life.* Washington, DC: The Catholic University of America Press, 1996.

Maestri, William F. *Do Not Lose Hope: Healing the Wounded Heart of Women Who Have Had Abortions.* New York: Alba House, 2000.

Magill, Gerard, and R. Randall Rainey. *Abortion and Public Policy: An Interdisciplinary Investigation Within the Catholic Tradition.* Omaha, NE: Creighton University Press, 1996.

McHugh, James T. "Health Care Reform and Abortion: A Catholic Moral Perspective." *Journal of Medicine and Philosophy* 19, no. 5 (1994): 491–500.

Ryan, Maura A. *Ethics and Economics of Assisted Reproduction.* Washington, DC: Georgetown University Press, 2003.

Shannon, Thomas A. "Prenatal Genetic Testing: The Potential Loss of Human Dignity Will Demand a Consistent Ethical Response from Catholic Health Care." *Health Progress* 82, no. 2 (2001): 33–35.

Smith, Herbert F., S.J. *Pro-Choice? Pro-Life? The Questions, the Answers.* Boston: St. Paul Books and Media, 1995.

Wildes, Kevin Wm., ed. *Infertility: A Crossroad of Faith, Medicine, and Technology.* Norwell, MA: Kluwer Academic Publishers, 1997.

PART III

Death and Dying

"God did not make death, and he does not delight in the death of the living. For he has created all things that they might exist .... God created man for incorruption, and made him in the image of his own eternity, but through the devil's envy death entered the world, and those who belong to his party experience it" (Wis 1:13–14; 2:23–24).

The Gospel of life, proclaimed in the beginning when man was created in the image of God for a destiny of full and perfect life (cf. Gen 2:7; Wis 9:2–3), is contradicted by the painful experience of death which enters the world and casts its shadow of meaninglessness over man's entire existence. Death came into the world as a result of the devil's envy (cf. Gen 3:1, 4–5) and the sin of our first parents (cf. Gen 2:17, 3:17–19).[1]

WITH THESE WORDS from the first chapter of his encyclical letter *The Gospel of Life,* John Paul II reminded the world that death was not part of God's original plan for humanity. Rather, death and the suffering that often accompanies it are both the result of our shared sin. As such, suffering and death have become part of the reality of our common human existence. Yet, the late Holy Father also reminded us that as human beings we were created "for incorruption," and have regained the promise of eternal life through the sacrifice of Jesus on the Cross. Within the Catholic tradition, then, what becomes important regarding death is how one approaches it and how we treat those who are dying.

In contemporary society, some argue that as rational beings we should be able to plan our deaths, take control of nature, and choose the time to end our life here on earth—indeed, it is argued that this is a fundamental right of all rational beings. Some suggest further that it is our duty to assist in the death of those who have made the choice to control their end. Finally, some even go so far as to claim that compassion demands that we end the lives of those who are not able to make this choice for themselves, yet whose quality of life has so diminished that there is little value left in living.

The Catholic perspective is quite different. As we explained in Part II on human reproduction, the Catholic tradition's specific understanding of human life rests upon two central tenets: (1) each human being is created in the image and likeness of God; and (2) the life of each human being is given as a free gift from God. It was further argued that these two points give rise to an obligation to respect all human life. This obligation also encompasses respect for one's own self, even in the face of death. And so, the fact that one chooses one's death does not, by itself, make that choice valid and good. Rather, the task here is to consider whether it is ever appropriate to actively end innocent human life.

The underlying concern for those who favor choosing one's death, or choosing death for one who is suffering, involves the fear of losing human dignity. The claim is that certain diseases, and certain stages of the dying process, strip a human being of our most fundamental abilities—most notably, our ability to think and act for ourselves—and so, in turn, rob the suffering person of her or his dignity.

However, to respond to this concern, we must be clear about what constitutes human dignity *and* what is the source of this dignity that we clearly recognize as part of human nature. Once again, the Catholic position here is clear—the source of human dignity is the fact that we are created in the image and likeness of God. However, this dignity is also recognized through the uniqueness found in each and every human being. This uniqueness is grounded empirically in each person's specific genetic code, as well as experientially in each one's particular personality. These are points that all of us can recognize, even if one is not inclined to accept the uniqueness of an individual as being rooted in the theological understanding of God as our Creator.

At the heart of our uniqueness is, of course, our rational nature. But one must be careful not to take too narrow a view here. The rational nature of humanity includes our ability to build and foster relationships with others, to communicate, and to love. The key word here is "ability." It is quite obvious that human beings do not carry out all of the aforementioned activities all the time—infants are limited in their ability to communicate, one who is unconscious cannot properly speaking love others, nor do any of us act in these ways while asleep. However, all human beings, regardless of development, age, mental disposition, health status, gender, etc., have the innate capacity to communicate, to share, and to love. These are endowments of human nature. In terms of our dignity it is not the actualization of these endowments that is significant, but rather the mere fact that human beings are so endowed. Disease and illness cannot strip these endowments away, although they certainly can hinder the active presentation of our endowments. Nor can any human being strip away her or his own dignity, or take away the dignity of another—our dignity always remains within us.[2]

However, this is not to say that death and dying do not present us with serious challenges to human dignity. Indeed, dying seems to be one of the greatest challenges humans face in life. But the problem does not come entirely from the external forces of disease and illness—rather, a major part of humanity's problem with death and dying comes from humanity itself, and the tendency to ignore the dignity within each other and within our own selves. To the extent that disease and illness mar our bodies and our minds, dignity becomes harder to recognize. Simply because society tells us that a human being is to be beautiful and useful, we conclude that those who are marred and/or ineffective in the production of goods for society have a diminished worth. This is the path that, as the late Holy Father noted in *The Gospel of Life,* was leading us into the "culture of death":

This culture is actively fostered by powerful cultural, economic and political currents which encourage an idea of society excessively concerned with efficiency. Looking at the situation from this point of view, it is possible to speak in a certain sense of a war of the powerful against the weak: a life which would require greater acceptance, love and care is considered useless, or held to be an intolerable burden, and is therefore rejected in one way or another. A person who, because of illness, handicap, or, more simply, just by existing, compromises the well-being or life-style of those who are more favoured tends to be looked upon as an enemy to be resisted or eliminated. In this way a kind of "conspiracy against life" is unleashed. This conspiracy involves not only individuals in their personal, family or group relationships, but goes far beyond, to the point of damaging and distorting, at the international level, relations between peoples and States.[3]

Those who are suffering through the dying process vividly remind us of the reality of our own frailty, thus tempting many into this "war" of one against the other and strengthening the "culture of death."

And so, the challenge that death and dying present is not to prevent people from losing their dignity. Simply put, no human being can ever lose her or his dignity—dignity is inherent in each of us. Rather, our challenge is to recognize the dignity that is always present within each and every human being. This is why, in part, euthanasia and assisted suicide are such affronts to the Catholic tradition. The American bishops capture this point well in their *Ethical and Religious Directives for Catholic Health Care Services* when discussing "Issues in Care for the Dying":

Above all, as a witness to its faith, a Catholic health care institution will be a community of respect, love and support to patients or residents and their families as they face the reality of death. What is hardest to face is the process of dying itself, especially the dependency, the helplessness and the pain that so often accompany terminal illness. One of the primary purposes of medicine in caring for the dying is the relief of pain and the suffering caused by it. Effective management of pain in all its forms is critical in the appropriate care of the dying.

The truth that life is a precious gift from God has profound implications for the question of stewardship over human life. We are not the owners of our lives and hence do not have absolute power over life. We have a duty to preserve our life and to use it for the glory of God, but the duty to preserve life is not absolute, for we may reject life-prolonging procedures that are insufficiently beneficial or excessively burdensome. Suicide and euthanasia are never morally acceptable options.[4]

In this light, to make the claim that it is better to actively end the life of a human being in order to preserve her or his dignity quite simply has confused the issue, thereby diminishing what human dignity is really all about.

This brings us back to the obligation to respect all human life—even while that life is being ravaged by disease and marred by illness, perhaps even fatally so. What, then, is the Catholic response to death and dying? As noted in the previous statement from the American bishops, it is stewardship. We are called to care for the life of each individual as a gift, from the beginning of life to the very end. Such care brings with it further responsibilities. We must continue to fight illness and disease, while still respecting the life of all human beings. We must be attentive to the needs of the dying, both within our own families and within the larger community. We must ease the physical pain of the dying, and not ignore or minimize the reality of the pain they feel. We must be present to the dying by visiting the sick, praying for them, and abiding with them in their suffering. As the Congregation for the Doctrine of the Faith so clearly explained in their *Declaration on Euthanasia:* "What a sick person needs, besides medical care, is love, the human and supernatural warmth with which the sick person can and ought to be surrounded by all those close to him or her, parents and children, doctors and nurses."[5] Society as a whole must become more open in regard to dying and strive to recognize the inherent dignity of persons throughout the entire dying process.

In saying all of this, there is no pretense that living through the dying process with a loved one is easy. Typed words on a page can rarely capture the anguish of watching a loved one die, or the utter helplessness that families feel when they begin to realize that with all of our technological advances, there are many ailments, diseases, and problems that modern medicine still cannot treat or alleviate. This is especially true when there is great suffering involved. What can we say regarding suffering? From the perspective of philosophy alone, not much, I fear—at least, not much that is truly meaningful. Our words, though well intentioned, often sound hollow and empty. That is because suffering is a mystery that we will never fully probe in this life. For many, this is where faith clearly helps support human reason in our quest for meaning and understanding. Yet, what we do know is that experience tells us that human suffering—while never something desirable for its own sake—can be transformative. And so, our words—though lacking—are not worthless. Nor are our loving actions of care for those who suffer and for those who are dying. In one of his early apostolic letters, *The Christian Meaning of Human Suffering*, John Paul II offered a beautiful and moving reflection on the salvific nature of the human experience of suffering and death within the Judeo-Christian tradition. In particular, he noted:

Those who share in Christ's sufferings have before their eyes the Paschal Mystery of the Cross and Resurrection, in which Christ descends, in a first phase, to the ultimate limits of human weakness and impotence: indeed, he dies nailed to the Cross. But if at the same time in this *weakness* there is accomplished his *lifting up*, confirmed by the power of the Resurrection, then this means that the weaknesses of all human sufferings are capable of being infused with the same power of God manifested in Christ's Cross. In such a concept, *to suffer* means to become particularly *susceptible*, particularly *open to the working of the salvific powers of God,* offered to humanity in Christ. In him God has confirmed his desire to act especially through suffering, which is man's weakness and emptying of self, and he wishes to make his power known precisely in this weakness and emptying of self.[6]

Thus, for Christians, part of the transformative power of suffering lies in the fact that Jesus suffered on the cross for our sins, and that God the Father allowed Christ to suffer for us in this manner. God knows both what it is to suffer as we suffer, *and* what it is like to experience the suffering and death of a loved one. This is part of the solace that faith and grace can bring, even in the absence of rational argumentation.

Now, does this mean that we must do everything possible in order to keep people alive, or that we are obligated to extend the dying process as long as our technological means allow? Certainly not. As we noted earlier in a quote from the *Ethical and Religious Directives* from the American bishops, "We have a duty to preserve our life and to use it for the glory of God, but the duty to preserve life is not absolute, for we may reject life-prolonging procedures that are insufficiently beneficial or excessively burdensome."[7] Thus, the Catholic tradition emphasizes that life is an important human good—but life is by no means the only good, nor is it absolute. Indeed, this is what allows police officers, firefighters, and military personnel to take the risks that their jobs require. It is also why we do not consider a parent who rushes into the way of a speeding vehicle or jumps into a raging river to save a child to be suicidal. A Catholic may rightly sacrifice her or his life for another important good if necessary. This further means that when it comes to our health—as the *Ethical and Religious Directives* specifically point out—we do not have to do everything possible to continue our physical existence. Instead, there are two criteria that can help guide our decision making on these difficult end-of-life issues, both individually and for society as a whole.

First, we can employ the well-established (though sometimes over-looked) principle of futility, which dates back to the very beginnings of medicine and the teachings of Hippocrates. Simply put, one is not obligated to continue with medical treatment that has been deemed futile. The determination that treatment is ineffective or futile is a medical judgment, to be rendered by those health care professionals involved with the person's care. As such, this is an objective judgment that must be able to be supported empirically. Only health care professionals are trained and licensed to make such a judgment. The reason I suggest the principle of futility is sometimes "overlooked" has to do with the contemporary focus upon patient autonomy within medicine today, by which many assume that health care providers must do whatever a patient—or the client—requests or demands (as long as they can pay for it!). The mantra of "do everything" is a common one in contemporary health care. To a degree, such requests and demands for futile care at the end of life are understandable given the psychological and emotional stress that patients and families come under as death draws near. Nonetheless, such an approach is inappropriate in the health care setting. As Dr. Edmund Pellegrino argued in his essay "Decisions to Withdraw Life-Sustaining Treatment":

The moral authority of the patient, the patient's surrogate, or a living will is not absolute. It is limited under the following conditions: (1) when the patient's decision produces identifiable, serious, probable harm to identifiable others; (2) when the physician is asked to violate his or her personal and professional ethical integrity; (3) when the patient deliberately attempts to injure himself or herself; or (4) when the treatment requested is clinically futile or contraindicated. The physician is not under obligation to comply with a request, however autonomous, that violates the physician's own beliefs or his or her conception of the best standard of care.[8]

And so, if current treatment will not alleviate or cure a person's pathology, there is no longer an obligation to continue that therapy. A clear example would be stopping CPR on a patient in the emergency room. Why will the doctor finally cease the efforts of the resuscitation team? Because their efforts are futile. However, continuation of such therapy could still be permissible for a short time to allow for other important goods to be achieved (i.e., to allow time for family to gather, to have a priest provide the sacrament of the sick, etc.).

The second criterion is more involved, and centers around the concept of grave burden. In Catholic teaching, the concept of burden as it relates to health care treatment is connected with the distinction between ordinary and extraordinary means. The roots of this distinction run very deep in the Catholic tradition, but were first formally stated by Pope Pius XII. For example, in his 1957 "Address of Reanimation," Pius noted that: ". . . normally one is held to use only ordinary means—according to circumstances of persons, places, times, and culture—that is to say, means that do not involve any grave burden for oneself or another. A more strict obligation would be too burdensome for most people and would render the attainment of the higher, more important good too difficult."[9] In statements such as this, Pius XII was arguing that one was obligated to do those acts deemed ordinary to promote a healthy life, such as eating, taking common medicines, exercising, etc. However, due to the potentially burdensome nature of some treatments, one was not obligated—though it was certainly permissible—to pursue more extraordinary means of prolonging life, such as attempting radical surgical procedures or taking experimental drugs.

Unfortunately, with the advances of modern medicine and the stepped-up pace of technological development, the concepts of ordinary and extraordinary means of medical treatment have become blurred, in part due to differences in how those terms are used today within medical practice and in the debates concerning bioethics. For example, most surgeons would consider transplants to be quite ordinary in the practice of medicine today. Yet, a husband might consider a heart transplant, which would require the prior death of someone else to procure the heart, to be a rather extraordinary way to continue living even in the face of his family's concerns for his own life. Of course, in neither case is the issue of "burden" upon the patient an explicit concern. This is why in the 1980 *Declaration on Euthanasia,* the Congregation for the Doctrine of the Faith employed the parallel concepts of "proportionate" and "disproportionate" means:

Everyone has the duty to care for his or her own health or to seek such care from others. Those whose task it is to care for the sick must do so conscientiously and administer the remedies that seem necessary or useful. However, is it necessary in all circumstances to have recourse to all possible remedies? In the past, moralists replied that one is never obliged to use "extraordinary" means. This reply, which as a principle still holds good, is perhaps less clear today, by reason of the imprecision of the term and the rapid progress made in the treatment of sickness. Thus some people prefer to speak of "proportionate" and "disproportionate" means. In any case, it will be possible to make a correct judgment as to the means by studying the type of treatment to be used, its degree of complexity or risk, its cost and the possibilities of using it, and comparing these elements with the result that can be expected, taking into account the state of the sick person and his or her physical and moral resources.[10]

Among Catholic scholars, and within the official teaching of the Church, both sets of terms can be found in contemporary discussions of death and dying. Even the late Holy Father employed both concepts in his March 20, 2004, allocution, in which he specifically touched on the use of artificial nutrition and hydration:

I should like particularly to underline how the administration of water and food, even when provided by artificial means, always represents a *natural means* of preserving life, not a *medical act.* Its use, furthermore, should be considered, in principle, *ordinary* and *proportionate,* and as such morally obligatory, insofar as and until it is seen to have attained its proper finality, which in the present case consists in providing nourishment to the patient and alleviation of his suffering.[11]

Thus, the "terms" employed in public debates regarding end-of-life issues must not be allowed to obscure the true focus of the Church's position here, which is the *burden* life-prolonging treatment may sometimes impose.

In the end, the determination of grave burden is a subjective judgment

that can only be made by the one who is dying, her or his family, or a designated surrogate. Since this judgment is subjective, it is not to be made
lightly, nor should it be taken lightly. Members of a health care team, as well
as family and friends, should attempt to make certain that an expression of
grave burden is not flowing from a fear of losing dignity or from a state of
depression. Nevertheless, it would be inappropriate to simply ignore a person's expression of grave burden. As such, there is no obligation to continue with burdensome treatment. Of course, this would still be permissible if
the person suffering were willing to accept even a very serious burden for
some other important good (i.e., participating in experimental therapy for
research purposes).

The criteria of futile treatment and grave burden do not necessarily simplify the issues surrounding death and dying—there are no black and white
answers here. Some Catholic scholars have even suggested that the concepts
of futility and grave burden are thrown around too loosely and too frequently to be of value any longer. However, that is *not* a demonstration of the in-
validity of such concepts, but rather an illustration of the failure of some
people to correctly apply them. And so, the concepts of futile treatment and
grave burden do provide a helpful basis from which to evaluate the obligation to continue life-prolonging treatment. In making such decisions, the
Catholic tradition would always err on the side of life, and would always encourage the continuation of life. Yet, the tradition also recognizes that it can
certainly be appropriate at times to withdraw and withhold medical treatment, thereby allowing a person to die as a result of a fatal pathology.

However, some bioethicists and doctors outside the Catholic tradition
have recently begun to argue that allowing a person to die is not essentially
different from euthanasia.[12] Euthanasia is defined as an act whereby one directly intends the death of a person, usually for the expressed motive of ending that person's suffering. Traditionally, euthanasia can take two forms—
active or passive. With active euthanasia, the intention to bring about death
is carried out through a direct action—that is, you do something to actually
kill the person (e.g., provide a lethal dose of medicine). It is argued by proponents that the death of the one suffering is necessary to prevent any further loss of dignity. With passive euthanasia, a direct action is not taken—
rather, one forgoes performing an action that normally should be carried
out, in order to cause death (e.g., not feeding a person). Allowing to die, by
contrast, arises only when there is no longer a moral obligation to continue
to resist death because—citing the two criteria discussed earlier—treatment

has been deemed futile, or treatment will bring about a grave burden for the patient. The key ethical issue here is the intention of the action—not simply the consequences or outcomes. The intention is not for the person to die, but rather to reduce suffering and allow a fatal pathology to take its natural course. Of course, in all three cases (euthanasia, stopping futile treatment, or avoiding grave burden), the end result is the death of a person. However, the intentions and causes involved are clearly different. The *Catechism of the Catholic Church* summarizes the difference by noting:

Discontinuing medical procedures that are burdensome, dangerous, extraordinary, or disproportionate to the expected outcome can be legitimate; it is the refusal of "over-zealous" treatment. Here one does not will to cause death; one's inability to impede it is merely accepted. The decisions should be made by the patient if he is competent and able or, if not, by those legally entitled to act for the patient, whose reasonable will and legitimate interests must always be respected.[13]

A few pertinent distinctions can help further clarify the ethical difference between allowing one to die and euthanasia.

First, active euthanasia, by definition, directly intends and causes the death of a person. This is referred to as an act of commission—that is, the goal of euthanasia is for the person to die, and so a direct action is taken to end the life of the person who is dying. There is no question about the fact that one must end a person's life by direct means with active forms of eutha-nasia. For their part, proponents of active euthanasia often attempt to jus-tify the act as the lesser of two evils. But this is not acceptable, because we must never directly intend and cause evil. In contrast, when one removes life-prolonging therapies or withholds further treatment in the face of a fa-tal pathology because treatment has been deemed medically futile, or be-cause it will result in a grave burden for the patient, death is *not* directly caused. The persons involved do not take any direct action to kill or harm the person who is dying. Rather, the fatal pathology has become so serious that it has made further treatment futile or burdensome. Furthermore, it is insisted that basic care (keeping the person comfortable, clean, as free of pain as possible, etc.) must be continued—the one who is dying is *not* being abandoned. The *Catechism* affirms this point by noting:

Even if death is thought imminent, the ordinary care owed to a sick person cannot be legitimately interrupted. The use of painkillers to alleviate the sufferings of the dying, even at the risk of shortening their days, can be morally in conformity with human dignity if death is not willed as either an end or a means, but only foreseen and tolerated as inevitable. Palliative care is a special form of disinterested charity. As such it should be encouraged.[14]

And so, the issue of what causes death here is an important distinction for evaluating the ethical difference between active euthanasia and allowing one to die.

The second difference still relates to active forms of euthanasia, but broadens our focus to include so-called passive forms of euthanasia. After all, given the previous point, it could be argued that passive euthanasia is identical to allowing one to die, since neither involves a direct action to bring about death. Nevertheless, there is also an important difference to be acknowledged here. When one is engaging in passive euthanasia, the intention remains to have the person die. As such, the only real difference between active and passive euthanasia involves the manner in which death is brought about. In passive forms of euthanasia, death is not achieved through direct means, but rather by forgoing an action that normally should be performed. What makes this euthanasia, then, is the fact that there is still an obligation to prolong life, either because no fatal pathology is actually present, or because treatment is still medically effective and is not imposing any serious burden. Death is caused here through a lack of action—this is also referred to as an act by omission. In contrast, with allowing one to die the intention is not to cause the death of the person, but rather to achieve some other important human good. Thus, with allowing a person to die, one is still choosing a good. This is also a point of contention, as some argue that it is not possible to separate out our intentions in this manner, and that when death is involved it is always intended.[15] To this we must respond by pointing out that only the one making a decision knows her or his true intentions. It is, therefore, inappropriate for proponents of euthanasia to tell all of us what our intentions are when we act—they simply cannot make such a claim. Further, it should be noted that within the judicial system the determination of intention is a crucial matter that can mean the difference between murder in the first and second degree, or between voluntary and involuntary manslaughter. Even though all would recognize the limitations of attempting to determine a person's intentions in court (since one could always lie), there remains the clear recognition that intentions are important for determining a person's responsibility for her or his actions. If indeed a person were to make a decision to withdraw or withhold treatment for a loved one with the direct intention of having that loved one die, then such an act would be euthanasia, regardless of what that person may "publicly" claim about the situation. However, if one recognizes that a loved one has been suffering greatly and that it is the medical therapy itself that is creating that suffering and thereby imposing a serious burden upon the person, then withdrawing treatment in order to end the suffering of the loved one—not to end her or his life *per se*—would be ethically permissible.

In the end, our response in the face of death should not be to eliminate pain—even in the presence of tremendous suffering—by intentionally eliminating those who are dying. All acts of euthanasia intend to eliminate the person—not the problem. Human compassion and respect for the dignity of every human being calls for so much more from us than the minimalistic solution of purposely hastening or causing someone's death.

To further develop these reflections, we have two excellent essays. We will begin with John Berkman's consideration of "Medically Assisted Nutrition and Hydration in Medicine and Moral Theology." In his introduction, Berkman notes, "Of the various ethical dilemmas surrounding decisions regarding the use of life support, none provoked more disagreement among both Catholic ethicists and the Catholic episcopacy than that of the use of medically assisted nutrition and hydration . . . . There were regular if not constant exchanges between Catholic ethicists on this question through the 1980s and early 1990s." To shed light on the issue and to help clarify the debate among Catholic scholars in particular, Berkman presents a comprehensive and detailed discussion regarding the use of medically assisted nutrition and hydration. In the first part of his essay, Berkman presents an overview of the history and use of this treatment within medical practice. He argues in part that ". . . inadequate understanding of the medical history, development, and varying roles of medically assisted nutrition and hydration has led moralists to overly rigid understandings of its place in medicine." As a result of this, Berkman points out that current attempts to classify medically assisted nutrition and hydration as either "basic care" or "medical treatment" in general will not work because such a determination can only be made on a case-by-case basis. After reviewing the medical history, Berkman then addresses the earliest considerations of medically assisted nutrition and hydration by American moral theologians, emphasizing that they saw it as part of the overall duty to preserve life. In his third section, Berkman focuses specifically upon the more recent Catholic debate over the appropriate uses of medically assisted nutrition and hydration, and the shift away from the traditional concern for the duty to preserve life toward more ambiguous issues such as quality of life. Berkman next proceeds to analyze four recent arguments used by moral theologians to justify withholding or withdrawing medically assisted nutrition and hydration in the case of comatose patients, including arguments based upon "quality of life" and "excessive burden." In the fifth section, however, Berkman takes what many readers may find an unexpected turn. Berkman addresses recent studies that have raised serious questions about the efficacy of medically assisted nutrition and hydration in contemporary medical practice. In particular, Berkman discusses the significance of current studies that indicate that specific classes of patients do not actually benefit from medically assisted nutrition and hydration, and that in some cases classes of patients can be harmed by the treatment. Berkman believes that as the results of these studies come to light, and their implications begin to sink in, medically assisted nutrition and hydration will be employed far less often. Berkman ends with a thoughtful Eucharistic reflection on the meaning of "feeding" and how this act goes well beyond simply providing nutrition. In his closing comments, Berkman remarks: "Feeding others and being fed by others are among the most significant acts that Christians do, and not only for nutritive reasons. As persons shaped by a Eucharistic vision of our eating practices, Christians know this well. If and when it is realized that MANH is not as effective in prolonging life as it was once thought to be, there will be an opportunity in nursing homes and other medical contexts to rethink the significance of feeding."

The second essay is Brendan Sweetman's "Two Arguments against Euthanasia." As Sweetman notes, next to abortion, euthanasia is one of the most discussed moral issues in America today, and many citizens will be asked to vote on this controversial issue in the next decade—thus, it merits careful study. For his discussion, Sweetman defines euthanasia as ". . . the intentional killing of a patient with the aim of bringing an end to that person's suffering." He explains that he is using the term in a broad enough sense to include both voluntary and involuntary euthanasia, as well as what is described today as physician-assisted suicide. The first of the "two arguments" presented by Sweetman is referred to as the "in principle" argument against euthanasia, and holds that euthanasia is intrinsically wrong and so should never be legalized even though some claim it can produce beneficial consequences. This first argument rests on the doctrine of the sanctity of life, which Sweetman argues has been a dominant value throughout all human culture and society. As such, this first argument is not essentially a religious argument, even though many who favor euthanasia try to cast arguments based on the sanctity of life only in that light. In his essay, Sweetman develops that "in principle" argument through a consideration of the main objections against it. Through this point/counterpoint, Sweetman lays out the overall debate regarding euthanasia clearly and intelligently. In the second part of his essay, Sweetman moves in a different vein and addresses what he calls the "practical argument" against euthanasia, which involves the concerns that many people have expressed over the practicality of trying to control something like euthanasia and keep it from being abused if it were legalized. Sweetman discusses eight particular areas of possible abuse that could arise from the legalization of euthanasia, including the danger of pushing the poor and elderly toward euthanasia and the pressure, not often discussed, this would place upon the doctor-patient relationship, which is already strained in many ways in contemporary health care. Sweetman speaks frankly about these "all-too-real" concerns that are rarely acknowledged in the euthanasia debate, which proponents try to keep exclusively focused upon the emotional aspects of human suffering. In the end, Sweetman points out that ". . . the 'in principle' argument is the strongest argument in the sense that it makes the stronger claim that euthanasia is wrong in itself, whereas the 'practical argument' says only that euthanasia would not work in practice." The insights Sweetman offers will provide readers with a broader perspective of the problems connected with the actual practice of euthanasia and the legitimate reasons for opposing it both ethically and legally.

As these essays help remind us, the Catholic perspective requires a very specific approach to human suffering and death. We are challenged to share in the pain and suffering of the human family in a manner that honors the dignity of every individual human being, just as we shared in the fullness of each individual life, while never forgetting that we are called to an eternal reality that lies beyond this earthly existence. As John Paul II reminded us in his letter *The Christian Meaning of Human Suffering*, this is what gives us the Christian hope in the face of death:

As a result of Christ's salvific work, man exists on earth *with the hope* of eternal life and holiness. And even though the victory over sin and death achieved by Christ in his Cross and Resurrection does not abolish temporal suffering from human life, nor free from suffering the whole historical dimension of human existence, it nevertheless *throws a new light* upon this dimension and upon every suffering: the light of salvation. This is the light of the Gospel, that is, of the Good News. At the heart of this light is the truth expounded in the conversation with Nicodemus: "For God so loved the world that he gave his only Son." This truth radically changes the picture of man's history and his earthly situation: in spite of the sin that took root in this history both as an original inheritance and as the "sin of the world" and as the sum of personal sins, God the Father has loved the only-begotten Son, that is, he loves him in a lasting way; and then in time, precisely through this all-surpassing love, he "gives" this Son, that he may strike at the very roots of human evil and thus draw close in a salvific way to the whole world of suffering in which man shares.[16]

NOTES

1. John Paul II, *Evangelium Vitae*, no. 7.

2. For an excellent discussion of the concept of human endowments, see John F. Kavanaugh, S.J., *Who Count as Persons?* (Washington, DC: Georgetown University Press, 2001), especially chapter 4, "Endowments of Embodied Persons," pp. 48–70.

3. *Evangelium Vitae*, no. 12.

4. United States Conference of Catholic Bishops, *Ethical and Religious Directives for Catholic Health Care Services*, 4th ed. (Washington, DC: USCCB, 2001), p. 29.

5. Congregation for the Doctrine of the Faith, *Declaration on Euthanasia*, 1980, II.

6. John Paul II, *Salvifici Doloris*, no. 23.

7. *Ethical and Religious Directives*, p. 29.

8. Edmund D. Pellegrino, M.D., "Decisions to Withdraw Life-Sustaining Treatment: A Moral Algorithm," *Journal of the American Medical Association* 283, no. 8 (February 23, 2000): 1066.

9. Pope Pius XII, "Address of Reanimation," *Acta Apostolicae Sedis* 49 (1957): 1027–33. See also "The Prolongation of Life: An address of Pope Pius XII to an International Congress of Anaesthesiologists," November 24, 1957.

10. *Declaration on Euthanasia*, IV.

11. John Paul II, "Address of John Paul II to the Participants in the International Congress on 'Life-Sustaining Treatments and Vegetative State: Scientific Advances and Ethical Dilemmas,'" paragraph 4. One will also see this combination employed in the *Ethical and Religious Directives*, directives 56 and 57, p. 31.

12. Timothy Quill, M.D., et al., "The Rule of Double Effect—A Critique of Its Role in End-of-Life Decision Making," *New England Journal of Medicine* 337, no. 24 (December 11, 1997): 1768–71.

13. *Catechism of the Catholic Church*, English Translation for the United States of America (New York: Catholic Book Publishing Company, 1994), 2278, p. 549.

14. Ibid., 2279, p. 549.

15. Quill et al., "The Rule of Double Effect."

16. *Salvifici Doloris*, no. 15.

Medically Assisted Nutrition and Hydration in Medicine and Moral Theology

JOHN BERKMAN

For a significant portion of the 1980s, ethical issues regarding the use of various forms of support to prolong life grabbed newspaper headlines in the United States. High-profile legal cases over the "right to die," such as those of Karen Ann Quinlan and Nancy Cruzan, became legal landmarks. Other highly publicized cases, such as those of Brophy, Conroy, Herbert, and Jobes, contributed to making the issue a commonplace part of the news. In the midst of the headlines generated by these and other related cases, many Catholic ethicists attempted to provide analysis and guidance. These cases also elicited frequent formal statements from the Catholic episcopacy, both from individual bishops and from episcopal conferences.[1]

Of the various ethical dilemmas surrounding decisions regarding the use of life support, none provoked more disagreement among both Cath-

This article originally appeared in *The Thomist* 68 (2004): 69–104. Thanks to Michael Baxter, Bill Mattison, Joyce McClure, Gilbert Meilaender, John Grabowski, and William Barbieri for helpful comments on earlier drafts of this paper. Thanks also to Jennifer Moore, M.D., and Heidi White, M.D., for insight on current medical practice with regard to MANH, and to Thomas Bender, M.D., for originally bringing to my attention the Kelly-Donovan debate. Finally, I wish to acknowledge with gratitude the support of the Duke Institute on Care at the End of Life, where I was Visiting Scholar in 2001–2, and where much of the research for this paper was conducted.

olic ethicists and the Catholic episcopacy than that of the use of medically assisted nutrition and hydration (henceforth MANH). Among the episcopacy, this disagreement gained a high profile in statements from the Texas and Pennsylvania bishops, as well as those of other groups of bishops. There were regular if not constant exchanges between Catholic ethicists on this question through the 1980s and early 1990s.[2]

The literature detailing various arguments for or against the use of MANH in caring for the dying and debilitated is extensive. Yet the thesis of this article is that a large part, if not the main thrust, of the debates over MANH has been inadequate and misguided on a number of different levels. I hope to reorient and redirect the debate by attending to the medical history of MANH (part 1) and recent medical developments with regard to MANH (part 5), examining and contextualizing the earliest debate (i.e., in the 1950s) over MANH among moral theologians (part 2) as well as a more recent debate over MANH involving numerous American Catholic bishops (part 3), and critically evaluating the types of moral arguments that preoccupy many of those who currently write on the ethics of MANH (part 4).

The first section—a brief history of nineteenth- and twentieth-century medical practice with regard to MANH—aims to show that inadequate understanding of the medical history, development, and varying roles of medically assisted nutrition and hydration has led moralists to overly rigid understandings of its place in medicine. One upshot of what I argue in this section is that, for example, attempts to define MANH as either inherently "basic care" or "a medical treatment" is an exercise in futility. Such descriptions are only legitimate in specific medical contexts and are "patient dependent."

With this history providing a sense of the medical context of MANH in the 1950s, the second section analyzes what I believe is the first discussion of MANH by American moral theologians, placing it in the context of their broader concern with "the duty to preserve life." The astute reader will surmise that the very different medical context for MANH at that time reveals both the achievement and the limitations and provisional character of the debate over MANH by the Catholic moralists (e.g., Gerald Kelly, S.J.) of that era. In view of the evolving medical context of MANH between the 1950s and the 1980s, one goal of this section is to show the problematic nature of appeals by some later Catholic moralists to the authority of earlier authors on the question of MANH.

The third section examines a more recent Catholic "debate"—one between two groups of American Catholic bishops in the early 1990s—over the appropriate uses of MANH. Even this relatively recent debate cannot be separated from its specific social and medical context. Their debate shows both continuity with and development beyond the earlier textbook debates, showing a greater sensitivity to the various contexts in which the question can arise. In this debate, the emphasis seems to be moving away from the preoccupation with how vigorously to preserve life, and toward asking which lives should be vigorously (or even not so vigorously) preserved. The concern over questions related to "quality of life" is seen in the inordinate attention this debate devotes to questions related to the preservation of the lives of patients in comas or in a persistent vegetative state (PVS). My point in this section is that the traditional question concerning the duty to preserve life has been to some extent preempted by new questions regarding what constitutes a dying person and the quality of life to be preserved. These new questions—especially those concerning quality of life—are full of conceptual ambiguity and at the same time deeply troubling.

In order to clarify the current status of the debate concerning MANH, the fourth section unpacks some of the arguments that have had significant currency in the last two decades when arguing that MANH should be discontinued from PVS and other coma patients. Focusing on four recent arguments regarding MANH for comatose patients, this section argues that while adequate decisions regarding the use of MANH must always be relative to the benefit received by the patient, those who wish to withdraw MANH from patients who are not terminally ill and whose lives will be extended by MANH bear the burden of proof, morally speaking.

In the light of the argument made in the fourth section, the fifth section is a reversal of sorts. This section evaluates recent studies on the efficacy of MANH, studies that raise serious questions about the medical benefit of MANH for many classes of patients. Having argued in the fourth section that the presumption should be to give MANH to all who can derive proportionate medical benefit from it, I postulate in the fifth section that many classes of patients who have been presumed to gain such medical benefit from MANH may not in fact have been benefiting from MANH, and some (as a class of patients) may even have been harmed by MANH. If these current studies hold up, the forty-year honeymoon between MANH and much of the medical community will be over. As questions continue to be raised about the medical benefits and burdens of MANH, we can expect that the future will bring greater attention to various means and general benefits of oral feeding, and less reliance on MANH.

In the light of the medical developments presented in section 5, the article concludes with some reflections on the eating practices of contemporary American culture, and their possible influence on assumptions about the moral appropriateness of MANH and feeding the dying and severely debilitated more generally. The debates over MANH in the 1980s and early 1990s focused almost exclusively on one aspect of eating practices, namely, their nutritive significance. In other words, concern was focused almost entirely on how morally to evaluate a death that resulted from a lack of nutrition.[3] While some contributors to the debate expressed intuitions about the symbolism of food as an expression of concern for one's parent or relative or friend, little was said about the significance of eating practices theologically—for example, for Eucharistic practices, for maintaining Christian community, for practicing hospitality, etc. For many of those involved in the debate, there was no significant moral difference between eating and receiving nutrition. I conclude this section and the article with observations as to how a Eucharistic vision and Eucharistic practices might guide Christian care of the dying and severely debilitated, including feeding practices. The purpose of this paper will be realized *not* if the reader's primary conclusion is that MANH is not as helpful as we have thought and we must use it less, *but only if* the reader's primary conclusion is that MANH often represents a failure truly to feed the patient, and if it leads to redoubled efforts to find a more holistic means of feeding all persons whenever it is beneficial to them.

1. A Short History and Summary of Recent Practice

From ancient times, people have received nutrition in ways other than through oral feeding.[4] Greek physicians made extensive use of nutrient enemas, delivering various broths as well as wine, milk, and whey through this means. Hippocrates was one of many who advocated rectal tube feeding. Devices were developed in the eighteenth and nineteenth centuries that delivered nutrients by such means as far along as the colon. Articles in British and American medical journals in the latter part of the nineteenth century discussed a wide variety of nutrients introduced in this way.[5] Perhaps the most high-profile recipient of rectal feeding in the nineteenth century was President Garfield, who was fed in this way every four hours for most of the seventy-nine days he survived after being wounded by an assassin.[6]

While the earliest recorded use of a tube for feeding directly into the esophagus, stomach, or jejunem is in the fourteenth century, it first came into widespread use in the nineteenth century.[7] At the time such methods were known as gavage or force-feeding. Their first common use was apparently for feeding patients of insane asylums in the first half of the nineteenth century. Such feedings were through tubes inserted either through the mouth (orogastric feeding) or the nose (nasogastric feeding). In the latter half of the nineteenth century, both nasogastric and rectal feedings were widely used.[8] By the end of the nineteenth century pediatricians were advocating such feedings for premature infants, and for infants and children with diphtheria and other acute ailments.[9] One physician noted that while such MANH was best carried out by a physician, any intelligent nurse or parent could be taught how to administer it.[10]

While numerous developments in both the techniques of tube feeding and the nutritional content of tube feeding occurred in the first half of the twentieth century, the first monograph devoted to the practice of tube feeding—in particular to scientifically demonstrating its positive effects—was published by Morton Pareira in 1959. Pareira noted that while knowledge of tube feeding had been commonplace, use of tube feeding had up to that time been "sporadic and limited."[11] Scientific studies of the beneficial effects of tube feeding were only begun in the early 1950s. Three large studies (at least 100 patients in each study), including one by Pareira and associates, showed the beneficial effects of tube feeding on a wide range of patients who were suffering from malnutrition.[12] Pareira classified the 240 patients in his 1954 study into nine categories. Since practically all of his patients showed improvement from tube feeding, he considered all categories as indications for tube feeding. For example, he considered patients suffering malnutrition because of localized mechanical impediments (e.g., maxillofacial surgery or paralysis of swallowing muscles) and because of the nature of their postoperative convalescence (e.g., whose malnutrition persisted because of anorexia) to be indications for tube feeding.

Pareira included patients unable to eat because of systemic mechanical impediments related to sensorial depression (i.e., patients in a prolonged coma) and patients suffering from terminal cancer as two other indications for tube feeding.[13] Although he referred to the beneficial effects of tube feeding for coma patients only in passing, he devoted a chapter of his short monograph to the benefits of tube feeding for patients with terminal cancer. Pareira studied sixty-four terminal cancer patients.[14] Most were bedridden, and all were malnourished and anorexic. After pursuing various means and incentives to get these patients to eat, such attempts were abandoned and the patients were tube fed. With the exception of the few patients who were imminently dying, anorexia disappeared in all of the tube-fed patients. The return of appetite occurred in these patients between one and three weeks after tube feeding was initiated. Evidence of the return of appetite was demonstrated by the number of patients who desired to "eat around the tube" and their action in doing so if permitted. Pareira found that while most of these patients were considered imminently dying when admitted, many who were thought to be terminal were rehabilitated for a period of many months prior to their eventual death. While initially almost all were bedridden, the majority of the tube-fed patients became at least partially ambulatory, more comfortable, and less dependent on nursing care. Pareira concluded that these patients were undernourished not because of any specific effects of the cancer, but because of anorexia. By restoring appetite through tube feeding, the condition of patients who were becoming progressively malnourished was reversed, with improved nutrition leading to the return of appetite. While Pareira was unable or unwilling to make claims about increased longevity, he considered the beneficial clinical effects of tube feeding, including a return of strength and increased sense of well-being as well as a return of appetite, to be clear. The resulting situation was also happier for patients and their families.

Extensive developments in MANH would go on in the 1960s and 1970s, leading to a widespread use of MANH. However, it suffices for our purposes to note that Pareira's conclusions about the therapeutic efficacy of MANH for a broad range of acutely and chronically ill patients and its palliative benefit for dying patients have been widely accepted up to the recent past. Later I will discuss recent medical studies that question these assumptions about the efficacy of MANH, but it is important that we be aware of this prevailing medical context for discussions and debates regarding the use of MANH from the 1950s through the 1990s. This context is important for three reasons.

First, we saw above that while alternatives to oral feeding were certainly employed in a large number of contexts in the first part of the twentieth century, the clinical benefits of MANH were not scientifically demonstrated until the mid-1950s and their use did not become routine until the 1960s. However, the first discussion of MANH by Catholic moral theologians took place in the late 1940s and early 1950s. Therefore, it is important carefully to contextualize the conclusions drawn by those moral theologians in relation to the medical status of MANH at that time.

Second, in considering how best to characterize tube feeding morally, the diverse purposes for which it is employed must be adequately considered. For example, tube feeding is sometimes employed not because oral feeding is no longer physically possible but as a supplement to or an improvement over oral feeding, and sometimes as a substitute for convenience rather than out of necessity.

Thus it is important to note that MANH, even for coma patients, is not necessarily employed because coma patients are "unable to chew and swallow." For example, long before tube feeding was widely available, at least some coma patients were sustained for many years. Though I have not been able to obtain data on the nutritional arrangements for coma patients from the nineteenth and early twentieth century with long-term survival, I presume that some of these patients were fed orally and others were fed via nutritional enemas. While some coma patients are unable to chew and swallow, this is not a universal feature of coma patients. Certainly, to feed coma patients—or patients with a wide variety of other debilities—orally often takes a great deal of time and effort and such patients may aspirate (i.e., choke on) their food. These kinds of difficulties often make oral feeding an extremely unpalatable choice for nurses or other health-care providers. While tube feeding may often be rightly instituted for efficiency and safety, we should not conclude that all such patients are unable to chew and swallow *simpliciter*.[15]

Third, this brings us to a further issue related to the cost and convenience of tube feeding. Whereas reference is sometimes made to the high cost of maintaining tube-fed patients in hospital, it is neither true that patients must be tube fed in hospital nor that tube feeding is necessarily a costly option. Tube-fed patients are more often than not in nursing homes and often at home.[16] Patients in nursing homes sometimes (unfortunately) come to be tube fed because they experience significant weight loss, and rather than hiring additional staff to supervise the patients' eating practices or to take the time to assist them in eating, tube feeding is prescribed. While a lack of assistance or supervision by no means accounts for all or even most cases of nursing-home patients' losing weight, the fact that it is often less costly to have a patient on a feeding tube than to hire additional staff to customize meal preparation or to supervise eating probably provides a disincentive to improve oral feeding efforts. Furthermore, Medicaid and other forms of insurance typically provide additional reimbursement for tube feeding but not for special meal preparation or assisted oral feeding.[17]

2. The Christian's Duty to Preserve Life

With this brief history and overview of tube-feeding practices in place, we are now in a position to turn to the first significant analysis of the ethics of tube feeding in moral theology. Of the various textbooks in medical ethics produced by Catholic moral theologians between the 1940s and 1960s, two of the most popular and significant were Gerald Kelly's *Medico-Moral Problems* and Charles McFadden's *Medical Ethics*.[18] While the majority of these texts focused on beginning of life issues, each dedicated a chapter to the topic of the duty to preserve one's life. This discussion was generated at least in part by the desire to help the dying distinguish suicide from acceptable forgoing of some medical treatments, and to help medical professionals distinguish euthanasia from appropriate withdrawals of treatment.

For Kelly and McFadden, the Catholic tradition's key principle for discerning the extent of the duty to preserve life was the distinction between ordinary and extraordinary means of preserving life.[19] Their texts include definitions of the principle, a history of the principle, and examples for its application.

In itself, the principle is straightforward. A patient is obligated gratefully to receive ordinary means of preserving life, but may decline extraordinary means. In defining what constitutes ordinary means, Kelly and McFadden note that physicians and moralists typically mean different things by the term. For a physician, "ordinary means" typically refers to those medicines or procedures that are, for example, commonplace, standard, and accepted. For a moralist, ordinary means of treatment includes "all medicines, treatments, and operations, which offer a reasonable hope of benefit for the patient and which can be obtained and used without excessive expense, pain, or other inconvenience."[20] Whereas for a physician "ordinary means" refers to a medicine or treatment in itself, for a moralist what constitutes ordinary means is always dependent upon the benefit gained from the particular treatment by the patient relative to his particular condition at a particular time. Thus, for a moralist, the same treatment may at one point in a patient's illness be considered ordinary, whereas at another stage it may be considered extraordinary or even useless, depending on its possible efficacy.

Kelly roots this principle in the difference between absolute and relative duties for the Christian. Whereas the prohibition on taking one's own life is absolute (the duty to avoid doing evil), the obligation to preserve one's own life is limited (the duty to do positive good). Since one's obligation to preserve one's life is limited, a number of different considerations can render a treatment extraordinary. Kelly cites three examples from the history of moral theology where a hardship or burden was regarded as rendering a means of treatment extraordinary: going into a debt that would place hardship on one's family, undergoing a tremendously painful surgery or amputation (e.g., prior to the development of anaesthesia), or moving to a far country to preserve or restore one's health (i.e., in a cultural context in which people's identities were firmly rooted in the land and their families and at a time when such travel was difficult, dangerous, and likely permanent).[21] Of course, some of what constituted serious burdens in centuries past (e.g., traveling to another country for a cure or undergoing an operation) are no longer a serious burden for most persons today. Such categories are in themselves always open to revision in relation to medical, technological, and cultural changes over time.

Kelly and McFadden consider the 1950s equivalent of MANH when they discuss the appropriateness of withdrawing intravenous feeding from a patient in the last stages of a painful death from cancer. The patient, though racked with pain, continues to linger on, sustained by the intravenous feeding.[22] In the case they discuss, the physician removes intravenous feeding, and the patient dies within twenty-four hours.[23] Presumably the patient dies from a complication related to a lack of hydration. Was such a decision appropriate? McFadden presents different answers from three moral theologians before presenting his own view.

Joseph Sullivan argues that means of preserving life must be seen in relation to the patient's condition. Since the patient has no hope of recovery and is suffering extreme pain, the intravenous feeding is to be classified as extraordinary.[24] J. P. Donovan argues that since the feeding nourishes the patient, it must be considered ordinary care and the removal of such sustenance is the equivalent of mercy killing.[25] G. Kelly says that, although he understands the prolongation of life in such circumstances as "relatively useless," he would continue with the intravenous feeding unless the patient objected to it. On the other hand, he also acknowledges that if the patient were incompetent and the physician and family thought that he was racked with pain to such an extent that he was not spiritually profiting from his state, they might reasonably presume that he does not want the feeding. Kelly is reluctant to propose this solution, out of fear that people might regard it as "Catholic euthanasia." Instead, he says that efforts should be directed toward better pain management. He does not insist on this as the only recourse, but advises the employment of extreme caution with possible instances of forgoing the preservation of life.

In response to these three alternatives, McFadden states his own view that while in theory such intravenous feeding would be considered extraordinary, in practice its withdrawal should be rejected. His objections include Kelly's arguments regarding scandal and the slippery slope to euthanasia, and the claim that a medically useless treatment may have other spiritual benefits.

In addition to the case of the imminently dying cancer patient, Kelly and McFadden comment on a case where a patient has lapsed into what appears to be a terminal coma.[26] If the patient is not spiritually prepared for death, then it is obligatory to maintain him with the hope that he will recover from the coma. If the patient is spiritually prepared for death, then both Kelly and McFadden consider it to be appropriate to cease intravenous treatments once it is medically established that the coma is in all likelihood irreversible. According to Kelly, intravenous feeding to terminal coma patients "creates expense and nervous strain without conferring any real benefit."[27]

While these analyses of the question of the use of MANH with dying and/or debilitated patients were the first attempts to address this question, and seemingly produced at best a provisional solution to this problem, they have been extremely influential. Kelly is well known to have been the primary author of the earliest editions of the *Ethical and Religious Directives for Catholic Health Care Services,* which influenced thinking about this question and continues to function authoritatively for Catholic healthcare services, albeit in an edition further revised by others. McFadden's and particularly Kelly's writings on MANH are widely cited by moral theologians who argue very different viewpoints about MANH, not least because some of the ambiguities in Kelly's response make it easy to see it as supporting one's own viewpoint. However, their writings on the subject of MANH reflected the medical practices of their day (i.e., regarding the immediate impact of withdrawing MANH from a cancer patient, or the nature of the coma state), practices significantly different from those of the present. In particular, their medical assumptions about coma states were different from those current four decades later, when the question of MANH for patients in coma and/or PVS states would become the focus of a major debate within the American Catholic episcopacy.

3. Recent Episcopal Interpretations of the Duty to Preserve Life

As we saw in the previous section, the key principle regarding the withdrawal of MANH from a dying person has traditionally been that of ordinary versus extraordinary means of medical treatment. While certainly a live issue in the 1950s and 1960s, the question of withholding or withdrawing life-supporting treatments such as MANH came to much greater prominence in the 1970s. In this dawning of an era of increasingly technological medicine combined with a zealous imperative to prevent death at all costs, the careful casuistry of the Catholic tradition on ordinary versus extraordinary means of treatment was seemingly overwhelmed by two competing viewpoints. On the one hand, there was the approach of a well-meaning but at times overzealous medical profession eager to use all the tools at its disposal to save lives. On the other hand, there was the approach of an increasingly large group of persons who began to see the medical establishment as infringing on their right to self-determination at the end of their lives. In response, the "right to die" movement was born.

In different ways, these two competing approaches departed from the classic "patient-dependent" understanding of ordinary treatment of the dying. While the medical establishment could be accused of sometimes forgetting the integral good of the individual patient in the quest to use all possible life-prolonging treatments, the "right-to-die" contingent substituted "patient autonomy" for a measured understanding of the good of the patient. Determinations of the good of the patient were increasingly subsumed in the question of who had the authority to make decisions regarding the patient's treatment. In the 1980s, these two different, competing viewpoints were played out in a number of very high profile legal decisions, in particular the Karen Ann Quinlan and Nancy Cruzan cases.

During the 1980s and early 1990s, a number of bishops and dioceses submitted briefs in these cases and/or made public comment on the legal decisions. Among these various statements, two are particularly noteworthy. In May 1990, sixteen of the eighteen Texas Catholic bishops issued an "Interim Pastoral Statement on Artificial Nutrition and Hydration." In January 1992, the Pennsylvania Catholic bishops issued "Nutrition and Hydration: Moral Considerations." These two episcopal documents follow closely the approach of Kelly and McFadden. Both see the issue as that of the appropriate care for and preservation of human life. Both appeal to the principle of ordinary and extraordinary means of treatment as the key principle for discerning appropriate efforts toward preserving life, and both examine the examples of providing nutrition and hydration for the dying cancer patient and the comatose patient.

With regard to the example of MANH for the dying cancer patient, the Texas and Pennsylvania bishops follow Kelly and McFadden in theory but not in practice, in that both argue that forgoing MANH can be acceptable in practice as well as in theory. The Texas bishops argue this implicitly when they follow the 1986 statement of the NCCB's Committee for Pro-Life Activities that "medical treatments may have to take account of exceptional circumstances, where even means for providing nourishment may become too ineffective or burdensome to be obligatory."[28] The Pennsylvania bishops argue the point explicitly, seeing this example as a "relatively easy" case of where it is appropriate to withhold or withdraw MANH:

> In the case of a terminally ill cancer patient whose death is imminent, for instance, the decision to begin intravenous feeding or feeding by nasogastric tube or gastrostomy may also mean that the patient is going to endure greater suffering for a somewhat longer period of time—without hope of recovery or even appreciable lengthening of life. Weighing the balance of benefits and burdens makes it relatively easy to decide that this could fall into the category of extraordinary means and that such feeding procedures need not be initiated or may be discontinued.[29]

Here we see an apparent change in practice (though not in principle) of Catholic teaching on the use of MANH for those imminently dying in significant pain.

When it comes to the example of the use of MANH for comatose (especially PVS) patients, the Texas and Pennsylvania bishops part company. Since the question of providing MANH for PVS patients has provoked perhaps the most medical and ethical disagreement among bishops' conferences and among Catholic moral theologians, the rest of this section and the next section will focus on this particular class of patient, before returning to a more general discussion in the final section.

According to the Texas bishops, patients in a PVS or an irreversible coma are stricken with a fatal pathology. Thus, decisions about when it is appropriate to withhold or withdraw MANH are to be judged individually, ascertaining the relative burdens or benefits of using MANH and deciding accordingly. According to the Texas bishops, in this situation the evaluation of benefits and burdens is to be made by the proxy based on the expressed wish of the patient. They do not say what should be done in the situation in which the express wishes of the patient are not known, but since they say that a person in PVS or an irreversible coma "has come to the end of his or her pilgrimage and should not be impeded from taking the final step," it would seem that they would have no principled objection to a proxy's withdrawing MANH.[30]

The Pennsylvania bishops diverge from the Texas bishops on this question at a number of points. Whereas the Texas bishops limit their discussion to irreversible comas and the PVS and define neither, the Pennsylvania bishops seek to avoid possible confusion by distinguishing a range of unconscious or seemingly unconscious states, not all of which are properly referred to as either a coma or a PVS. For example, they describe two forms of apparent unconsciousness, the psychiatric pseudocoma and the locked-in state, where a person is not actually unconscious, but is for different reasons entirely or almost entirely unable to show the typical signs of consciousness. In addition, the Pennsylvania bishops consider the term "irreversible coma" an oxymoron, since a true coma is "never permanent." Eventually, a person will either emerge into consciousness or sink into a deeper form of unconsciousness known as a PVS. Furthermore, the Pennsylvania bishops argue that regardless of which state of unconsciousness a patient is in, in none of these states is the patient dead or imminently dying, but is rather debilitated to varying degrees. While they acknowledge that the dominant medical opinion is that patients in a PVS are unlikely to recover, they note that some patients have been known to recover consciousness, and also note that there is debate in the medical literature regarding the likelihood of the recovery of PVS patients.[31]

Having provided a description of varying degrees of unconsciousness, the Pennsylvania bishops go on to argue that since, unlike the cancer patient, the PVS patient is not "imminently terminal," MANH can serve a life-sustaining purpose and thus prima facie constitutes ordinary care. Although it usually will not contribute to restoring a patient to health, it does serve to preserve the patient's life in its current debilitated state. Involved here are two key claims: first, that PVS is not a fatal pathology because the "natural history" of the condition (independently of not receiving nutrition and hydration) is not imminently or even routinely terminal; second, that preserving the life of a person, no matter how debilitated his state, is a benefit. There is no such thing as a life that is of itself of greater burden than benefit—that is, a life not worth living.

Having accepted that feeding a PVS patient is a benefit to him, the Pennsylvania bishops then engage in an extended examination of potential burdens that might outweigh the benefits of MANH. Interestingly, while they consider primarily the possible burdens imposed by the procedure of MANH itself, they also consider, secondarily, the burdens of continued existence in a PVS state. Possible burdens are considered first in relation to the patient himself and second in relation to the family, loved ones, and society. In general, the Pennsylvania bishops conclude that neither the feeding of a PVS person, nor continued existence in that state, is a serious burden to the patient. Furthermore, while acknowledging the potential strain on the patient's family, they do not think that in most cases this justifies a decision to remove MANH from a PVS patient. However, they acknowledge that in some instances a family "may have reached the moral limits of its abilities or its resources. In such a situation they have done all that they can do, and they are not morally obliged to do more."[32] While willing to acknowledge such possible "exceptions," they do not wish such exceptions to be the basis for a general acceptance of the practice.

Initially, the main difference between the positions of the Texas and Pennsylvania bishops seems to be descriptive: what constitutes an appropriate description of the PVS patient? Do such patients have a fatal pathology (i.e., the inability to chew and swallow, as one ethicist puts it)? Or are they simply particularly debilitated patients who require significant care?

Upon a closer reading of the two documents, deeper disagreements emerge. For example, in citing examples of reasonable benefits for a patient, the Texas bishops include "maintenance of life with reasonable hope of recovery." Maintenance or preservation of life itself is not included on their list, and this is reinforced by their next statement: "Even without any hope of recovery it is an expression of love and respect for the person to keep the patient clean, warm and comfortable." Feeding incurable patients is not included as necessarily an expression of love. Further on in the document, when discussing patients with a lethal pathology, the question of MANH is presented in such a way that arguments must be provided as to why it should be given, rather than why it may not. This is a viewpoint that seems to follow logically from the viewpoint in which human life—independently of the degree of function or debilitation—is not considered something worthwhile to be preserved in itself.

The disagreements implicit in these episcopal statements are given a much clearer articulation in arguments presented by numerous theologians in the years leading up to them. In order better to understand the underlying disagreements that existed both in these episcopal statements and in the more general debate among theologians, I will characterize what I take to be the four types of arguments that were typically presented as moral justifications for withholding or withdrawing MANH from patients in a PVS or other coma-like states.

4. Four Kinds of Arguments for Withdrawing or Withholding MANH

However much the episcopal statements we looked at above may differ, even more starkly different viewpoints on these questions can be found (as might be expected) in the writings of moral theologians. Identifying the key arguments which encapsulate rival viewpoints requires some effort, since there is no consensus on the meaning and use of key terms such as "benefit," "burden," "fatal pathology," "quality of life," and so on. In this section, I will parse out and summarize the four most influential justificatory arguments for withholding or withdrawing MANH for PVS or other seriously ill patients who are unable to be or have difficulty being fed by mouth.

First, there is the "fatal pathology" argument. On this view, the severely debilitated patient who is unable to chew and swallow is considered to have a fatal pathology. Morally speaking, an "existing fatal pathology may be allowed to take its natural course."[33] By "fatal pathology," one may mean one of two things. If one means "fatal if no treatment is given," then this argument on its own establishes very little, if anything. For without someone having at least a potentially fatal pathology, the conversation concerning the duty to preserve one's life never arises. Furthermore, while it is clearly acceptable in some circumstances for a person with a fatal pathology to refuse particular medical treatments, the simple recognition of a person's having a fatal pathology does not provide criteria for morally evaluating treatment decisions.

On the other hand, if one means "fatal regardless of the treatment given," then this would seem to mean that the patient is imminently dying, or at least terminally ill. The terms "imminently dying" and "terminally ill" more unambiguously constitute a prognosis of a particular patient's condition than does "fatal pathology," and thus function better as criteria for evaluating the choice to withhold or withdraw MANH. Unsurprisingly, these terms have been much more widely accepted in the theological and particularly the medical community as appropriate criteria.

This distinction sheds light on differences between the debate about MANH by Kelly and others in the 1950s and the debate as it played out in the 1980s. When Kelly and McFadden addressed the issue of "terminal coma," a coma condition as they understood it in light of the medical practices and possibilities of their day was indeed akin to what could be considered "imminently dying." However, by the 1980s, whether for good or ill, PVS patients could not for the most part be accurately defined as being imminently dying or even terminally ill.

A second justification for withholding or withdrawing MANH from PVS patients is the "inability to pursue the spiritual purpose of life" argument.[34] According to this argument, the obligation to prolong human life comes from the need and desire to strive for the purpose of life. Pursuing the spiritual purpose of life requires one to be able to perform human acts *(actus humanus)*. However, since PVS patients cannot and probably will not be able to perform human acts, they can no longer pursue the spiritual purpose of life. Since "the ability to strive for the purpose of life [is] the touchstone for using or forgoing life support for persons with serious . . . pathologies . . . when people are in a PVS, there is no moral mandate to utilize MANH on their behalf."[35] This argument—when made in a specifically Catholic context—appeals to a particular interpretation of Aquinas regarding the *telos* of a human life, and also finds support in a widely quoted address by Pius XII.[36] In terms of the traditional appeal to the benefits and burdens of a medical treatment, the argument is essentially that MANH does not benefit PVS patients, and thus is a useless treatment which may not or even should not be administered.

The "spiritual purpose of life" argument has considerable appeal, not least because we tend to identify ourselves with the activities that distinguish us as human beings. Advocates of this view tend to distinguish sharply between biological and personal life, arguing that "biological" life only has significance to the extent it enables personal life.[37] However, critics of this argument claim that it assumes a dualistic anthropology, requiring persons to disassociate "themselves" and their spiritual purpose from their character as bodily creatures. Critics further note that humans are not "in" their bodies, but that their bodies are in some sense constitutive of who they are.[38] The "spiritual purpose of life" argument typically assumes functional criteria for "personhood" and thus leads to the exclusion of certain classes of human beings from care typically extended to all persons. The argument seems logically to legitimate withdrawal or withholding of MANH not only from PVS or other coma patients, but also from various classes of patients who through genetic disease or other debility are unable to perform human acts. Since these classes of patients cannot benefit from MANH or other medical treatments, there is no purpose to treating them should they develop any kind of life-threatening (but manageable) illness.

Thus, in the 1980s, some theological ethicists accepted the discontinuance of MANH to those in a PVS for reasons similar to that articulated by James Gustafson, that for such patients "the qualities that distinguish human beings and are the basis of human valuing of, and respect for, persons no longer exist."[39] However, other theological ethicists argued that "withholding or withdrawing food and fluids *on this rationale* is morally wrong because it is euthanasia by omission. The withholding or withdrawing of food or fluids carries out the proposal, adopted by choice, to end someone's life because that life itself is judged by others to be valueless or excessively burdensome."[40]

The above reference to "excessive burden" in fact constitutes a third distinct argument. This argument also has two discernible varieties. The first focuses on the burden to the patient, the second focuses on the burden to the caregiver, to the family, and to society. Of the four kinds of arguments distinguished in this section of the paper, arguments from "excessive burden" are those most closely rooted in the traditional principle of ordinary versus extraordinary means of treatment. Thus, this argument is the basis for Kelly's and McFadden's acceptance—at least in theory—of withdrawing intravenous feeding from a comatose patient. It is also the basis for the Pennsylvania bishops' acknowledgment that in some instances MANH for a PVS patient could be considered extraordinary treatment and thus morally optional.

The first type of "excessive burden" argument emphasizes the burden of MANH for the PVS patient himself. This burden is sometimes expressed in terms of the patient's autonomous choice: that the patient would not have wanted to be kept alive in such a state. It is also expressed in terms of the aesthetic disvalue of such a state of existence, described as "offensive" or "repugnant." However, when the burden is described in this way, it is unclear whether what is being objected to is the burdensomeness of MANH as a form of treatment or care, or rather the form of life of the PVS patient, which MANH helps sustain.

Traditional "excessive burden" arguments for withholding or withdrawing MANH depend on the discernment that the burden being considered excessive is the burden of the treatment, not the burden of life itself. Discerning the motives of patients or their proxies is difficult at best. However, since some PVS patients can be fed orally, one means of engaging in such discernment is to inquire whether the proxy would think it a good thing to feed the PVS patient orally if that were possible. If that is the case, then it is more likely that what is being rejected is the treatment. However, if the receiving of nutrition by any means is rejected, and there is no reason to believe that the nutrition itself would harm or poison the patient, then there is significant reason to believe that what is being rejected is not a treatment but life in that state. However, as such, this is not a form of the traditional "excessive burden" argument against MANH as it is understood in terms of the principle of ordinary versus extraordinary treatment, and is more properly seen as what is typically referred to as a "quality of life" argument, which is discussed below.

The second type of "excessive burden" argument is one in which MANH for the PVS patient is considered burdensome to the family, the caregivers, or society. This is not only the most common justification for withdrawal of MANH from PVS patients, but also the kind of argument which defenders of the classic distinction between ordinary and extraordinary treatment are likely to accept as legitimate in the tradition. More strident advocates of withdrawing MANH from PVS patients tend to make this appeal by referring to the financial costs to society of maintaining PVS patients, and thus make a generalized argument that the burdens of caring for such patients typically or always outweigh the benefits. Those who more reluctantly acknowledge the legitimacy of the argument that in some situations the burdens of maintaining a PVS patient make MANH an extraordinary treatment—such as the Pennsylvania bishops—focus on the limits of a family's ability to care for a PVS patient in a limited number of difficult or unfortunate situations.

The fourth and final argument is the "quality of life" argument. We can again distinguish two varieties of argument, which are distinguishable by their different understandings of "quality of life." On the one hand, "quality of life" may refer to choices about the quality of living. For example, when one has a particular form of heart disease, having an angioplasty now might result in a stroke and a very debilitated future existence, whereas not having the operation may mean that one will likely die from a heart attack before too long. In making a choice whether or not to undergo angioplasty, a person is making a choice about what kind of life he wants. While these kinds of choices are not strictly commensurable, it is still possible to evaluate them, arguing that some are better and others worse, some morally acceptable and others morally unacceptable.

For instance, when a person is making a choice whether or not to receive a medical treatment, or between two different possible medical treatments, there are at least three different ways in which we can evaluate the nature of his decision. We may understand him to be (a) choosing between two reasonable alternatives, as in the example of the previous paragraph; (b) making a seemingly imprudent but perhaps defensible choice; and (c) choosing to die by omission. To take another example, with an elderly but somewhat demented man whose last remaining pleasure is eating, but who is beginning to have problems chewing and swallowing, one could defend a choice to keep feeding him orally, despite the risk of death by aspiration.[41]

The second kind of "quality of life" argument is a determination that there is insufficient "quality" in life itself. Like the first variety of "excessive burden" argument discussed above, this argument is typically not a rejection of a treatment because it does not improve or maintain the quality of life that one now has, but is rather a rejection of a treatment because it sustains a life that is not considered to have sufficient quality to be maintained. As such, to withdraw MANH because of this kind of "quality of life" concern is not in fact a choice about appropriate medical care, which is always ordered to benefiting the life a patient has, but a non-medically determined choice about living itself.

In this section, I have examined what I take to be the four most significant arguments put forward by moral theologians as a rationale for limiting or forgoing the administration of MANH to PVS and other comatose or severely debilitated patients. While not using or withdrawing MANH from PVS or other severely debilitated patients can be justified in some circumstances, the burden of proof lies with establishing that the burden of the treatment outweighs the benefit to the patient of maintaining and prolonging his life.

Of course, perhaps the strongest rationale for the widespread administration of MANH to patients over the last forty years has been the accepted belief that MANH does extend the life of a broad range of patients. This underlying assumption about the efficacy of MANH has recently begun to be questioned by the medical profession, and it is to this that I turn in the next section.

5. Changing Medical Practices with Regard to MANH

In the previous section the focus was on arguments for and against withdrawing MANH from PVS patients. In this final section we return to a more general discussion of changing medical practice with regard to MANH for dying and debilitated patients. In the first section I discussed medical practice over the last thirty years with regard to MANH, how often it is instituted for a variety of reasons that combine perceived safety, cost, and convenience for caregivers. In this section, we look at recent changes in the use of MANH among medical practitioners.

Two of the key assumptions that have governed the use of MANH among the elderly and debilitated are that it increases longevity (e.g., for comatose patients) and that it improves quality of life (e.g., Pareira's cancer patients). This assumption has led to the use of MANH for large numbers of elderly patients in nursing homes, VA hospitals, and other facilities across America, which continues to the present.

One of the shared assumptions about MANH by almost all the moral theologians who discuss the ethics of MANH is that it increases longevity for almost all classes of patients. This assumption has been held for the last forty years with little empirical verification. Until recently it was assumed that tube feeding was almost always a relatively safe, effective, and valuable therapy. This assumption has been particularly strong in the United States, where the use of tube feeding is four to eleven times more common than in other industrialized nations.[42] However, the assumption that MANH increases longevity has been challenged by recent studies on a number of different classes of patients.

In one study published in 1998, 5,266 elderly nursing-home residents with chewing and swallowing problems were followed, to compare the rates of mortality of those with a feeding tube versus those without.[43] Overall, the study found a significantly higher mortality rate for patients with a feeding tube. On the other hand, a significant portion of those patients who employed a feeding tube were later able to be weaned from the tube, though the study does not indicate why this was the case, or whether the patient's chewing and swallowing problems were resolved. The study is aware of the possibility that the increased mortality may be because the tube-fed population was sicker, but also offers a number of other potential explanations for the increased mortality. First, while feeding tubes are often inserted to prevent aspiration, the efficacy of this intervention has never been proven.[44] Second, tube-fed patients have a tendency to be more agitated, which leads to the use of other medications or restraints. Third, tube-fed patients may have a number of other local complications, such as increased diarrhea leading to fluid and electrolyte imbalances, and increased infections from the feeding tube itself, or from its being dislodged.

In another study published in 2000 of 2,149 patients receiving nutritional support who were seriously ill (e.g., almost all were also on a ventilator), enteral or tube feeding was associated with increased longevity for patients in a coma. However, it was also associated with decreased longevity for patients with acute respiratory failure, with multiorgan system failure with sepsis, with cirrhosis, and with chronic obstructive pulmonary disease.[45] The authors of the study acknowledge that the significance of their results might be limited because of an inability to adjust for the relative severity of their patients' illnesses (i.e., those receiving nutritional support might have been relatively sicker and thus likely to die sooner). While they do not wish to draw definitive conclusions about the cause for increased mortality among certain classes of patients, the authors of this study do conclude that certain classes of patients who receive tube feeding may be at increased risk of mortality.

At the same time as these studies have been going on, an increasing number of geriatricians have been finding that there are alternatives to overcoming many kinds of chewing and swallowing problems in the elderly. There is currently much work on matching individual patients with appropriate diets, making meals that are appetizing to particular patients, and also finding the kind of consistency of food that patients with chewing and swallowing problems can assimilate without aspiration. For example, while some patients will choke on solids but not on liquids, other patients will choke on liquids, but not on thickened liquids. Whereas in the past a patient's tendency to aspirate a typical menu might have been an indication for tube feeding, now in some places efforts are going toward tailoring menus to the specific swallowing abilities of a particular patient.

This brings us to the question of the future of MANH in medicine. If the studies discussed above are reinforced by other studies, there will undoubtedly begin to be a considerable change in the use of MANH. The previous two sections of this paper focused on MANH for PVS and other coma patients, and the argument put forth there was that since (a) this class of patients is not in any ordinary sense "terminally ill" or "imminently dying," and (b) MANH has been shown to prolong the life of this class of patients, the burden of proof is on those who wish to argue that such patients should not receive MANH. Thus the reader may assume that this paper is strongly advocating the use of MANH for all classes of patients. It is not. While undoubtedly preserving the lives of many persons, MANH also has many deleterious qualities, which have not been addressed widely in either the medical or the ethical literature. Some of these deleterious qualities are medical burdens in the narrow sense: MANH in some classes of patients may result in reduced longevity, add other medical complications, and increase patient discomfort. On these grounds alone, we are seeing the reduction in the use of MANH for dying and debilitated patients in various medical settings in the United States. In the final section, I will argue that moral theologians have a broader and more holistic perspective to offer to the question of the use of MANH for dying and debilitated patients, a perspective that is rarely presented in the moral and theological literature.

6. Feed Me Till I Want No More?

The perspective to be presented in this last section is encapsulated in a verse by the Welsh poet and hymn writer William Williams. His most famous hymn begins as follows:

> Guide me, O Thou great Jehovah,
> Pilgrim through this barren land.
> I am weak, but Thou art mighty;
> Hold me with Thy powerful hand.
> Bread of heaven, bread of heaven,
> Feed me till I want no more;
> Feed me till I want no more.

In Williams's verse, we can see three implicit claims. First, eating is placed in the context of Christian pilgrimage and discipleship. The hungers of a Christian can and should always draw him to the Provider of his daily bread, which by God's grace will fulfill those hungers. Second, Williams's reference to "being fed" signals the importance of the communal element in Christian eating: Christians not only pursue their daily bread, but also accept being fed, and in doing so accept gifts given to them. Thus Christians accept the gift of the Eucharist as sustenance for their lives. Third, in the ambiguity of the term "want" in Williams's verse, we are drawn to the realization that "being fed" is adequately grasped neither as merely a satiation of human desires nor as the fulfillment of bodily needs. Rather, Christians' desires and needs for food are to be integrated with—and if and when necessary, subordinated to—the ultimate end of the Christian. For the Christian, "feed me till I want no more" is ultimately neither a cry of gluttonous self-assertion, nor a medical request for the most efficient delivery of nutrition as long as medical benefits are to be had, but an exclamation of a commitment to recognize that one's daily bread comes from God and God's people.

It is remarkable how little has been written about the theological significance of eating practices. The human practices of dining and/or feeding others has not been a significant topic for most moral theologians. A notable exception to this is a recent article by Patrick McCormick, which focuses on the theological—and especially Eucharistic—significance of eating practices in relation to some of the culinary pathologies endemic in American culture.[46] McCormick seeks to recover a holistic theological perspective on Christian eating practices in light of "Diet America's" current preoccupation with dieting. However, McCormick's insights are also applicable, as I will seek to show, to Christian reflection on feeding those who are dying and severely debilitated.

McCormick seeks to move us toward a more adequate theological understanding of our eating practices. He emphasizes a theological understanding of the significance of the bodily, and challenges contemporary eating practices—specifically those of "Diet America"—in the light of a Eucharistic theology. Thus he asks:

if our ability to participate in the mystery of this sacrament depends at least in part on our grasp of the symbols employed in the breaking, sharing, and eating of this bread and wine, then just how does our being immersed in the rituals and customs of "Diet America" affect our experience of the Eucharist? And second, what, if anything, does the Eucharist have to say to our contemporary food culture and larger practices of table fellowship? In what ways does this sacrament of God's creative, redemptive and reconciling love inform and/or challenge the attitudes, practices, and structures of "Diet America"?[47]

McCormick's theological account of the significance of our eating practices begins with an appeal to Wendell Berry's claim that with food becoming an ever more efficiently produced, processed, and packaged commodity, we find it increasingly harder to eat with an understanding of our food as a gift of God that involves the labors of others. When we are involved with the growing and/or the preparing and cooking of our food, "we experience and celebrate our dependence and our gratitude, for we are living from mystery, from creatures we did not make and powers we cannot comprehend."[48] This insight is particularly relevant for the situation of the person receiving MANH. Although tube feeding has always in some sense circumvented eating, at one time it was simply hospital food inserted into a tube and transported into the body. At present it is highly processed, and perhaps the exemplification of the alienation of "food" from its sources, and the mystery and gratitude that food should call forth from us. As we noted earlier, patients are often tube fed not strictly out of medical necessity, but for a variety of conveniences and benefits, which sometimes do not take into account the pleasures and joys of eating of the person who is to be tube fed.

McCormick also seeks to show how "Diet America's" approach to food alienates us from the pleasures of eating, and on a deeper level, from an adequate recognition of our embodiment. The culture of dieting rejects the pleasures of the palate, and, in typically promoting an idealized conception of the body, produces a rejection and/or hatred of real human bodies. McCormick cannot see how this can be reconciled with a Eucharistic vision that tells us to "taste and see the goodness of the Lord." He also notes that "Diet America" is particularly ill at ease with bodies that "grow old, get sick, and die," and with women's bodies, which it constantly seeks to "reduce," often "to a number on their bathroom scales, a number which is always too large."[49] In contrast, McCormick notes that by our participation in the Eucharist, we are transformed into the body of Christ, and we are to "celebrate our bodies and the bodies of our neighbors . . . our bodies are glorious creation . . . [which] have been fashioned by God to savor and enjoy that world—indeed they have become God's dwelling place."[50] McCormick's insights with regard to the diet culture's perception of imperfect bodies is clearly present in many discussions of the bodies of the dying and severely debilitated. Such discussions never rejoice in such imperfect and debilitated bodies, but typically speak of the "repugnance" or "burdensomeness" of life itself when it is lived in such bodies. Our culture, which prizes efficiency and bodily perfection, is often unable to find anything redeeming in the process of dying of a severely debilitated person.

McCormick also powerfully recognizes the communal and social elements of our eating practices. Humans do not merely eat; they dine. Dining is a place of companionship, and cooking is an opportunity to display artistry and hospitality. McCormick states this eloquently:

For these tables are not only the places where we share our food and drink, they are also where we bring our stories, raise a toast to our dreams, thank God for our blessings, welcome new family members, and remember old friends. And they are the places we bring the good that has been grown, harvested, and delivered by others, as well as the places where we bow our heads to recall those without tables. They are places for sharing and breaking bread, for making sure that everyone has enough and that no one hoards all the good stuff; for it is a tough thing to enjoy a meal next to someone who is hungry. They are places for reconciliation, for forgiving and making peace with a simple toast or a piece of bread since it is much too hard and stilted a thing to sit around these tables and eat with enemies. And they are places to bring new acquaintances and fashion them into friends or family, because dining is not something we can do well with strangers. If there are things more important than how we behave at our tables—both personal and public—there are not many of them.[51]

Herbert McCabe echoes McCormick's argument that our eating practices create our communities, claiming that eating alone (and living alone) are somehow unnatural for humans.[52] In breaking bread and sharing the cup with others, we become reconciled and brought into community with others.

The importance of the communal dimension of eating is also usually ignored in ethical discussions of MANH for dying and debilitated patients. For example, as was noted earlier in the paper, nursing-home patients are sometimes started on tube feeding because they are not eating sufficiently by mouth, for whatever reason. While the choice to tube feed may mean improved nutrition given the existing situation, the choice to administer tube feeding may signal the end of efforts to feed the patient by mouth. In such cases, it is also the end of one of the main forms of human contact and attention that such a patient may expect to receive. From then on, the nurse or attendant is typically "feeding" a machine, and contact with the patient is likely to be more remote. In addition, a nursing-home patient who is tube fed typically no longer goes to the dining room to eat with others. As such, she is deprived of another main source of human contact and socialization. Finally, the patient is now deprived of a ritual that typically regulates her days and hours, and further alienates him from the typical human activities that are part of defining who we are.

McCormick alludes to one other deficiency with the culture of "Diet America" in its preoccupation with "reducing" human bodies—its rejection of hospitality. In the quest to control and reduce the body, "Diet America" is preoccupied with control over all that goes in the body, and so is suspicious of others' offers of hospitality. McCormick notes that "the Christian story is littered with saints like Vincent de Paul, William Booth, and Dorothy Day who spent their lives honoring and caring for the suffering bodies of neighbors and strangers alike."[53] For Christians, the centrality of the command to perform the corporal works of mercy is a stark reminder not only of the Christian responsibility to show hospitality in caring for the sick and suffering and debilitated bodies of the sick and dying, but also to be willing to receive hospitality when we are debilitated and dying. In the culture of "Diet America," a culture that emphasizes autonomy and self-mastery, we should not be surprised to see the spiritual pathology of the refusal to receive hospitality.

The Christian witness of hospitality also speaks to the situation of many patients who receive or have received MANH. In most of the contemporary debates about MANH, it is assumed that if MANH is removed, the person will not be fed because she should not or cannot receive any substantive nutrition. While there are certainly many situations when a patient is dying where it is indeed necessary and even best for her not to be fed, it should not be a general assumption that patients who are taken off of MANH are no longer to be fed by mouth. Feeding others and being fed by others are among the most significant acts that Christians do, and not only for nutritive reasons. As persons shaped by a Eucharistic vision of our eating practices, Christians know this well. If and when it is realized that MANH is not as effective in prolonging life as it was once thought to be, there will be an opportunity in nursing homes and other medical contexts to rethink the significance of feeding. It can be hoped that a Eucharistic vision of the significance of feeding the dying and debilitated will be embodied in these settings, recalling what it might mean to hear the cry of even the dying and severely debilitated to "feed me till I want no more."

NOTES

1. For example, "Guidelines for Legislation on Life-Sustaining Treatment," U.S. bishops' Committee for Pro-Life Activities, *Origins* 14, no. 32 (January 24, 1985): 526ff.; "Providing Food and Fluids to Severely Brain-Damaged Patients," friend-of-the-court brief by the New Jersey Catholic Conference in the Nancy Ellen Jobes Case, *Origins* 16, no. 32 (January 22, 1987): 582ff.; "Georgia Man Asks to Turn Off Life-Supporting Ventilator," friend-of-the-court brief by the archdiocese of Atlanta in the case of Larry James McAfee, *Origins* 19, no. 17 (September 28, 1989): 273ff.; "The Nancy Cruzan Case," Bishop John Leibrecht, *Origins* 19, no. 32 (January 11,

1990): 525ff.; "Treatment of Dying Patients," bishops of Florida, *Origins* 19, no. 3 (June 1, 1989): 47ff.

2. For examples of such exchanges, see John Connery, "The Clarence Herbert Case: Was Withdrawal of Treatment Justified," *Hospital Progress* (February 1984): 32–35, 70; and John Paris, "Withholding or Withdrawing Nutrition and Food: What Are the Real Issues," *Hospital Progress* (December 1985): 22ff. See also Richard McCormick, S.J., "'Moral Considerations' Ill Considered," *America* 166 (March 14, 1992): 210–14; and Kevin McMahon, "What the Pennsylvania Bishops Really Said," *Linacre Quarterly* 59 (August 1992): 6–10. For an exchange between William E. May and Kevin O'Rourke, see William E. May, "Tube Feeding and the 'Vegetative' State," *Ethics & Medics* 23, no. 12 (December 1998): 1–2; Kevin O'Rourke, O.P., "On the Care of 'Vegetative' Patients: A Response to William E. May's 'Tube Feeding and the "Vegetative" State,'" *Ethics & Medics* 24, no. 4 (April 1999): 3–4.

3. Some saw failing to feed as allowing the patient to be "starved" to death. Others saw feeding (specifically comatose) patients as a failure of faith with regard to Christian belief in the resurrection of the body.

4. Good general histories of alternatives to oral feeding include Henry T. Randall, "The History of Enteral Nutrition," in *Clinical Nutrition*, vol. 1: *Enteral and Tube Feeding*, ed. J. L. Rombeau and Michael D. Caldwell (Philadelphia: W. B. Saunders Company, 1984), pp. 1–9; and Laura Harkness, "The History of Enteral Nutrition Therapy: From Raw Eggs and Nasal Tubes to Purified Amino Acids and Early Postoperative Jejunal Delivery," *Journal of the American Dietetic Association* 102 (2002): 399–404.

5. See C. E. Brown-Séquard, "Feeding per rectum in Nervous Affections," *Lancet* 1 (1878): 144. Also Y. M. Humphreys, "An Easy Method of Feeding per rectum," *Lancet* 1 (1891) 366–67.

6. W. D. Bliss, "Feeding per Rectum: As Illustrated in the Case of the Late President Garfield and Others," *Medical Record* 22 (1882): 64–69.

7. Such tubes were also used for removing poisons or other unwanted contents of the stomach. The first reported use of a tube for aspirating the contents of the stomach was in 1813 by a professor of surgery at the University of Pennsylvania. P. S. Physick, "Account of a New Mode of Extracting Poisonous Substances from the Stomach," *Eclectic Repertory and Analytical Review* 3, no. 1 (October 1812): 111–13; also see Morton D. Pareira, *Therapeutic Nutrition with Tube Feeding* (Springfield, IL: Charles C. Thomas Publisher, 1959), p. 11. Combining lavage and gavage was being done by 1939, when Stengel and Ravdin reported on inserting twin tubes at the time of gastric surgeries, one into the jejunum for feeding and the other into the stomach for removing gastric contents. See A. Stengel, Jr., and I. S. Ravdin, "The Maintenance of Nutrition in Surgical Patients with a Description of the Orojejunal Method of Feeding," *Surgery* 6 (1939): 511–19.

8. Randall, "The History of Enteral Nutrition," p. 2.

9. Gavage feeding of premature infants was popularized by the first modern authority on the feeding of premature infants, the French physician Stephane Tarnier (1828–97), and furthered in America by the work of Julius Hess (1876–1955), who in 1913 opened the first continuously operating center for premature infants in the United States. See Frank Greer, "Feeding the Premature Infant in the 20th Century," *Journal of Nutrition* 131 (2001): 426S–430S.

10. W. A. Morrison, "The Value of the Stomach-tube in Feeding after Intubation, Based upon Twenty-eight Cases; Also Its Use in Post-diphtheritic Paralysis," *Boston Medical and Surgical Journal* 132 (1894): 127–30.

11. Pareira, *Therapeutic Nutrition with Tube Feeding*, p. 13.

12. T. Boles, Jr., and R. M. Zollinger, "Critical Evaluation of Jejunostomy," *Archives of Surgery* 65 (1952): 358–66; L. S. Fallis and J. Barron, "Gastric and Jejunal Alimentation with Fine Polyethylene Tubes," *Archives of Surgery* 65 (1952): 373–81; M. D. Pareira, E. J. Conrad, W. Hicks, and R. Elman, "Therapeutic Nutrition with Tube Feeding," *Journal of the American Medical Association* 156 (1954): 810–16.

13. See Pareira, *Therapeutic Nutrition with Tube Feeding*, pp. 8, 16–17.

14. Pareira notes that none of the patients had tumors that involved the gastrointestinal tract (ibid., p. 34).

15. A neurologist well known for advocating the withdrawal of MANH from PVS patients acknowledges that "[b]ecause PVS patients often have an intact involuntary swallowing reflex in addition to intact gag and cough reflexes, it is theoretically, and in rare cases practically, possible to feed these patients by hand. However, this usually requires an enormous amount of time and effort by health-care professionals and families. If the patient is positioned properly, and food is carefully placed in the back of the throat, the patient's involuntary swallowing reflex will be activated." Ronald Cranford, "The Persistent Vegetative State: The Medical Reality," *Hastings Center Report* 18 (February/March 1988): 31.

16. See Catherine H. Bastian and Richard H. Driscoll, "Enteral Tube Feeding at Home," in Rombeau and Caldwell, eds., *Clinical Nutrition*, 1: 494–511.

17. Note that "in most states, there is a higher reimbursement rate for tube-fed patients, and hand-feeding a disabled resident takes considerably more staff time than operating a feeding tube pump." Susan Mitchell, D. K. Kiely, and L. A. Lipsitz, "Does Artificial Enteral Nutrition Prolong Survival of Institutionalized Elders With Chewing and Swallowing Problems?" *Journal of Gerontology* 53A, no. 3 (1998): M212. The authors are citing B. Leff, N. Cheuvront, and W. Russell, "Discontinuing Feeding Tubes in a Community Nursing Home," *Gerontologist* 34 (1994): 130–33.

18. Gerald Kelly, S.J., *Medico-Moral Problems* (St. Louis, MO: Catholic Health Association of the United States and Canada, 1958), pp. 128–41; Charles McFadden, *Medical Ethics*, 5th ed. (Philadelphia: Davis and Company, 1961), pp. 227–32. For further elaboration of Kelly's viewpoint, see Gerald Kelly, S.J., "The Duty of Using Artificial Means of Preserving Life," *Theological Studies* 11 (June 1950): 203–20. For a history of these texts in medical ethics by Catholic moral theologians and claims about the centrality of the work of Kelly and McFadden, see David F. Kelly, *The Emergence of Roman Catholic Medical Ethics in North America* (New York: Edwin Mellen Press, 1979). For a more extensive examination of the principle of ordinary and extraordinary means of treatment from the same period as Kelly and McFadden, see Daniel Cronin, *The Moral Law in Regard to the Ordinary and Extraordinary Means of Conserving Life* (dissertation; Rome: Gregorian University, 1958).

19. This traditional distinction between ordinary and extraordinary means of treatment continues to function normatively and institutionally in Catholic health care in the United States, with its inclusion in the fourth edition of the *Ethical and Religious Directives for Catholic Health Care Services* (2001). Directives 56 and 57 read as follows:

> 56. A person has a moral obligation to use ordinary or proportionate means of preserving his or her life. Proportionate means are those that in the judgment of the patient offer a reasonable hope of benefit and do not entail an excessive burden or impose excessive expense on the family or the community.

> 57. A person may forgo extraordinary or disproportionate means of preserving life. Disproportionate means are those that in the patient's judgment do not offer a reasonable hope of benefit or entail an excessive burden, or impose excessive expense on the family or the community.

We find four key elements in these two directives. First, discernment of whether a treatment is ordinary or extraordinary requires the judgment of the patient. Second, the patient needs to judge what constitutes a treatment's offering a reasonable hope of benefit. Third, the patient needs to judge whether a proposed treatment entails a severe or excessive burden. Fourth, the patient needs to judge whether a proposed treatment imposes an excessive expense on the family or the community.

20. Kelly, *Medico-Moral Problems*, p. 129. Compare this statement of ordinary treatment with that of *Ethical and Religious Directives* 56, above.

21. Kelly, *Medico-Moral Problems*, p. 132.

22. With intravenous feeding, nutrients are introduced into veins rather than into the stomach or jejunum. Such forms of feeding (now referred to as total parenteral nutrition) are used

with some patients (e.g., patients who have had their small intestine removed and cannot adequately absorb nutrients received enterally). However, intravenous feeding is typically not the nutritional therapy of choice because of its negative effects on the veins through which they are delivered. While I do not have definitive data on the efficacy of intravenous feeding as it would have been done in the 1940s, I believe that such feedings would have been very limited in terms of delivery of calories and nutritional balance, and would have likely led to numerous other medical complications. However, delivery of simple hydration intravenously would have been provided with greater ease and fewer complications.

23. See McFadden, *Medical Ethics,* pp. 229–30.

24. J. V. Sullivan, *Catholic Teaching on the Morality of Euthanasia,* Catholic University of America Studies in Sacred Theology, 2d ser., 22 (Washington, DC: Catholic University of America Press, 1949), p. 72.

25. J. P. Donovan, "Letting Patients Die; Plight of a Vasectomized Man," *Homiletic and Pastoral Review* 49 (August 1949): 904.

26. It is not exactly clear what Kelly means by "terminal coma." Some moral theologians have interpreted this as being a patient in a persistent vegetative state, but this is by no means clear.

27. Kelly, "The Duty of Using Artificial Means of Preserving Life," p. 230, cited in McFadden, *Medical Ethics,* p. 232.

28. Texas Catholic Bishops, "Interim Statement on Withdrawing Artificial Nutrition and Hydration," *Origins* 20, no. 4 (June 7, 1990): 54, quoting from NCCB Committee for Pro-Life Activities, "The Rights of the Terminally Ill," *Origins* 16, no. 12 (September 4, 1986): 222ff.

29. Pennsylvania Catholic Bishops, "Nutrition and Hydration: Moral Considerations," *Origins* 21, no. 34 (January 30, 1992): 547.

30. Texas bishops, "Interim Statement on Withdrawing Artificial Nutrition and Hydration," p. 54.

31. For examples of patients who have revived from a PVS, see Pennsylvania bishops, "Nutrition and Hydration," p. 551, n. 14. For the viewpoint that recovery from a PVS after six months "does occur, but is rare," see the Multi-Society Task Force on PVS, "Medical Aspects of the Persistent Vegetative State: Part II," *New England Journal of Medicine* 330, no. 22 (June 2, 1994): 1575; for evidence that recovery from a PVS is more likely, see Keith Andrews, "Recovery of Patients after Four Months or More in the Persistent Vegetative State," *British Medical Journal* 306 (June 12, 1993): 1597–600.

32. Pennsylvania bishops, "Nutrition and Hydration," p. 549.

33. Kevin O'Rourke, "The A.M.A. Statement on Tube Feeding: An Ethical Analysis," *America* 155 (1986): 321–23, 331, at 322.

34. An alternative name for this argument is the "no hope of benefit" argument. On this view, "hope of benefit" is understood as a recovery of cognitive or relational functioning that allows a person to perform human acts *(actus humanus).*

35. O'Rourke, "On the Care of 'Vegetative' Patients," pp. 3–4.

36. Pius XII, "The Prolongation of Life: An address of Pope Pius XII to an International Congress of Anaesthesiologists (November 24, 1957)," appendix IV in *Conserving Human Life,* ed. R. E. Smith (Braintree, MA: The Pope John Center, 1989), pp. 312–18.

37. With regard to the biological life/personal life distinction, "[I]t is necessary to distinguish clearly and consistently between physical or biological life and personal life (personhood). When this important distinction is not made, quality of life judgments can equivocate between the value of biological life and the value of personhood." Thomas Shannon and James J. Walter, "The PVS Patient and the Forgoing/Withdrawing of Medical Nutrition and Hydration," *Theological Studies* 49 (1988): 635. With regard to the significance of this distinction for the care of PVS patients, Callahan argues that MANH can be withdrawn from PVS patients because "neither provides any genuine benefit: there is not meaningful life of any kind—it is a mere body only, not an embodied person." Daniel Callahan, "Feeding the Dying Elderly," *Generations* 10 (Winter 1985): 17.

38. Thus Gilbert Meilaender argues: "Yet for many people the uselessness of feeding the

permanently unconscious seems self-evident. Why? Probably because they suppose that the nourishment we provide is, in the words of the President's Commission, doing no more than 'sustaining the body.' But we should pause before separating personhood and body so decisively. When considering other topics (care of the environment, for example) we are eager to criticize a dualism that divorces human reason and consciousness from the larger world of nature. Why not here? We can know people—of all ranges of cognitive capacity—only as they are embodied; there is no other 'person' for whom we might care. Such care is not useless if it 'only' preserves bodily life but does not restore cognitive capacities. Even if it is less than we wish could be accomplished, it remains care for the embodied person." Gilbert Meilaender, "On Removing Food and Water: Against the Stream," *Hastings Center Report* 14 (December 1984): 12.

39. James Gustafson, in a May 22, 1985, letter to John Paris, cited by Richard McCormick in "Nutrition-Hydration: The New Euthanasia," in *The Critical Calling* (Washington, DC: Georgetown University Press, 1989), p. 377.

40. William E. May et al., "Feeding and Hydrating the Permanently Unconscious and Other Vulnerable Persons," *Issues in Law and Medicine* 3 (Winter 1987): 206.

41. For an interesting discussion of why the Catholic tradition does not advocate the protection of one's life and health at all costs, see Bernadette Tobin, "Can a Patient's Refusal of Life-prolonging Treatment Be Morally Upright When It Is Motivated Neither by the Belief That the Treatment Would Be Clearly Futile Nor by the Belief That the Consequences of Treatment Would Be Unduly Burdensome?" in *Issues for a Catholic Bioethic*, ed. Luke Gormally (London: The Linacre Centre, 1999), pp. 334–40.

42. See L. Howard, M. Ament, C. R Fleming, and others, "Current Use and Clinical Outcome of Home Parenteral and Enteral Nutrition Therapies in the United States," *Gastroenterology* 109 (1995): 355–65. Cited in M. L. Borum, J. Lynn, Z. Zhong, and others, "The Effect of Nutritional Supplementation on Survival in Seriously Ill Hospitalized Adults: An Evaluation of the SUPPORT Data," *Journal of the American Geriatrics Society* 48 (2000): S35.

43. Mitchell, Kiely, and Lipsitz, "Does Artificial Enteral Nutrition Prolong Survival of Institutionalized Elders With Chewing and Swallowing Problems?," M207–M213.

44. See Thomas Finocane and Julie Bynum, "Use of Tube Feeding to Prevent Aspiration Pneumonia," *Lancet* 348 (November 23, 1996): 1421–24.

45. Borum, Lynn, Zhong, and others, "The Effect of Nutritional Supplementation on Survival in Seriously Ill Hospitalized Adults," S33.

46. See Patrick T. McCormick, "How Could We Break the Lord's Bread in a Foreign Land? The Eucharist in 'Diet America,'" *Horizons* 25 (1998): 43–57. For other suggestive articles on ways in which Christians might understand their eating practices Eucharistically, see Mark Allman, "Eucharist, Ritual, and Narrative: Formation of Individual and Communal Moral Character," *Journal of Ritual Studies* 14, no. 1 (2000): 60–67; and especially William T. Cavanaugh, "The World in a Wafer: A Geography of the Eucharist as Resistance of Globalization," *Modern Theology* 15, no. 2 (April 1999): 181–96.

47. Ibid., p. 47.

48. Ibid., p. 48, quoting from Wendell Berry, "The Pleasures of Eating," in *Not for Bread Alone*, ed. Daniel Halpern (Hopewell, NJ: Ecco, 1993), p. 17.

49. McCormick, "The Eucharist in 'Diet America,'" p. 52.

50. Ibid., p. 53.

51. Ibid., p. 54.

52. Herbert McCabe, *The New Creation* (London: Fontana, 1964).

53. McCormick, "The Eucharist in 'Diet America,'" p. 51.

CHAPTER 7

Two Arguments against Euthanasia

BRENDAN SWEETMAN

In addition to abortion, the subject of euthanasia is one of the most discussed and controversial moral topics in contemporary American society. At present, the practice is legal in only one state, Oregon, following passage of that state's Death with Dignity Act in 1997, and its subsequent survival of several court challenges.[1] But the issue has appeared on the ballot in several other states over the past decade or so, where it has always been defeated. It is almost certain that it will be on the ballot in those same states and in other states in the not too distant future. In fact, it is not an exaggeration to say that many citizens will be called upon to vote on the issue of euthanasia in the next decade. It is therefore imperative to consider the moral and legal issues surrounding the topic.

I will argue that euthanasia is immoral, and so should be illegal. Before elaborating my argument for this conclusion, I wish to be clear about what I mean by the term "euthanasia." It will also be helpful to distinguish my understanding of the term from other possible uses of the term, and also to note the relationship between my use of the term and other terms that are germane to the debate. By "euthanasia," I am referring to the *intentional* killing of a patient with the aim of bringing an end to that person's suffering. I would like to use the term broadly to include cases where euthanasia is requested

I wish to thank Edward Furton and Doug Geivett for helpful comments on an earlier version of this paper.

by the patient (voluntary euthanasia), and cases where it is not requested by the patient (involuntary euthanasia). I am also including in this understanding of the term cases more recently described as "physician-assisted suicide"; my argument makes no distinction between whether a patient commits suicide himself for the purposes of ending suffering, or whether the patient is assisted in killing himself by medical personnel, or whether medical personnel fully carry out the act with no assistance from the patient. I do not deny that differences between these cases may have moral significance, but they will not be significant for our argument because we are mainly interested in the general question of whether suicide in end-of-life cases is moral.

Two other important points are worth emphasizing before we move on to the main argument. First, I do not think that there is a morally significant distinction between active and passive euthanasia; since active euthanasia is wrong, so is passive euthanasia.[2] The term active euthanasia describes cases where there is an act of commission—where the doctor actively kills the patient, say, by administering a lethal injection that directly brings about death, whereas passive euthanasia describes cases where there is an act of omission—where the doctor removes a treatment, say, by switching off a life-support machine or ending a drug treatment, and allowing the patient to die. Some argue that the moral difference between these two forms of euthanasia is that, depending on the type of treatment being removed or ended, passive euthanasia lets nature take its course in the sense that the patient might *not* die, whereas active euthanasia actively involves intervention in the course of nature to insure that death does take place. In some cases—for example, in switching off a machine—it is often argued that we are letting nature take its course, and sometimes the patient does not die. However, passive euthanasia is just as wrong as active euthanasia because the *intention* of the doctor is to kill the patient (this is also the intention of the patient who requests euthanasia). If this is the doctor's intention, then he switches off the machine to bring about the patient's death, and if the patient lives, nature thwarts his intention.

However, second, I fully accept the distinction that is sometimes made in the debate on euthanasia between extraordinary and ordinary means. This distinction was initially based on the insight that it is not morally necessary for medical personnel to use extraordinary means to keep a person alive, but it is morally necessary to use ordinary means to keep a person alive.[3] But with the increasing advances in technology in the field of medicine, this terminology is perhaps a little out of date, and is now generally broadened to include cases that may involve excessively burdensome treatment (as noted by Pope John Paul II in *Evangelium Vitae*). This is treatment that a patient could reasonably refuse because it is disproportionate to any expected result, or because it would be physically and mentally demanding for the patient, or the patient's family, to tolerate. Patients are not morally bound to undergo excessively burdensome treatment. All participants in the debate recognize, I think, that what counts as extraordinary and ordinary means, and even as excessively burdensome treatment, can vary with culture, economic conditions, and circumstances (although the core moral principles do not vary). My concern here is with the motivation behind these concepts. I want to emphasize that cases where a patient dies because she, in good conscience, refused excessively burdensome treatment (or less commonly nowadays, cases where the hospital was unable to employ extraordinary means of treatment) are not to be classified as cases of (passive) euthanasia. This would include those cases where a doctor made the decision to switch off a machine that was keeping a patient alive but was not leading to the recovery of the patient. In this case, the doctor is bringing medical treatment to an end, and does not intend to kill the patient, and the death is regretted. The passive nature of the action is important, because the patient may continue to live. Indeed, when the doctor switches off the machine perhaps he hopes that the patient will continue to live, and although the patient's death may be foreseen, it is not intended. In short, cases where a patient refuses excessively burdensome treatment (or where a hospital cannot provide extraordinary means) and the patient dies are not to be classified as cases of passive euthanasia.[4]

Cases involving patients who are kept alive by artificial nutrition and hydration are more difficult. Although these cases are outside the scope of this paper, in general the removal from a patient of artificially administered hydration and nutrition would be an instance of euthanasia (as in the Terri Schiavo case), and so would be wrong, according to the arguments of this paper. This is true *except* in those cases where the nutrition and hydration treatment would likely cause extreme pain, which can occur with certain illnesses, or in certain cases where the patient is dying and very near death (as noted in Pope John Paul II's March 2004 statement on this matter).[5]

The "In Principle" Argument against Euthanasia

The first argument against euthanasia might be referred to as the "in principle" argument. According to this argument, euthanasia is wrong in principle, wrong in itself, is intrinsically wrong, and so should not be made legal. This argument does not say that euthanasia is wrong because its introduction will lead to some undesirable consequences or problems; rather it holds that—regardless of its consequences—it is wrong in itself. And because it is wrong in itself, it can never be moral no matter what perceived benefits might come from it. The reason euthanasia is wrong in itself is that *human life is sacred, of supreme value, is the most cherished value in human existence, has intrinsic worth, is a fundamental value.* Human life is such a highly valued good that allowing people to commit suicide, or assisting them in committing suicide, for whatever reason, compromises the value of life, and is therefore immoral. Throughout recorded history human life has been recognized by almost all societies as the highest valued good. Even though one can point to some notorious exceptions, even though there were many abuses, and even though some people (e.g., children) were sometimes not regarded as full human beings, this does not detract from the general point that human life has been regarded as by far the highest value in human history. The doctrine of the sanctity of life has been dominant not only in the Western tradition but also in the Eastern tradition. In the language of rights, the right to life has been regarded as the highest right, and is higher than other rights such as the right to freedom, the right to own property, the right to security, and the right to vote. Philosophers, theologians, and others have not always agreed on why life is the highest value (there are several theories offered), but they have agreed that it *is* the highest value. In any case, this is not the place to rehearse this debate, but simply to emphasize the point that the "in principle" argument against euthanasia is based on the argument that life is the most fundamental value, and that the practice of euthanasia would be incompatible with this value.

It is important to emphasize that the "in principle" argument is not essentially a *Christian* or a *religious* argument in a narrow or sectarian sense. This is because it need make no specific appeal to doctrinal religious beliefs in its general outline, need make no appeal to religious texts to support its premises and conclusions, and need make no appeal to religious authority or inspiration. Even the use of the phrase "human life is sacred" is not meant to suggest that this is essentially a religious argument; rather the phrase is widely used in our society to underscore the intrinsic value of life, even by secularists (though official secularist arguments might employ more religiously neutral language). Moreover, the argument that euthanasia is intrinsically wrong because human life is of intrinsic value is an argument that would obviously be accepted by many atheists and secular humanists. What are the main objections to this argument? I will briefly consider four here, and indicate how we may reply to them; this will also help us to elaborate further the "in principle" argument.

First, there is what we might call the "pluralism" objection. This is the argument that since we live in a pluralist society, with many different worldviews and many different moral codes, it is wrong to impose our beliefs about what is intrinsically wrong in principle on those who do not agree with us. Surely the essence of a free society is that people should be free to make up their own minds about these kinds of matters? It is perfectly okay for me to believe that euthanasia is wrong in itself, so the argument goes, but it is problematic for me then to impose this view on others who do not hold it. This would subordinate the freedom of people to choose moral values for themselves in favor of an arbitrary imposition of values from some select worldview or group. So those who advance this objection believe that the correct solution to disagreements about euthanasia at the level of principle is to legalize euthanasia, and let people choose for themselves whether or not they wish to avail themselves of it. That way nobody gets to impose his or her view on anybody else, and everyone will have the right to develop their own moral response to the issue.[6]

This objection sounds interesting, and the language in which it is expressed (concerning freedom to choose, rights, etc.) has considerable influence in our society, and can often put the unsuspecting euthanasia opponent on the defensive. Yet a little probing beneath the surface quickly reveals that this objection involves a too-superficial analysis of the moral issues. The problem with this argument is that it *presupposes* moral relativism about moral values, a thesis that those who advance it usually do not wish to commit to, and a thesis in any case that cannot be defended. This objection presupposes moral relativism because it suggests that everyone should be able to make up their own minds on moral values, and that nobody can impose his or her moral values on another, and this is usually the definition of what I call extreme moral relativism (i.e., where moral values are relative to the individual). In the particular case at hand, this general theory about the applicability of moral values (relativism) is then applied to the issue of euthanasia.

This objection therefore presupposes moral relativism in a way that a pro-euthanasia argument which simply claims that euthanasia as a *specific practice* is moral, and makes *no general claims about moral knowledge,* does not.

The problem with this objection then is that it is based on moral relativism, and moral relativism is impractical and contradictory. Moral relativism is impractical because it is impossible to live without making objective moral judgments (e.g., that racism is immoral, that kindness is moral, that stealing is immoral, etc). Relativism is also self-contradictory because, while the relativist argues that there are no moral values, he usually goes on to make objective moral judgments! For example, he usually believes that those who would deny the choice of euthanasia to patients in distress are doing something immoral! He holds that this is an objective moral wrong. It leads to a contradiction because the relativist is saying at one and the same time that nobody should be able to impose his "in principle" values on anyone else, and yet that is exactly what he wants to do: he believes that euthanasia is morally acceptable in principle and therefore should be legal; he wants to impose this view on those who believe it is wrong in principle and therefore should be illegal. The relativist's position is also not neutral because once a practice is legalized one is forcing the practice on those who do not accept it in the crucial sense that they must *live in a society where the practice is legally acceptable,* a practice which, to a significant extent, will shape the society in which we live.

It is also important to emphasize that those who propose this objection are not really relativists at all, and do not really wish to portray themselves as such. That is to say, they do not really hold that all moral values are relative; moreover, they do not even usually try to avoid making objective moral judgments (in order to be consistent). They simply employ this strategy—a strategy I call "the rhetoric of relativism"—because they know that it is often effective in our culture in moral debates, especially if one is debating with someone not well versed in the logic of moral arguments. They may not even know themselves *how* the strategy works, but only that it *does* work. The strategy involves, as we have seen, employing a general attack on the objectivity of moral knowledge, *as a way of arguing for the morality of a specific issue,* in this case euthanasia, instead of simply arguing for the specific case *on its own merits.* I suspect that one might have been laughed out of court for employing such a debating strategy in a moral argument in the Middle Ages, but in our society it is quite remarkable how far one can get in a moral debate by adopting this approach.[7]

The second objection to the "in principle" argument is the argument that life is not supremely valuable, perhaps not even our highest value. Some liberal thinkers might want to reserve that honor for the value of freedom. In any case, what this objection is saying is that human life is not the most fundamental value, and so there may be cases where it is morally acceptable to end life, and these would include cases of euthanasia.[8] This argument is problematic because it seems contradictory to say that freedom is more valuable than life itself, especially since one must be alive to experience freedom. This is not to deny that freedom is a very great value, it is simply to point out that it seems inherently contradictory to argue that we should be free to end our own lives. After all, we regularly restrict freedom in order to protect life, so the argument that freedom actually can outweigh the value of life is an odd argument.

It is sometimes objected that the willingness of people to die to protect freedom could be used as an argument to show that freedom is a higher value than life. Otherwise, would it make sense for a person to give up his or her life to protect freedom? This raises the case of martyrs and others who have died for a cause, in this case the cause of freedom. While I agree that one can give one's life for the cause of freedom, I don't think it follows from this that freedom must be regarded as a higher value than life. It is important to emphasize that when one commits to a (dangerous) cause, one is not intending by this action to commit suicide. A member of the Jewish ghetto in Warsaw who took on the Nazis might well believe this would mean almost-certain death. Yet they are not committing suicide, for the Nazis would be the cause of their death. Thus they are not intentionally dying to protect freedom. Yet we might still wonder whether being *willing* to die for the cause of freedom shows in some way that freedom is a higher value than life. I believe it shows only that freedom is a very important value, but not the highest value. This is why slaves in general throughout history did not commit suicide. Further, when U.S. soldiers give their lives in battle to preserve the freedom of American society, they are doing this to preserve a society in which life, liberty, and the pursuit of happiness are very high values, with life being the highest. People do sometimes die to protect the freedom of others, but this does not show that freedom is the supreme value. The vast majority of people value their lives more than they value their freedom.

A modification of this objection might be to accept the principle that all life is sacred, of intrinsic value, but to argue that this does not preclude the taking of life. The taking of life in euthanasia-type cases, it might be argued, is not inconsistent with affirming the supreme value of life (indeed, some of those who support euthanasia may not wish to claim that life is not supremely valuable). Yet this argument is also vulnerable to contradiction in that to affirm that life is intrinsically valuable and yet at the same time to say that suicide is permissible seems, on any reasonable reading, to be a contradiction in terms. In general terms, the argument that the intrinsic value of life excludes the permissibility of suicide seems much more reasonable than an argument like that offered by Margaret Battin, in which she says that human beings have a right to rational suicide "simply by virtue of being human."[9] Battin's argument is a fairly typical argument employed to support euthanasia, but it seems to me to be more of an assertion than an argument, especially since Battin admits she has no theory of natural rights to support it (a theory which in any case would be very difficult for her to defend because it usually requires appeal to the notion of human nature, a notion which most liberal thinkers today reject).

The third objection to the "in principle" argument might be called the "suffering objection," and it is perhaps the strongest objection. Sometimes supporters of euthanasia come across as not having much regard for the value of life (as in the Terri Schiavo case). But the stronger face of their argument is based on an appeal for compassion for those who are suffering. This is the argument that the needless suffering of a patient is sufficient reason to override the argument that life is the supreme value, a principle that we otherwise may generally affirm. In short, the argument is that we have a moral obligation to have compassion for people who are terminally ill and suffering needlessly, and this obligation (perhaps coupled with the value we place on freedom of self-determination) extends to allowing them to end their suffering by giving them the option of suicide. This, it should be said, is the main motivation behind many arguments in favor of euthanasia, and it is a good motivation in the sense that it is borne out of a genuine desire to end needless suffering.

Some have replied to this argument by saying that it assumes that all suffering is needless, or by arguing that modern palliative care is so advanced that no one now need suffer intolerably, but I shall not give either of these replies. My reply is that, while we recognize that we would like to do all we can to end the suffering of a patient, and would see this as a moral obligation, there are nevertheless grave dangers in saying that the suffering of a patient is a justification for suicide. First, how do we decide how much suffering is too much, and which types of suffering are included (physical, mental)? This is a very difficult question to answer; the usual answer from euthanasia supporters is to allow the patient to decide this issue for him or her self. But this answer is also fraught with problems (I will come back to why at the end of the paper). The second danger is that allowing euthanasia for the reason of ending suffering would virtually commit us to a new principle in ethics: that one's suffering can trump the value of one's life. Acceptance of this principle opens up at least two further ethical possibilities: if one's suffering can trump the value of one's life, could other people's suffering trump the value of one's life (in the case of, say, a husband abusing his wife and children; would their suffering give them a right to kill him)? Also, might something other than suffering (say the personal happiness or well-being of others) trump the value of one's life? In short, there is a utilitarian dimension to the argument that suffering trumps the value of life, and it is problematic for the reason that all utilitarian arguments are problematic—they open the door to saying that nothing is wrong or right *in itself* but only in whether or not it can be shown to contribute to the overall good.

The fourth objection to the "in principle" argument is that it would also require outlawing the death penalty, but supporters of the "in principle" argument against euthanasia often support the death penalty. Isn't there a possibility of inconsistency here, since one is relying upon the supreme value of life in one area (euthanasia) but apparently compromising it in another (capital punishment)? This objection does underscore the necessity of insuring that one's views on life issues (abortion, euthanasia, capital punishment, etc.) are consistent. However, in general it is not inconsistent to favor capital punishment and to be against euthanasia, because committing oneself to the principle that all life is supremely valuable does not mean and has never meant that one is against *all* killing. Usually, one still holds that killing in self-defense and in a (just) war are justified, i.e., support for the supreme value of life does not imply pacifism. Although the right to life is fundamental and supreme, it is not generally held to be an *absolute* right, but one that applies only to innocent life.[10]

The Practical Argument against Euthanasia

The second line of argument against euthanasia we might call the "practical" argument. This argument is motivated by a concern for the *practical abuses* that would inevitably result if euthanasia were to be legalized. It relies on the general point that euthanasia is impractical because it could not be adequately regulated through legislation. The key point of the argument is that the legalization of euthanasia would lead to serious abuses; these abuses would be immoral, and so it would be wrong to legalize euthanasia for this reason alone. The practical argument need make no appeal to the "in principle" argument, but can stand by itself. The legalization of euthanasia, according to the practical argument, leads to an increase in human misery, misery that the introduction of euthanasia was supposed to prevent. The main points of the practical argument have been well documented in a variety of sources;[11] I will not elaborate them in detail here, but simply provide an overview of the main abuses that should give us great cause for concern if euthanasia were to be legalized.

First, one of the major problems with health care in many countries, and especially in the United States, is that it is frequently linked to the ability to pay. Those with good financial resources often get better medical treatment than those with lesser resources. Indeed, those who are very well off can often get the best medical treatment available in the world. And there are millions without health insurance whose medical coverage is not very good; even the medical coverage of many people with insurance is often less than adequate. We all know of insurance companies raising one's premiums or even stopping one's health insurance altogether as soon as one begins to make large claims on the company (i.e., as soon as one gets a serious illness). We all know of HMOs that use profit motives to reduce services. Now the question is: what effect would euthanasia have if introduced into such a system?

It is a good bet that euthanasia would soon become linked to the ability to pay for health care, with the poor far more likely to be euthanized than the rich. We can be fairly sure that euthanasia would be quite cheap, especially when compared to the cost of other types of medical treatment. Given this, many poor patients faced with spending all of their savings on various treatments, often with questionable success rates, will likely opt for euthanasia as a cheaper choice (will insurance companies pay for euthanasia?). The important point is that the less well off may voluntarily opt for euthanasia for financial reasons, and not because of undue suffering. Opting for death for financial reasons—because one cannot afford medical treatment—would be an abuse, I contend; it would be an immoral consequence of the introduction of legalized euthanasia.[12]

Second, another likely area of abuse is that the elderly ill, who are often very vulnerable, might be pushed into euthanasia against their will. They might be pressured by family, relatives, or medical staff (or perhaps even by cultural peer pressure). I have in mind here subtle pressure of the kind that families are especially skilled at! One of the universal truths of the human condition which almost every human being has experienced is that family members possess myriad ways to put subtle pressure on other family members to bring about certain actions they deem desirable! If euthanasia is legalized, we can expect to see cases where elderly people, in particular, opt for euthanasia because they feel this is what their family would prefer, or because they feel they are a burden on their families (just as elderly people sometimes decide to move to retirement homes for the same reason). Their decision may look like it was freely arrived at in the sense that they may go through the official procedure for voluntarily requesting euthanasia, but it is not what they really want. And, of course, to further complicate things their perception of family pressure or of being a burden may be mistaken. In an ideal world, this would not happen if euthanasia were to be legalized, but in the real world I think we have to acknowledge that it is bound to happen on quite a significant scale. It will occur frequently, I believe, especially if a "euthanasia culture" develops in fifty or a hundred years (a euthanasia culture might be defined as one not only in which euthanasia is widely accepted, but where a significant number of those who die every year do so by means of euthanasia; perhaps many hospitals will have staffed "euthanasia wings").

Third, it is inevitable that some people will be even directly pressured into euthanasia by medical staff, especially by unscrupulous doctors who wish to speed things up a little. Are there such doctors? There are unscrupulous members of almost every profession, and medicine is no exception. There are lawyers who significantly overcharge their clients, banks who mislead their customers about loan rates, food companies who fudge on food safety, drug companies who falsify drug safety tests, car salesmen who sell lemons, professors who never grade an exam, and doctors who will kill patients against their will.[13] One hopes that the number of such cases will be small, that such an evil practice will be very rare, but it is hard to estimate the mental anguish and increase in misery that would accompany such cases. (And those who advocate euthanasia better pray that this does not happen in their own cases! The utilitarian argument that there may be one case of abuse in a hundred cases of euthanasia is all well and good, unless the case of abuse happens to be your own!)[14] Some members of the medical profession are bound to abuse the practice, as has happened in other countries, most notably the Netherlands (a worry to which the U.S. Supreme Court referred in its 1997 decision that there is no general legal right to euthanasia). This will always be a temptation for some in an already overburdened health system that currently has to refuse some people even basic health care. One particular difficulty will be in distinguishing between those cases where a doctor administers a pain-relieving, but potentially life-shortening, drug with the sincere intention of relieving suffering only, and cases where the intention is to relieve suffering *and* kill the patient, or just to kill the patient. Cases of the first kind are well defended by the doctrine of double effect, I believe, but cases of the second kind, since they require access to the *intention* of the moral agent in order to determine the morality of the action, would be very difficult to safeguard against, and to regulate.

Fourth, a concern for many about the legalization of euthanasia, and one of the main reasons that the American Medical Association opposes it, is that it may lead to a change in the ethics of the medical profession. It would challenge the current practice, reflected in the Hippocratic Oath, where the doctor is concerned absolutely and without qualification for the health and welfare of the patient, and does all he or she can, within reason, to cure the patient. The worry is that if euthanasia were legalized it would eventually result in putting a limit on the doctor's concern for the health and welfare of the patient—the limit would be up to the point where euthanasia becomes a "serious" option. At this point, some doctors might do less than they could do, because they might feel that euthanasia is a more sensible option, especially in a euthanasia culture.

Another feature of this argument is that euthanasia might lead to a breakdown of trust between patient and doctor, because the patient might feel that the doctor is doing less than he or she could to cure them, knowing that euthanasia is an option. Of course, this feeling on the part of the patient could be mistaken, but it would nonetheless be real. It would surely become a feature of many doctor/patient relationships if euthanasia were to become fairly widely established. The practice of euthanasia may well lead to an erosion of trust between some patients and some medical personnel. Again, this would lead to an increase in the mental anguish of an already anguished, vulnerable patient.[15]

Fifth, the actual practice of euthanasia will place a moral burden on doctors that they are not trained to cope with, and that will add to the already considerable pressures they are under. This will result in further stress in the lives of doctors, which will inevitably lead to undesirable consequences for patients. In addition, doctors may attempt to find a way to avoid this moral burden. One obvious way is to require their subordinates (e.g., nurses) to administer fatal doses. This already happens to some extent with the administering of pain-relieving (and potentially life-shortening) drugs. The regulations for the legalization of euthanasia would hopefully prevent this kind of abuse, but it would be very difficult to police in a lot of cases because many people's jobs depend on carrying out the orders of their superiors.[16]

Sixth, another concern is that the regulations under which euthanasia is introduced will be eventually loosened, and that the floodgates will open. When euthanasia is first legalized the legislation will have to be carefully crafted and the criteria for euthanasia tightly defined, with strict controls and safeguards included. For example, euthanasia is likely to be restricted to cases where it satisfies three criteria: (1) it is voluntarily requested; (2) the patient is suffering intolerably; and (3) the patient is terminally ill. These criteria will have to be further specified, and the procedure for establishing that each one has been met will have to be clearly provided for in the legislation. However, it is inevitable that a patient will eventually bring a court challenge to this legislation for the right to euthanasia in cases where he or she is suffering, but not terminally ill, or vice versa. We have seen a loosening of the law in other areas of life such as divorce and abortion, and euthanasia will probably be no exception. And while suffering is usually restricted to physical suffering, eventually this will be broadened to include cases of mental suffering as well.[17] There is less chance perhaps that the law will be widened to include cases of involuntary euthanasia, but the other cases are worrying enough. In general, our society has become more and more liberal on a variety of issues, and it is reasonable to suggest that euthanasia laws will be influenced by this trend.

Seventh, there is the whole question of misdiagnoses of illnesses. We all like to think that medicine is an exact science, because it reassures us and gives us more confidence in our doctors. However, we know that medicine is not an exact science, and the diagnosis of terminal illness, and of how long a patient has left to live, is often particularly difficult and frequently inaccurate. One man who argued against the legalization of euthanasia in Oregon was told on three separate occasions many years earlier that he had six months to live. The strongest form of euthanasia legislation will probably require a second opinion on whether a patient is terminally ill or not. Nevertheless, because this is an inexact area of medicine it may lead to people committing suicide who would otherwise have lived and recovered from their illnesses.

Eighth, the effect of a euthanasia culture on society in general is also something that one has to consider in the debate concerning the morality of euthanasia. The effect could be very negative. The worry is that euthanasia would lead to a further erosion of respect for human life, an erosion that many would argue is an increasing characteristic of our contemporary culture. It might lead to a further cheapening of the value of life overall in society, not just because of the fact that a form of suicide is now legally available, but also because we would be committing to the principle that one can take one's own life if one judges that one's quality of life is not sufficient to make life worth living. This seems to introduce a quantitative, materialistic attitude toward the value of life, which many will find disturbing. This attitude is already in evidence in other areas of life (e.g., cosmetic surgery), so it is not perhaps an exaggeration to say that it might become worse in a euthanasia culture.

The main objection to the practical argument from those who support euthanasia is the general objection that the abuses I have mentioned are exaggerated; they either would not happen, or would not be nearly as serious as I have stated them. The objection also emphasizes that the legislation introducing euthanasia would be carefully crafted and tight enough to minimize these abuses.[18] The objection further states that all law is abused to some extent; that the sought-after standard of an abuse-free law, implied perhaps in the practical argument, is too idealistic; that if we insist on such a strict standard we could not legalize anything. Human beings are imperfect, it is argued, so we will inevitably end up with laws that are imperfectly applied; we need to do the best we can in a difficult situation.[19] This is an interesting objection, and the point about all law involving abuse is undoubtedly correct. Nevertheless, leaving aside the "in principle" argument for a moment, I am not at all convinced that the abuses mentioned would not occur, and have no confidence that built-in safeguards would work. It is difficult to be precise, of course, about which abuses might be more likely to occur than others, or about how bad the abuses might be. Nevertheless, I am convinced that the legalization of euthanasia would lead to some fairly serious abuses and worrying trends (such as tying the value of life to a person's sense of independence),[20] and it is too big a risk to take. Let us not forget that once we make a practice legal, it is very difficult, if not impossible, to

reverse the practice if we do not like the results (and for the patient successful euthanasia is irreversible, of course; unlike other slippery slope issues,
this *is* a life or death issue). The availability of euthanasia is supposed to lead
to a decrease in human misery, but I think it may well lead to an increase
in human misery overall, and it is this concern for the common good of society that we must consider in our laws when we are trying to do the best
we can. I agree with Stephen Potts that the burden of proof in this matter
falls on those who support the legalization of euthanasia. Potts argues that
those who support the legalization of euthanasia "should demonstrate beyond reasonable doubt that the dangers listed will not arise, just as chemical
companies proposing to introduce a new drug are required to demonstrate
that it is safe as well as beneficial."[21] An argument in favor of euthanasia that
relies almost entirely on compassion for the individual patient is looking at
only one side of the issue, as Potts points out, and ignores the real danger
that will result from abuses of the practice.[22]

The Relationship between the Arguments

It is helpful to consider the relationship between the "in principle" argument and the "practical" argument against euthanasia for a moment, because their relationship has implications for the public debate in a democratic society.

Usually when an individual is against euthanasia they are against it both
in principle and in practice. That it to say, they believe that it is wrong in
itself, but also that it would lead to serious abuses if legalized. This is the
standard view of most anti-euthanasia groups, for example, and it is the
strongest argument against euthanasia (assuming that both are good independent arguments, of course). However, it is logically possible to be against
euthanasia in principle, but to hold that it would not lead to abuses if legalized. Yet, one would still be against its legalization because one is against it
in principle. This particular view on euthanasia, while logically possible, is
quite rare.

But a far more common position, and one with relevance to the contemporary debate, is the position whose proponents either are in favor of euthanasia in principle, or are unsure about whether it is moral or immoral in
principle, but who are very worried about possible abuses that would follow
the legalization of euthanasia. Consequently, while not sure of their final
view on the "in principle" argument laid out above, they are still against the

legalization of euthanasia because they find the practical argument persuasive. This is the position of many people in American society, and partly explains why euthanasia bills were defeated in liberal states like California.

It is also important to note that the actual debate in contemporary society about euthanasia, especially at the level of public policy, more frequently concerns the practical argument against euthanasia rather than the "in principle" argument. This is because in a pluralist society a debate about in principle matters usually takes us back to a debate about which worldview is true; this is a very difficult debate in which to engage in modern culture, and it is very difficult to make progress in such a debate. Therefore, at least in the public debate, people tend to avoid their differences of principle. The practical argument is more easily debated because the suggested abuses mainly concern matter-of-fact issues, and it is much easier to debate about matters of fact than about matters of principle. Nevertheless the "in principle" argument is the strongest argument in the sense that it makes the stronger claim that euthanasia is wrong in itself, whereas the practical argument says only that euthanasia would not work in practice. If one were against euthanasia in practice, but not in principle, and one became satisfied that the practical abuses would not occur (say, through proposed built-in safeguards, etc.) then one could consistently support the legalization of euthanasia.

Conclusion: Value of Life versus Quality of Life

Euthanasia is a practice that brings into focus the question of which has more moral weight: the value of life or the quality of life? Traditionally, it has been argued that human life is the supreme value, and that one's quality of life can never trump it and justify the taking of one's life. But end-of-life issues raise the question anew: could the quality of one's life sink so low that one could rationally judge that one's life had no or very little value, and so one's suicide would be justified? This is another version of the objection to the "in principle" argument that life may not be the supreme value—its value, rather, should be defined in terms of various activities and projects which human beings want to pursue; when they can no longer pursue these activities and projects, their life has no value.

This argument prompts us to consider how we might go about defining the quality of life (an issue that came up in considering the third objection above to the "in principle" argument). One could try to define it as a certain level of independence, a certain amount of freedom, absence of debilitating pain, a certain range of rational choices, etc. But one can see that these matters can be quite subjective, and that it will be very difficult to get a working definition on this matter for the purposes of legislation. In response to the obvious problems that accompany any attempt to define quality of life, modern liberal political theorists—with their strong emphasis on freedom, rights, and their relativistic inclinations—are inclined to argue that "everyone should be allowed to determine how and when they die" (i.e., everyone should be able to decide for themselves their own quality of life). Daniel Brock, James Rachels, Margaret Battin, Helga Kuhse, and Ronald Dworkin have all offered versions of this argument. Indeed, it is a fairly typical liberal argument in the debate over euthanasia, and other controversial moral issues.[23]

While this line of reasoning might apply in some areas of life, I do not think it can apply in the case of euthanasia. To be consistent, a proponent of the above view could not object if someone in almost perfect health, in body and mind, nevertheless opted for suicide (after a temporary or trivial setback, say). However, it is likely that most people would not regard a decision like this as morally right, and would seek to *exclude* it from any law permitting euthanasia. But this means that the proponents of the above view would place some *restrictions* on how and when people can choose their own death. Given this, they will then be obliged to engage in debate about what these restrictions should be. And this means that they will be obliged to *reenter* the debate concerning the appropriate definition of quality of life. And it is when we enter this debate that I think the practical objections to the legalization of euthanasia represent a very strong argument against its legalization.

The debate about euthanasia often comes down, for some liberal thinkers (i.e., those who accept John Stuart Mill's approach to liberty), to the question of whether there is a general human right to suicide. And it is in discussion of this issue that the liberal position, inspired by Mill, is at its weakest. For the notion that suicide is "a fundamental human right," as Margaret Battin claims,[24] is very difficult to defend in the light of the suffering the suicide of an individual can cause for that person's family and friends. No example shows better, I believe, the inadequacy of Mill's harm principle. Further, liberals tend to defend the view that suicide is a fundamental right, not by appeal to any general theory of natural rights, but by appeal to the relativistic move that one should be free to make the decision about suicide for oneself. But as I pointed out in our discussion of the "in principle" argument above, it is inconsistent, even dishonest to imply moral relativism about ethics in general as a way of arguing for the morality of a specific practice, namely, euthanasia. This is because moral relativism is a thesis that applies to all moral values. All this strategy achieves is to obscure by means of the rhetoric of relativism the serious moral issues involved in the debate over euthanasia.

NOTES

1. For an overview of the Oregon debate, see Daniel Hillyard and John Dombrink, *Dying Right: The Death with Dignity Movement* (New York: Routledge, 2001).

2. See Benedict Ashley, O.P., and Kevin O'Rourke, O.P., *Health Care Ethics: A Theological Analysis,* 4th ed. (Washington, DC: Georgetown University Press, 1997), pp. 411ff., for a valuable discussion of these and other related matters.

3. See Pope Pius XII, "Prolongation of Life," *The Pope Speaks* 4, no. 4 (1958): 393–98.

4. I believe that cases of administering morphine to relieve suffering, but which may shorten the patient's life, are also morally acceptable. Such cases are well defended by the doctrine of double effect. For a very good discussion of the distinctions between active and passive euthanasia, between extraordinary means and ordinary means, and of how extraordinary means cases differ from ordinary means cases, see Bonnie Steinbock, "The Intentional Termination of Life," in *Killing and Letting Die, ed. Bonnie Steinbock* (Englewood Cliffs, NJ: Prentice Hall, 1980), pp. 69–77. For more on the definition of extraordinary means, see the Congregation for the Doctrine of the Faith, *Declaration on Euthanasia* (Vatican City, 1980), pp. 10ff.

5. John Paul II, "Address of John Paul II to the Participants in the International Congress on 'Life-Sustaining Treatments and Vegetative State: Scientific Advances and Ethical Dilemmas,'" March 20, 2004.

6. This argument, as it is applied to the quality of life versus value of life debate, is further elaborated in the last section of the paper.

7. I explain and illustrate this debating strategy in more detail in chapter 8 of my *Why Politics Needs Religion: The Place of Religious Arguments in the Public Square* (Downers Grove, IL: InterVarsity, 2006).

8. See James Rachels, *The End of Life* (New York: Oxford University Press, 1986), where he argues that the Western tradition has valued life too much, that there "are times when the protection of human life has no point," p. 24.

9. Margaret Battin, *The Least Worst Death: Essays in Bioethics on the End of Life* (New York: Oxford University Press, 1994), pp. 279ff.

10. For a further discussion of this point, see Alan Donegan, *The Theory of Morality* (Chicago: University of Chicago Press, 1977), pp. 87ff.

11. An indispensable study, based on comprehensive knowledge of the medical field, of the various abuses that might occur if euthanasia were to be legalized, including a study of the actual practice of euthanasia in the Netherlands, is Herbert Hendin's *Seduced by Death: Doctors, Patients and Assisted Suicide,* rev. ed. (New York: Norton, 1998).

12. Even when euthanasia is not legal, patients might be motivated to request it because the quality of their life is low due primarily to lack of financial resources. Depending on the illness in question, the Christian view of the human person requires that the state take the responsibility to provide a reasonable quality of life for persons who are permanently ill, long-term disabled, and so on. This is because we *are* our brother's keepers.

13. Hendin reports that, in a significant number of cases in the Netherlands, the doctor was the first to suggest suicide to the patient. Also, the Remmelink study carried out in the Netherlands to assuage public fears about euthanasia only exacerbated them, because the commis-

sion reported that one thousand patients were euthanized without explicit request. Some doctors defended this by saying that many of these patients were "already in the dying phase"; see Hendin, *Seduced by Death*, pp. 104ff.

14. Euthanasia is frequently defended in utilitarian terms by arguing that the suicide of a patient leads to an increase in the overall good. Whether or not this is true is obviously debatable, but the main problem with this argument is that it is not an argument *specifically* for the morality of euthanasia; rather it is based on the assumption that the utilitarian thesis that morality should promote the greatest happiness for the greatest number of people is correct. Therefore, this argument for euthanasia stands or falls with that thesis, and since the thesis faces insuperable difficulties the utilitarian approach to euthanasia is similarly afflicted. For an example of the utilitarian argument applied to euthanasia, see Joseph Fletcher, "Ethics and Euthanasia," in *Ethical Issues in Death and Dying*, ed. Robert F. Weir (New York: Columbia University Press, 1977), pp. 348–59.

15. For an analysis of the ethics of the doctor/patient relationship, see Edmund Pellegrino, "The Internal Morality of Clinical Medicine: A Paradigm for the Ethics of the Helping and Healing Professions," *Journal of Medicine and Philosophy* 26, no. 6 (December 2001): 559–79.

16. For further discussion of the moral burden euthanasia places on doctors, from which it sometimes takes them months to recover, see David Thomasma et al., eds., *Asking to Die: Inside the Dutch Debate about Euthanasia* (Dordrecht, Holland: Kluwer, 1998), pp. 312ff.

17. There have been several cases in the Netherlands of patients who requested, and were granted, euthanasia who were suffering from mental, but not physical, illness (i.e., whose doctors were psychiatrists). See Hendin, *Seduced by Death*, pp. 155ff.

18. For an overview of the kinds of controls those who favor the legalization of euthanasia have in mind, see Battin, *The Least Worst Death*, pp. 173ff.

19. Daniel Maguire raises this objection, among others, to the practical argument against euthanasia. Maguire acknowledges that possible abuses have to be taken seriously, but then mistakenly argues that this does not show that euthanasia is wrong in principle. But the point of the practical argument is not to show that euthanasia is wrong in principle, but to show that the abuses it might lead to are serious and likely to occur, and so are good reasons in themselves to make euthanasia illegal. See Maguire's "Deciding for Yourself: The Objections," in *Ethical Issues in Death and Dying*, pp. 325ff.

20. Thomasma et al. report that the most often cited reasons for euthanasia in the Netherlands are loss of dignity, and loss of independence. They suggest that because of this, even if adequate pain control were present, there would still be a need for euthanasia. However, they fail to consider that this fact also changes the nature of the debate from a concern about ending insufferable pain to a concern about what constitutes human dignity, a much more contentious issue. See Thomasma, *Asking to Die*, pp. 12ff.

21. Stephen G. Potts, "Looking for the Exit Door: Killing and Caring in Modern Medicine," *Houston Law Review* 25 (1988): 510. See also Potts' detailed practical objections to euthanasia in the same article, pp. 504–11.

22. This is true of James Rachels' very interesting discussion of euthanasia, a discussion that nevertheless focuses almost totally on the point that euthanasia will relieve suffering, and pays very little attention to the practical problems which may accompany its legalization (problems which will contribute to suffering in my view). See Rachels' *The End of Life*.

23. Brock gives this answer to the question of quality of life, but does not address the issue of what limits, if any, he would put on it. See Daniel Brock, "Voluntary Active Euthanasia," in *Social Ethics: Morality and Social Policy*, 5th ed., ed. Thomas Mappes and Jane Zembaty (New York: McGraw-Hill, 1997), pp. 70–73. A similar response is given by James Rachels, in what he calls the argument from liberty, but again he does not discuss what limits one might put on this (though terminal illness appears to be one of them); but Rachels mainly considers whether or not the limits would include assistance from a third party. See Rachels, *The End of Life*, pp. 180ff. A version of this argument is also given by Margaret Battin, who acknowledges that the "autonomy" argument, as she calls it, protects all cases of "rational" suicide, and she ap-

pears to want to limit suicide to only rational cases, but does not define how this limitation is to be specified. See Battin, *The Least Worst Death,* pp. 277ff. Helga Kuhse also argues that rational, autonomous subjects should decide their own quality of life, but again provides no discussion of any limits she would put on this, though she does seem to want to restrict it to euthanasia-type cases; see her *The Sanctity-of-Life Doctrine in Medicine: A Critique* (New York: Clarendon Press, 1987), pp. 211ff.

In *Life's Dominion* (New York: Knopf, 1993), Ronald Dworkin actually raises a hypothetical case of a healthy young person committing suicide while in a temporary depression as a case most would disapprove of, and yet he still provides no discussion of what limits we should put on quality of life decisions (thereby implying that the young man's suicide would be moral). Instead of facing the issue directly, Dworkin offers a convoluted account of a person's interests, which he divides into two types: experiential and critical (pp. 201ff.), but fudges on the crucial issue of whether there are critical interests which are universal to all (pp. 206ff.), and ends by saying that individuals should make euthanasia decisions on the basis of their own critical interests, or, if they are not able to do this, family and relatives may do it for them on the basis of *their* judgments of the individual's interests (p. 213). Dworkin's avoidance of the crucial issues is egregious, as is his tendency to express his argument in carefully crafted rhetorical flourishes, like the following: "Making someone die in a way that others approve, but he believes a horrifying contradiction of his life, is a devastating, odious form of tyranny" (p. 217). Unfortunately this kind of sophistry only serves to obscure the philosophical issues.

Among those who have questioned whether there can be such a thing as autonomous, rational suicide is John Kavanaugh, S.J.; see his *Who Count as Persons? Human Dignity and the Ethics of Persons* (Washington, DC: Georgetown University Press, 2001), pp. 132ff.

24. Battin, *The Least Worst Death,* pp. 279ff.

SELECTED BIBLIOGRAPHY ON
DEATH AND DYING

Barry, Robert Laurence, O.P. *Breaking the Thread of Life: On Rational Suicide.* Somerset, NJ: Transaction Publishers, 1994.

Callahan, Daniel. *The Troubled Dream of Life: Living with Mortality.* New York: Simon and Schuster, 1993.

Callahan, Sidney. "The Moral Case against Euthanasia." *Health Progress* 76, no. 1 (1995).

A Catholic Guide to End-of-Life Decisions. Boston: National Catholic Bioethics Center, 1997.

Catholic Health Association of the United States. *Care of the Dying: A Catholic Perspective.* Part 3. St. Louis, MO (1993).

DeBlois, Jean, C.S.J. "Changing the Way We Care for the Dying." *Health Progress* 75, no. 2 (1994): 48–49.

DeBlois, Jean, C.S.J., and Kevin D. O'Rourke, O.P. "Issues at the End of Life." *Health Progress* 76, no. 8 (1995).

The Dignity of the Dying Person: Proceedings of the Fifth Assembly of the Pontifical Academy for Life. Vatican City: Libreria Editrice Vaticana, 2000.

Gilham, Charles, and Peter Leibold. "A Voice against Physician-Assisted Suicide." *Health Progress* 78, no. 3 (1997): 44–47.

Gormally, Luke, ed. *Euthanasia, Clinical Practice, and the Law.* London: St. Augustine Press, 1994.

Gregory, Wilton. "The Church and the Public Discussion of Assisted Suicide." *Health Progress* 78, no. 2 (1997).

Gula, Richard M., S.S. *Euthanasia and Assisted Suicide: Positioning the Debate.* St. Louis, MO: Catholic Health Association of the United States, 1994.

———. *Euthanasia: Moral and Pastoral Perspectives.* Boston: Paulist Press, 1995.

Jeffreys, Derek S. "Euthanasia and John Paul II's 'Silent Language of Profound Sharing of Affection': Why Christians Should Care about Peter Singer." *Christian Bioethics* 7, no. 3 (2001): 359–78.

Kilner, John F., Arlene B. Miller, and Edmund D. Pellegrino, eds. *Dignity and Dying: A Christian Appeal.* Grand Rapids, MI: Eerdmans Publishing, 1996.

Manning, Michael. *Euthanasia and Physician-Assisted Suicide: Killing or Caring?* Boston: Paulist Press, 1998.

May, William E. *Testing the Medical Covenant: Active Euthanasia and Health Care Reform.* Grand Rapids, MI: Eerdmans Publishing, 1996.

O'Rourke, Kevin D., O.P. "Pain Relief: The Perspective of the Catholic Tradition." *Journal of Pain and Symptom Management* 7, no. 8 (1992): 485–91.

Stempsey, William E. "Laying Down One's Life for Oneself." *Christian Bioethics* 4, no. 2 (1998): 202–24.

Talone, Patricia A. *Feeding the Dying: Religion and End-of-Life Decisions.* New York: Peter Lang Publishing, 1996.

Tuohey, John F. "Mercy: An Insufficient Motive for Euthanasia." *Health Progress* 74, no. 8 (1993): 51–53.

PART IV

Genetics, Stem Cell Research, and Cloning

THE CATHOLIC POSITION on the ethics of research on human genetics, cloning, and embryonic versus adult stem cells flows out of the twofold concern to respect human dignity and protect human life that we have discussed in the first three parts of this book. Promoting and improving human life is clearly part of the Catholic mission in health care. Thus, the Catholic Church recognizes that, as part of improving human life, research upon human subjects is permissible. As the *Catechism of the Catholic Church* states: "Scientific, medical, or psychological experiments on human individuals or groups can contribute to healing the sick and the advancement of public health."[1] This is an important point to emphasize at the outset of our reflections here because the Catholic Church is often unfairly criticized today as being anti-science. However, the Catholic tradition has always been cautious and reflective whenever considering actions that affect the dignity of human persons. Thus, while areas of research such as human genetics, cloning, and embryonic/adult stem cells "might" promise new treatments, cures, and improved health for millions, these areas of biomedical science also create important ethical dilemmas because they involve research on human subjects that is often harmful or destructive, and which threatens the dignity of the very people it seeks to help. And so, the *Catechism* goes on to remind us:

Basic scientific research, as well as applied research, is a significant expression of man's dominion over creation. Science and technology are precious resources when placed at the service of man and promote his integral development for the benefit of all. By themselves however they cannot disclose the meaning of existence and of human progress. Science and technology are ordered to man, from whom they take their origin and development; hence they find in the person and in his moral values both evidence of their purpose and awareness of their limits.[2]

In short, the goal of promoting and improving human life must be tempered by attention to the dignity owed to the human subjects we propose to experiment upon. More simply, there are limits to scientific research—regardless of the nobility of one's motives.

To begin with, many Catholics raise questions regarding cloning, genetic engineering, and stem cell research at least in part because such activity is perceived as bordering on interference with God's providential creation. But similar concerns are also voiced in secular arenas. In regard to genetic research, fears are often expressed that scientists might interfere with the "gene pool" or manipulate the genome inappropriately, with disastrous results. Concerns are also raised over the proposed intentional destruction of human embryos for embryonic stem cell research. With cloning, many are troubled by the fact that it took scientists well over two hundred attempts to successfully clone the sheep known as Dolly and that Dolly went on to experience long-term side effects from the cloning procedure and died prematurely. The expressed "motives" behind these various forms of research are all (at least "officially") pretty much the same—to improve human life overall. However, one's motive is not the only thing that matters in ethics—we are responsible for the actions and means that we choose as well. To all of these concerns, the Catholic Church would add its interest in protecting the dignity of the embryos, clones, and people being experimented upon to advance this research. After all, many researchers try to argue that most of the secular concerns voiced above will eventually be diminished as our scientific understanding of each of these processes grows. But improved efficiency in cloning or genetic research will not diminish the ethical obligation to respect human dignity and protect human life which these techniques threaten.

To be clear, the genetic information we have been discovering is not, by itself, problematic. Nor, in general, is research into the vast possibilities of stem cells inherently immoral. Rather, it is the manner in which all of this research is being conducted that raises a series of ethical questions. There are also ethical dilemmas related to the outcomes of these types of human research. For example, in human genetics, concerns arise from the status given to the knowledge gathered, and the manner in which our genetic information will be used in the future by the scientific community as well as the larger human community. As for some forms of stem cell research, concern focuses on the status of the embryo from whom researchers want to "harvest" stem cells—a process that destroys the embryo itself. There is also the related problem of so-called "therapeutic" cloning, which proposes to produce cloned human embryos for the sole purpose of developing an unlimited supply of stem cells for continued research and eventual (researchers hope!) therapeutic application. The Catholic approach calls for careful reflection upon these controversial forms of research, which threaten to harm so many vulnerable human beings—good motives notwithstanding. On this point, the *Catechism* is emphatic: "Research or experimentation on the human being cannot legitimate acts that are in themselves contrary to the dignity of persons and to the moral law."[3]

Let us first consider the question regarding the status of genetic knowledge. What have we really learned from the Human Genome Project, for example? Some would claim that we have learned everything there is to know about human life because they believe that the totality of human existence is contained within our genes. This attitude is a form of *reductionism*, limiting a human being's lived experience to the physical/material level of DNA coding—an approach which at best "brackets" the spiritual dimension of the human person, and at worst outright denies its reality. Without ignoring the importance of our genetic makeup, the Catholic tradition continues to affirm that there is a reality deeper than genetics in the human person. Indeed, as the Congregation for the Doctrine of the Faith affirmed in *The Instruction on Respect for Human Life*, humanity cannot be reduced to the biological level:

For it is only in keeping with his true nature that the human person can achieve self-realization as a "unified totality": and this nature is at the same time corporal and spiritual. By virtue of its substantial union with a spiritual soul, the human body cannot be considered as a mere complex of tissues, organs and functions, nor can it be evaluated in the same way as the body of animals; rather it is a constitutive part of the person who manifests and expresses himself through it. The natural moral law expresses and lays down the purposes, rights and duties which are based upon the bodily and spiritual nature of the human person.[4]

In the specific case of our genome, this is but one element of our existence. Each human being is more than a collection of (speaking loosely) height genes, weight genes, eye color genes, cancer genes, heart disease genes, etc.

There is more to us than meets the eye—or the microscope. And so, the Catholic perspective resists any attempt to reduce human beings to the level of simple materiality and biology.

In addition to *reductionism,* an attitude of *determinism* is also often present among those researching human genetics. *Determinism* is the view that everything in reality is already set or fixed, which also means that there is no freedom within the universe, let alone within human activity. Rather, it is argued that since (in their perspective) each and every human being is simply a product of her or his DNA, our lives are programmed by our genetic makeup. It is suggested that very soon we will be able to determine a person's entire future life at the moment of birth based on an analysis of her or his DNA. But after a few moments' reflection, one can see that this attitude is too simplistic. Human history is filled with examples of human beings who overcame tremendous limitations imposed upon them physically to achieve great things. We can recall stories of deaf musicians, blind artists, athletes who should not have been athletic, children who should not have lived into adulthood, and so on—people like Beethoven and Helen Keller. At the same time, even if researchers were to discover a "violence gene," that by itself would not really explain crime. The Catholic perspective, of course, does not deny the influence of genetic makeup upon the human race. However, Catholics would resist efforts to deny human freedom, and thereby reduce human responsibility for action, as suggested by attitudes of *determinism* regarding human genetics. Free will is not something that can be verified empirically in the pure sense. Nevertheless, lack of scientific evidence does not mean that free will does not exist—this is a fallacy of reasoning. Further, in the absence of scientific data, there is evidence of freedom within the larger scope of human experience, as well as within reflection upon our own actions in life. Once again, there is much more to humanity than what the scientific eye can behold on its own.

And so, the Catholic perspective resists the *fatalism* that flows in the undercurrents of much of contemporary genetic research. Instead, as we have noted before in this volume, Catholics maintain respect for the individuality of each human person with the recognition that: (1) each human being is created in the image and likeness of God; and (2) the life of each human being is given as a free gift from God. Genetics remains but one part of our knowledge of the human condition, along with other studies such as history, psychology, literature, art, philosophy, and theology. From the Catholic perspective, then, the attitudes of *reductionism* and *determinism* are dehumanizing in that they ignore the totality of human personhood.[5]

With its broader perspective of human personhood, the Catholic approach is also able to resist the dangers of "labeling" that seem to be following upon the heels of genetic research. Genetic screening identifies our potential weaknesses: "cancer," "heart failure," or "low I.Q." But it must be emphasized that conclusions based upon genetic screening can only be expressed in terms of probability. Gene research thus far has identified only "markers" for genetic diseases (an area in which there is still vast work to be done). Everyone with a family history of heart disease does not develop heart disease. While carrying a genetic marker may not be insignificant knowledge for a person when making future health decisions, there is no evidence to date of a direct causal link between carrying a genetic marker and actually developing the problem associated with that marker. It is also evident, although there is dispute as to what degree, that environment and lifestyle choices are relevant factors in developing genetic diseases. Further, recent studies are beginning to suggest that the more important factor is not the presence of a genetic marker, but rather the location of that marker on the genome—especially in relation to other genetic markers—or the absence of specific other markers. And so, ignoring the crucial distinction between direct causality and probability gives rise to the *fatalistic* attitude within genetic research noted earlier. The Catholic approach strives to avoid the pitfalls of "labeling" that such *fatalism* in regard to research may lead to. Instead, the only "labels" a Catholic would accept are "child of God" and "a being deserving respect." Regardless of each human being's genetic makeup, these "labels" always hold true.

In addition to these general concerns regarding attitudes underlying genetic research, Catholics also raise specific questions about various forms of proposed genetic intervention in human beings. Generally speaking, there are two main goals that are the focus of genetic intervention. First, researchers want to cure genetic diseases. Second, there is interest in enhancing specific genetic characteristics or qualities.

Curing disease has a twofold dimension. One approach focuses solely upon an affected individual suffering from a genetic disorder. The person's nonreproductive *(somatic)* cells are treated to "repair" the faulty gene or genetic sequence, thereby eliminating the expression of the disease or its future occurrence. However, it also seems possible to remove specific genetic disorders from the gene pool by treating the reproductive *(germ-line)* cells of people who are carriers of genetic diseases. The goal of this latter approach is to eradicate genetic disease from the human gene pool.

There is also a twofold dimension of genetic enhancement that parallels the attempt to cure disease. On the one hand, by manipulating the genome it seems that one would be able to basically "select" specific characteristics for a "new" person—gender, intelligence, height, weight, eye color, perhaps certain dispositions toward music, art, athletics, etc. Parents, it is suggested, could then give their children the best possible chance of succeeding in life, just as they might attempt by sending their child to the best schools, or giving them special training in activities such as music, art, school work, etc. And, of course, if such alteration could be done on an individual's non-reproductive cells, it could also be done upon the reproductive cells and passed on to future generations.

Now most of what was just discussed is only *speculative* at this point. However, science fiction novels, television shows, and movies are digging into these possibilities so enthusiastically that it almost seems like genetic intervention is "science fact." For many, this is an exciting new frontier to be explored—and exploited—for all it is worth. And so, it is not premature to go beyond expressing concern for the attitudes expressed in genetic research and question the ethical nature of genetic intervention and its two-fold goals of curing disease and enhancing personal characteristics, since this seems to be the direction in which the field is moving.

To begin with, the overriding and unbending concern of the Catholic tradition is that genetic research must not do anything to hinder or harm human beings. This would fall in line with the general norms regarding respect for human persons and scientific research addressed in the *Catechism:*

> It is an illusion to claim moral neutrality in scientific research and its applications. On the other hand, guiding principles cannot be inferred from simple technical efficiency, or from the usefulness accruing to some at the expense of others or, even worse, from prevailing ideologies. Science and technology by their very nature require unconditional respect for fundamental moral criteria. They must be at the service of the human person, of his inalienable rights, of his true and integral good, in conformity with the plan and the will of God.[6]

Of special concern here would be interventions that might threaten our basic human endowments of *reason* and *sociability.* This will be a delicate issue, since there is still so much about the human genome we do not know. The temptation to "experiment" blindly in this area must be resisted—the hope for "great good" from genetic intervention does not outweigh the respect owed to human beings at all stages of life. Respect for persons requires that scientific certitude regarding the consequences and benefits of genetic intervention be obtained before anything is actually done to human subjects. If anyone objects that such certitude cannot be obtained without human trials and experimentation, then the ethics of proceeding with such research must be questioned. How can we reasonably claim to be helping the human race when we are unaware of the possible harm that might be done to some humans? This is simply too important for the future of humanity as a species, let alone for each of us as beings destined for a higher happiness than found in this temporal order, to take risks. Nor would such forms of research be acceptable just because some might come forward who are willing to participate—exploitative research fails to embody respect for the worth and dignity of human beings.

In this light, the Catholic perspective would be open to efforts to use genetic knowledge to cure or prevent particular diseases within an individual. Again, all care must be taken to avoid harm to a person's *rational* and *social* nature (so, for example, genetic intervention on brain cells would be more problematic than intervention on heart tissue to reduce the likelihood of heart disease). The effort to heal is well within the Catholic understanding of medicine as a healing ministry. Also, in practical terms, the potential for harm in this case would be limited to just the one person upon whom the intervention is being tried. On the other hand, attempting to reduce genetic disease in the germ-line is much more problematic. A potentially larger number of affected individuals could be involved, and the ability to predict outcomes would be considerably more complicated due to the complex nature of the human genome. We must remember that the mere presence of a problematic gene is only part of the picture—other issues such as placement on the genome and relation to other genes are also factors. Further, since not all genetic anomalies show up in the first or even second generation, and since the influence of another being's DNA in reproduction must be considered, unexpected consequences—perhaps even irreversible—could occur without detection for decades. When dealing with the human species, the risks must be confronted. Indeed, our current experiences with animal cloning should give us great pause regarding genetic intervention in germ-lines. Finally, if it is indeed possible to treat an individual and manipulate a person's genome to cure or prevent disease, the need to remove genetic diseases from the genome itself, with the added risk of altering the whole genome, become much less pressing. Prudence seems to dictate avoiding genetic intervention in germ-lines.

As for the issue of enhancement, the concerns are even greater. Fears of creating a super-race and visions of Nazism still permeate our shared human experience in this regard, and rightly so. Yet, there is a reasonable medical basis suggested in support of genetic enhancement, both for individuals and for the human species. The argument is that enhancing human beings would make us more resistant to disease, and therefore lead to a higher quality of life in general. If one steps away from fears of creating super-soldiers and super-cops, and focuses instead upon creating stronger immune systems, the picture looks quite different. After all, it could be argued, we enhance livestock and farm produce to resist disease—if such intervention is good enough for corn, why would it be wrong for human beings? Furthermore, some would surely be willing to pay for enhancements for themselves and for their children, and freedom of choice arguments based on radical notions of autonomy could sway many to say, "Why not?" Of course, if such interventions became possible, it would likely be impossible to control and limit the types and amounts of enhancements people would seek. Thus, for some the very *possibility* of misusing genetic technology provides sufficient grounds for preventing any further research into human genetics. It is not clear that this argument works, however. Jesus healed the sick—can we ignore the potential to increase global health out of fear of misuse?

In the end, however, concerns similar to those regarding genetic research for curing disease also hold for enhancement. To enhance a person's genetic makeup in a manner that improves resistance to disease could be justified on the same grounds as exercising and taking vitamins to improve one's health, provided that any intervention attempted would not adversely affect human *reason* and *sociability*. If such negative consequences cannot be avoided, then such intervention would not be permissible. As noted before regarding curing disease, the level of concern is so much higher when focused on the germ-line that prudence would caution against such therapy. But it does not seem that research on enhancement for health reasons is impermissible out of hand. Needless to say, technology for genetic enhancement will need very careful attention if it ever becomes available.

As for the concern over potential abuses, the Catholic perspective would acknowledge that the mere fact something can be done does not mean that it should be done—some actions are simply impermissible, while others, as we have suggested, are grossly imprudent. As a human community, our responsibility would be to identify those types of intervention that are impermissible and/or imprudent, and to do everything possible to keep them from happening. In part, this requires putting the burden of proof regarding potential genetic therapies upon researchers themselves. So much of bioethics today involves trying to show why certain actions are wrong and should not be permitted—the challenge to those who question certain types of research is, "Why not?" But the Catholic approach, following the direction of reason, would require that one *demonstrate the benefit of a therapy or intervention first,* while also *clearly showing how harm will be avoided.* In many ways, those involved in bioethics have allowed "the cart to be put before the horse," thereby keeping much of the ethical discussion playing the role of catch-up to genetic science. When the research is still in the "theoretical" phase, researchers often argue that ethical critiques are premature. However, when the research moves toward application, the call for ethical reflection is then characterized as impeding scientific progress. We need to reverse this trend and make those who know the science share the burden of demonstrating that their research is as ethically sound as it is theoretically viable. Consider the number of FDA-approved pharmaceuticals that have recently been recalled because they have caused unexpected harm. In the end, the cause is often the insufficiency of the research protocols intended to determine all the effects of the drugs. Such an approach with human genetic intervention would be disastrous, and would threaten the dignity of all human beings.

Finally, a word must be added regarding the broader scope of genetic enhancement. Why do some people want to be taller, thinner, or more intelligent, have a different eye color, or hair color, or skin color? What really lies behind the push for "enhancements" that go beyond basic health? People are expressing concerns about life, about their worth, about success and acceptance in the human community through these desires for improvement of their genomes. Perhaps before we rush to satisfy demands for enhancement, and spend significant amounts of money (both private and public) on genetic interventions that enhance characteristics, we should spend time as a community questioning the origin of these desires. Human beings will always have limitations and flaws—is that so bad? If our goal is perfection, we will never be satisfied in this earthly existence.

But what about stem cell research? Here the concerns are, admittedly, different. The goal of stem cell research in general is clearly therapeutic, seeking to draw cures for the sick and the ailing from these remarkable cells that have the ability (in theory) to become any tissue in the human body. There are no fears here of super-races or of destroying the gene pool. Rather, very noble goals are asserted for the cure of some of humanity's most fearful diseases and disorders: Parkinson's, leukemia, spinal cord injuries, etc. Indeed, some segments of society wonder how the Catholic Church—or *anyone* for that matter—could possibly oppose such important and helpful research as that being done on human stem cells. If the Catholic Church is *pro-life,* how can it stand in the way of research that will save and extend life?

The simple and direct answer to this question is that the Catholic tradition does *not* oppose stem cell research that is done ethically and appropriately. To understand the Catholic perspective, one must first recognize that there are two forms of stem cell research—a distinction rarely brought out in any adequate fashion by the contemporary media. Most of the current focus both scientifically and politically is upon embryonic stem cells—these are stem cells harvested from a developing embryo when it is at the blastocyst stage, or seven to eight days into its development. This research raises serious ethical concerns because the act of harvesting the embryonic stem cells destroys the embryos from which the cells are being obtained. A further problem is the recent emphasis on developing embryos for the specific purpose of harvesting stem cells for research either through *in vitro* fertilization or cloning techniques. Nevertheless, in all such cases the Catholic Church opposes any embryonic research that is harmful and destructive as an affront to the dignity of human life at one of our most vulnerable moments. John Paul II eloquently stated the Church's position regarding the respect owed to the human embryo in his encyclical letter *The Gospel of Life*:

Although "one must uphold as licit procedures carried out on the human embryo which respect the life and integrity of the embryo and do not involve disproportionate risks for it, but rather are directed to its healing, the improvement of its condition of health, or its individual survival," it must nonetheless be stated that the use of human embryos or fetuses as an object of experimentation constitutes a crime against their dignity as human beings who have a right to the same respect owed to a child once born, just as to every person.

This moral condemnation also regards procedures that exploit living human embryos and fetuses—sometimes specifically "produced" for this purpose by in vitro fertilization—either to be used as "biological material" or as providers of organs or tissue for transplants in the treatment of certain diseases. The killing of innocent human creatures, even if carried out to help others, constitutes an absolutely unacceptable act.[7]

The Church's consistent position maintains that from its very beginning, a human zygote deserves the full respect we would give to any other member of the human family—we cannot, therefore, destroy its life, even for precious stem cells which might be able to help another human being. What is more, embryonic stem cell research has had no real success in animal trials after more than twenty years of research, and faces serious problems with tumor formation and unstable genetic expression in the cells that researchers are attempting to develop. In terms of public policy, these factors will also be important—although they do not overshadow the ethical argument against embryonic stem cell research.

The second, and completely unproblematic source of stem cells is what are more commonly referred to as adult stem cells. Before any confusion arises, it should be noted that adult stem cells are basically those stem cells obtained from any source other than a human embryo before eight days of development—the term "adult" here is meant to illustrate that these stem cells have begun to "mature" in their developmental process. One general source of these adult stem cells that we have been tapping into for many years now—although without fully realizing what we were doing—is from bone marrow. Essentially, a bone marrow transplant is used to help restore a patient who has become dilapidated from the serious side effects of treatments for diseases such as leukemia. What we have come to realize is that what makes the bone marrow transplant effective are the adult stem cells present in the donor marrow. Another rich source of adult stem cells is umbilical cord blood. Such cells are usually referred to simply as cord blood cells, but they are indeed stem cells (the term "adult" simply becomes confusing here). Indeed, ongoing research is showing that human beings have stem cells in every major organ of their bodies, and that these stem cells can even be used from one organ or area of the body to help regenerate altogether different parts of the body. Now, it must be pointed out that even though there seem to be stem cells throughout the whole body, this does not necessarily mean it will be easy to isolate and harvest these adult stem cells—nevertheless, the stem cells are there! And, given the incredible advances that are being made almost daily with adult stem cell research, embryonic stem cell research is years and years behind (perhaps even decades) the current therapeutic application of adult and cord blood stem cells for human patients. Thus, even looking at this as just a practical matter for public policy, there is no need to gather "leftover" embryos, as some call them, or to create new "genetically matched" embryos from cloning, in order to "harvest" their stem cells—a process that results in the destruction of the embryo.

However, what if there were no successes or advances coming from adult stem cell research? What if cord blood contained no useful stem cells? In short, what if embryonic stem cells were our only source of hope for fighting the devastating diseases cited earlier? The Catholic position remains clear. Harvesting stem cells from an embryo—cloned or otherwise—destroys a human being, a living member of the human community. This is tantamount to taking the vital organs from one person, resulting in her or his death, in order to transplant those organs into other persons to save their lives. Although one's motives may be noble, the act itself is objectively evil. We cannot actively and directly harm or kill one human life to save another—or even multiple others. And so, even if embryonic stem cell research were the only way to fight many human diseases, these destructive procedures would still be unethical because they violate respect for persons—which includes all human beings as worthy of respect from the moment of conception on—and because they fail to promote the true common good.

In many respects, these topics are among the most technical ones discussed in this book, and it is easy to be overwhelmed by both the scientific and the ethical sides of these dilemmas. But the authors in this fourth part of the book will help guide readers through these difficult issues, exploring the deeper nuances of the ideas previewed in this introduction. These essays also help correct the mistaken notion that the Catholic Church is old-fashioned, anti-science, and out of step with the contemporary world. Indeed, the Church's wise caution regarding genetics, cloning, and stem cell research flows out of its ongoing study of these issues—an ongoing study that reflects the Catholic commitment to living *in* the world, though never living *for* the world. And so, we will begin with Kevin D. O'Rourke, O.P., and his essay titled "Genetics and Ethics." Throughout his discussion, O'Rourke provides a helpful overview for readers of the future prospects for genetic therapies, including the specific connection between genetic research and stem cell therapy. However, O'Rourke focuses on three pressing ethical issues that will have a direct impact upon Catholic health care providers: genetic testing and counseling, stem cell research and Church teaching, and stem cell research and the desire to prolong life indefinitely. The issue of testing raises caution over what genetic screening actually tells us— O'Rourke reminds us that genetic tests can provide indicators, but not certitude regarding future diseases. Thus, the concern related to testing is genetic counseling, and addressing how genetic information should be presented to patients. Unfortunately, as O'Rourke notes, trained genetic counselors are few, and so Catholic health care providers need to address ways to appropriately fill this void as genetic research grows and expands. In regard to stem cell research and Church teaching, the specific concern arises over embryonic research and problems of cooperation. Again, O'Rourke provides a helpful overview of the Catholic tradition's position, while also noting that more development of Church teaching will be needed as genetic and embryonic research advance in the secular forum. How will Catholic health care respond to the "knowledge" gained from these forms of research? Finally, O'Rourke ends his essay by reflecting on the "deeper" issue that seems to be at the heart of contemporary medicine—the desire to prolong our lives indefinitely. O'Rourke sums up his concerns regarding the increasing focus upon genetic research as the means to extend human life in this manner: "It seems entirely possible that health care providers will neglect our nation's more important health priorities: universal health care coverage and compassionate care of the dying. Spiritual values are not strongly present in our health care efforts. The poor and severely debilitated do not receive much attention. Moreover, the health care community could become so concerned about enhancing and extending the life of U.S. citizens that it neglects the more basic health care needs of the rest of the world."

In the second essay in this part, Catherine Green leads the reader in a reflection called "Genetic Enhancement as Freedom of Choice: The Myth." Green organizes her careful and detailed discussion of the ethical issues associated with genetic enhancement technologies around three general categories. First, she address several foundational questions regarding what we mean in the public forum by terms such as "disease," "health," and "abnormality," which in turn affects our understanding of "enhancement" versus "treatment"—a distinction which she notes is far from clear. Next, Green addresses the popular argument that genetic enhancement is simply a matter of personal rights and freedom of choice. In particular, genetic enhancement can be viewed as increasing current parenting options for improving the lives of our children—so much so, that given the state of technology in society, enhancement could quickly become viewed as a moral obligation for parents. Unfortunately, the language of choice and obligation ultimately leads to the legalistic approach of rights—an approach that is inherently adversarial. For her part, Green argues, "The problem of the good use of genetic technology, however, is not automatically a problem of law, but rather a problem of morality." In this light, Green begins her ethical reflection on genetic enhancement as an issue of freedom of choice with a consideration of what it means to be a human person and what constitutes genuine human happiness. Green makes a special appeal here to the work of the noted French philosopher Yves R. Simon. In particular, Green argues that rather than adding to our freedom of choice, the availability of genetic enhancement could in actuality limit our freedom instead, especially as social pressures come to bear upon individuals to seek out such enhancements. In the end, Green makes it clear that she is not arguing against genetic enhancement in general, while also pointing out that the proper discernment regarding the ethics of such research will not always be easy or clear. And so, while there may be some good to gain, she warns: "Because of the complexity of the natural environment and the limitations of our human understanding we may never know enough about the impact of our genetic enhancements to make it reasonably safe to use them well." Nevertheless, Green maintains that the best approach to take in looking for the "good" in genetics begins with keeping in mind what we are as human persons.

The final essay in this part of the book is my own, and provides an in-depth analysis of stem cell research and its connection to what some want to term "therapeutic" cloning. In "Stem Cells, Cloning, and the Human Person," I begin with an explanation of the basic science involved in stem cell research. A key element of my discussion is highlighting the distinction between *embryonic* stem cell research (which destroys the embryos from which the cells are obtained) and *adult* stem cell research (which does not harm the donor of the stem cells)—a distinction that is crucial to understanding the ethical nature of these two separate forms of research. I also review the current progress of both embryonic stem cell research and adult stem cell research, and explain the challenges that both avenues of research still have to face. The particular issue of "therapeutic" cloning is addressed at this point in the essay because it is raised as a means for solving one of the most serious difficulties facing embryonic stem cell research—the problem of immune rejection. Once the basics of the research have been laid out, I then present a twofold argument against both embryonic stem cell research and "therapeutic" cloning. First, based upon the discussion of the current therapeutic advances in both embryonic and adult stem cell research, it is shown that human regenerative medicine can be promoted through the use of adult stem cell research alone, thus obviating the need for embryonic stem cell research. And, if embryonic stem cell research is not necessary, then neither is "therapeutic" cloning. As such, continued funding for this research is drawing away valuable resources that could be used to find legitimate cures for serious human diseases. The thrust of this first argument is that, based on scientific grounds alone, there is no need to continue with embryonic stem cell research and "therapeutic" cloning. However, beyond these serious scientific shortcomings of the research on embryonic stem cells, I also present an ethical argument from the *personalist* perspective that any form of destructive human research goes against the common good, and so must be banned in human society. In the end, I point out: "If we continue to bow to the pressure of utilitarian arguments regarding the 'hope' and 'promise' of cures to deadly diseases, we risk a further erosion of the dignity of our common human personhood. However, if we stand against these attacks upon the most marginalized of all human beings—those only a few 'days' old in terms of the true start of our existence—our efforts can serve as a renewal in the struggle for restoring human dignity in our world today."

As the human community considers these various issues, the Catholic tradition reminds the world that opposition to the various forms of destructive human research addressed here flows from the shared dignity of all humanity, too easily forgotten in contemporary culture. As *The Instruction on Respect for Human Life* from the Congregation for the Doctrine of the Faith argued:

> . . . the fruit of human generation, from the first moment of its existence, that is to say from the moment the zygote has formed, demands the unconditional respect that is morally due to the human being in his bodily and spiritual totality. The human being is to be respected and treated as a person from the moment of conception; and therefore from that same moment his rights as a person must be recognized, among which in the first place is the inviolable right of every innocent human being to life.[8]

We must constantly assert this truth in our world today, and hold accountable those who would undermine our common dignity by attempting to reduce human beings to mere products.

NOTES

1. *Catechism of the Catholic Church,* English Translation for the United States of America (New York: Catholic Book Publishing Company, 1994), #2292, p. 552. Regarding the Church's stance toward science, it is also helpful to recall the following passage from the Introduction, Part I, of *Donum Vitae:*

> The Church's Magisterium does not intervene on the basis of a particular competence in the area of the experimental sciences; but having taken account of the data of research and technology, it intends to put forward, by virtue of its evangelical mission and apostolic duty, the moral teaching corresponding to the dignity of the person and to his or her integral vocation. It intends to do so by expounding the criteria of moral judgment as regards the applications of scientific research and technology, especially in relation to human life and its beginnings. These criteria are the respect, defence and promotion of man, his "primary and fundamental right" to life, his dignity as a person who is endowed with a spiritual soul and with moral responsibility and who is called to beatific communion with God.

2. Ibid., #2293.

3. Ibid., #2295.

4. Congregation for the Doctrine of the Faith, *Donum Vitae,* 1987, Part I, 3. John Paul II also warned of the dangers of this line of thinking, and those related to forms of physicalism and naturalism, in his encyclical letter *Veritatis Splendor.*

5. For more on this see John Paul II, *Veritatis Splendor,* especially nos. 46–48.

6. *Catechism of the Catholic Church,* #2294, p. 552.

7. John Paul II, *Evangelium Vitae,* no. 63.

8. *Donum Vitae,* Part I, 1.

CHAPTER 8

Genetics and Ethics

Questions Raised by the Human Genome Project

KEVIN D. O'ROURKE, O.P.

Few enterprises have been as grand as the Human Genome Project (HGP). According to its leaders, the project is "an ambitious effort to understand hereditary instructions that make each of us unique."[1] It is intended "to find the location of the 30,000 or so human genes and to read the entire genetic script, all three billion bits of information, by the year 2005."

Researchers have announced that, although some chores remain, the task of identifying and sequencing the human genome is substantially complete. The ultimate goal of the HGP is to decode, letter by letter, the exact sequence of all three billion nucleotide base pairs that make up the human genome. Researchers hope this knowledge will lead to new technologies that can, first, identify defective genes, and, second, either neutralize their debilitating qualities or replace them entirely with "good genes." In the future, genetic science may even be able to wipe out some diseases altogether. The HGP's potential benefits seem endless.

In the past, physicians diagnosed an illness as the result of a clinical examination, confirming it through biomedical testing. Those procedures are becoming obsolete, according to the HGP's leaders:

This article originally appeared in *Health Progress* (March–April 2001): 28–32. Copyright © 2001 by the Catholic Health Association. Reprinted with permission.

On the horizon is a new era of molecular medicine characterized less by testing symptoms and more by looking to the most fundamental causes of diseases. Rapid and more specific diagnostic tests will make possible earlier treatments of countless maladies. Medical researchers will be able to devise novel therapeutic regimens based on new classes of drugs, immunotherapy techniques, avoidance of environmental conditions that trigger disease, and even replacement of defective genes.[2]

Francis S. Collins, M.D., the HGP's director, has long maintained that medicine would make amazing strides as a result of genetic research. Some of the developments Collins predicted are already in motion. They include the following:

- Each year clinical labs in this country perform millions of tests aimed at detecting potential or actual diseases caused by genetic defects.
- Newborn infants are screened for sickle cell anemia, a metabolic illness called phenylketonuria, and congenital thyroid diseases.
- Other tests reveal whether people predisposed by family history to develop cancer have in fact inherited dangerous genetic mutations.

Early detection of such genes allows people to begin therapy before symptoms occur. Genetic therapy for potential diseases discovered through genetic testing may be applied in one of three different ways: through splicing into human cells a healthy gene to displace the defective gene, by administering pharmaceuticals containing altered cells, or by stifling harmful genes by interfering with their protein production.

Still, we know that, although genetic makeup determines human physiology, it contributes only a *predisposition* to human behavior.[3] Human personhood "is embodied intelligent freedom, with many levels of human activity most clearly manifest and definable by its maximum activity, the power to integrate these activities."[4] Collins has borrowed the words of another intrepid scientist, Copernicus, to suggest that the HGP itself may be part of God's plan: "To know the mighty works of God, to comprehend His wisdom and majesty and power, to appreciate the wonderful working of His laws, surely all this must be a pleasing and acceptable mode of worship to the Most High to whom ignorance cannot be more grateful than knowledge."[5]

Genetic Screening and Stem Cell Therapy

Two dramatic applications of genetic knowledge have already made news.

Preimplantation Genetic Screening

One news story concerned a six-year-old Colorado child who had been born with Fanconi anemia, a genetically caused disease that normally results in death at an early age.[6] Her parents sought advice from medical scientists familiar with the illness. The scientists suggested that if the parents were to have a second child without the defective gene, that child's blood might be transfused into their daughter and save her life.

Because both parents had the Fanconi gene, their chances of producing a child who did not have the illness were only one in four. But the scientists were able (before implantation) to examine the newly conceived embryo, select from it a totipotent cell (one capable of generating a complete organism) that did not have the defective gene, and implant that cell in the womb of the mother. (They also destroyed those totipotent cells that did carry the defective gene.)

When the second child was born, blood stem cells from his umbilical cord were transfused into his sister. It is not yet clear whether the procedure, which cost more than $100,000, will save the girl's life. However, it *is* now clear that preimplantation genetic screening makes it possible to produce children without Fanconi anemia.

Stem Cell Therapy

Stem cells are pluripotent, capable of developing into any of the 210 types of cell that make up the human body. Researchers are conducting experiments to determine whether stem cells can be manipulated to develop in vitro in the same way they do in a normally developing human embryo. If scientists can develop stem cells outside the body, they may be able to use them in stem cell therapy—replacing defective organs in the human body. "Culture of the cells in the laboratory could be nudged down different developmental pathways to become heart, bone marrow, or pancreatic cells," as one observer has noted.[7]

The stem cells needed for such research are available. Scientists originally harvested the cells from "spare embryos" developed through in vitro fertilization and from recently aborted human embryos, but today they can cultivate them in the laboratory.

Stem cell therapy already seems to be an effective treatment for certain diseases, especially diseases of the autoimmune system. Researchers report that some patients with lupus erythematosus have improved significantly as a result of being transfused with their own blood stem cells.[8] In this procedure, physicians collect some of the patient's blood stem cells and subject them to intense chemotherapy, after which they transfuse the cells back into the patient. The treated stem cells migrate to the patient's bone marrow, where they repopulate the deficient cells. Researchers hope someday to use patients' own blood stem cells to treat such neurological disorders as Parkinson's disease, Huntington's disease, and Alzheimer's disease; stroke; and problems resulting from spinal cord injuries.

How will health care providers deal with these new developments? Ethicists have discussed a number of issues arising from genetic mapping, especially those involving hiring practices and insurance coverage.[9] However, three ethical issues sure to affect Catholic health care providers have *not* been much considered. They are:

- Genetic testing and counseling.
- Stem cell research and Church teaching.
- Stem cell research and the desire to prolong life indefinitely.

Genetic Testing and Counseling

Any person planning to undergo genetic testing should first have counseling so that he or she can make good decisions based on its results. Counseling is vital because most people (including, unfortunately, members of the health care professions) are uninformed about the new genetic science and its developing technology. As a result, myth rather than fact dominates many discussions of genetics. Three facts in particular are often overlooked.

Disease Has Social Roots

The causes of ill health are social as well as genetic. As one observer has put it:

Poor health runs in families, but usually this has little to do with genes. The best predictor of health and disease is class. Tuberculosis and lung cancer may soon be diseases of the poor, and even for cancer, the chances of survival are related to income. Wealth and poverty are inherited, and most people who are born poor stay that way.

As important as this is to public health, nobody sees this as falling within the province of genetics.[10]

Testing Is Not a Crystal Ball

Knowing that one has a susceptibility to an illness, rather than certainty that one will develop it, is the best that can be expected from genetic testing. Some scientists were saying a few years ago that research would soon detect the genes that "cause cancer" and find a way to replace them with more dependable substitutes. Today, however, scientists see the development of a disease, especially an inherited one, as a much more complex phenomenon:

Nobody doubts that cystic fibrosis is a single illness. However, most inherited diseases are not due to errors in a single or a few genes: instead they are symptoms of a great constellation of failures. Sometimes a single error is involved in certain cases, but not others: sometimes inherited changes whose individual effects are imperceptible may together produce a disease . . . . Because some conditions have a largely environmental origin in some patients and a mainly genetic one in others, to unravel the causes will not be easy. Even then, it is not clear how useful the information will be.[11]

A Shortage of Genetic Counselors Exists

For a person undergoing genetic testing to respond intelligently and maturely to test results, he or she will need counseling from a professional equipped to consider the ethical implications. Unfortunately, few such professionals are available. The United States currently has only 1,600 certified genetic counselors; no more than 120 new professionals join their ranks each year.[12] Many of these, moreover, are untutored in the Catholic tradition. It is common, for example, for genetic counselors to recommend abortion in cases where amniotic screening suggests that a fetus has a genetic defect. How many Catholic hospitals have qualified genetic counselors in their obstetric-gynecological departments? And even if counseling is provided, how "Catholic" is it?

Because we have so few counselors, the job of explaining to patients the risks involved in genetic screening often falls to physicians. But physicians are not prepared to be adept counselors. A recent study revealed that, although 70 percent of the physicians and other health care professionals surveyed had discussed genetics with their clients, only 10 percent felt confident in their ability to do so.[13] In another study, nearly a third of the physicians who had received results from a test detecting serious mutations misinterpreted the findings.[14] A concerted effort is under way to teach physicians how to talk empathetically to patients about the results of genetic research and technology.[15] But no one should assume that a physician is necessarily competent to discuss genetic information or to conduct genetic counseling.

Stem Cell Research and Church Teaching

A second ethical issue, especially related to embryo stem cell research, concerns the manner in which such pluripotent cells are obtained.[16] Most are currently derived from two sources:

- Embryos declared "extra" in the process of in vitro fertilization.
- Newly aborted embryos.[17]

In either case, obtaining embryo stem cells in this manner is contrary to the teaching of the Church because it involves the destruction of human beings or close cooperation with those who destroy human beings (even if the persons destroyed were in but the initial stage of existence). When scientists first began using fetal tissue in research some years ago (before stem cell research became so prominent), they tried to do it with spontaneously aborted fetuses. But those efforts were not successful.[18] Spontaneously aborted fetuses do not seem to be a viable source of supply for research and therapy involving fetal tissue.

Not all embryo stem cells currently available for research are directly obtained from the remains of human fetuses. Some, called "cultured" stem cells, are developed from those thus obtained and sold to researchers.[19] In other cases, stem cells may be harvested from adults. The latter source is recommended by spokespersons for the Catholic Church because it does not involve the direct destruction of human beings.[20] Adult stem cells are effective in some therapeutic procedures, including those mentioned above for lupus erythematosus and other diseases of the autoimmune system. But the prospects for developing adult stem cells as a plentiful source of stem cell research and therapy are not encouraging. According to the National Institutes of Health, "There are some significant limitations to what we may or may not be able to accomplish with them (adult stem cells). First of all, stem cells have not been isolated for all tissues of the body . . . . Secondly, adult stem cells are often present only in minute quantities, are difficult to isolate and purify, and their numbers decrease with age."[21]

Would it be possible to carry on research or therapy in Catholic health care facilities or university laboratories with stem cells cultured from stem cells originally derived from aborted fetuses? The *Ethical and Religious Directives for Catholic Health Care Services* says that "Catholic health care institutions should not make use of human tissue obtained by direct abortions even for research and therapeutic purposes."[22] This statement (Directive 66) was promulgated at a time when research with fetal cells concentrated on transplanting brain cells for the cure of Parkinson's disease. Stem cell research had not yet become widespread. It seems, nevertheless, that the prohibition would apply to any human tissue used for research or therapy if the cells in question were obtained *immediately* from aborted fetuses.

But would Directive 66 prohibit the use of fetal tissue not immediately harvested from direct abortions? Would it apply to embryo stem cells obtained by the culturing of fetal stem cells? Although those using such material would not themselves be involved in the immediate and direct misuse of human fetuses, they would be cooperating with the persons who originally harvested the stem cells. What kind of cooperation would this be? Would it be prohibited because it was too closely associated with the killing of innocent human beings? In other words, would this type of cooperation be formal (intending the evil) or material (not intending the evil but involved in the action in some way)? And if it was material, would it be immediate (involved in the action in an essential way) or mediate (involved in a non-essential way)?[23]

A recent document from the Pontifical Academy of Life offers some insight into answering this question. The Pontifical Academy asked: "Is it morally licit to use ES (embryo stem) cells, and the differentiated cells obtained from them, which are supplied by other researchers or are commercially obtainable?"[24]

The answer is negative because (prescinding from participation—formal or otherwise—in the morally illicit intention of the principal agent) the case in question would entail a proximate material cooperation in the production and manipulation of human embryos on the part of those producing or supplying them.[25]

The Pontifical Academy's declaration, although not the official teaching of the Church, was developed within the tradition of prior Church teaching, and thus must be respected. However, two things may be noted concerning this statement. First, the response seems to grant that cooperation with the person originally obtaining the cells need not be formal cooperation (that is, one does not intend the evil of obtaining the cells from aborted fetuses). If it possible that material cooperation is involved, is it immediate or mediate? Immediate cooperation has a different proximate intention *(finis operis)* from that of the principal wrongdoer, but it is *integrally* involved in the sinful act. Mediate cooperation also has a different proximate intention from that of the principal wrongdoer, but is only *accidentally* involved in the sinful act. Distinguishing immediate cooperation from mediate cooperation is often difficult.[26] If the cooperation is judged to be immediate, then it could never be justified because the original act of harvesting the embryo stem cells from aborted fetuses is intrinsically evil.[27]

The Pontifical Academy's statement maintains that any cooperation "in the production and manipulation of human embryos on the part of those supplying them is proximate material cooperation."[28] This statement is not entirely helpful. The academy uses the term "proximate cooperation," but this term is usually used to specify a type of mediate material cooperation. Our concern is not with those who originally salvage or produce embryo stem cells, but rather with those who avail themselves of the opportunity to use cultured stem cells for research or therapy. Could we envision the person using cells developed in culture being so far removed from the original procurement of the cells that he or she would be cooperating with the original harvesting of the cells—but in a manner that could be judged mediate rather than immediate?

Mediate material cooperation is legitimate if there is a sufficient reason for it. This reasoning is based on the principle of double effect. In this case, the good effect would be the research or therapy that could be accomplished through the use of the cells.[29] The bad effect, not intended but nevertheless foreseen, is accidental cooperation with the original process. The issue is not a new one. People have asked, for example, about the ethics of using information gathered by physicians working in Nazi concentration camps. Though much of this "science" was worthless, it did seem to include some useful information concerning human reaction to hypothermia. Could such knowledge be used licitly by researchers who had no sympathy for Nazis and no connection with their crimes? The question was hotly debated. The use of cultured embryo stem cells will likely be hotly debated as well.

Stem Cell Research and the Desire to Prolong Life

Some HGP research and the technologies resulting from it may make it possible to extend human life well beyond the average life span.[30] Indeed, this phenomenon has already begun. The notion that only a long life is a good life is rampant in our society. Yet a sixteenth-century theologian, one of the first to consider aging and our moral responsibility to prolong life, maintained that "God does not want us to worry about a long life" and that "directly terminating our life is one thing, but not striving to prolong it is another thing."[31]

According to Catholic teaching, human life is not an absolute good. Charity, or friendship with God, is the only absolute good, so far as human life is concerned. Catholic health care providers are encouraged to foster this mentality, especially as they care for the dying.[32] Death is not the enemy but the gateway to eternal life for those who love God.

But how will a mentality that concentrates on extending human life to 150 or 200 years for those who can afford it influence our desire to serve God and neighbor? Will our culture try to deny that death is a part of life? We are mortal; death is not a regrettable accident. The philosopher Leon Kass has said, "To argue that human life is better without death is to argue human life would be better without being human."[33]

It seems entirely possible that health care providers will neglect our nation's more important health priorities: universal health care coverage and compassionate care of the dying. Spiritual values are not strongly present in our health care efforts. The poor and severely debilitated do not receive much attention. Moreover, the health care community could become so concerned about enhancing and extending the life of U.S. citizens that it neglects the more basic health care needs of the rest of the world.

People committed to the stewardship of scarce resources must be concerned about the products and programs emerging from HGP research. Attempts to extend life may well deplete the resources needed for basic health care. The ministry's leaders, our sponsors and bishops, have an obligation to keep our priorities in order so that the extension of human life does not become a primary goal of Catholic health care.

NOTES

1. *The Human Genome Project,* National Center for Human Genome Research, National Institutes of Health, 1995.

2. Ibid.

3. See S. Pope, *The Evolution of Altruism and the Order of Love* (Washington, DC: Georgetown University Press, 1994); "Colloquy Explores Genetic Predisposition," *Human Genome News* 7, no. 2 (1995).

4. Benedict Ashley, O.P., and Kevin O'Rourke, O.P., *Health Care Ethics,* 4th ed. (Washington, DC: Georgetown University Press, 1997), p. 7.

5. Francis Collins, "Human Genetics: Where Do We Stand?" *Origins* 26 (November 1996): 468.

6. E. Goodman, "Adam Nash Was Designed to Save His Sister," *St. Louis Post-Dispatch,* October 12, 2000; L. Platt and D. Carlson, "Prenatal Diagnosis, When and How," *New England Journal of Medicine* 327, no. 9 (August 27, 1992): 327.

7. N. Wade, "Scientists Cultivate Cells at Root of Human Life," *New York Times,* November 6, 1998, p. 1.

8. R. Kotulak, "Lupus Therapy Stirs Hope for Patients," *Chicago Tribune,* August 25, 2000, p. 1.

9. See R. Hubbard and R. C. Lewontin, "Pitfalls of Genetic Testing," *New England Journal of Medicine* 334, no. 18 (May 2, 1996): 334; American Medical Association Council Report, *Journal of the American Medical Association (JAMA)* (1991): 266; P. Reilly et al., "Ethical Issues in Genetic Research: Disclosure and Informed Consent," *Nature Genetics* 15, no. 1 (January 1997): 16–20.

10. S. Jones, "Genetics in Medicine: Real Promises and Unreal Expectations," *Milbank Reports* (New York: Milbank Foundation, 2000), p. 4.

11. Ibid., p. 8.

12. P. Boyle, "Pastoral Counseling Faces Genetics," *Park Ridge Center Bulletin,* September–October 2000, p. 13.

13. V. Lapham, "Genetics: Blind Spot in Medical Training," *Genetics in Medicine* 2, no. 3 (June–July 2000): 16.

14. J. Stephenson, "Group Drafts Core Curriculum for What Docs Need to Know about Genetics," *JAMA* 279, no. 10 (March 11, 1998): 735.

15. Ibid.

16. "Stem Cells: A Primer," *National Institutes of Health,* December 1999, p. 2. Available at http://stemcells.nih.gov/infoCenter/stemCellBasics.asp (updated September 2002).

17. Ibid.

18. See K. O'Rourke, "Research on Human Embryos: Ethical Perspective," *Ethical Issues in Health Care,* Center for Health Care Ethics, Saint Louis University Medical Center, January 1998; D. Dickson, "Europe Split on Embryo Research," *Science* 242, no. 4879 (November 1998): 1117.

19. See "Human Primordial Stem Cells: A Symposium," *Hastings Center Report* 29, no. 2 (March–April 1999): 34.

20. See R. Doerflinger, "Destructive Stem Cell Research on Human Embryos," *Origins* 28 (April 29, 1999): 770.

21. "Stem Cells: A Primer," p. 4; see also "Government Urged to Consider Stem Cell Banks," *The Royal Society of Great Britain,* March 8, 2000.

22. National Conference of Catholic Bishops, *Ethical and Religious Directives for Catholic Health Care Services* (Washington, DC: United States Catholic Conference, 1995), p. 24.

23. See B. Merklebach, *Summa Theologiae Moralis,* vol. 1, 8th ed. (Brussels: Desclee de Brouwer, 1946), pp. 487ff.

24. "Declaration on the Production and the Scientific and Therapeutic Use of Human Embryonic Stem Cells," Pontifical Academy for Life, Vatican City, August 25, 2000.

25. Ibid.

26. D. Prummer, *Manuale Theologiae Moralis*, vol. 1, 13th ed. (Rome: Herder, 1958), pp. 447ff.

27. John Paul II, *Veritatis Splendor*, nos. 80–81.

28. "Declaration on the Production."

29. B. Merkelbach, *Summa Theologiae Moralis.*

30. S. Hall, "The Recycled Generation," *New York Times Magazine*, January 20, 2000, pp. 30ff.

31. F. de Vittoria, *On Homicide*, ed. J. Doyle (Milwaukee: Marquette University Press, 1997).

32. *Ethical and Religious Directives*, General Introduction, p. 5.

33. Quoted in N. Wade, "Arguments over Life and the Need for Death," *New York Times*, March 7, 2000, section F, p. 4.

CHAPTER 9

Genetic Enhancement as Freedom of Choice

The Myth

CATHERINE GREEN

The Human Genome Project is essentially complete, with 99 percent of the human genome successfully sequenced.[1] Scientists and commercial institutions predict a bright future for the use of this information. For example, James Watson argues that knowledge of how the "DNA code works is the path by which human health will be reached,"[2] while marketers for corporations such as Monsanto and Eli Lilly pharmaceuticals tell us that genetically modified foods and drugs will allow us to combat world hunger and cure our most dreaded diseases. On the other hand we also hear voices of caution and fear. Genetic manipulation could cause irreparable harm to our environment or irrevocably alter what it means to be a human person.

The two goals of science are to understand the world in which we live and to manipulate that world in order to make it more congenial to our needs and desires.[3] The successful sequencing of the human genome may provide another basis for doing this. The problem for thoughtful people is

I would like to express my gratitude to Professors Lisa Felzien and Mary Haskins for their generous review of this manuscript and suggestions for improving its biological accuracy and readability, and to Professor Teresa Reed for her generous review and suggestions for improving the philosophical arguments. Also thanks to my husband, Thomas Taylor, for his careful editing of the manuscript.

to move beyond the rhetoric and the marketing to carefully consider whether and how to make use of this knowledge. Most people agree that the treatment or prevention of genetic conditions such as Tay Sachs or Huntington's disease is a good thing. Many people would also argue that the treatment of disease is an appropriate use of our scientific knowledge while the enhancement of our otherwise "healthy" human capacities would be wrong.[4] Genetic enhancement, they tell us, would be like the social eugenics of the 1920s and '30s, when Americans of low intelligence or those caught in a cycle of poverty and ignorance were sterilized as a matter of social policy.[5] Further, the atrocities of social eugenics carried out by Hitler's Third Reich remain frightening reminders of the horrors of the misuse of scientific knowledge. We would not wish to revisit any of those abuses. At first glance it seems clear, then, that genetic manipulation for the treatment of disease is a good thing while genetic enhancement is to be avoided.

A cursory review of both popular and academic literature, however, shows that the best use of such technology is far from clear. As a matter of fact, the amount of debate and discord might suggest that the issues are not amenable to much clarification or resolution. However, knowing how easily scientific knowledge can be misused, our problem is to explore what would constitute its good use.

In this paper we will specifically explore the argument that enhancement genetics provide opportunities for increased personal freedom of choice. We will begin by identifying several of the difficulties raised by the treatment/enhancement distinction. These include questions about what we mean by terms like "health," "disease," and "abnormality," and thus what we might mean by "enhancement." After briefly reviewing these issues, we will identify two common mistakes in thinking that serve to make the problems appear more intractable than they need be. We will next review the major aspects of the understanding of what it means to be a human person explicated by the contemporary philosopher Yves R. Simon.[6] This theory is deeply rooted in the classical theory of man that we argue is still relevant today. We will argue that this stable account of human nature helps us to think systematically about what uses of genetic technology might be conducive to our happiness as individuals and as members of the larger human community. In doing so we will respond specifically to the claim in favor of widespread use of genetic enhancement technology: that enhancement is an issue of personal choice. We will not argue against genetic technology in general nor will we argue that the good use of it will always be clear. We will argue that when we keep in mind what we are as human persons, we often can see more clearly those actions that we ought to avoid.

Treatment or Enhancement?

The first problem is to understand what terms such as "normal," "health," "disease," and "enhancement" mean. Is the child who is born of parents of short stature and likely to be significantly shorter than the average population "normal," where the child with a deficiency of growth hormone and likely to be equally short in stature is "abnormal"? We ask this question for two rather different reasons.[7] The first is the medical question of treatment as opposed to enhancement. Here the problem is to identify the proper domain of medicine. Would it be appropriate for medical professionals to treat both children and would it be appropriate for insurance companies or government agencies to cover the cost of such treatment? The second is the problem of whether "enhancement technologies" might create or exacerbate other social tensions.[8] Some of the concern here would be that people who are identified as "abnormal" might be placed at serious risk for social and financial isolation. People with disabilities currently struggle to maintain their place in the mainstream of society. With genetic testing, manipulation, and selective abortion of "abnormal" fetuses, would people with existing disabilities become more marginalized?

In the mid-1990s, the National Institutes of Health sponsored a task force to inquire into the use and misuse of various sorts of "enhancement technologies."[9] Their thought was that they would be able to develop guidelines for the use of genetic enhancement manipulations that would indicate techniques that would be more medically and socially appropriate and those that would be less so. After considerable debate the group arrived at the conclusion that the term "enhancement" was itself too ambiguous to allow for any clear account of its use or misuse. One problem is that most genetic technology interventions can be understood to be enhancements since they make a situation better. Certainly vaccines can be understood to be enhancements since they enhance our ability to avoid specific diseases.[10] Further, the question of the meaning of enhancement is grounded in the contentious understanding of the term "health," which can be understood restrictively as the "absence of disease," the definition favored by the medical community, or expansively as "a state of complete physical, mental, and social well-being," which is the definition adopted by the World Health Organization. If health is "the absence of disease," the person with HIV but without AIDS will be understood to be healthy, as would the person with the gene for Huntington's disease who has yet to exhibit symptoms. If genetic technology is only appropriate for people with disease, both of these persons could be barred from therapy! On the other hand, if health is understood to be "the state of complete physical, mental, and social well-being," almost all genetic manipulations could be seen as treatments rather than enhancements. There seems to be no clear distinction between the two.

Robert F. Murray would argue that to try to define genetic health is futile and even dangerous. He argues that health can only be defined in terms of specific persons, under specific conditions, and at certain times.[11] This takes into account the idea that an 80-year-old person with mild hypertension is considered healthy, where a 35-year-old in the same state would be considered not very healthy. It also makes sense of the idea that a person with otherwise serious genetic abnormalities may yet be healthy, for example, an active person with Down syndrome. The term "health," he argues, is descriptive of a person and cannot be understood except in the context of particular people. Further, if the term "genetic health" refers to the absence of genetic characteristics that would lead to potentially destabilizing relations within the person or in the relation between the person and his/her environment, then no person would/could be understood to be healthy.[12] It is estimated that each individual carries at least four or five genetic "abnormalities" that will actually or could, under the right circumstances, lead to some disease or troublesome pathology. It is "normal" to be "abnormal" in some ways.

Evelyn Fox Keller notes that we are increasingly trying to define "normal" in terms of the human genome "where 'health' is defined in reference to a tacit norm, signified by '*the* human genome,' and in contradistinction to a state of unhealth (or abnormality), indicated by an ever growing list of conditions characterized as 'genetic diseases.'"[13] The human genome is not, however, the genetic makeup of any one person. It is the compilation of genetic material from an undisclosed number of undisclosed people. When scientists say that they know 99 percent of the human genome they mean they know a great deal about the sequence of the persons whose genetic material was used in the genome project. This information cannot necessarily tell us much about health or disease in any individual person. Scientists estimate that there is greater diversity among individual human persons within a racial or ethnic group than there are differences between groups.[14]

What this means is that there is a great deal more we do not know about the relationship between any one person's genetic makeup and the "human genome" than we do know. We may know a great deal about humans as a species and yet know little about the role or importance of the vast individual variations found among human persons. Thus the distinction between genetic health and disease can make sense only in the context of specific people with specific differences in specific situations.

Further, a genetic difference is not necessarily a problem. There are some genetic "abnormalities" that clearly confer an advantage for the carrier under certain circumstances. For example, one copy of the mutated gene responsible for sickle cell anemia confers resistance to malaria.[15] In equatorial regions where malaria is epidemic there is a significantly higher rate of sickle cell trait in the general population, up to 10 percent of the total population.[16] In this case, "abnormality" is generally a good thing! From the point of view of the individual, to have the sickle cell trait is clearly an advantage. Only where a person inherits two alleles for sickle cell anemia do they develop the debilitating disease. When we look at the group then, the presence of sickle cell trait, even with the presence of devastating disease among those with two alleles, provides for the continuation of the group. There is some evidence to suggest that there is a similar protection from typhoid fever conferred by the presence of the cystic fibrosis allele.[17] We are just beginning to understand the relation between our genetic makeup and disease, while we currently know even less about the relation between our genetic makeup and health. The notion of "genetic" health or abnormality, then, does not seem to provide a reliable guide for deciding which genetic traits to prevent or which to enhance.

One thing we do know is that this biodiversity is important for the survival of the species. Also, for every change we effect, there will be one or more unintended correlative effects that will occur. This is called the law of unintended consequences. For example, when scientists selectively breed poultry for an increase in egg size they find a correlative decrease in number of eggs produced.[18] From a simply pragmatic point of view this suggests that we ought to be exceedingly cautious about manipulating our genetic structure for any but the most pressing of reasons.

We have seen that the distinction between treatment and enhancement is far from clear. All treatments make things better and can thus be seen as enhancements, and most preventive therapies such as vaccines enhance our abilities to ward off illness or death. It looks as if the terms "health" and "disease" make real sense only in the context of specific persons and situations while genetic differences are not necessarily problems. Even with all these ambiguities in the terminology, we would follow Erik Parens in arguing that the common-sense distinction between treatment and enhancement is a good place to start thinking about the ethical nature of genetic enhancement.[19] For the purposes of this paper we will use a restricted understanding of the meaning of the term "enhancement," more consistent with the common understanding of the term. The term "enhancement," then, will cover "any interventions designed to produce improvements in human form or function that do not respond to legitimate medical needs."[20]

Enhancement as Free Choice: The Myth

Many today would argue that enhancement genetic engineering is not an issue of social eugenics as it was practiced in the 1920s and '30s. Rather, they say, it is about individual freedom to choose our genetic future. Evelyn Fox Keller argues that most people take it to be true that genetic manipulation is only about individual human health. "Genetics merely provides the information enabling the individual to realize an inalienable right to health."[21] Walters and Palmer note, "Genetic enhancements that are freely chosen by consenting adults can be distinguished from enhancements that might be chosen by parents on behalf of their young children."[22] They argue that there would be little moral objection to enhancements chosen by adults. In his book *Children of Choice,* John Robertson extends this argument about choice to parents as well. He argues, "It has become a matter of choice . . . whether their children have certain genetic characteristics."[23] To deny people "procreative freedom" is "to deny or impose a crucial self-defining experience, thus denying persons respect and dignity at the most human level."[24] Arthur L. Caplan argues, "In so far as coercion and force are absent and individual choice is allowed to hold sway, then, presuming fairness in access to the means of enhancing our offspring, it is hard to see what exactly is wrong with trying to create more perfect babies or better adults."[25] According to these authors, genetic manipulation is about private choices that increase individual freedom. The goal of genetic manipulation is to allow us to make good choices about how to live a healthy life and to make good choices for our children. In this view genetic enhancement techniques would be like other forms of medical therapy and people should be free to use them or not. So long as there are no social policies mandating certain genetic interventions, the thoughtful adult, at least, would have more options and thus more freedom.

It is also argued that decisions about the genetic future of our children, both as individuals and for future generations, are similar to the decisions we now make when choosing a school or a summer camp. Arthur Caplan argues that the pressures of our competitive contemporary society will tend parents toward using genetic information and enhancement technologies to provide better opportunities for their children.[26] He concludes that there is no clear ethical problem with doing so. "It is not so clear that it is any less ethical to allow a parent to pick the eye color of their child or to try and create a fetus with a propensity for mathematics than it is to permit them to teach their children the values of a particular religion, try to inculcate a love of sports by taking them to games and exhibitions or to require them to play the piano in order that they acquire a skill."[27] Robert N. Proctor argues that while there are many legitimate concerns that arise with the use of genetic manipulation in the context of procreation, perfection is not one of them. As Evelyn Fox Keller suggests above, Proctor couches the issue in terms of freedom of choice. "Arguably, perfection is no more the goal of genetic than of any other therapy. No one seems to mind when parents provide their children with balanced diets or stimulating day care; why isn't the spectre of perfection an issue here?"[28] With this he dismisses the subject. In this view, then, genetic manipulation for the enhancement of our children is simply another means to give them an advantage in an increasingly difficult world.

From here it is an easy step to the position that we would owe it to our children to provide such genetic "insurance." Several authors take precisely this position. Ronald M. Green, in his article "Parental Autonomy and the Obligation Not to Harm One's Child Genetically," argues that parents are morally obligated to make sure their children have genetic advantages similar to those enjoyed by other children in their surrounding environment. "Parents have a *prima facie* obligation not to bring a child into being deliberately or negligently with a health status likely to result in significantly greater disability or suffering, or significantly reduced life options relative to the other children with whom he/she will grow up."[29] He argues that this position is not about social policy. There should be no rules or regulations that specify genetic obligations for parents. Rather it is a matter of individual freedom and responsibility. Arthur Caplan argues that in order to prevent social stratification as a result of individual choices about genetic manipulation and enhancement, it may be necessary for society to take measures to assure that genetic enhancement opportunities are open to all.[30] It is an obligation of parents to provide genetic enhancement for their children and the obligation of society to make sure that access to such interventions is distributed evenly!

Philip Kitcher and John A. Robertson both argue even more radically that the reality of the advances in molecular biology and genetics make it virtually impossible for anyone now planning children to avoid its impact on their decision making.[31] The problem, according to them, is not whether social eugenics, as an exercise of individual choice, will occur, but rather how we will use it to shape our children's futures.

Like Caesar crossing the Rubicon, there is no turning back from the technical control that we now have over human reproduction. The decision to have or not have children is, at some important level, no longer a matter of God or nature, but has been made subject to human will and technical expertise. It has become a matter of choice whether persons reproduce now or later, whether they overcome infertility, whether their children have certain genetic characteristics, or whether they use their reproductive capacity to produce tissue for transplant or embryos and fetuses for research.[32]

According to Kitcher and Robertson, then, our real choices today are about how to use genetic technology to make our children healthier and more competitive. To do this we would have to investigate which types of genetic manipulations will achieve these goals. One sign that there is significant truth in these claims is seen in the increasing pressure that is brought to bear on women to undergo genetic testing through amniocentesis and to abort the fetus where genetic abnormalities are identified. Such arguments are often couched in terms of the best interest of the child, while the practice has the effect of negative eugenics—that is, determining the characteristics of future generations by preventing birth or reproduction of individuals with certain traits. At issue here are economic as well as social and political factors. A study on genetic mapping, published in 1988 for the U.S. Congress by the Office of Technology Assessment, noted that "human mating that proceeds without the use of genetic data about the risks of transmitting diseases will produce greater mortality and medical costs than if carriers of potentially deleterious genes are alerted to their status and encouraged to mate with non-carriers or to use artificial insemination or other reproductive strategies."[33]

We began with the idea that we currently have some knowledge about human genetics, and an increasing ability to test for certain traits in our children with limited ability to prevent or enhance them. We envisioned a multitude of ways genetic enhancement might be used to make a better life for our children and heard arguments that genetic enhancement is an issue of personal freedom of choice and is not really different from current parenting choices. From there it seemed an easy move to the moral obligation to do so, and finally to the conclusion that, given the state of technology, we cannot avoid doing so. All we can do, Kitcher and Robertson have argued, is to try to make good choices about *which* traits to prevent and which to enhance. We will argue, however, that the debate is far from over and that we do have many choices available to us. However, it is crucial to find some stable criteria to help us make our choices well.

Two Errors in Thinking

In the contemporary rhetoric about ethical issues in general and issues of genetic treatment and enhancement in particular, there are two presuppositions that are common and misleading. As we saw in some of the arguments about the nature of genetic enhancement and our obligation to provide genetic enhancement where it is available, the language used is in terms of rights and duties. Consenting adults have a right to use genetic enhancement techniques to improve their quality of life. Children have a right to be born free of genetic defects and have the best chance of a successful life. Where one person has a right, other persons or institutions have a duty to make sure that right is preserved.[34] Language of rights is essentially legal language designed to allow one person to press a case against another. This, then, is inherently adversarial language which pits one person against another and individuals or groups against society as a whole. It is not that a discussion of questions about genetic enhancement technologies ought never to be in terms of rights or duties. Rather, we argue that this language is only appropriately used after we already know what is good or bad in the situation and where we have reason to believe that the good of the person or group is not being adequately achieved due to the negligence or failure of other people. It is quite appropriate to speak of rights and duties where a social system has broken down or where historically a social system tends to break down. For example, because governments historically want to limit unfavorable political discourse, it is appropriate to legislate the right of free speech.

The problem of the good use of genetic technology, however, is not automatically a problem of law, but rather a problem of morality. That is, what is it that we ought to do because it is *good for us?* The prominent philosopher and ethical theorist Robert Sokolowski argues that "moral action" is where the agent reflectively takes the good of the other to be his or her own good.[35] It is not simply a question of good intention, since we can have good intentions without actually investing our particular actions with that intention. Rather, it is the expression of that intention in a particular action that changes the character of the action. Truly moral action expresses the goal and the reality that what is good for the other is also good for the moral agent. For example, in writing this paper, my good as the author will be achieved to the extent that I have developed an argument that is adequate to the reality of the problem and have clearly developed the argument such that you, the reader, can understand and recognize what is true in it. This is like the rather "old-fashioned" view of business that is behind the adage "the customer is always right." That is, what is good for the customer is also good for the businessperson. This is not, however, another way of expressing the more modern business goal of trying to find a "win-win" solution. This language of "win-win" does not necessarily prevent the possibility of losers; it simply assures that any losers would be outside the formal group where "win-win" is being pursued. The nature of winning is precisely that it is measured against losing. It is *essentially* competitive. To take the good of another to be our own good requires no such negative standard by which to be measured. This stance is *essentially* collegial or communal. Morality, then, is about trying to achieve what is good for everyone involved. Where language of rights asserts a duty someone owes us, language of goods allows the possibility that the good is mutual. It is not necessarily about my good over yours, but rather about our unified good.

We would argue that what is *good* for us is what is both logically and ontologically prior. We each begin by pursuing what we understand to be the good for us. Often, perhaps always, what is truly good for us is also good for others. This is because we are social and limited beings and we live in a limited world. What is truly good for us, then, must be achieved within this social and limited context. When we ask what we ought to do in a situation, generally we mean, what would make us happy or what would be better for us? This is the language and action characteristic of human freedom. The question of rights and duties arises when, as a result of actions or failures of action by others, we are prevented from pursuing or achieving our good.

Then we turn to someone for help. This is characteristically a problem of a *lack* of personal freedom. We would argue that what is good for our genetic future and that of our children is a problem of rights and duties only where our ability to act morally has failed or is likely to fail. Thus to conceive of all issues of our genetic future in terms of rights and duties is to place the problem in an adversarial domain and to preclude the possibility of actually achieving what is good for everyone. Where many people today decry the invasion of law into morality, they unwittingly reinforce this invasion when they make their arguments in terms of rights rather than in terms of what is good. Language of rights and duties is both helpful and necessary in certain cases, but the realm of rights is only a small part of the realm of morality.

People might argue that they prefer the language of rights over that of goods because rights are codified in law and have an objective character, where what is good for people is really known only to that person. This leads us to our second issue. This is often called the problem of "relativism" and is a problem of reduction. In many ways what is good for one person is quite different from what is good for others. Because we are radically unique beings acting in unique circumstances of time and place, what will be good for us in one situation may not be good in another and may not be good for other people here and now. The reduction we make is to assume, then, that there are no *common features* of what is good for us *as human beings* that can serve to help us think about what is good for us both as a group and as individual persons. We will argue that there are significant characteristics that have been understood to be important to our human function and happiness since the beginning of recorded history. These characteristics are stable across centuries, across cultures, and across genders. The development of these human characteristics is good for people. Analogously, we know that the characteristics of plants are such that they require nourishment, water, and sunlight in order to thrive. We can see and measure when they are thriving. Thriving is a largely objective characteristic. This is true for human persons as well. We can often, perhaps usually, see when a person is thriving or failing to thrive. Thus, people regularly say things like, "you look tired today," or "marriage seems to be agreeing with you." They are not simply noting that marriage often makes people happy, but that some aspect of our countenance conveys to them our happiness. The thriving of a human person, then, is both largely objective and to a large extent brought about by the satisfaction of those characteristics that are common to us as human persons. If we pay attention to these human characteristics we are much more likely to be able to discern some general principles that will guide our thinking about our good human genetic future.

Human Nature and the Pursuit of Happiness

The classic definition is that man, a human person, is a "rational animal." That is, human persons share much of the biology and determinations of animals but also have the ability to think about their own being, their past and future, and to manipulate themselves and their environment in very complex ways. While there is much dispute about whether there is a distinctly "human" nature, most agree that there are certain characteristics of those beings that we call human that allow us to distinguish them from other human-like beings such as monkeys or chimpanzees.[36] Further, from a strictly genetic point of view, scientists are able to distinguish human genetic material from other non-human sources. Thus even at the developmental stage of one cell, the being that is a human zygote is distinctly different from other one-celled beings.

Insofar as we are biological beings we are determined by that biology to express certain tendencies. There is a tendency to stay alive exhibited in our various physiological compensatory mechanisms. There is a tendency toward mortality exhibited in our cellular and structural decay. There is a tendency to satisfy our need for food, water, rest, and activity in limited amounts simply to maintain our biological nature. From a biological point of view we are limited creatures. We are subject to all the laws of physics and chemistry. We are, like all living beings, mortal.

We are also intensely social creatures. As infants and children we are essentially dependent on other human persons for our survival and our education. Isolation from other humans leads to a failure to thrive and, in severe cases, to death. We come together in communities to provide goods and services for each other, to provide protection from lawless beings, and for mutual comfort and support. However, our social tendencies are not limited to those that compensate for our personal deficiencies, but are also directed toward simple enjoyment and opportunities for altruism. In order to be fully human we "need" friends and loved ones to share our joys and our play, and to be the beneficiaries of our largesse.[37] In true friendship we are enriched both in giving and in receiving.

We also have the capacity for reasoning and reflection about ourselves and about our lives. We can recall our past, contemplate our future, and manipulate our world. We clearly do not all operate at the same level of rationality, but we belong to that species of being for which rationality is the norm. Just as we would identify a tomato plant devoid of leaves and fruit as a tomato plant, people with limited or absent rational capacities still belong to the category of human person. The pursuit of science derives directly from this aspect of our human nature. As a result of our ability to think about ourselves and about our reality, we raise questions that science, among other disciplines, attempts to answer. Further, this capacity for reasoning and reflection allows us to foresee, in a way, our own death as no other beings seem able to do. This foresight can bring with it both hope and despair and serves as a motivation for both science and suicide.

From our ability to reason and reflect derives our ability to make choices. We are clearly determined by our biological nature in many, perhaps most, of the kinds of things we need and desire. But we are not fully determined to act to satisfy any particular desire at any given time nor are we determined in the means we will use to do so. While my physiologic status may determine that I am thirsty, I must choose how to respond to that need. Because we can, even must, make choices about how to satisfy our various tendencies, we are free to choose or avoid acting to pursue genetic enhancement technology. It is precisely to this aspect of our human nature that the arguments in favor of adult use of various enhancement technologies are directed. Freedom to choose, however, is not without its responsibilities. We all know that where we have fewer options it is often easier to make a choice. Thus as the development of technology offers more opportunities, we must be more careful in our evaluation of the options.

Classical philosophy and personal experience tell us that we always act to try to achieve our own happiness, what we understand to be good for us. About this we have no choice, it is given as part of our being human. Thus the teenager who steals a car in order to join a gang and the person who murders an enemy are both trying to bring about their own happiness. Clearly, however, we can be radically mistaken about what kinds of actions will actually make us happy, will actually be good for us. Yves R. Simon tells us that some actions are more consistent with *human* happiness than others.[38] The kind of happiness we all desire is both unlimited in scope and in duration. We do not simply want to be happy with our choice of beverages, but with all aspects of our lives and we want this happiness to last forever. Thus our desire for happiness inclines us to want to acquire everything, achieve everything, know everything, and live forever. Again, it is precisely because our nature disposes us to unlimited desires that we pursue genetic research and other forms of scientific exploration. Thus any argument against genetic enhancement or science as a whole on the grounds that it is somehow "unnatural" will quickly fail.

However, every particular thing that might bring us happiness is, by its very nature, limited and temporary. What we want is unlimited, where each particular object of our desire is precisely limited to the satisfaction of one particular tendency. For example, I want to be happy. A big piece of chocolate cake will certainly bring immediate, if brief, happiness. Everything we can really have will only satisfy part of our desires; money, spouse, children, even physical immortality is only a part of what we want.

Simon argues that our real freedom of choice is achieved precisely when we recognize that any particular thing we desire is limited, while the good we truly desire is unlimited.[39] In the moment of that recognition, any material determination we might have had that would make us act to achieve the good thing is absent. Whatever the particular good is, it would not make us fully happy. Why then act at all? This is the dilemma of the depressive person who sees only the limitation of the particular thing that could be chosen. Freedom, however, is clearly not a passive acceptance of the limitations of being and a failure to act, but is a power to achieve being. It is the recognition that the particular good is truly good even as it is both partial and temporary. With this recognition comes the power to overcome the inertia and to act to satisfy our particular desire.

Simon argues that many, if not most, of our actions are, in fact, determined by our material nature and our prior history precisely because we fail to acknowledge the limitations of the thing that is before us.[40] Freedom of choice is an exercise of the peculiar power that human beings have to *see* the limits of a reality and choose to accept it *precisely in its limited form.*[41] Thus we say of people who are addicted to drugs that they are *determined* by their physiology to keep using drugs. When they make the choice to avoid drugs, we say they are *free* from the addiction and acting more rationally. They have used reason to examine the limitations of both actions, to use or avoid drugs, and have chosen one that goes against their biological tendencies while supporting their rational tendencies. Our common language here takes note of this existential difference.

To sum up, then, as human persons, we have a variety of tendencies that we are characteristically trying to fulfill. We desire to satisfy our tendency for knowledge and exploration and to have an adequate and accurate account of our reality. We desire to satisfy our biological needs for food, water, rest, sex, and the like. We desire to satisfy our social tendencies for friendship, love, and generosity. We desire to be active and pursue our own happiness rather than to be passive or to be acted on by others. We are limited beings and we desire to know our limitations even as we desire to overcome them. We are not arguing that these natural tendencies are good because they are natural; rather, we are arguing that what is good for us is the development of those capacities that are most uniquely human: reasoning, free choice, and ethical action toward others. The evidence that this is true is in our lived experience of our own actions.

We said above that we desire unlimited happiness. While we desire unlimited happiness we are aware that there are limitations in all aspects of our life. One of our desires is to learn how to come to grips with this fact of our finitude. Hans Jonas discusses the importance of this need in his article "The Burden and Blessing of Mortality." Here he examines the philosophical meaning of the distinction between living and non-living beings that rests in metabolism. He argues that for living beings existence is procured by "doing." "Doing" here means metabolism as a biological function as well as the "doings" of higher organisms. The difference between living and non-living beings is in their intrinsic ability to change. With this ability is the necessity of change, where a failure to keeping doing and changing is death.[42] The ability to change is intrinsic to the being but is modified and limited by its environment. He argues that this possibility of death is a burden, in that living beings are always fighting against the possibility of death. He also argues that it is precisely in this struggle that all value is found. Prior to life there is merely existence. Stones exist but experience no "value" of their existence. With life comes concern at the most primitive level about nonexistence. Life, then, is intrinsically better than death and sentient life is better than simple life, as evidenced by the evolutionary motion toward life and toward high levels of sentience as well as by the subjective reports of people whose lives are or might be limited.[43] In sentience higher life forms bring with them an increasing capacity for concern about death. The burden of life is the ever-pressing *possibility* of death.

The blessing, Jonas argues, rests in the *certainty* of death. Biological diversity is achieved precisely by the death of some species or traits. "The term *evolution* itself already reveals the *creative* role of individual finitude, which has decreed that whatever lives *must* also die. For what else is natural selection with its survival premium, this main engine of evolution, than the use of death for the promotion of novelty, for the favoring of diversity, and for the singling out of higher forms of life with the blossoming forth of subjectivity?"[44] If all value in the world is found in the concern about living and death, all meaning in human life comes from the recognition of this concern and the meaning one sees in it. Jonas argues that "mortality" and its correlative "natality"[45] (birth) are the source of creativity in human history. From many points of view—environmental, political, and social—we can see the good that comes from one generation passing along the torch to the next. Materially, our world cannot support unlimited numbers while politically and socially we need both the energy and creativity of the youth and the skepticism and inertia of the elderly to maintain vibrant yet stable social environments where people of all ages can thrive.

Individually, he argues, mortality is also a blessing. We are finite beings in a finite environment, subject to finite laws of nature. Identity, he argues, rests with our connection to our self. Since our physical being is constantly changing, human identity rests with our relation to the past. To live interminably is to lose the connection to the past and thus to lose our identity. Conversely to maintain the connection to the past is to lose the present, an equally unhappy outcome.[46] Jonas notes that none of this discussion relieves the burden of the ever present possibility of death nor is the reality of death a blessing except after a completed lifetime.[47] Mortality, then, is an important aspect of our human being. It is the limit from which we can and must draw meaning. Again, then, the characteristics of our human person include the capacity to think rationally, to act from choices, to live in society, and to achieve meaning from our mortality.

As we mentioned above, Simon argues that some actions are more compatible with what it takes to achieve human happiness than others.[48] Given that human beings are complex organisms with multiple tendencies, human happiness is never assured. Simon argues that actions compatible with human happiness are characterized in four ways: (1) they must be compatible with our specifically human nature; (2) they must arise from within our own being; (3) they must be enjoyable in peace; (4) they must be enjoyable in common.

We will briefly discuss each in turn. First, actions that are compatible with human happiness must be compatible with our specifically human nature. This means that actions that go against any one of our characteristic tendencies will tend to bring unhappiness. For example, if we act irrationally, or fail to care for our physical needs, if we are asocial or antisocial or if we ignore the limits of our finite being, we will not tend to be happy. He gives a very instructive account of the relation between pleasure and happiness here. Pleasure, he argues, usually attends the satisfaction of any tendency. Thus we experience pleasure when we learn new things, make our own choices, achieve a goal we have set, and when we satisfy our bodily-sensual tendencies. Sometimes however, real achievement leads to pain. This, he argues, is a problem of order. Given that human beings are complex organisms there is *necessarily* a hierarchy in the order of the satisfaction of the various tendencies. We see this biologically in the physiologic compensatory mechanisms that assure blood to the brain as the priority under adverse conditions.

The pain that results from the satisfaction of a tendency is the sign that this action has disrupted the good order of the organism as a whole. Thus if we satisfy our desire for food to too great a degree, we gain weight, which leads to heart and joint problems. If we satisfy our desire for sex under imprudent conditions we get unwanted pregnancies or STDs. This follows for all the human tendencies, even that of reasoning and searching for knowledge. This is what Plato is getting at in Book VII of the *Republic*, where he argues that the philosopher must return to the cave. It is not possible to survive if we pursue knowledge to the exclusion of all else. As humans we still have to eat, sleep, and live in the world.

Because our human desires, as such, are not naturally limited, and because we humans have the capacity to reflect on our good, we can, we *must,* make judgments about how, when, and to what degree we should act to satisfy these tendencies. Again, since human desires are not naturally limited, each individual desire can become the source of an addiction. Simon argues that the problem of addiction is a problem of mistaking the necessary relationship between a part (one tendency) and the whole human person. The part is for the sake of the whole and necessarily subjugated to it. In addiction, then, when we experience pleasure at the satisfaction of a tendency and recognize the pleasure as limited, we mistakenly believe that unlimited pleasure or happiness will come with unlimited satisfaction of the tendency. Where drugs bring us pleasure we pursue more drugs. Where thrills bring us pleasure we seek more thrilling situations. In reality, however, only an accurate judgment about the relationship of a particular tendency to our whole good and the rendering of the proper order of the whole will bring about happiness. It is important to note that this requires the recognition of the natural limits of the satisfaction of each tendency and recognition of the limited nature of the whole person. Thus, like Jonas, Simon would argue that the recognition of our mortality is essential to our human happiness.

The second principle Simon offers is that actions conducive to human happiness characteristically arise from within the agent. This principle speaks to the human characteristic of being able to make choices and pursue what we believe is good for us. What this means is that we are happier when we are active in situations rather than passive, when we act of our own accord rather than under coercion or threat, and when we conceive our own goals rather than having them set for us. Human happiness arises in part, then, from the exercise of this unique human power of free choice.

The third and fourth principles are closely related. Actions conducive to human happiness are enjoyable in peace and in common. These speak to our nature as limited and as social. Actions that are enjoyable in peace are ones that are not conducive to agitation, frenzy, addiction, and the like. Here, he is talking about both internal peacefulness and peaceful relations with those around us. Internally, this could include things such as not drinking so much caffeine that we become jittery, or not putting ourselves into situations that cause unnecessary or unremitting anxiety. Personally and socially it means avoiding actions that might result in the violent expression of our own or other people's ideas and desires. Actions that are not enjoyable in common are those that we would feel inclined to hide from others or actions that make it more difficult for us to interact with the whole community of human persons. This would include things like exercising unnecessary power over others, or using other people as the instruments of our desires or of our success.

Our language about these matters is instructive. We tend to say that there is something "wrong" with a person who never bothers to use his or her intelligence to think through problems, or with the person who allows others to make all the decisions, or the person who is totally isolated from the community, or the person who has to be on the move all the time and can never sit still. This "wrong" is not simply a moral statement, but a statement about the nature of what it means to be a human person and how the particular individual fails to live up to what he or she is. It is the recognition of the ontological reality the person fails to express adequately. We would argue that this understanding of what leads to happiness is true for all people, all cultures, and all the time. Thus people with severe developmental or physical disabilities will be happier to the extent that they are able to learn, to interact with others, to love and be loved, and to do things for themselves. Of course this applies to people in developing countries, in remote villages of Africa or China as well. Having the possibility to satisfy our human tendencies to the extent that we are really able to do so makes us happier.

Given our characteristic tendencies as human persons, then, and the necessary order among those tendencies demanded by the complexity of our organic being, we can begin to think more fruitfully about what kinds of genetic manipulation and enhancements might actually be good for us, that is, actions that would be conducive to our individual and our collective human good.

Enhancement Genetics and Freedom of Choice

As we saw above, much of the rhetoric in favor of genetic enhancement is in terms of personal freedom. It is argued that so long as people are able to freely choose or avoid enhancement techniques, such techniques simply add to their available options. This is a very attractive claim and calls for investigation. I would argue that there are several reasons why this claim ought not be accepted at face value.

Perhaps the most important concern here is that it presupposes that individuals who exercise their genetic enhancement options do so in isolation from their biological and social environments. If we cannot exercise these choices in isolation then genetic enhancement would not be a simply "personal" choice. It is important to recall that Newton's second law of physics—"for every action there is an equal and opposite reaction"—has its analogue in biology and in social sciences. In genetics the reaction may be neither equal nor opposite, but may in fact be exponential. This is clearly true in germ-line (egg and sperm cell) enhancement techniques, where technology would alter the genetic structure not only of the individual but also of all offspring. Thus, while it might make economic sense to think about correcting or enhancing a trait for all future generations, this clearly moves the issue outside the realm of "personal" choice and freedom. Further, it is increasingly clear that individual genetic expression, that is, the expression of a particular genetic possibility in a person, is influenced in very complex ways by the environment.[49] We saw above the example of sickle cell trait as a genetic mechanism for protecting people from malaria. Clearly the environment alters the expression of our genetic makeup in other ways as well. We are taller because we have a better diet. We also have direct genetic alterations in the form of a variety of mutogenic compounds that have been introduced into the environment. Some of these environmental influences on genetic expression and genetic makeup we understand, if in a limited way. Many we do not.

Conversely, alterations even in individual genetic characteristics may have an impact on the environment of our body, of the world around us, or on society. For example the techniques used in gene therapy for cases like severe combined immune deficiency syndrome (SCIDS), as well as Parkinson's disease, involve inserting "corrected" genetic material into the bloodstream or the brain of a patient with the disease. The goal is that the corrected genetic material will grow and foster the development of healthy immune cells or healthy brain cells in the patient. One potential problem, noted by some researchers but considered to be unlikely, is that there are no means available to specify where the new genes locate in the body and thus the danger exists that they could associate with and activate a proto-oncogene (a gene that might cause cancer).[50] In fact, two patients in the SCIDS study developed leukemia, which is the unregulated production of white blood cells. The genetic material inserted to stimulate their ability to fight infection seems to have caused an overproduction of other cells that fight infection. Unregulated cell growth, of course, is cancer. As a result the study was halted and other studies using similar techniques given more strict review until more is known about the issues.[51] In this case the risk was known and research moved ahead with some caution. The study was small, oversight was present, and the resulting outcome was devastating to those directly involved, but limited to them. Clearly, then, even somatic cell enhancement alters the environment within the individual person.

Is there also alteration of the more general physical and social environment? To my knowledge there has been none demonstrated to date. However, this might be understood in terms of the limited number of genetic alterations that have been attempted in humans. Moreover, it is clear that there are unintended environmental consequences of genetic alteration in plants. There are data to show that genetic material from genetically modified corn has been identified extensively in two remote regions of Mexico, far from places where genetically modified corn was being grown.[52] The effects of this genetic contamination are continuing to be investigated. Further, there is the much reported case of Star Link corn, where genetically modified feed corn that was considered likely to cause allergic reactions in humans contaminated the commercial corn being used to make various corn-based foods. In this case more than three hundred kinds of corn-based foods had to be recalled. What this suggests is that we must be very cautious in our genetic enhancement research, since the result may have effects beyond the intended effect and perhaps far beyond the particular people involved as well. For example, it is hypothetically possible that the genetically modified material that is inhaled by patients being treated for cystic fibrosis may be exhaled or coughed into the environment and inhaled by other persons, resulting in an alteration of the genetic material of their lung mucosa. To my knowledge this has been neither reported nor studied. However, given the environmental "drift" by cross-pollination that has been reported in genetically modified plants, there is reason to believe that similar "drift" might occur in some human genetically modified materials.

A second concern with genetic enhancement as an exercise of "personal" freedom is that it may alter the relationship between the person and other members of society. This can happen in two ways. It can change the nature of any particular relationship and it can serve as an impetus for others to pursue enhancement technologies. One goal of enhancement technology discussed in the media is competitive advantage. Currently there is an ongoing problem of the use of performance enhancing drugs by professional athletes. Genetic enhancement could be targeted in the same way. However as it increases the competitive advantage of one person enhanced, there is increased pressure on other members of the society to utilize enhancement techniques to restore equality.[53] Dan Brock argues that where enhancement technologies used for the sake of a competitive advantage become widespread, the effect of the competitive advantage would be washed out. That is, the field would eventually become more level again. The technique then becomes self-defeating.[54] This suggests that the effect could be exponential but perhaps self-limiting when all or most people shared the enhanced feature. However, this would be costly, both in personal and in economic terms.

Eric Juengst notes that one argument against enhancement in general is that it is a form of cheating.[55] As in the example of steroid use among athletes, there are social norms and practices that are undercut when enhancement techniques are employed. The enhanced athlete has an unfair advantage over the rest of the competitive group and alters his or her social relations by eschewing societal values and norms. Further, enhanced athletes change their relation to themselves. To win a marathon by taking drugs misses the point of the project. Juengst suggests that while competition and winning, certainly in athletic events and within certain limits and situations in social and political contexts, are a part of the goal, they are far from the whole of it. That is, there is a measure of good human action and a failure to live up to that measure ends up cheating oneself as well as society. I would suggest that the standard that is truly at issue here is not *simply* social norms but rather social norms that arise from our somewhat inchoate understanding of what it means to be a human person.

Again we would suggest that much of our difficulty in this debate rests with our difficulty in identifying a standard measure by which to evaluate our actions. As I suggested earlier, if we measure in terms of rights and duties, the standard we are using is legal norms and precedents. When we use the language of competition and advantage we take other people to be the standard by which we measure ourselves and our actions. Both these norms are essentially adversarial and therefore essentially contentious. A powerful and destructive myth of the Human Genome Project, I would argue, is to position "the human genome" as the standard by which we measure what is human. This is what Evelyn Fox Keller is suggesting is happening when she says "health is defined in reference to a tacit norm, signified by the 'human genome,' and in contradistinction to a state of unhealth (abnormality), indicated by an ever growing list of conditions characterized as 'genetic disease.'" The molecular biologist Walter Gilbert is reported to have argued that it is through knowledge of the human genome that we can respond to the ancient commandment "know thyself."[56] This again suggests that the human genome would be the standard for what it means to be human. If we use the human genome as the norm, we would measure ourselves only in terms of our biology and even then not against a norm, but rather against an impossible ideal! No one could be "normal." More importantly, in such a measure, we would utterly fail to address what it means to be a person, a self.

One problem, then, with competition-enhancing genetic techniques is that they tend to work against our human nature as social and as measured by what it means to be a human person. The athlete who uses steroids diminishes the real good of the accomplishment. That good could include the physical strength and endurance developed by the training and the activity of the race, the habit of discipline and hard work that attend the training and race, the sense of self-control and self-mastery that follow the intense preparation and competition, and the respect of fellow competitors and fans.

Further, we would argue that the use of genetic enhancement techniques is not only *not* an exercise of simply "personal" freedom, it is not really an exercise of freedom at all! Margaret Little warns us about what she calls the "ethics of complicity."[57] Her concern is that there exist very powerful social pressures that coerce young women, for example, into evaluating their bodies in terms of norms that are distorted, unjust, and cruel.[58] Thus women are drawn to various surgical enhancement techniques because their sense of individual self-worth is measured by these unjust norms. The ethics of complicity come into play when the medical community takes advantage of this lack of self-worth by encouraging expensive treatments while ignoring and thus tacitly condoning the unjust social norms that cause the problem to begin with.

I would suggest that this argument is true in a variety of arenas, including male beauty (e.g., baldness and height) and athletics. Where the emphasis in sports is moved from fair and disciplined competition to winning and obtaining multimillion-dollar product endorsement contracts, athletes feel pressured to do whatever is necessary to win. As Thomas Aquinas points out to us, the end or the goal in large part determines the means that must be used to achieve it.[59] Where the goal is simply to win, there are no inherent limitations on the means that can be used to achieve the goal. Thus the athlete can mistakenly believe that steroids are simply "useful," while the rest of us can be led to believe that genetic enhancements are necessary in order for us to prosper and to assure a bright future for our children.

However this position actually decreases our individual freedom, precisely by allowing our actions to be covertly influenced by these unjust and destructive external social norms. The athletes in this situation, or Margaret Little's young women, are free to do what they want—what they believe will make them happy—but they are precluded from doing what is good for them as persons and what is more likely to make them truly happy. That is, they are less free to act with integrity. Integrity means, in this instance, acting in such a way as to maintain the unity and function of the various aspects of their individual and social human character. Susan Bordo points out that the rhetoric of freedom in these arenas is subtly misleading and sometimes deliberately so.[60] Enhancement technologies may be explained as opportunities for individual people to exercise control over their lives, to make free choices, where, in fact, they are marketing strategies or Margaret Little's suspect social norms that subtly coerce people into seeking the enhancement. "Thus," Bordo notes, "we are not permitted to feel satisfied with ourselves and we are 'empowered' only and always through fantasies of what we *could* be."[61] This is what Peter Kramer, in his book *Listening to Pro-*

zac, calls "free choice under pressure."[62] This is not, of course, what any one of us means by freedom.

Yves Simon argues, rightly, that there are several levels of human freedom.[63] Initial freedom, he tells us, is simply the freedom to choose what is good for us or what is not so good for us. Our athletes and young women have this initial level of freedom. However, because one of our important characteristics as a human person is to act of our own accord, free from coercion and pressure, to the extent that we "choose" to go along with social pressure rather than act as we truly believe to be right or because we fail to take the opportunity to think carefully about what is truly good for us, we damage our own nature. We make it easier for us to be coerced or to act without due consideration in the future. In a perverse way we "choose" to give up our freedom.

It is the case that every time we act in any particular way we increase the likelihood that we will act that way in the future.[64] The experience of plastic surgeons suggests that this is true with enhancement plastic surgery. "Some surgeons acknowledge that once you begin 'correcting' for age, it is all too easy to start sliding down the slope of habituation. 'Plastic surgery sharpens your eyesight,' says one. 'You get something done, suddenly you're looking in the mirror every five minutes—at imperfections nobody else can see.'"[65] To the extent that we allow ourselves to be coerced by rhetoric and marketing techniques that tell us we must use various enhancement techniques to become or remain more competitive or financially successful or beautiful or even more healthy, we "choose" to limit our real freedom. We fail to recognize that our true good encompasses all the aspects of our human nature and can be realized only when these aspects are functioning in harmony within us, allowing us to function in harmony with our society and our environment. Thus, under certain circumstances, enhancement technology may limit our freedom of choice, not as a result of social policy as occurred in the 1920s and '30s, but from social pressure, an equally powerful force.

Simon argues that there are higher levels of freedom as well.[66] When we make choices that are truly good for us as complete human persons, we open up new possibilities for achieving what is good. For example, the person with a drug habit might make the difficult choice to avoid the desired "fix." While she may suffer from a withdrawal syndrome she also benefits in several ways. She has the money that would have been used to pay for the drug and she has the reality of being drug-free ... having avoided it once it is easier to do so the next time the desire arises. She has a sense of self-control, however fragile. Also she has the sense of physical health that goes with being drug-free. There are likely to be many other benefits as well, such as a renewed respect of family or friends. Each time she avoids the "fix" she increases each of these goods such that even if she breaks down, she now has this existential reality of having succeeded before. Simon argues that as we make choices against things that are not truly good for us we increase the real goods available. After a while the person is no longer choosing between good and not good, but between things that are all good. This is a new and more robust form of freedom. This kind of choosing becomes itself habitual, but in a new and very different way. He calls this the difference between "freedom of choice" and "freedom of autonomy." This becomes a habit developed as a result of rational deliberation and choice and is directed toward the good of the person as a whole. An example of this kind of habit is safe driving. When people are committed to safe driving and develop the habit of practicing the various techniques, they are able to drive safely without thinking about all the particulars, checking the view mirrors, watching their speed, etc. They can be thinking about many things, but the nature of this sort of habit is that when something occurs out of the ordinary, the direction of the habit toward the good pulls them immediately back to the situation. Thus they are driving along and see children in an unfenced yard playing with a ball, they "automatically" slow down and increase their awareness of the possibility of a child's darting into the street. Actions that support this habitual way of thinking and being are never without their connection to this thoughtfulness and the search for the true good.[67] Thus they are precisely not mechanical or determined only by physiologic "need." In the case of enhancement activities, then, those that would truly enhance our freedom and our personhood would be those *activities* that increase our own development and use of our various faculties, rather than technologies that are visited upon us.

We are arguing, then, that genetic enhancement technologies, while discussed as opportunities to exercise individual freedom, may be, in fact, the opposite. First, they are not likely to be simply matters of individual importance. Because we are social beings, our actions have an impact on others around us and may put pressure on them to follow our path. Because we are biological beings and operate in a complex and diverse biologic environment, we must take care that our genetic enhancement technologies not put stress on that biologic diversity. Because of the complexity of the natural environment and the limitations of our human understanding we may never know enough about the impact of our genetic enhancements to make it reasonably safe to use them well.

Neither, we argue, is genetic enhancement essentially or necessarily an exercise of freedom. It seems theoretically possible, at least, that some acts of genetic enhancement might support a person's real freedom to choose. But this would require serious reflection about the goals of the person and the providers involved. Since we are, in part at least, products of our culture, in which suspect cultural norms of beauty, perfection, and health are held, we will need to be exceedingly cautious about whether we are falling victim to subtle coercion in the rhetoric and the marketing of these techniques. We would not argue that all scientists, physicians, and biotechnology companies are trying to "seduce" us for their own gain rather than ours. We would argue, however, that there are increasingly many real and essential conflicts of interest between what these people are trying to achieve and what we might be trying to achieve by any particular enhancement technology.

Conclusion

We have argued that there is much ambiguity in the meanings of the terms "health," "disease," "treatment," and "enhancement." Given the inadequacy of our understanding of the role of genetic alterations in the promotion and prevention of disease (e.g., sickle cell trait) and the clear advantage of genetic diversity and some genetic mutations, the idea of a genetic "health" makes little sense. Further, we argued that this lack of knowledge along with our lack of knowledge about the effects of genetic manipulations on the individual and general environment should induce us to be extremely cautious in our pursuit of genetic technologies that would respond to any but the clearest cases of genetic disease. We argued that our best course in thinking about genetics and our future is to begin with the common distinctions between health and disease and between treatment and enhancement as they pertain to particular people in the context of their own life. These concepts are most significant when used to think about real people in real situations.

We also argue that the common adversarial language that is used in thinking about genetic enhancement, the language of rights and duties, is about winning, and makes it difficult to come to solutions that are good for both the individuals involved and the community as a whole. The goal of people is to live a good and happy life. There is no necessity for conflict in that goal. Thus we argue that the first order of business in thinking about genetic enhancement technology is to fix our attention on the particular people who are to be helped and to examine in what manner their good can be achieved. The questions are not about our goals as ethicists or philosophers or researchers. They are about the particular people for whom the technology is intended. What is their good as full and complete human persons, rather than as biological bundles of DNA? What actions would foster their relation to themselves and their lives and to the society within which their good must be achieved? We argue that to think in competitive and adversarial terms precludes the possibility of any really good use of enhancement or other genetic technology. It necessarily limits the good to some and not to others.

We have argued that a clear understanding of what it means to be a human person, to be the sort of being who has a tendency to think and reflect about past and future, to want to act freely and to make judgments about that past and future, and whose good is necessarily tied up with the good of others helps us think more clearly about how genetic enhancements might help or harm people. Thus we argued that while genetic enhancement for ourselves is often discussed in terms of the exercise of personal freedom, this may be a very mistaken and misleading view of the reality. That is, the use of genetic technology is not simply a personal issue because of the social and environmental impacts it might have. Further, we argued that it is likely that such action would not even be an exercise of freedom, but rather the result of significant social pressure that is subtle yet pervasive, what Peter Kramer calls "free choice under pressure."

Genetic manipulation and enhancement is not by its nature bad. There are many good uses for genetic manipulation in the treatment of diseases that cause us suffering. There may well be good uses of genetic enhancements in such areas as eyesight and the like. In order to think well about any use of genetic enhancement technology we will have to think about it in the context of a particular person in a particular situation, paying particular attention to the real goals of the enhancement and to the likely results such enhancement will have for them biologically, personally, and socially. Again, it seems possible that some enhancements under particular situations will be a good use of the technology. But again, we must keep in mind that here as with all other actions, there will be unintended consequences. Thus, we must be exceedingly cautious in our pursuit of these technologies.

NOTES

1. National Human Genome Research Institute, "International Consortium Completes Human Genome Project," www.genome.gov/11006929 (cited June 12, 2003), p. 1.

2. Richard Lewontin, *Biology as Ideology: The Doctrine of DNA* (New York: Harper Perennial, 1991), p. 67.

3. Ibid., p. 8.

4. Leon Kass, "NOW with Bill Moyer," PBS broadcast of July 24, 2003.

5. Justice Oliver Wendell Holmes argued in his 1927 Supreme Court decision in the case of Carrie Buck, "It is better for all the world if, instead of waiting to execute degenerate offspring for crime, or to let them starve for their imbecility, society can prevent those who are manifestly unfit from continuing their kind . . . three generations of imbeciles are enough!"

6. Simon's writings consistently utilize and reinterpret the best arguments from Aristotle, Thomas Aquinas, and modern realist philosophers to examine issues of modern science and to show the deep affinity between modern science and philosophy.

7. Erik Parens, "Is Better Always Good?" in *Enhancing Human Traits: Ethical and Social Implications,* ed. Erik Parens (Washington, DC: Georgetown University Press, 1998), p. 4.

8. Ibid.

9. Ibid., p. 1.

10. Ibid., p. 5.

11. Robert F. Murray, Jr., "Genetic Health: A Dangerous, Probably Erroneous, and Perhaps Meaningless Concept," in *Genetic Counseling: Facts, Values, and Norms,* ed. Alexander M. Capron et al. (New York: Alan R. Liss, 1979), p. 79.

12. Charles Culver, "The Concept of Genetic Malady," in *Morality and the New Genetics: A Guide for Students and Health Care Providers,* ed. Bernard Gert et al. (Sudbury, MA: Jones and Bartlett Publishers, 1996), p. 151.

13. Evelyn Fox Keller, "Nature, Nurture and the Human Genome Project," in *The Code of Codes: Scientific and Social Issues in the Human Genome Project,* ed. Daniel Kevles and Leroy Hood (Cambridge, MA: Harvard University Press, 1992), p. 295.

14. Joseph L. Graves, Jr., *The Emperor's New Clothes: Biological Theories of Race at the Millennium* (New Brunswick, NJ: Rutgers University Press, 2001), p. 204.

15. Daniel L. Hartl and Elizabeth W. Jones, *Essential Genetics: A Genomics Perspective,* 3rd ed. (Sudbury, MA: Jones and Bartlett Publishers, 2002), p. 253.

16. Ibid., p. 526.

17. Ibid., p. 537.

18. Ibid., p. 557.

19. Parens, "Is Better Always Good?" p. 25.

20. Eric Juengst, "What Does Enhancement Mean?" in *Enhancing Human Traits,* p. 31.

21. Keller, "Nature, Nurture and the Human Genome Project," p. 295.

22. Leroy Walters and Julie Gage Palmer, *The Ethics of Human Gene Therapy* (New York: Oxford University Press, 1997), p. 111.

23. John A Robertson, *Children of Choice* (Princeton, NJ: Princeton University Press, 1994), p. 5.

24. Ibid., p. 4.

25. Arthur L. Caplan, "What's Morally Wrong with Eugenics?" in *Controlling Our Destinies: Historical, Philosophical, Ethical and Theological Perspectives on the Human Genome Project,* ed. Phillip R. Sloan (Notre Dame, IN: University of Notre Dame Press, 2000), p. 222.

26. Ibid., p. 216.

27. Ibid., p. 222.

28. Robert N. Proctor, "Genomics and Eugenics: How Fair Is the Comparison?" in *Gene Mapping: Using Law and Ethics as Guides,* ed. George J. Annas and Sherman Elias (New York: Oxford University Press, 1992), p. 66.

29. Ronald M. Green, "Parental Autonomy and the Obligation Not to Harm One's Child Genetically," *Journal of Law, Medicine and Ethics* 25 (1997): 10.

30. Caplan, "What's Morally Wrong with Eugenics?" p. 221.

31. Philip Kitcher, *The Lives to Come: The Genetic Revolution and Human Possibilities* (New York: Simon and Schuster, 1996), p. 284; John A. Robertson, *Children of Choice,* p. 5.

32. Ibid..

33. U.S. Congress, Office of Technology Assessment, *Mapping Our Genes—The Genome Projects, How Big, How Fast?* OTA-BA-373 (Washington, DC: U.S. Government Printing Office, April 1988), p. 84.

34. Milton A. Gonsalves, *Fagothey's Right & Reason: Ethics in Theory and Practice,* 9th ed. (Columbus, OH: Merrill Publishing Company, 1989), pp. 230–31.

35. Robert Sokolowski, *Moral Action: A Phenomenological Study* (Bloomington: Indiana University Press, 1985), p. 61.

36. Lewontin, *Biology as Ideology,* p. 99. Francis Fukyama argues that our human nature is "the sum of the behavior and characteristics that are typical of the human species arising from genetics rather than environmental issues." *Our Posthuman Future: Consequences of the Biotechnology Revolution* (New York: Picador, 2003), p. 130.

37. Aristotle, *Nicomachean Ethics,* VIII, iv.5.

38. Yves R. Simon, *Freedom of Choice,* ed. Peter Wolff (New York: Fordham University Press, 1969), p. 46.

39. Ibid., pp. 115, 148.

40. Ibid., p. 124.

41. Ibid. Simon calls this "dominating indifference." That is, the person is indifferent to acting to pursue a particular good because that good is only partially good. There is no determination to act. This determination to act comes, then, from the power of the agent to act in the face of this "indeterminacy." Freedom is in recognizing that we do not have to act and then choosing to act or refrain from acting.

42. Hans Jonas, "The Burden and Blessing of Mortality," *Hastings Center Report* 22 (1992): 34.

43. Ibid., p. 38.

44. Ibid.

45. Ibid., p. 39.

46. Ibid., p. 40.

47. Ibid.

48. Simon, *Freedom of Choice,* pp. 44–52.

49. Hartl and Jones, *Essential Genetics,* pp. 550ff.

50. Jaan Suurküla, M.D., "The Failure of Gene Therapy," www.gene.ch/gentech/1997/Jul-Aug/msg00375.html.

51. Brandan A. Maher, "More Gene Therapy Trials Halted," *The Scientist,* www.biomedcentral.com/news/20030116/06.

52. Ignacio Chapela and David Quist, Seventh International Symposium on the Biosafety of Genetically Modified Organisms, ed. Ariel Alvare-Morales, www.worldbiosafety.net/title%20paper.html.

53. Dan W. Brock, "Enhancements of Human Function: Some Distinctions for Policymakers," in *Enhancing Human Traits,* pp. 59–63.

54. Ibid., p. 60.

55. Eric T. Juengst, "What Does Enhancement Mean?" *Enhancing Human Traits,* p. 39.

56. Daniel Kevles, "Out of Eugenics: The Historical Politics of the Human Genome," in *The Code of Codes,* p. 19.

57. Margaret Olivia Little, "Cosmetic Surgery, Suspect Norms, and the Ethics of Complicity," in *Enhancing Human Traits,* p. 162.

58. Ibid., p. 167.

59. Thomas Aquinas, in *An Aquinas Reader,* ed. Mary T. Clark (New York: Fordham University Press, 2000), p. 51.

60. Susan Bordo, "Braveheart, Babe, and the Contemporary Body," in *Enhancing Human Traits,* pp. 189–221.

61. Ibid., p. 209.

62. Peter Kramer, *Listening to Prozac* (London: Fourth Estate Limited, 1994), p. 273. He is here quoting from Thomas H. Murray, "Drugs, Sports and Ethics," in *Feeling Good: Ethics and Nontherapeutic Drug Use,* ed. Thomas Murray et al. (Totowa, NJ: Humana Press, 1984).

63. Yves R. Simon, *Freedom and Community,* ed. Charles P. O'Donnell (New York: Fordham University Press, 2001), pp. 36–46.

64. This is one reason why gangs have initiates steal a car or carry out a crime. Beyond bonding them to the other members of the gang, it makes them more "useful" in the future when illegal activities are in question. In this sense, human persons are like other physical things where actions reinforce themselves, e.g. the rope long coiled returns to its coiled shape. Our character, the "what we are" morally, is determined step by step by the particular actions we carry out. This is not simply a psychological reality, but an ontological/existential one.

65. S. O. Davis, "Knifestyles," *Marie Claire,* May 1996, p. 46, quoted in Susan Bordo, "Braveheart, Babe and the Contemporary Body," p. 204.

66. Simon, *Freedom and Community,* pp. 16–19.

67. Yves R. Simon, *Moral Virtue* (New York: Fordham University Press, 1986), pp. 58–61.

CHAPTER 10

Stem Cells, Cloning, and the Human Person

JOHN F. MORRIS

In this chapter I will explore the contemporary controversy surrounding stem cell research and cloning, and, from the perspective of the Aristotelian-Thomistic personalist tradition, how these technologies are impacting human persons both individually and in society.

Now, immediately some may object that as a philosopher, and not a scientist, I have no business addressing these growing areas of scientific research. I have been told that I, and others like myself who raise questions about the ethics of cloning and the destructive aspects of some forms of stem cell research, should simply "leave science to the scientists."

The thrust of this statement is, I believe, twofold. First, the implication is

Readers will note the numerous Internet sources referenced here. Given the open-ended nature of the Internet and the problem of "disappearing" postings, there has been a growing debate over the scholarly use of web-based resources. While I acknowledge the reality and serious nature of the concerns that are being raised, I have included such references here for two key reasons: First, the wide variety of websites referenced offers a better understanding of just how broad the debate over stem cell research is, including its international dimensions. Second, the field of stem cell research has expanded so much and so quickly over the last few years that many professional and scientific research journals, experiencing a growing backlog of articles waiting for publication, have begun to use the Internet for "pre-publishing" or "web-publishing" papers and research findings well before they appear in print. Thus, to keep up on the very latest advances in the field, it is necessary to reference these web-based resources. However, whenever possible, I have cited hard-copy sources, or provided future publication information.

that science and technological development are, and must remain, autonomous and pure in order to maintain the integrity of the scientific process. It has even been suggested to me and others that questioning the work of scientific research *at all* comes dangerously close to repeating the Galileo affair (at least as perceived by some in the scientific community) and hindering the pursuit of scientific knowledge.[1] Second, the more subtle implication is that if problems do arise with science or technology, scientists will police themselves and prevent harm from being done to society. In sum, the suggestion is that the world of science and research ought to be a "morally free" zone.

My response to this *laissez faire* attitude of "leaving science to the scientists" is simple and direct—ABSOLUTELY NOT! In the late 1950s, the English philosopher Bertrand Russell led an effort known as "the Pugwash movement," with the goal of global nuclear disarmament. Russell himself noted:

My purpose was to secure cooperation between Communist and anti-Communist scientists on matters lying within their technical competence, and, if possible, also on international measures related to nuclear weapons. I thought that a statement signed by some twelve of the ablest men living at that time would, perhaps, have some effect upon Governments and the public.[2]

Among the signatories was none other than Professor Albert Einstein. Certainly Russell led a noble cause here. Yet, Russell was by no means the only person concerned with the development of weapons of mass destruction. Countless other groups of people from all walks of life protested and fought for the same goal of nuclear disarmament—indeed, that struggle continues today. My point is this: was Russell's document any more valid than the multitude of other protests simply because he gathered the signatures of prominent physicists involved with atomic theory to point out the dangers of nuclear warfare? Such a suggestion is ludicrous. The development of nuclear weaponry is more than a matter of atomic physics—it involves *ethical* issues that are appropriate for all human beings to be concerned about.

In the same vein, I argue that I, as well as every human being, have both a *right* and an *obligation* to become involved with the debate regarding the destruction of embryos for some forms of stem cell research, and regarding human cloning as a method for obtaining more embryonic stem cells for such research. The destruction of embryos for research and the technology of cloning both affect the nature and future of humanity. These are issues for all of us, not scientists alone. Nor does the involvement of non-scientists hinder or impede the "freedom" of scientific researchers to do their work. Rather, this is simply a call for scientific and technological research to be conducted in an ethically responsible manner.

And so, in this chapter I will take a two-step approach to addressing these areas of human research. First, I will review the basic science behind various forms of stem cell research and what is referred to as "therapeutic" cloning that are at the heart of today's debates. A key element in this discussion will be the distinction between embryonic stem cell research and adult stem cell research—a distinction that is rarely emphasized in the media coverage of these issues, yet which is crucial to understanding the ethics of such research. I will also explain the connection between embryonic stem cell research and cloning—yet another issue that is clouded over by the media. It will be shown that not only are many public people concerned with where these technologies are leading us, but many within the scientific community condemn them as well.[3] Thus, this critique is not simply a "knee-jerk," "anti-science" reaction, as many try to portray it in the public debate. Indeed, part of my argument will demonstrate that embryonic stem cell research and cloning are not necessary for the purposes advocates claim. As such, continued funding for this research is drawing away valuable resources that could be used to find legitimate cures for serious human diseases.

However, beyond the mere scientific problems with embryonic stem cell research and human cloning, I will also present as the second part of this chapter an ethical argument against these destructive forms of research from the *personalist* perspective. Although there are many grounds on which to condemn such research, I will argue in particular that all forms of destructive human research go against the common good, and so must be banned in human society. If we continue to bow to the pressure of utilitarian arguments regarding the "hope" and "promise" of cures for deadly diseases, we risk a further erosion of the dignity of our common human personhood. However, if we stand against these attacks upon the most marginalized of all human beings—those only a few "days" old in terms of the true start of our existence—our efforts can serve as a renewal in the struggle for restoring human dignity in our world today. We must remind the world that opposition to destructive human research flows from the shared dignity of all humanity, and seek to hold accountable those who would undermine our common dignity by attempting to reduce human beings to mere products. In the end, even if embryonic stem cell research and "therapeutic" cloning were leading to effective cures for human diseases, this chapter will demonstrate that they are still unethical and so should be banned.

The Basics of Stem Cell Research

Our first task is to explain exactly what a "stem cell" is, and thereby understand why these special cells have become the focus of so much research and controversy. It should be pointed out that there are a number of sources from which one could draw to explain the technical aspects of stem cell research in its various forms. In the last several years numerous web pages have been developed to explain the research. There have also been informational pieces in magazines such as *Time* and *Newsweek,* and we have all probably seen and heard a variety of TV and radio programs attempting to explain some of the details involved in stem cell research. Finally, underlying all of these popular media sources are the "specialty" scientific journals, many of which, with the growth of these new fields of research, are booming, yet are not always the most accessible (both literally and figuratively) to the public. On the one hand, such wide exposure of the public to this issue has been helpful in raising everyone's awareness about stem cells. On the other hand, such exposure has been far from complete, especially regarding the ethical issues at stake— many people simply do not understand how anyone could oppose research aimed at eliminating human illness and disease. A particularly troubling aspect of all this media attention has been a variance in the "facts" being reported, whether in terms of the success of specific types of research, ambiguity regarding whether the research has been conducted with human subjects or is still only at the animal stages, or the dates given for when a zygote enters into the blastocyst phase (the preferred time for harvesting embryonic stem cells). And so, to bring some consistency to this first part of our discussion, I will follow the basic information regarding stem cells presented by the National Institutes of Health on their official web page.[4]

A. What Is a Stem Cell?

As noted by the NIH:

Stem cells have two important characteristics that distinguish them from other types of cells. First, they are unspecialized cells that renew themselves for long periods through cell division. The second is that under certain physiologic or experimental conditions, they can be induced to become cells with special functions such as the beating cells of the heart muscle or the insulin-producing cells of the pancreas.[5]

Thus, in general, stem cells are undifferentiated cells that have the twofold ability to divide for indefinite periods of time in culture and to give rise to more specialized cells. They are referred to collectively as "stem cells" because they are what all other cells in our body "stem" from. Indeed, perhaps referring to them as "root cells" would have been more appropriate. Now some people in the debate label these special cells "generic" or "blank" cells, since they have not undergone any differentiation in the developmental process.[6] The choice of rhetoric here is important—after all, a "generic" cell cannot represent a unique human person, right? However, if these cells truly were "blank," they would be of no value to the researchers who are working with them. Indeed, it is precisely the fact that these cells are loaded with human genetic information that makes them of value—they contain all of the information needed to become every cell in the body. Rather than being "generic" cells, then, stem cells are more properly understood as "master" cells which contain all of our complex biological/genetic information. Much of the basic research involved with stem cells is focused on unlocking the double puzzle of why these cells are able to remain undifferentiated for so long, but also what then finally turns them on to begin to develop into more specialized cells in the body.

B. The Two Categories of Stem Cells: Embryonic and Adult

1. Embryonic Stem Cells

The first key distinction to be made regarding stem cells involves the source from which they are derived. Perhaps the stem cells most familiar to the general public are those harvested from human embryos, which are thus referred to as embryonic stem cells.[7] As the NIH primer explains:

The embryos from which human embryonic stem cells are derived are typically four or five days old and are a hollow microscopic ball of cells called the blastocyst. The blastocyst includes three structures: the trophoblast, which is the layer of cells that surrounds the blastocyst; the blastocoel, which is the hollow cavity inside the blastocyst; and the inner cell mass, which is a group of approximately 30 cells at one end of the blastocoel.[8]

The important issue here is how these embryonic stem cells are obtained. All the NIH primer says is this: "Human embryonic stem cells are isolated by transferring the inner cell mass into a plastic laboratory culture dish that contains a nutrient broth known as culture medium."[9]

This sounds very nice, and relatively simple. And yet, the crux of the ethical objection to embryonic stem cell research lies in this act of harvesting the "inner cell mass" from the embryo. As noted, the embryo is at the blastocyst stage when the cells are harvested. The trophoblast, or outer shell, is a delicate structure at this point. When the "inner cell mass" is "transferred," a pipette is inserted into the trophoblast and ends up breaking it apart. What this means in layman's terms is that the act of harvesting embryonic stem cells *destroys* the embryo itself. In fact, because of its delicate structure at this phase, there is no way to obtain embryonic stem cells without destroying the embryo. If it were possible to obtain some of an embryo's stem cells by somehow pulling them through the trophoblast while leaving it intact, embryonic stem cell research would be viewed in an entirely different manner. But this is not the case—and so, we must not gloss over this crucial issue of how embryonic stem cells are obtained.

As the embryonic stem cells replicate in the culture medium, they are removed to other culture dishes as the process of subculturing continues. Finally, as explained in the NIH primer: "After six months or more, the original 30 cells of the inner cell mass yield millions of embryonic stem cells. Embryonic stem cells that have proliferated in cell culture for six or more months without differentiating, are pluripotent, and appear genetically normal are referred to as an embryonic stem cell line."[10] These stem cell lines can then be frozen and transferred anywhere in the world for further research and experimentation.

2. Adult Stem Cells

However, embryos are not the only source of stem cells. It is now known that there are stem cells in every major organ of the human body—but stem cells can also be obtained from umbilical cord blood,[11] placentas,[12] amniotic fluid,[13] the mouth,[14] the nose,[15] baby teeth,[16] human cadavers,[17] and even human fat tissue.[18] All of these are generally referred to as "adult" stem cells. Unfortunately, this often causes confusion. For instance, most of us would not think of stem cells obtained from the placenta and umbilical cord after a birth in terms of something "adult." Nor would we commonly think of the use of a twelve-year-old's bone marrow in a transplant to save her brother as being part of "adult" stem cell research. Nonetheless, all stem cells not derived from embryos fall into this category and are therefore part of adult stem cell research. The term "adult" here simply refers to the fact that these cells have undergone some degree of differentiation and maturation within the body.

Research on adult stem cells has actually been going on for much longer than that on embryonic stem cells. As the NIH notes:

The history of research on adult stem cells began about 40 years ago. In the 1960's, researchers discovered that the bone marrow contains at least two kinds of stem cells. One population, called hematopoietic stem cells, forms all the types of blood cells in the body. A second population, called bone marrow stromal cells, was discovered a few years later. Stromal cells are a mixed cell population that generates bone, cartilage, fat, and fibrous connective tissue.[19]

In fact, bone marrow transplants have been in therapeutic use for over thirty years now. It was not originally understood that it was the presence of "stem" cells in the bone marrow that made such transplants successful. However, with increased research the medical and scientific communities are gaining clearer insights into the role of our adult stem cells as the root of the body's own natural healing processes.

Another important factor that must be kept in mind is that even though researchers are finding adult stem cells in every major organ of the body, those cells are not necessarily present in large numbers. As the NIH points out: "One important point to understand about adult stem cells is that there are a very small number of stem cells in each tissue. Stem cells are thought to reside in a specific area of each tissue where they may remain quiescent (non-dividing) for many years until they are activated by disease or tissue injury."[20] Of course, this is not the case with stem cells harvested from umbilical cords and placentas, which yield a much higher number of stem cells than even embryo harvesting in a simpler and more efficient manner.[21] And, with the progress being made in helping adult stem cells to proliferate in culture, the "numbers" issue may not be important for much longer.[22]

C. The Potency/Plasticity of Stem Cells

The second key distinction to be made regarding stem cells involves their ability to become other cells. This is referred to as the *potency* or *plasticity* of the stem cell. As the NIH notes: "Embryonic stem cells can become all cell types of the body because they are pluripotent. Adult stem cells are generally limited to differentiating into different cell types of their tissue of origin. However, some evidence suggests that adult stem cell plasticity may exist, increasing the number of cell types a given adult stem cell can become."[23] To clarify this notion of "plasticity," one must understand the various levels of "potency" researchers refer to regarding stem cells. The most "potent" stem cells are referred to as *totipotent*—the idea being that such cells have the potential to become not only every cell in the human body, but a whole human being on their own. By the second to third day of human development, the zygote is composed of four cells. Each of these four cells is totipotent, and could in theory become a complete human being on its own under the proper circumstances. Between days four and seven, the cells of the embryo are described as *pluripotent.* A cell that is pluripotent has the ability "to develop into many different cell types of the body."[24] It is generally thought that a pluripotent cell can become any of the more than two hundred different types of cells in the human body. Finally, after the first eight days of development, the stem cells that remain in the human body are referred to as *multipotent.* A multipotent cell can become only a limited number of other cell types. The implication here is that after a certain amount of differentiation, stem cells lose their ability to be pluripotent—hence, the reference above from the NIH that adult stem cells are limited in their ability to differentiate.[25] In fact, if one goes back just two to three years one will find spread liberally throughout discussions of the need for increased funding in embryonic stem cell research the claim that adult stem cells are not as plastic as the pluripotent embryonic stem cells.[26]

However, if one examines the literature carefully, it becomes clear that this claim was really just an assumption made by researchers—primarily embryonic stem cell researchers—that was offered with no real scientific data to support the claim. Fortunately, not everyone in the scientific community accepted this assumption, and so research on adult stem cells has continued. Current research shows clear evidence that adult stem cells—even if not technically labeled "pluripotent"—are indeed "plastic," and therefore just as useful for therapeutic purposes, as embryonic stem cells. As noted by the NIH in their primer on stem cells: "A number of experiments have suggested that certain adult stem cell types are pluripotent. This ability to differentiate into multiple cell types is called plasticity or transdifferentiation."[27] Thus, as David Prentice, Ph.D., one of the founding members of Do No Harm—The Coalition of Americans for Research Ethics, a group that opposes embryonic stem cell research, noted in a paper presented to the President's Council on Bioethics in July of 2003:

... our current knowledge regarding adult stem cells has expanded greatly over what was known just a few short years ago. Results from both animal studies and early human clinical trials indicate that they have significant capabilities for growth, repair, and regeneration of damaged cells and tissues in the body, akin to a built-in repair kit or maintenance crew that only needs activation and stimulation to accomplish repair of damage. The potential of adult stem cells to impact medicine in this respect is enormous.[28]

Proponents of embryonic stem cell research continue to challenge these findings,[29] but the evidence of adult stem cell plasticity is growing.[30]

Current Therapeutic Applications of Human Embryonic Stem Cell Research

Simply put, to date there have been no therapeutic applications for human subjects using embryonic stem cells. This is confirmed by the NIH in
the list of Frequently Asked Questions (FAQs) posted on its official website:

*Have human embryonic stem cells been used successfully to treat
any human diseases yet?*

Scientists have only been able to do experiments with human embryonic stem cells
(hESC) since 1998, when a group led by Dr. James Thomson at the University of Wisconsin developed a technique to isolate and grow the cells. Moreover, Federal funds
to support hESC research have only been available since August 9, 2001, when President Bush announced his decision on Federal funding for hESC research. Because
many academic researchers rely on Federal funds to support their laboratories, they
are just beginning to learn how to grow and use the cells. *Thus, although hESC are
thought to offer potential cures and therapies for many devastating diseases, research
using them is still in its early stages.*[31]

The point is put more directly by Wesley J. Smith, a senior fellow at the
Discovery Institute, in commentary for the *National Review Online*: "How
many humans have been treated by embryonic stem cells? Zero."[32] Note that
the NIH cites a lack of funding prior to Bush's 2001 decision regarding embryonic stem cells as a key reason for the limited progress with the research.
However, no such restrictions affected research in the private sector. Yet to
date no human therapies have been developed by private companies either.
As noted in a review piece on the business aspects of stem cell research published February 25, 2000, in the journal *Science:*

While Geron has nabbed the early lead in exploiting embryonic and primordial fetal
stem cells, almost a dozen other biotech firms are elbowing their way into a crowded
field to develop therapies using so-called "adult" stem cells. Once thought to be less
versatile than primordial stem cells because they have already made a commitment
to become particular cell types, these cells are now turning out to have greater than
expected capabilities. What's more, they pose fewer ethical problems because they
can be obtained from sources other than embryos or aborted fetuses. And the companies using them argue that it may require less work to transform them into specialized cells for transplantation.[33]

Over a year later the *Wall Street Journal* published a similar review in its online *Opinion Journal* that noted:

Adult stem cells appear to be easier to control than embryonic cells, are closer to commercial application, and have a history of proven benefits—including bone-marrow applications. . . . Little wonder, then, that the private sector is focusing almost exclusively on adult stem-cell research. Of the 15 U.S. biotech companies solely devoted to developing cures using stem cells, only two focus on embryos. . . . That the market is speaking so loudly against embryo stem-cell research probably explains why embryo researchers are so eager to reverse the ban on *government* funding.[34]

Regardless of the funding issue, the fact remains that lying behind the current lack of therapeutic application using embryonic stem cells are several major scientific and technical problems. First and foremost, it must be noted that the bulk of research using embryonic stem cells—whether human or non-human—has been conducted only on mice.[35] This is true even in cases where the stem cells are from a human embryo—the research subject is still a mouse or some other animal! And, as noted by the NIH in their primer:

Most of the evidence that stem cells can be directed to differentiate into specific types of cells suitable for transplantation—for example, neurons, heart muscle cells, or pancreatic islet cells—comes from experiments with stem cells from mice. And although more is known about mouse stem cells, not all of that information can be translated to the understanding of human stem cells. Mouse and human cells differ in significant ways, such as the laboratory conditions that favor the growth and specialization of specific cell types.[36]

And so, the primary goal of this stage of the research is to develop a "proof of concept" regarding possible applications of embryonic stem cell research.[37]

Yet, even with progress being made in "proofs of concept," numerous obstacles remain for embryonic stem cell research. Here are some of the major hurdles identified throughout the NIH literature impeding the successful development of embryonic stem cell research into therapies that can actually be applied to human patients:

1. *Tumor formation*—". . . if undifferentiated embryonic stem cells are removed from the culture dish and injected into a mouse with a compromised immune system, a benign tumor called a teratoma can develop."[38]

2. *Obtaining pure cultures*—"Depending on the culture conditions, embryonic stem cells may form clumps of cells that can differentiate spontaneously to generate many cell types."[39]

3. *Immune rejection*—"Another important aspect of developing therapies based on stem cells will be devising ways to prevent the immune system of recipients from rejecting the donated cells and tissues that are derived from human pluripotent stem cells. Modifying or evading the immune rejection of cells or tissues developed from embryonic stem cells will not be able to be done exclusively using mouse models and human adult stem cells."[40]

4. *Unstable genetic expression*—"Once the purity profile has been established for a population of human stem cells generated using standardized procedures, derivations that occur outside what is expected due to normal biological variation serve as a harbinger that significant, and possibly deleterious, changes may have occurred. Such alterations could reflect the introduction of genetic mutations as a consequence of culture conditions used to promote expansion and to induce differentiation of the progenitor cell population."[41,42]

Although research continues and small steps forward are touted by those in favor of embryonic stem cell research, these obstacles are formidable. Obviously, the formation of tumors—even if deemed benign—is not a positive outcome for a therapy aimed at curing or alleviating disease. Pure cultures of cells for transplantation are a must to avoid more than one cell type growing at a site and thereby undoing the therapeutic benefit that is sought. This relates to the problem of unstable genetic expression as well—transplanting cells that have genetic errors will clearly have counterproductive results. But perhaps the single largest obstacle is the problem of immune rejection. To date, the primary way to combat immune rejection is with large doses of immunosuppressant drugs. Yet, even with the recipient's immune system suppressed, many transplants are still rejected by their hosts.

A. Cloning as a Solution to Problems with Embryonic Stem Cell Research

When discussions about the limitations and problems of embryonic stem cells arise—especially immune rejection and obtaining pure cell cultures—one of the most often mentioned "solutions" is *"therapeutic" cloning*. On the one hand, developing clones as a source for harvesting embryonic stem cells would provide an opportunity to create new stem cell lines. These new lines could then be developed under better, standardized procedures in order to attain pure cultures of cells for "eventual" human therapeutic application. As it is right now, most of the existing stem cell lines on which President Bush allowed federal research money to be spent are unsuitable for use in human treatment, in part because they were grown on mouse feeder cells or using other animal-based serums that contaminated the lines.[43] Thus, new stem cell lines, it is argued, need to be created—and cloning is held up as the best method for developing the new lines. The other major advantage of using cloned cells is that if genetic material from a patient is cloned, and the stem cells are then harvested from the developing embryo, those cells should be able to be transplanted back into the patient without any immune rejection. Thus, cloning in both cases is referred to as "therapeutic" because someone will benefit from the stem cells. Much has already been written on what a glaring misnomer it is to call such a procedure "therapeutic," since the clone will obviously not benefit here, as well as pointing out that "therapeutic" cloning uses exactly the same methods as "reproductive" cloning, therefore leaving no meaningful distinction between the two actions.[44] This is, in part, why some want to refer to "therapeutic" cloning in some other fashion, such as the President's Council on Bioethics, whose members have chosen to call this "Cloning-for-Biomedical-Research," while "reproductive cloning" is referred to "Cloning-to-Produce-Children."[45] But moving beyond the rhetoric, it will help to clarify the ethical issues at stake with cloning by discussing how a clone is developed.

To begin, let us define the term "clone." According to the National Academy of Sciences a "clone" is: "(1) An exact genetic replica of a DNA molecule, cell, tissue, organ, or entire plant or animal; (2) An organism that has the same nuclear genome as another organism."[46] The President's Council on Bioethics defines the process of "cloning" as:

... a form of asexual reproduction (parthenogenesis is another), the production of a new individual not by the chance union of egg and sperm but by some form of replication of the genetic makeup of a single existing or previously existing individual. (In biological or functional terms, the core of sexual reproduction is not bodily intercourse but the fusion of male and female *germ cells;* thus IVF [in vitro fertilization], though it takes place outside the body, is—biologically speaking—a form of sexual reproduction.) Cloning is the activity of producing a clone, an individual or group of individuals genetically virtually identical to the precursor that is being "replicated."[47]

Overall, there are three primary methods of developing a "clone." Let us briefly review each general method.[48]

First, the cloning process most often discussed in the news media, and which is most often held up as the best solution for problems with embryonic stem cell research, is called somatic cell nuclear transfer, or SCNT. At present, there are three techniques for SCNT. The basic procedure was first explored by Hans Spemann in the 1920s.[49] Second is the Roslin technique, named after the Roslin Institute in Edinburgh, which brought us Dolly.[50] The third technique currently in use is the Honolulu technique, developed at the University of Hawaii.[51] With SCNT, two cells are used: an egg cell, or oocyte, and any other somatic (nonreproductive) cell. The nucleus is removed from the egg cell (i.e., it is enucleated). Then the nucleus from the somatic cell is "transferred" into the empty egg cell. Since the nucleus of the somatic cell had a complete genetic code, the egg cell reacts as if it has been fertilized. The new embryo is, therefore, now a clone—or genetic replica—of the person from whom the somatic cell was obtained. The variations in methods of SCNT noted above arise from varying techniques for how the somatic cell nucleus is actually transferred into the empty ovum.

A second method for developing a clone mimics the natural process of twinning. Identical twins are formed when the developing embryo—at a very early stage—splits and becomes two embryos. This occurs while the cells of the embryo are still in the totipotent stage, thus both embryos possess a complete genetic code, and can develop independently of each other. This process can be artificially induced in the lab, and is referred to as "artificial twinning," "embryo splitting," or more precisely, "blastomere separation."[52] The technique is rather involved, but comes down to separating an embryo at either the two-cell, four-cell, or eight-cell stage of its development. The embryo is treated in such a manner that the cells can be separated through the embryo's membrane without destroying the integrity of the cells. The process has been used in animals, but only recently has it been suggested as a method for cloning humans. One particular area of interest involves in vitro fertility treatments—embryo splitting could double or quadruple the number of developing embryos a couple achieves.[53] Some claim this is not the same as "cloning," but the difference is one of semantics—in either case, you forcibly produce a replica of an existing being.[54]

The final method is known as parthenogenesis, the technique reportedly used by Advanced Cell Technology, the Massachusetts-based biotech company that announced on October 13, 2001, that they had successfully cloned the first human embryo.[55] In this method one needs only an egg cell, or oocyte, to produce a clone. The egg is stimulated—either through electrical shock, or sometimes using chemical treatments—in order to initiate embryonic development. This method takes its name from the Greek term *parthenos,* which means "virgin." Hence, this method has become known in recent literature as the "virgin birth" method of cloning.[56] The basic idea here is that a new human being can be produced only from a female egg, and so males are not needed. To understand how this is possible, we need to remember that all of our cells contain our genetic code. This includes our reproductive cells (sperm and eggs). Thus, even though our reproductive cells present with only half of the chromosomes needed to develop a human being, within the DNA of the egg cell is a blueprint of the mother. The purpose of the electrical shock or chemical treatment is to make the egg cell recognize the woman's DNA and thereby begin acting as if it had been fertilized. And so this method produces a clone of the woman whose egg cell is used. Parthenogenesis has only recently been discussed as a possible method for cloning humans because it had not been very successful in lower forms of mammalian life. However, recent experiments with mice and monkeys have shown greater promise.[57] Plus, proponents of this form of cloning argue that the method provides an "ethical" source of stem cells because, to date in human experiments, none of the embryos survive much past the blastocyst stage. As one article put it:

... even though an electric or chemical stimulus can induce parthenogenesis in mammals, the resulting embryos die after a few days. And that, according to its proponents, is the beauty of the technique as far as stem cells are concerned: it produces embryos that could never become human beings. So destroying these embryos to obtain stem cells would avoid the ethical concerns that have led to restrictions or bans on embryonic stem cell research in many countries.[58]

Some scientists and ethicists are beginning to suggest that this might be the best method for obtaining greater numbers of embryonic stem cells for research, since these parthenotes will not survive. In part, they argue that these types of clones may not even really be "human beings" because they lack the "potential" to live. For my part, I believe that if parthenogenesis were used on human egg cells, the result would indeed be human beings— albeit defective human beings. Thus, the same ethical problems involved with the other forms of "therapeutic" cloning still remain.[59]

Regardless of which method of cloning is being discussed, the reason for pursuing "therapeutic" cloning is the same across the board: to produce embryos for the sole purpose of destroying them for their prized "inner" cell mass—i.e., their stem cells. The advantage that this offers for stem cell research, as noted above, is that stem cells derived from one's clone would not trigger—it is hoped—an immune rejection response. As noted by the NIH in their report on the scientific progress of stem cells:

The potential immunological rejection of human ES-derived cells might be avoided by . . . using nuclear transfer technology to generate ES cells that are genetically identical to the person who receives the transplant. It has been suggested that this could be accomplished by using somatic cell nuclear transfer technology (so-called therapeutic cloning) in which the nucleus is removed from one of the transplant patient's cells, such as a skin cell, and injecting the nucleus into an oocyte. The oocyte, thus "fertilized," could be cultured in vitro to the blastocyst stage. ES cells could subsequently be derived from its inner cell mass, and directed to differentiate into the desired cell type. The result would be differentiated (or partly differentiated) ES-derived cells that match exactly the immunological profile of the person who donated the somatic cell nucleus, and who is also the intended recipient of the transplant—a labor-intensive, but truly customized therapy.[60]

Given the "hope" and "promise" of embryonic stem cell research, and the advantage of using cells obtained from a genetically matched donor (your clone) for reducing immune rejection, the call for "therapeutic" cloning has been slowly rising from various sectors in the medical field over the past several years, including the American Medical Association.[61]

Current Therapeutic Applications of Human Adult Stem Cell Research

Whereas embryonic stem cell research has yet to yield any direct therapeutic applications for human patients, but instead has only provided a few "proof of concept" results, adult stem cell research has made concrete advances toward curing and alleviating human disease. The actual results that have been achieved up to this point are simply too long to review in this chapter.[62] Just listing the headlines of a few recent stories discussing successes in adult stem cells gives one a sense of the genuine "promises" that are being fulfilled by such research: "Muscle Stem Cells May Cure Incontinence"; "Chemotherapy plus Stem-Cell Transplantation May Reduce Relapse of High-Risk Breast Cancer"; "Bone Marrow Holds Promise in Treatment of MS"; "Paralyzed Woman Walks Again after [Umbilical Cord] Stem Cell Therapy"; "New Hope for Children with Eye Tumors Using Own Stem Cells"; "Adult Stem Cell Transplants Offer New Hope in Some Cases of Blindness"; "Stem Cells Repair Brain after Stroke"; "Bone Marrow Found to Have Cells to Repair the Pancreas"; "Tests of Cell Transplants Offer Hope to Diabetics"; "Stem Cells from Fat Used to Repair Skull."[63] Rather than try to sort through all of the successes in adult stem cell research, I will focus on several key areas of concern and discussion in the public debate: Parkinson's disease, leukemia, and cardiac tissue function and repair. I will also limit my discussion to treatments that have been conducted on human patients (the research involving animal trials is even more extensive!).

A. Adult Stem Cells Used to Treat Parkinson's Disease

Although the results have not yet been peer-reviewed, Dr. Michel Levesque of Cedars-Sinai Medical Center in Los Angeles, California, reported at the April 8, 2002, annual meeting of the American Association of Neurological Surgeons an 80 percent reversal of symptoms in the first Parkinson's patient treated using his own neural stem cells.[64] The patient was Dennis Turner, a fifty-seven-year-old engineer and former fighter pilot who had been diagnosed with Parkinson's in his late forties. His disease progressed rapidly, to the point where he had to give up flying at age fifty-two—traditional regimens of drug therapy had not slowed down the progression of his disease. Dr. Levesque performed a routine brain biopsy procedure to obtain stem cells. The cells were then cultured into becoming mature dopamine-secreting cells—since the lack of dopamine is considered to be one of the primary factors in Parkinson's disease. Finally, in March of 1999, the newly cultured cells were transplanted back into Mr. Turner's brain in six different locations. After three months, the patient's dopamine levels had improved more than 50 percent. After one year, the patient's Unified Parkinson's Disease Rating Scale was improved by 83 percent, in the absence of any medication. Interestingly enough, at the one-year mark the patient's dopamine levels had fallen back to nearly where they were before the transplant was done—yet, as of 2002 when Dr. Levesque presented these findings, the Parkinson's symptoms had not returned. In short, the patient had been free of Parkinson's symptoms for over three years before his doctor even publicized the research! As noted by Dr. Levesque in a report in American Medical News—the newsletter of the American Medical Association: "What we have is a protocol in which we don't have to harvest 12 or 15 fetuses, we don't have to give immunosuppressant therapy, and we don't have to worry about viral disease transmission."[65]

Now, as many have been quick to point out, one "cure" does not guarantee a successful treatment protocol, and the findings still need to be peer-reviewed. Dr. Levesque is aware of this: "At this point, it's not a 100% pure culture.... We predict only 10% of the transplanted cells will survive."[66] Yet, this is amazing news in the development of treating such a devastating disease as Parkinson's, and Levesque has been authorized by the U.S. Food and Drug Administration to conduct a Phase II trial of the stem cell therapy in more human patients once several specific animal studies are completed. Nor is this the only successful research involving Parkinson's that is currently under way. Another study being conducted at Emory University has also shown promising results using retinal stem cells with six patients suffering from advanced Parkinson's disease—after one year, results showed an average of 50 percent improvement in motor function in all six patients.[67] Even more recently, in May of 2003 *Nature Medicine* published reports of a Phase I trial that relied, in part, on infusions of a transforming growth factor into the brains of five Parkinson's patients to stimulate their endogenous neural stem cells to help repair damage caused by the disease. After one year, Steven Gill of the Institute of Neurosciences in Bristol, England, noted a 61 percent improvement in the patients' activities, as reported in their daily living scores, with an accompanying increase in dopamine storage noticed in the brain and no serious clinical side effects.[68]

B. Adult Stem Cells Used to Treat Leukemia

In July of 2001, Nathan Salley from Arvada, Colorado, testified before a House subcommittee regarding the issue of stem cell research as part of the debate leading up to President Bush's decision on federal funding of research on embryonic stem cell lines. Nathan was diagnosed on March 4, 1997, at the age of eleven with acute myeloid leukemia. His disease was unfortunately already at an advanced stage before it was finally diagnosed by his doctors, and so he did not respond well to initial treatment. By age fourteen, Nathan and his parents were told he needed a bone marrow transplant, and the doctors believed that a cord blood transplant offered the best chance for recovery. In the summer of 1999, Nathan received his transplant using stem cells from umbilical cord blood, which as noted earlier falls into the category of adult stem cell therapy. To this date, Nathan has remained in complete remission, with a functioning immune system rebuilt by the transplanted cord blood stem cells.[69] Nathan himself remarked: "I am honored to represent some of the children that proponents of embryonic stem cell research insist they are trying to save. Yet embryonic stem cell research did not save me—cord blood research did. I am living proof that there are promising and useful alternatives to embryonic stem cell research and that embryos do not need to be killed to achieve medical breakthroughs."[70] Again, Nathan is but one example of success with adult stem cells derived from umbilical cord blood. Dr. Mary Laughlin, at Case Western Reserve University in Cleveland, reported high success rates in treating older adults with various forms of leukemia and lymphoma with cord blood stem cells. In a workshop presented to the Food and Drug Administration, a division of the Department of Health and Human Services, Dr. Laughlin put a human face on her research by speaking of one of her patients:

Chris is twenty-eight years old, likes to ski in Colorado, was diagnosed with Hodgkin's disease, and attained complete remission status. However, he presented to our transplant program with thyroid-related AML fourteen months [after he went into remission]. For this individual, no sibling match was identified and the pace of his disease precluded the necessary time to identify and mobilize a MUD donor [matched unrelated donor]. I think as we learn more about this new stem cell source, we can be assured that even in adult recipients a proportion of patients can derive direct benefit from use of this allogeneic stem cell source. This patient is now two and a half years out from his cord blood transplant.[71]

In general, the success of umbilical cord stem cell transplants in treating various diseases is a major medical advance. One of the largest obstacles in successful transplantation is finding compatible donors. However, the stem cells derived from umbilical cord blood are showing evidence of being able to adapt to patients' bodies with few immunological problems.[72] On many fronts, progress is being made in fighting the terrible disease of leukemia.[73]

C. Adult Stem Cells Used for Cardiac Function and Repair

Another area of increasing success in using adult stem cells for human therapy is the treatment of cardiac problems, including repairing heart damage. One dramatic story from February of 2003 involved a Michigan teenager, Dimitri Bonnville, who suffered a massive heart attack after being shot in the heart with a nail gun. The damage to Dimitri's heart was so severe that it appeared he would survive only if he received a new heart. Given the tremendous odds against getting a transplantable heart, doctors at Beaumont

Hospital in Royal Oak, Michigan, considered other options to save Dimitri's life. The actual research protocol was developed by one of Beaumont's cardiologists, Cindy Grines, M.D., along with William O'Neill, M.D., Beaumont's chief of cardiology. Dr. Grines explained the rationale for the experimental therapy: "The unique treatment was considered on an emergent-use basis in consultation with Beaumont's Human Investigation Committee. We based the treatment protocol on laboratory studies that have shown stem cells from the blood hold promise in helping to bring new life to damaged hearts, and on limited patient trials that indicate stem cells from bone marrow may also improve heart function."[74] On February 17, doctors began the treatment by giving Dimitri a drug called Neupogen, which stimulates the production of stem cells in the blood. The doctors then harvested Dimitri's own stem cells on February 21 using a specially designed blood machine, and then transplanted them directly into his left anterior descending artery (which feeds the front part of the heart) using a heart catheter. Several days later a defibrillator was also transplanted into Dimitri's chest to help him maintain a normal heartbeat.[75] Now, to be honest, it is too early to tell just how much of Dimitri's improvement came from the stem cell therapy—more research and study needs to be done. However, three months after the initial treatment, Dimitri continued to show signs of improved heart function. As noted by Dr. Grines in a press conference held in May of 2003, "Dimitri has made significant improvement. . . . Most patients who have a massive heart attack like Dimitri's would be headed toward congestive heart failure or a heart transplant. Dimitri is playing sports with his friends and becoming more physically active each day."[76] Pleased with the success, doctors at Beaumont were seeking FDA approval to conduct this therapy on four hundred more patients, but the FDA has withheld permission for now, wanting better evidence of the efficacy of the stem cells in the actual improvement of Dimitri's heart functioning.[77]

As noted by Dr. Grines, the idea to use adult stem cells to help repair the heart was based upon prior research. For example, in July of 2001, Reuters Health posted a report on work being conducted by German researchers. They harvested stem cells from a heart attack patient's bone marrow and then injected them back into his heart. They reported a 20–30 percent increase in his heart function after just ten weeks. They also had clear evidence that the improvement, in this case, was due to the adult stem cells which had actually repaired portions of the damaged part of his heart.[78]

French researchers had similar success in transplanting stem cells derived from a patient's skeletal muscles back into his heart.[79] And, not to be outdone, several hospitals in the United States have been conducting a Phase I trial focused on congestive heart failure using autologous skeletal stem cells called myoblasts, which are harvested from the patient's own leg, and then injected back into the heart. Since they are Phase I studies, the numbers of patients have been limited—but the results are very positive.[80] A different protocol is being used at St. Luke's Episcopal Hospital in Houston, Texas, where researchers have published results of using autologous bone marrow cell transplants to treat severe heart failure. In the published study, the researchers conclude: "Thus, the present study demonstrates the relative safety of intramyocardial injections of bone marrow–derived stem cells in humans with severe heart failure and the potential for improving myocardial blood flow with associated enhancement of regional and global left ventricular function."[81]

These stories do not just represent "hype," nor are they reflections of an "idealistic" hope. These are stories of real people, with real families, who have suffered tremendously. Yet, in all these cases genuine therapeutic benefit has been gained from adult stem cell treatments. These studies provide more than just "proof of concept." They have saved lives!

Adult versus Embryonic Stem Cells Based on Clinical/Scientific Data

And so, even before an ethical argument is raised, based upon the measures and standards of science, there is little reason to continue with embryonic stem cell research. Given all of the above, the demarcation between the actual therapeutic benefits of adult stem cells and those of embryonic stem cells is patently clear. Indeed, when one examines all of the obstacles facing the move to human trials and applications with human embryonic stem cells, one begins to wonder why any money or effort is being spent on such research at all. As noted by Marie-Louise Labat of the Jerome Lejeune Foundation in Paris at a recent meeting of the World Federation of the Catholic Medical Associations: "In the present state of knowledge concerning embryonic stem cells, the political debate is just nonsense."[82]

Thus, as Wesley J. Smith points out regarding the development of embryonic stem cell therapies in his commentary for the *National Review Online*:

... before human trials can even be safely undertaken researchers will have to over-come two serious difficulties that stand between patients and embryonic-cell regen-erative medicine: (1) ES cells cause tumors, and (2) ES cells may be rejected by the immune system. Surmounting these difficulties—if they can be surmounted at all—will take a very long time and much expense. There is no risk of rejection with adult cells, by contrast, because they come from the patients' own bodies. Nor, at least so far, does adult-stem-cell therapy appear to cause tumors. This puts adult therapies years ahead of the game.[83]

In the same vein, Maureen L. Condic, assistant professor of neurobiolo-gy and anatomy at the University of Utah, points out in an article in *First Things*:

The final argument against using human embryonic stem cells for research is based on sound scientific practice: we simply do not have sufficient evidence from animal studies to warrant a move to human experimentation. While there is considerable debate over the moral and legal status of early human embryos, this debate in no way constitutes a justification to step outside the normative practice of science and medicine that requires convincing and reproducible evidence from animal models prior to initiating experiments on (or, in this case, with) human beings. While the "potential promise" of embryonic stem cell research has been widely touted, the data supporting that promise is largely nonexistent.[84]

Now the comments from Smith and Condic were written in 2002, and so one might object that advances in embryonic stem cell research since then have surely prepared us by now to begin human trials—at least in the very near future. Indeed, all of us have continued to hear about "breakthroughs" with embryonic stem cell research. But this is simply not the case. Even with all of its "breakthroughs," embryonic stem cell research is lagging far behind the proven success of adult stem cell research, and at this point will proba-bly never catch up. It is a simple matter of noting how research and develop-ment works in the field of medicine. As Dr. Anton-Lewis Usala explains in a paper posted on the United States Conference of Catholic Bishops' website:

There is also a huge difference between promising research and the ability to turn research into a medical product. It takes years to conduct the basic science research, and many more years to turn discoveries into a usable medical therapy. Products that are now in human clinical trials are years ahead of any new basic science effort in, for example, embryonic stem cell research, now being proposed for federal fund-ing.[85]

The "reality" of the current status of embryonic stem cell research as being years away from human application was also admitted—albeit, somewhat reluctantly—at the September 2003 meeting of the Presidents' Council on Bioethics. In the published transcript of the Council's third session, held on September 4 and titled "Stem Cells: Moving Research from the Bench Toward the Bedside: The Role of NIH and FDA," the council chairman, Leon Kass, asked the director of the National Institutes of Health, Elias A. Zerhouni, M.D., regarding embryonic stem cell research, ". . . how do you square the sense that on the one hand we are at a very, very early stage, and on the other hand the field might be ripe already for certain kinds of clinical trials. What message should we take away on that particular point?"[86] To this, Dr. Zerhouni replied:

. . . science, as you can imagine, advances by leaps and bounds, and investigators have passions and sometimes believe there is a shortcut or not a shortcut. So that the two areas of research that I think are driven to applications are those that, through what I call . . . recipes or lucky strikes or understandings of pathways, whatever it is, try to find an application, a path to application, in a proof of concept fashion, usually in animal systems. . . . Even if you showed today that there was a recovery of cardiac function through some pathway, you still will have to do the demonstration that you understand the host cell interaction, you understand immune response, you understand all of the safety considerations, and so on.[87]

Later in the same session, these points were echoed by Mark B. McClellan, M.D., the Commissioner of the U.S. Food and Drug Administration: ". . . as is the case with all of the biologicals, especially complex new technologies like this, ultimately it's nature that determines whether the products are really going to benefit the needy . . . whether those benefits can be demonstrably given to patients. And we're still very early on in that process."[88] Later in the discussion, Dr. McClellan was more specific regarding the time it will take to bring embryonic stem cell research to the point of human application:

I think, you know, with some reason that we are going to be able to bring new benefits, important new benefits, to many millions of patients that don't have effective treatments available today. But as with so many other areas of emerging technologies, moving from ideas that seem to work well even at the proof of concept stage, to treatments that demonstrably can be shown reliably to be safe and effective in patients is very difficult. And we are early in that process now for these complex biological treatments. . . . [T]here are a host of other important safety issues and effectiveness issues that also need to be much better understood before these treatments can be used reliably and confidently by the public to improve the health of the public . . . But this is a difficult process. You know, a lot of people talk about the fact that it takes over a decade for going from—for something as simple as a small molecule drug, just a simple chemical, from the time that it's first identified and people first suspect that it's going to have a benefit in patients. It can take well over a decade to go from that proof of concept to a product being commercially available to the public.[89]

In terms of research and development, then, once one gets beyond the hype, it becomes clear that embryonic stem cell research is years away from human application. However, in the current atmosphere of the political side of this debate, this may soon change. The pressure is on to start conducting embryonic research on human subjects—even in the absence of good animal models. This pressure is coming from celebrity spokespersons, as well as some scientists, who favor "trying everything" as we look for a cure. The claim is made that, even though adult stem cells are starting to show "plasticity" and are leading to actual therapeutic applications in human trials, we must still keep "all avenues open" as we search for cures to humanity's deadly diseases.

Consider the comments of Charles Jennings, editor of the scientific journal *Nature Neuroscience*:

Opponents of embryonic stem cell research will presumably continue to cite studies with adult cells . . . in support of their position. . . . However, stem cell research is still a very new field, and it will probably be many years until its full therapeutic potential becomes clear. . . . I think much more work is required before we can make a strong statement about the therapeutic potential of adult versus embryonic stem cells.[90]

The same sentiment is echoed by George Q. Daley, M.D., Ph.D., in the *New England Journal of Medicine* when he writes:

A worthy goal of biomedical research is to reprogram an adult cell directly, without having it pass through the intermediate stage of the preimplantation embryo. Reaching this objective would eliminate ethical challenges to such research. One day, direct reprogramming of an adult cell may prove feasible through a combination of chemical and genetic means. But this goal will be achieved more quickly if we are allowed to explore reprogramming with the use of currently available methods, which entail nuclear transfer and the creation of new lines of embryonic stem cells.[91]

The editors of *Scientific American* also add their support for continuing embryonic stem cell research in the following manner:

Opponents of the research might retort, Why not continue using only adult stem cells? Some stem cells can be found in adult tissue as well, after all. The scientific answer is that we don't yet know whether the adult cells necessarily retain the full plasticity of the embryonic ones. Research should and will continue on the adult stem cells, and if they ultimately prove as capable as or better than embryonic ones, it might then be wise to forsake the embryonic cells in deference to the moral debate over whether an embryo is really a human being. Until then, however, adult stem cell work can only be an adjunct to the embryonic work.[92]

Finally, the NIH tells us:

The development of stem cell lines that can produce many tissues of the human body is an important scientific breakthrough. This research has the potential to revolutionize the practice of medicine and improve the quality and length of life. Given the enormous promise of stem cell therapies for so many devastating diseases, NIH believes that it is important to simultaneously pursue all lines of research and search for the very best sources of these cells.[93]

Yet this call for continuing research on human embryos in light of mounting success using adult stem cells flies in the face of the National Bioethics Advisory Commission's statement in its 1999 report, *Ethical Issues in Human Stem Cell Research:* "In our judgment, the derivation of stem cells from embryos remaining following infertility treatments is justifiable only if no less morally problematic alternatives are available for advancing the research."[94] It is true that the report goes on to advocate continuing embryonic stem cell research, but this "might" be somewhat understandable given that there had not been much research done with adult stem cells at that point. However, the case is far different today, and the facts do not warrant continued research into embryonic stem cells.

Moving Beyond the Science—The Ethical Arguments against Destructive Embryonic Stem Cell Research and Cloning

A. Basic Ethics

If you were to peruse your "average" textbook in ethics, you would most likely find a general distinction being made between two primary approaches to ethics—deontology (duty) and utilitarianism (consequences). There might be a nod given to virtue ethics and religious morals, but the key theories are most often presented as autonomy versus social consequences.

The great champion of duty ethics was the German philosopher Immanuel Kant (1724–1804).[95] According to Kant, the duty of every rational being was to become autonomous, and to follow only that moral law discovered through the application of one's own pure reason. Or, more simply, to obey reason. In this approach, *what* one does is irrelevant—all that matters is *why* one acted; that is, one's motivation must be out of a sense of duty to reason. Thus, Kant went so far as to argue that one must tell the truth about the location of a friend to a murderer who is trying to kill said friend (some friend!). The duty to truth is absolute. The primary virtue of deontological ethics, then, is the absolute notion of autonomy.

On the other hand, we have utilitarianism, which was championed by the English philosopher John Stuart Mill (1806–1873).[96] Mill's dictum has become rather famous: always act to promote the greatest happiness of the greatest number of people. In this approach, all that matters is the ultimate outcome, however one chooses to measure that, of one's action. If one produces good for others, then the action has moral worth. *What* one actually does is again irrelevant—consequences are the key. But in the end, the individual becomes subsumed into the community, becoming only one part of the larger—more important—whole. As such, society becomes more important than the individual. The majority stands superior to any individual or minority.

The reason it is worthwhile to mention and clarify these two approaches is that they stand behind much of the argumentation being used to support human embryonic stem cell research and cloning. On the one hand, utilitarian arguments are offered at every turn—the great hope and promise of benefit from the technology has become a well-worn mantra, even in the absence of any real evidence that such promises will ever come to fruition. Looking forward to all the good that may someday come from cloning and human embryonic stem cell research is, at root, a utilitarian view. On the other hand, we are also met with arguments that individuals have the right to be treated with human embryonic stem cells or to use stem cells derived from human clones for medical reasons, *if* they so choose. If you do not like cloning, then do not have a clone made—but at the same time, do not take away someone else's right to such research. Such an attitude reflects the absolute belief in radical autonomy.

However, as one considers the views of deontological ethics and utilitari-

anism, one can begin to recognize a serious problem. These theories are opposed to each other—one advocates autonomy while the other places value
only on the community. Hence, we encounter the primary conflict of ethics—the individual versus the community; or more directly, the good of the
one versus the good of the many. This conflict stuns many people. After all,
which approach should we choose? Is there any way to judge which is better? Or, do we simply pick one and go with it? Some even use this conflict
as a springboard to justify relativism (since no one seems to know the truth
anyway). The unfortunate consequence of this oversimplification of ethics
into either the one or the many leads some to conclude that ethics is mere
rhetoric—or worse, a game.

But there is a third alternative that is not often represented clearly and
completely in contemporary textbooks or discussions of ethics. It is an approach that has been known as the Natural Law tradition, rooted in the
work of philosophers such as Aristotle, St. Thomas Aquinas, and more recently Jacques Maritain, but which today is usually referred to as *personalism* (to clarify it from notions of "legalism" or from confusions about what
"natural" means).[97] What *personalism* recognizes, which both deontology
and consequentialism fail to recognize, is that human beings are *both* individuals and social beings. As such, duty ethics and social ethics each fall
short of representing our moral obligations because they fail to fully represent who and what we are as human beings.

Overall, the primary goal of *ethical personalism* is to achieve the common good, which flows out of our common human nature. As Jacques Maritain aptly notes in his influential work *The Person and the Common Good,*
the human person is drawn into society "because of its very perfections,
as person, and its inner urge to the communication of knowledge and love
which require relationship with other persons."[98] Without society, the human person would not be able to survive in the world, nor would the human person be able to attain the fullness of human life. Thus, Maritain concludes: "Society appears, therefore, to provide the human person with just
those conditions of existence and development which it needs. It is not by
itself alone that it reaches its plenitude but by receiving essential goods from
society."[99]

Understanding the correlation of the person to society, Maritain explains,
is central for understanding the common good: "the common good is common because it is received in persons, each of whom is as a mirror of the
whole. Among the bees, there is a public good, namely, the good functioning

of the hive, but not a common good, that is, a good received and communicated."[100] As such, the mission of social living for human beings involves the promotion of the common good, together with the development of each individual as she or he pursues that common good. The point is explained by Maritain in this manner: "We have emphasized the sociability of the person and the properly *human* nature of the common good. We have seen that it is a good according to the requirements of justice; that it must flow back upon persons, and that it includes, as its principal value, the access of persons to their liberty of expansion."[101]

The reality of daily life reveals that human society is not simply composed of autonomous individuals, isolated from all other existing beings in time and space. A human thrives and flourishes in relationships, embodied in a range of societies, each with their own proper integrity, whether it be on the level of family, faith community, profession, or politically organized state. Human communities are composed of persons who are both unique individuals *and* social beings. Thus, even across the diversity of various societies, human beings share a common good—not as individuals, but as members of the totality of the human community. The true mark of the common good, argues Maritain, is that it universally flows back upon all human persons, assisting each one in the pursuit of the good human life. In this light, then, we can see why human embryonic stem cell research and therapeutic cloning are unethical—to the extent that these activities harm or destroy human beings, they violate the common good of all humanity. Simply put, human beings should not be used in a manner that deprives them of their life and dignity. Even though it can be argued that some material benefit can be gained from such research, that "potential good" is outweighed by the embryo's participation in the common good as a member of the human community.

B. *The Weakness of the "Personhood" Argument*

Unfortunately, it is at this point that disagreement begins to arise. Many proponents of human embryonic stem cell research, and the use of cloning for deriving stem cells, would say that they completely agree with this *personalist* view of the common good. Their argument, however, is that zygotes, blastocysts, and pre-embryos are not "persons," and so they do not count as part of society, nor is there any obligation on society's part toward these beings. Thus, they *could* argue, the common good does not include zygotes, blastocysts, or pre-embryos. The confusion arises over what I term the "personhood" argument, which is actually *contrary* to the conclusions of Natural Law ethics and *personalism*.

What exactly is the "personhood" argument, then, and how does the position of personalism differ regarding zygotes and embryos? Typically the "personhood" argument begins by establishing a set of criteria for what constitutes human "personhood." If a being fails to meet these criteria for "personhood," then that being is *not* considered a person. Proponents of the "personhood" argument contend that only persons have rights and deserve respect. Therefore, non-persons can be used for research purposes, aborted, taken off life support, etc. There are actually a number of versions of the "personhood" argument, because there is no universally accepted criteria for what constitutes a human person. Some place the moment of "personhood" at the formation of the primitive streak (about eighteen days), others point to when the heart starts beating (approximately twenty-five days), or at the time brain waves can be detected (approximately six weeks), or at viability (approximately twenty-four weeks), and finally, some point to birth.[102] A few, such as Peter Singer, even place the criteria of "personhood" past live birth, and base it on fairly sophisticated activities of reason including self-awareness and voluntary decision making. However, in *all* of these cases, a zygote, blastocyst, or pre-embryo would not meet the requirements of "personhood," and so do not deserve the same level of respect or protection from harm as other human beings who do qualify as persons.

Now certainly the term "person" is an important one in our contemporary vocabulary. However, the major weakness of the "personhood" argument overall is revealed in the fact that it has so many variations. Since "personhood" is given numerous social, political, and philosophical definitions, it is too vague and too subjective to be of value in determining the ethics of embryonic stem cell research and "therapeutic" cloning. A further problem is that various versions of the "personhood" argument, if applied across society as a whole, would exclude a great many more human beings from the status of person than many in the public realize. As Sidney Callahan, the noted pro-life feminist and author, once noted:

[C]ertain philosophers set the standard of personhood so high that half the human race could not meet the criteria during most of their waking hours (let alone their sleeping ones). Sentience, self-consciousness, rational decision-making, social participation? Surely no infant, or child under two, could qualify. Either our idea of person must be expanded or another criterion, such as human life itself, be employed to protect the weak in a just society.[103]

Thus, given its multiplicity of meanings in contemporary society, "person-hood" is incapable of serving as a clear criterion for determining our social and ethical responsibility toward embryos and clones—and even humanity in general.

In response to the "personhood" argument, *ethical personalism* takes a very different approach. *Personalism* is based upon our common, shared human nature, and takes as its primary ethical principle that all human beings deserve the respect worthy of a person.[104] The implication here is that we all know how to respect "persons"—that is, we know how to treat people that we think deserve our respect. *Personalism,* however, takes this one step further and challenges us to see that all human beings in reality are "persons," whether they fit our preconceived biases of who counts or not. Therefore, *personalism* presents us with a much more inclusive approach in ethics than most other ethical theories. In the end, this means that respect is owed to all human beings from the very moment human life begins. Now, under the various "personhood" arguments, at the very early stages of human development a zygote, blastocyst, or embryo at best represent only "potential" human life. But *personalism* disagrees. While a zygote, blastocyst, or embryo may potentially one day be an astronaut, a musician, a future president of the United States, or a philosopher, what it IS is quite clear—it is ACTUAL life. While it is true that an actual being also possesses many future possibilities or potencies, an existing thing cannot be described solely in terms of its potencies—for, by definition, the potency does not yet exist (that is why it is only a potency). What this means, practically speaking, is that if one were to say that a human zygote was only "potential" human life, then that same zygote would have to have at the same time the potency to become something else entirely—which contemporary genetics points out is untrue.[105] In fact, contemporary embryology affirms that from the very moment of fertilization, a human ovum is distinguishable from a mouse ovum, a cow ovum, and even from a chimpanzee ovum—which we are told bears only a 5 percent genetic difference from a human being. And so, a fertilized ovum coming from human gametes is at its very moment of fertilization something actual, and so it must have a real, definable status. Thus, we can conclude that an embryo or clone is "human" due to the presence of human genetic material, and an embryo or clone is "life" because it is a self-developing entity. This is the reality of human nature. It is true that, like all organisms, zygotes of all types (cloned or not) depend upon their environment for sustenance. But the program of development is internal, although still capable of being influenced externally. Once a complete genome is actuated, a new, self-developing entity begins to unfold (even when there are errors present in the chromosomes as in Down syndrome, or with defective genes). On this point, there is clear agreement among embryologists—regardless of the claims raised by other researchers, ethicists, and politicians.[106]

Thus, the *personalist's* view that all human beings should be treated with the respect befitting a person brings the debate over embryonic research and "therapeutic" cloning to a common ground, especially since the criterion of when human life begins is scientifically verifiable, and does not fall into the confusions regarding the subjectivity of "personhood" noted above. Judge John T. Noonan clarified the *personalist* argument quite well when he wrote:

Humanity does not depend upon social recognition, though often failure of society to recognize the prisoner, the alien, the heterodox as human has led to the destruction of human beings. Anyone conceived by a man and a woman is human. Recognition of this condition by society follows a real event in the objective order, however imperfect and halting the recognition. Any attempt to limit humanity to exclude some groups runs the risk of furnishing authority and precedent for excluding other groups in the name of the consciousness or perception of the controlling group in the society.[107]

Reflecting on Noonan's point here, we can easily see that any attempt to employ the notion of "personhood" in public controversies within a pluralistic society will necessarily exclude certain individuals or groups from the larger group. Such exclusion marks those not deemed as persons as vulnerable to the whims and desires of the larger group. But *personalism's* focus on the very beginning of human life avoids this exclusiveness, and is instead an inclusive approach to ethics. Further, since life has been determined to be an inalienable right, we avoid the danger of letting society—via common assent or actual legislation—arbitrarily determine who counts and who does not. Our obligation is to respect all human beings as equals. It should also be pointed out that this debate over "personhood" is *not* simply a matter of rhetoric. The dangers involved with allowing society to employ subjective criteria for "personhood" are quite real, and jeopardize all of the vulnerable within a society. In this sense, then, an embryo or a clone clearly falls within the human community. As members of our community, they deserve respect in light of the common good. To the extent that embryos and clones are destroyed for the benefit of others, the common good suffers—and we are all worse off for the destruction of life that occurs

Conclusion: Call for a Total Ban on Destructive Human Embryonic Research and Human Cloning

In this chapter, I have argued that all human beings have a right and an obligation to be involved with the debate over human embryonic stem cell research and its extension to human cloning. I have reviewed the current progress of both embryonic stem cell research and adult stem cell research. It has been demonstrated that human regenerative medicine can be promoted through the use of adult stem cell research alone, thus obviating the need for embryonic stem cell research as a matter of public policy. And, if embryonic stem cell research is not necessary, then neither is therapeutic cloning. I have also explained that an embryo or a clone, indeed any zygote, is not simply "potential," but actual human life. I have further argued that as an actual human life, a clone or zygote is part of the human community, and thus is included under the umbrella of the common good. Finally, I have addressed the shortcomings of "personhood" as an appropriate criterion for determining who does and does not count within human society. Instead, I have argued for the objective approach offered by *ethical personalism* as a guide in determining our obligations toward other human beings, which focuses on the very beginning of human life as the moment at which respect and protection from harm must be given. From this perspective we can argue that all human beings must be treated as equals. Further, all human beings must be allowed to share in the common good of humanity.

Based upon the above reasoning, I conclude by arguing that there should be a total, worldwide ban on destructive human embryonic research and human therapeutic cloning. The development and use of human embryos and clones for research purposes—even those deemed therapeutic—is unethical. Taking the needed stem cells from a blastocyst—cloned or otherwise—destroys a human being, a member of our living community. This is tantamount to taking the heart from a living person, resulting in death, in order to transplant that heart into another person to save their life. Even if one tried to argue that in the case of a clone, only "spare organs" (a kidney) or "partial organs" (a lobe of the lungs or half of the liver) would be used, this would still be untenable because the clone would not have true freedom in the decision process, which is an ethical requirement of informed consent. Such cloning, then, would not truly be "therapeutic," because the clone itself never benefits from any of the procedures done to it. In the end, the ethical argument is quite simple and direct—we cannot actively and directly harm or kill one human life to save another. And so, according to *ethical personalism,* the process of destroying an embryo for its stem cells, or developing a clone and destroying it for the sole purposes of using its tissue in research or therapy is unethical.[108]

A Final Thought: Stimulating Our Own Cells

As one can see, adult stem cells have already been providing therapeutic benefit to living human patients. The promise is concrete, and can be measured with names and faces—all without destroying embryos, cloned or otherwise. This is research whose human application is well under way. And with emerging evidence of fewer immunological reactions using various types of adult stem cells, the threat of immune rejection or the need for large amounts of immunosuppressive drugs—two of the key drawbacks of embryonic stem cell transplants in animal models—is considerably less using adult stem cells.[109] Indeed, in the end, perhaps the most promising therapies will be those that do not even rely on any transplant, but instead harness the power of each person's own stem cells. As Dr. David Prentice, co-founder of the Do No Harm coalition, noted in his draft report to the President's Council on Bioethics in July of 2003:

The indications from the previous examples suggest that direct stimulation of endogenous stem cells within a tissue may be the easiest, safest, and most efficient way to stimulate tissue regeneration. Such stimulation need not rely on any added stem cells. This approach would circumvent the need to isolate or grow stem cells in culture, or inject any stem cells into the body, whether the cells were derived from the patient or another source. Moreover, direct stimulation of endogenous tissue stem cells with specific growth factors might even preclude any need to mobilize stem cells to a site of tissue damage.[110]

The implications of adult stem cell research, then, provide amazing hope for the future of human health. This, in my opinion, is where our focus should be. Every day we are learning more clearly that the power to heal ourselves and each other has been inside of us all along.

NOTES

1. For one interesting illustration, see the story by Kevin Clarke, "Unnatural selection: How biotechnology is redesigning humanity," *U.S. Catholic* 65, no. 1 (January 2000), posted online at USCatholic.org, accessed at www.uscatholic.org/2000/01/cov0001.htm on September 15, 2003.

2. Bertrand Russell, *Has Man A Future?* (Baltimore: Penguin Books, 1970), pp. 54–55.

3. See Do No Harm: The Coalition of Americans for Research Ethics website, especially their founding statement at www.stemcellresearch.org/statement/statement.htm#text40.

4. The National Institutes of Health's (NIH) official website, "Stem Cell Basics," at http://stemcells.nih.gov/infoCenter/stemCellBasics.asp#1. Note that if one were to look at other sources in either the popular media or in the specialty journals, one would probably find some variation in the facts being presented here. In the end, these differences and variations may not be relevant to the ethical issues that are the ultimate concern of this paper. However, it is interesting that the "scientists" are not always in agreement about their facts, which only adds to the confusion in the public debates regarding stem cell research.

5. Ibid., accessed at http://stemcells.nih.gov/infoCenter/stemCellBasics.asp#2 on August 6, 2003.

6. For a few noteworthy examples, see CNN.com, "Stem cells show promise in treating neurological diseases": "In November 1998, scientists announced for the first time that they were able to isolate stem cells, or blank cells, that could specialize into any kind of cell for the body—neurons, blood, muscle, bone," posted July 29, 1999, 2:02 p.m. EDT, and accessed at www.cnn.com/HEALTH/9907/29/stem.cell.advance on August 13, 2003; Elizabeth Cohen, CNN medical correspondent based in Atlanta, Georgia, in a July 18, 2001, interview posted on CNN.com, "Elizabeth Cohen: Ethics of Stem Cell Research": "They are essentially blank cells that potentially can be turned into pretty much any type of body tissue." posted: 7:20 a.m. EDT, and accessed at www.cnn.com/2001/HEALTH/07/17/cohen.otsc on August 13, 2003; and Juvenile Diabetes Research Foundation International, "Restoring normal blood sugar: Stem Cell Research": "Stem cells are 'blank' cells with the ability to grow into any other type of cell—such as insulin-producing islets. These cells could then be transplanted into someone with juvenile (type 1) diabetes and potentially cure the disease," updated August 12, 2003, posted at www.jdrf.org/index.cfm?fuseaction=home.viewPage&page_id=02DBD384-2A5E-7B6E-1AA3637745700722 and accessed on August 13, 2003.

7. See James A. Thomson et al., "Embryonic Stem Cell Lines Derived from Human Blastocysts," *Science* 282 (November 6, 1998): 1145–47, and John Gearhart, "Cell Biology: New Potential for Human Embryonic Stem Cells," *Science* 282 (November 6, 1998): 1061–62. These were the first two researchers to actually isolate human embryonic stem cells using two different methods.

8. NIH, "Stem Cell Basics," accessed at http://stemcells.nih.gov/infoCenter/stemCellBasics.asp#3 on August 6, 2003.

9. Ibid.

10. Ibid., accessed at http://stemcells.nih.gov/infoCenter/stemCellBasics.asp#4 on August 6, 2003.

11. See L. Gore et al., "Successful cord blood transplantation for sickle cell anemia from a sibling who is human leukocyte antigen-identical: implications for comprehensive care," *Journal of Pediatric Hematology and Oncology* 22 (September–October 2000): 437–40; M. J. Laughlin et al., "Hematopoietic Engraftment and Survival in Adult Recipients of Umbilical-Cord Blood from Unrelated Donors," *New England Journal of Medicine* 344 (June 14, 2001): 1815–22; Sei Kakinuma et al., "Human Umbilical Cord Blood as a Source of Transplantable Hepatic Progenitor Cells," *Stem Cells* 21 (2003): 217–27; and H. E. Broxmeyer et al., "High-efficiency recovery of functional hematopoietic progenitor and stem cells from human cord blood cryopreserved for 15 years," *Proceedings of the National Academy of Sciences USA* 100 (January 12, 2003): 645–50.

12. See the story regarding the official press release from Anthrogenesis Corporation of Cedar Knolls, New Jersey, by Anne Harding, "Company Finds Stem Cell Source in Placen-

tas," posted on the company's official website on April 12, 2001, accessed at www.anthrogenesis.com/asp/news0412.asp on August 30, 2003. Also see Miriam Falco, CNN Medical Unit: "Placenta source of stem cells, researchers say," posted on CNN.com on April 12, 2001, at 11:20 a.m. EDT, accessed at http://edition.cnn.com/2001/HEALTH/04/12/placenta.stemcells on August 13, 2003; and Kyodo News: "Scientists Develop Bone, Nerve Cells from Placenta," April 15, 2002, accessed at www.lef.org/newsarchive/disease/2002/04/15/ky/0000-4797-stem-cell.html on August 13, 2003.

13. See H. Okawa et al., "Amniotic epithelial cells transform into neuron-like cells in the ischemic brain," *NeuroReport* 12 (2001): 4003–4007; A. R. Prusa et al., "Oct-4-expressing cells in human amniotic fluid: a new source for stem cell research?" *Human Reproduction* 18 (2003): 1489–93; and Shaoni Bhattacharya, from New Scientist Online News, "Amniotic fluid may hold 'ethical' stem cells," posted on June 30, 2003, accessed at www.newscientist.com/hottopics/cloning/cloning.jsp?id=ns99993886 on August 30, 2003.

14. See K. Okumura et al., "Salivary gland progenitor cells induced by duct ligation differentiate into hepatic and pancreatic lineages," *Hepatology* 38 (July 2003): 104–13; and Richard Black, BBC Science Correspondent, "Mouth cells treat eyes," posted on BBCi on March 17, 2003, accessed at http://news.bbc.co.uk/2/hi/health/2856541.stm on August 13, 2003.

15. See S. F. Pagano et al., "Isolation and Characterization of Neural Stem Cells from the Adult Human Olfactory Bulb," *Stem Cells* 18 (2000): 295–300; David Wroe, Health Reporter, "Stem cell research led by the nose," posted on theage.com.au on January 31, 2003, accessed at www.theage.com.au/articles/2003/01/30/1043804464986.html on August 13, 2003; and Laurance Johnston, Ph.D., "Within the Realm," part 1 of a two-part series regarding the use of olfactory tissue for treatment of spinal cord injuries, *PN/Paraplegia News,* March 2003.

16. See S. Gronthos et al., "Postnatal human dental pulp stem cells (DPSCs) in vitro and in vivo," *Proceedings of the National Academy of Sciences USA* 97 (December 5, 2000): 13625–30; and Songtao Shi et al., "SHED: Stem cells from human exfoliated deciduous teeth," *Proceedings of the National Academy of Sciences USA* 100 (May 13, 2003): 5807–12.

17. See T. D. Palmer et al., "Progenitor cells from human brain after death," *Nature* 411 (May 3, 2001): 42–43; Janet McConnaughey, "Life from Dead Brains: Cadavers Provide Crucial Source of Stem Cells," ABCNews.com on November 6, 2000, and accessed at http://abcnews.go.com/sections/science/DailyNews/stemcells_cadavers001106.html on August 13, 2003; and CBSNews.com, "New Findings in Stem Cell Research," accessed at www.cbsnews.com/stories/2000/11/06/tech/main247182.shtml on August 13, 2003.

18. See Patricia A. Zuk, Ph.D., et al., "Multilineage Cells from Human Adipose Tissue: Implications for Cell-Based Therapies," *Tissue Engineering* 7, no. 2 (April 2001): 211–28; K. M. Safford et al., "Neurogenic differentiation of murine and human adipose-derived stromal cells," *Biochemical and Biophysical Research Communications* 294 (2002): 371–79; and Julia Sommerfeld, "Liposuction a novel source of stem cells," accessed at www.msnbc.com/news/747030.aspp on August 13, 2003.

19. NIH, "Stem Cell Basics," accessed at http://stemcells.nih.gov/infoCenter/stemCellBasics.asp#4 on August 6, 2003.

20. Ibid.

21. See National Marrow Donor Program, "Umbilical Cord Blood Stem Cell Transplantation, basic," accessed at www.marrow.org/MEDICAL/cord_blood_transplantation_basic.html on August 22, 2003; *Scientific American,* "Ask the Experts": "For which diseases or conditions is umbilical cord blood stem cell therapy most effective?" accessed at www.sciam.com/askexpert_question.cfm?articleID=00087759-141E-1CC7-B4A8809EC588EEDF&catID=3 on August 22, 2003; and March of Dimes, "Umbilical Cord Blood," accessed at www.marchofdimes.com/search/MsmGo.exe?grab_id=52579504&extra_arg=&page_id=894&host_id=1&query=umbilical+cord+blood&hiword=UMBILICAL+CORD+BLOOD on August 30, 2003.

22. The issue of whether or not adult stem cells can be made to proliferate efficiently is one of the most hotly contested problems in the debate over using *embryonic* versus *adult* stem cells. Proponents of embryonic stem cell research insist that adult stem cells are simply not

able to provide an adequate supply of cells for actual therapeutic application. However, as noted, continued advances in this area are clearly showing that adult stem cells can indeed replicate efficiently enough for therapeutic purposes. See G. Bhardwaj et al., "Sonic hedgehog induces the proliferation of primitive human hematopoietic cells via BMP regulation," *Nature Immunology* 2 (February 2001): 172–80; M. Reyes et al., "Purification and ex vivo expansion of postnatal human marrow mesodermal progenitor cells," *Blood* 98 (November 1, 2001): 2615–25; Y. Jiang et al., "Pluripotency of mesenchymal stem cells derived from adult marrow," *Nature* 418 (July 4, 2002): 41–49; and Jennifer Jaroscak et al., "Augmentation of umbilical cord blood (Ucb) transplantation with ex-vivo expanded UCB cells: results of a phase I trial using the Aastrom Replicell system," *Blood*, pre-published online as a Blood First Edition Paper on February 20, 2003; DOI 10.1182/blood-2001-12-0290, accessed at www.bloodjournal.org/cgi/content/abstract/2001-12-0290v1 on August 30, 2003. In particular, it has been shown that lithium, a common antidepressant, also helps stimulate adult stem cells to grow faster in culture: G. J. Moore et al., "Lithium-induced increase in human grey brain matter," *Lancet* 356 (2000): 1241–42; and R. Hashimoto et al., "Lithium stimulates progenitor proliferation in cultured brain neurons," *Neuroscience* 117 (2003): 55–61.

23. NIH, "Stem Cell Basics," accessed at http://stemcells.nih.gov/infoCenter/stemCellBasics.asp#5 on August 6, 2003.

24. Ibid., accessed at http://stemcells.nih.gov/infoCenter/stemCellBasics.asp#3 on August 6, 2003.

25. Ibid. Also, for further references on the issue of stem cell potency, see WebMD's page "Q&A on Stem Cells," accessed at http://my.webmd.com/content/article/16/1728_86306.htm?lastselectedguid={5FE84E90-BC77-4056-A91C-9531713CA348} on August 6, 2003.

26. For a few noteworthy examples see the following—but note as well that a "lack" of evidence or experimental data is NOT the scientific norm for drawing conclusions. Juvenile Diabetes Research Foundation International, "JDRF Issues New Stem Cell Research Q&A," on March 22, 2000: "Why not derive stem cells from adults? There are several approaches now in human clinical trials that utilize stem cells isolated from adults. These adult-derived stem cells do not have the same capacity for proliferation as those obtained from embryonic sources. Moreover, the adult-derived stem cells are likely to be more limited in their potential. For example, skin stem cells are predisposed to become skin and not other tissues. Unlike adult stem cells, embryonic stem cells contain two salient features important to diabetes research: (1) they can divide to a great extent because their proliferative capacity is far greater than stem cells isolated from adults; and (2) they can form (virtually) any cell type. The potency of adult stem cells is less well established." Accessed at www.jdrf.org/index.cfm?fuseaction=home.viewPage&page_id=65A091EC-DE4F-4696-8C3E40493A4101E8 on August 30, 2003. Also, from TIME.com by Jessica Reaves, "The Great Debate over Stem Cell Research," on July 11, 2001: "Adult stem cells taken from the blood or organs of healthy adults have recently demonstrated an unexpected adaptability in lab experiments. But these cells are marginally helpful to scientists, and do not show the same promise as those culled from embryos. Adult cells are fairly set in their ways, and don't seem to grow or replicate themselves as quickly as their younger counterparts." Accessed at www.time.com/time/health/article/0,8599,167245,00.html on August 30, 2003. And, from the University of Wisconsin–Madison, copyrighted 2001, "Embryonic Stem Cells": "Why not derive stem cells from adults? There are several approaches now in human clinical trials that utilize mature stem cells (such as blood-forming cells, neuron-forming cells and cartilage-forming cells). However, because adult cells are already specialized, their potential to regenerate damaged tissue is very limited: skin cells will only become skin and cartilage cells will only become cartilage. Adults do not have stem cells in many vital organs, so when those tissues are damaged, scar tissue develops. Only embryonic stem cells, which have the capacity to become any kind of human tissue, have the potential to repair vital organs." Accessed at http://news.wisc.edu/packages/stemcells/index.html?get=facts#1 on August 30, 2003.

27. NIH, "Stem Cell Basics," accessed at http://stemcells.nih.gov/infoCenter/stemCellBasics.asp#4 on August 30, 2003.

28. David A. Prentice, Ph.D., "Adult Stem Cells," presented to the President's Council on Bioethics, July 2003, draft, accessed at http://bioethics.gov/background/prentice_paper.html on August 30, 2003.

29. For an excellent discussion of the tension over embryonic versus adult stem cell plasticity, see Nadia Rosenthal, Ph.D., "Prometheus's Vulture and the Stem-Cell Promise," *New England Journal of Medicine* 349 (July 17, 2003): 267–74. Also of note is the recent concern being raised in the literature regarding the effectiveness of adult stem cells for therapeutic application in humans due to the phenomenon of cell fusion. Although the question of stem cell "fusion" is not exactly new, for a discussion regarding why this is now considered a potential "problem" see George Q. Daley, M.D., Ph.D., "Cloning and Stem Cells—Handicapping the Political and Scientific Debates," *New England Journal of Medicine* 349 (July 17, 2003): 211–12; also see the story by Steve Mitchell, "Study casts doubt on adult stem cells," published online on October 12, 2003, accessed at www.upi.com/view.cfm?StoryID=20031012-121339-2906r on October 13, 2003 (Mitchell reports on a study conducted by Arturo Alvarez-Buylla that raises questions about the efficacy of adult stem cells, which the journal *Nature* published online October 12, 2003—however, it is worth noting that the study was conducted on mice, and as we are reminded on all fronts, the differences between mice trials and human trials are significant and so the results of the study do not necessarily apply to current research using human adult stem cells). However, the whole issue of adult stem cell fusion may not be clinically relevant. Some studies indicate that cell fusion may be part of how stem cells actually help repair damage to the body. For an excellent rebuttal to the "cell fusion" problem, see Prentice, "Adult Stem Cells." For specific research regarding the question of stem cell fusion from 1961 to the present, see S. Sorieul and B. Ephrussi, "Karyological demonstration of hybridization of mammalian cells in vitro," *Nature* 190 (1961): 653–54; J. W. Littlefield, "Selection of hybrids from matings of fibroblasts in vitro and their presumed recombinants," *Science* 145 (August 14, 1964): 709–10; R. L. Ladda and R. D. Estensen, "Introduction of a heterologous nucleus into enucleated cytoplasms of cultured mouse L-cells," *Proceedings of the National Academy of Sciences USA* 67 (November 1970): 1528–33; G. Köhler and C. Milstein, "Continuous culture of fused cells secreting antibody of predefined specificity," *Nature* 256 (1975): 495–97; M. Tada et al., "Embryonic germ cells induce epigenetic reprogramming of somatic nucleus in hybrid cells," *EMBO Journal* 16 (1997): 6510–20; N. Terada et al., "Bone marrow cells adopt the phenotype of other cells by spontaneous cell fusion," *Nature* 416 (April 4, 2002): 542–45; H. M. Blau, "Stem-cell fusion: A twist of fate," *Nature* 419 (October 3, 2002): 437; G. Vassilopoulos et al., "Transplanted bone marrow regenerates liver by cell fusion," *Nature* 422 (April 24, 2003): 901–904; J. L. Spees et al., "Differentiation, cell fusion, and nuclear fusion during *ex vivo* repair of epithelium by human adult stem cells from bone marrow stroma," *Proceedings of the National Academy of Sciences USA* 100 (March 4, 2003): 2397–2402; and P. N. Newsome et al., "Human cord blood-derived cells can differentiate into hepatocytes in the mouse liver with no evidence of cellular fusion," *Gastroenterology* 124 (June 2003): 1891–900.

30. See D. Woodbury et al., "Adult Rat and Human Bone Marrow Stromal Cells Differentiate into Neurons," *Journal of Neuroscience Research* 61 (2000): 364–70; Neil Theise et al., "Derivation of hepatocytes from bone marrow cells in mice after radiation-induced myeloablation," *Hepatology* 31 (January 2000): 235–40; A. Gritti et al., "Adult neural stem cells: plasticity and developmental potential," *Journal of Physiology*, Paris, 96, nos. 1–2 (January–March 2000): 81–90; Neil Theise et al., "Liver from Bone Marrow in Humans," *Hepatology* 32 (July 2000): 11–16; Malcolm Alison et al., "Cell Differentiation: Hepatocytes from Non-Hepatic Adult Stem Cells," *Nature* 406 (July 20, 2000): 257; E. Kaji and J. Leiden, "Gene and Stem Cell Therapies," *Journal of the American Medical Association* 285 (February 7, 2001): 545–50; Luchuan Liang and Jackie R. Bickenback, "Somatic Epidermal Stem Cells Can Produce Multiple Cell Lineages During Development," *Stem Cells* 20 (2002): 21–31; Stuart H. Orkin and Sean J. Morrison, "Biomedicine: Stem-cell competition," *Nature* 418 (July 4, 2002): 25–27; and Sylvia Pagan Westphal, "Greater potential of adult stem cells revealed," from New Scientist Online News, posted on May 17, 2003, accessed at www.newscientist.com/hottopics/cloning/cloning.jsp?id=ns99993723

on August 30, 2003. Also, for a specific response to some of the claims made against adult stem cell plasticity, see Michael Fumento, "Celling Lies: More spurious stem-cell claims," posted on National Review Online on September 25, 2002, and accessed at www.nationalreview.com/comment/comment-fumento092502.asp on August 30, 2003.

31. NIH, "Stem Cell Information," Frequently Asked Questions, accessed at http://stemcells.nih.gov/faqs.asp#15 on August 30, 2003 (emphasis added).

32. Wesley J. Smith, "Spinning Stem Cells," in the National Review Online, posted April 23, 2002, accessed at www.nationalreview.com/comment/comment-smith042302.asp on August 30, 2003.

33. Eliot Marshall, "The Business of Stem Cells," *Science* 287 (February 25, 2000): 1418–19.

34. Richard Miniter, The WallStreetJournal.com Opinion Journal, "Hard Cell," posted on July 23, 2001, accessed at www.opinionjournal.com/columnists/rminiter/?id=95000857 on October 13, 2003 (emphasis added).

35. NIH, "Stem Cells: Scientific Progress and Future Research Directions," Executive Summary, p. 3, accessed at http://stemcells.nih.gov/stemcell/pdfs/execsummary.pdf on August 30, 2003: "Most of the basic research discoveries on embryonic and adult stem cells come from research using animal models, particularly mice."

36. Ibid.

37. See the testimonies of Elias A. Zerhouni, M.D., director, the National Institutes of Health, and Mark B. McClellan, M.D., commissioner, Food and Drug Administration, speaking before the President's Council on Bioethics, from the official meeting transcript, "Stem Cells: Moving Research from the Bench Towards the Bedside: The Role of NIH and FDA," Thursday, September 4, 2003, accessed at www.bioethics.gov/transcripts/sep03/session3.html on October 6, 2003.

38. NIH, "Stem Cells: Scientific Progress and Future Research Directions," Executive Summary, p. 9, accessed at http://stemcells.nih.gov/stemcell/pdfs/execsummary.pdf on August 30, 2003. It is interesting to note that the NIH report goes on to add: "A teratoma typically contains a mixture of partially differentiated cell types. For this reason, scientists do not anticipate that undifferentiated embryonic stem cells will be used for transplants or other therapeutic applications." This is an incredibly significant point. The whole force behind using embryonic stem cells is their pluripotency—which proponents of this research argue adult stem cells lack. However, the NIH points out that researchers are having trouble controlling these pluripotent stem cells derived from embryos—because of their pluripotent nature, they tend to form all sorts of tissues in addition to the ones being sought, and there is some indication that these cells may be attempting to turn back into stem cells once transplanted. All of which means that "pluripotency" is not all it was thought to be, and that already differentiated cells—i.e., multipotent cells like adult stem cells—are what will be needed for actual therapeutic applications. As noted by University of Pennsylvania bioethicist Glenn McGee in an interview with MIT's *Technology Review,* "The emerging truth in the lab is that pluripotent [embryonic] stem cells are hard to reign in. . . . The potential that they would explode into a cancerous mass after a stem cell transplant might turn out to be the Pandora's box of stem cell research," quoted by Richard Miniter in "Hard Cell," The WallStreetJournal.com Opinion Journal, posted on July 23, 2001, accessed at www.opinionjournal.com/columnists/rminiter/?id=95000857 on October 13, 2003. So, again, one must ask, do we really need embryonic stem cell research? It appears, when one carefully examines the findings being presented in the literature, that embryonic stem cells will never be useful for actual therapeutic benefit. For more on the problem of tumor formation, see J. S. Odorico et al., "Multilineage differentiation from human embryonic stem cell lines," *Stem Cells* 19 (2001): 193–204: "[T]he possibility arises that transplantation of differentiated human ES cell derivatives into human recipients may result in the formation of ES cell-derived tumors," posted on the Do No Harm website, accessed at www.stemcellresearch.org/facts/quotes3.htm on September 6, 2003.

39. NIH, "Stem Cells: Scientific Progress and Future Research Directions," Executive Summary, p. 4, accessed at http://stemcells.nih.gov/stemcell/pdfs/execsummary.pdf on August 30,

2003. Also see J. S. Odorico et al., "Multilineage differentiation from human embryonic stem cell lines," *Stem Cells* 19 (2001): 193–204: "Rarely have specific growth factors or culture conditions led to establishment of cultures containing a single cell type," accessed at www.stemcell-research.org/facts/quotes3.htm on August 30, 2003. Also see Wolfgang Lillge, M.D., "The Case for Adult Stem Cells," *21st Century: Science & Technology Magazine,* Winter 2001–2002, "So far there has been no solution to the problem of developing in the laboratory an unmistakable identifier for stem cells that can distinguish them unequivocally from cancer cells. For this reason, it is also not possible to produce sufficiently pure cell cultures from stem cells. So far, with embryonic mouse stem cells, a purity of only 80 percent has been achieved. That is in no way sufficient for cell transplantation as a human therapy. In a cell culture for therapeutic purposes, there must not be a single undifferentiated cell, since it can lead to unregulated growth, in this case to the formation of teratomas, a cancerous tumor derived from the germ layers. This problem would not be expected with adult stem cells, because of their greater differentiation," accessed at www.21stcenturysciencetech.com/articles/winter01/stem_cell.html on August 30, 2003. Also see M. J. Shamblott et al., "Human embryonic germ cell derivatives express a broad range of developmentally distinct markers and proliferate extensively in vitro," *Proceedings of the National Academy of Sciences USA* 98 (January 2, 2001): 113–18. There has been one recent report, from April of 2003, that some pure cultures of embryonic stem cells have been obtained by Geron, a biopharmaceutical company in California; see "Geron Reports Advances in Its Human Embryonic Stem Cell Programs" posted on Bioexchange.com: "Geron scientists presented new data showing that cardiomyocytes (heart muscle cells) can be derived from hESCs and enriched by a serum-free culture formulation that prevents the growth of unwanted cell populations," accessed at www.bioexchange.com/news/news_page.cfm?id=16801 on October 6, 2003. Nevertheless, developing pure cultures remains one of the key obstacles in pushing toward human application with embryonic stem cell research.

40. NIH, "Stem Cells: Scientific Progress and Future Research Directions," Executive Summary, p. 6, accessed at http://stemcells.nih.gov/stemcell/pdfs/execsummary.pdf on August 30, 2003. At this point in the research, large amounts of immunosuppressant drugs are required to ward off rejection of the transplanted cells—this is basically the same problem faced by all forms of transplant. Thus, even though these embryonic stem cells are often referred to as "generic" and "blank," they still trigger immune rejection because they carry the donor's DNA, which is recognized as foreign by the recipient's immune system. So, as the NIH notes later in Chapter 3 of its report titled "The Human Embryonic Stem Cell and the Human Embryonic Germ Cell": "Human ES derived cells would also be advantageous for transplantation purposes if they did not trigger immune rejection," p. 17, accessed at http://stemcells.nih.gov/stemcell/pdfs/chapter3.pdf on August 30, 2003. Also see Dr. Mae-Wan Ho, "Adult versus Embryonic Stem Cells," posted on the Institute of Science in Society's website, accessed at www.isis.org.uk/stemcells2.php on August 30, 2003.

41. NIH, "Stem Cells: Scientific Progress and Future Research Directions," p. 96, accessed at http://stemcells.nih.gov/stemcell/pdfs/chapter10.pdf on August 30, 2003. Also see D. Humphreys et al., "Epigenetic Instability in ES Cells and Cloned Mice," *Science* 293 (July 2001): 95–97: "The epigenetic state of the ES cell genome was found to be extremely unstable," from the abstract, accessed at www.ncbi.nlm.nih.gov/entrez/query.fcgi?holding=npg&cmd=Retrieve&db=PubMed&list_uids=11441181&dopt=Abstract on September 6, 2003. Also, Rachel B. Cervantes et al., "Embryonic stem cells and somatic cells differ in mutation frequency and type," *Proceedings of the National Academy of Sciences USA* 99 (March 19, 2002): 3586–90: "Therefore, the possibility that ES cells suffer UPD involving multiple chromosomes should be of concern. Because UPD allows all recessive loci on a given chromosome to manifest, including alleles encoding tumor suppressors, the accumulation of UPD in cultured stem cells raises a concern regarding clinical use of stem cells continuously maintained in culture. This concern does not constitute an argument against the therapeutic use of stem cells but rather indicates the need for screening such cultures to ensure the absence of UPD," accessed at www.pubmed-central.nih.gov/articlerender.fcgi?artid=122567 on September 6, 2003. And, W. Dean et al., "Al-

tered imprinted gene methylation and expression in completely ES cell-derived mouse fetuses: association with aberrant phenotypes," *Development* 125 (May 19, 1998): 2273–82. However, it should be noted that some researchers do not think that embryonic germ cells, which seem to have the same general properties as embryonic stem cells for proliferation and differentiation of other tissues, do not have epigenetic problems. See Carmen Sapienza et al., "Imprinted gene expression, transplantation medicine, and the 'other' human embryonic stem cell," *Proceedings of the National Academy of Sciences USA,* published online before print July 30, 2002, 10.1073/pnas.172384299, August 6, 2002, vol. 99, no. 16, pp. 10243–45, accessed at www.pnas.org/cgi/content/full/99/16/10243 on October 6, 2003.

42. One other problem still brought up in the literature involves the fear of transferring animal viruses to humans via xenotransplantation. As noted by the NIH, "Stem Cells: Scientific Progress and Future Research Directions," p. 95: ". . . the culturing of human embryonic stem and embryonic germ cells involves the use of mouse embryonic fibroblast feeder cells to keep the embryonic cells in a proliferating, undifferentiated condition. . . . Transplanting into humans stem cell preparations derived from founder cells that have been indirect, intimate contact with nonhuman animal cells constitutes xenotransplantation—the use of organs, tissues, and cells derived from animals to treat human disease. The principal concern of xenotransplantation is the unintended transfer of animal viruses into humans," accessed on August 30, 2003, at http://stemcells.nih.gov/stemcell/pdfs/chapter10.pdf. However, as the report from the NIH goes on to note: "Researchers are devoting considerable attention to developing culture conditions that do not use mouse feeder cells." The report specifically cites research conducted by Geron Corporation, a major biotech company based in California, that shows human embryonic stem cells can be proliferated under "feeder-free conditions." See Geron's own press release posted on Geron.com, "Geron Develops and Files Patents on Feeder-Free Growth Conditions for Human Embryonic Stem Cells," October 2001, accessed at www.geron.com/pr_20011001b.html on August 30, 2003. Also see the related story posted on Bioexchange.com on April 3, 2003, "Geron Reports Advances in its Human Embryonic Stem Cell Programs," accessed at www.bioexchange.com/news/news_page.cfm?id=16801 on October 6, 2003. Geron's successful "proof of concept" is noteworthy regarding this major obstacle in advancing embryonic stem cell research. Nevertheless, the research has not been peer-reviewed, nor validated, thus keeping the problem of animal feeder cell transfer a genuine obstacle for most embryonic stem cell research at this point in time. For other efforts to solve the animal feeder cell problem, see Ariff Bongso et al., "Human feeders support prolonged undifferentiated growth of human inner cell masses and embryonic stem cells," published online in *Nature Biotechnology,* vol. 20, no. 9, pp. 993–96, posted on August 5, 2002, accessed at www.nature.com/nbt/press_release/nbt0902.html on August 30, 2003; and L. Cheng et al., "Human Adult Marrow Cells Support Prolonged Expansion of Human Embryonic Stem Cells in Culture," *Stem Cells* 2 (2003): 131–42. For more on the risks of animal to human viral transfer see Emma Young, "Stem cells face xenotransplantation risk," from New Scientist Online News, posted on August 24, 2001, and accessed at www.newscientist.com/hottopics/cloning/cloning.jsp?id=ns99991196 on August 30, 2003; and Justin Gillis and Ceci Connolly, "Stem Cell Research Faces FDA Hurdle: With Mouse Cell Base, Tough Rules Apply," posted on Washingtonpost.com on August 24, 2001, and accessed at www.washingtonpost.com/ac2/wp-dyn/A53580-2001Aug23?language=printer on August 30, 2003.

43. For references to this issue, see Judith A. Johnson of the Congressional Research Service, specialist in life sciences, Domestic Social Policy Division, "Report to Congress, Stem Cell Research," submitted on February 24, 2003, and posted through the Congressional Research Service, accessed at www.house.gov/israel/issues/crs_hea_stemcells_022403.pdf on October 6, 2003: "The human embryonic stem cell lines that have been isolated to date have all been grown on beds of mouse 'feeder' cells. The mouse cells secrete a substance that prevents the human embryonic stem cells from differentiating into more mature cell types (such as nerve or muscle cells). Infectious agents, such as viruses, within the mouse feeder cells could transfer into the human cells. If the human cells were transplanted into a patient, these infected hu-

man cells may cause disease in the patient which could be transmitted to close contacts of the patient and eventually to the general population. Public health officials and regulatory agencies such as the FDA are specifically concerned about retroviruses, which may remain hidden in the DNA only to cause disease many years later, as well as any unrecognized agents which may be present in the mouse cells." Also see Ted Agres, "Senators urge stem cell expansion," posted on The-Scientist.com, April 25, 2003, accessed at www.biomedcentral.com/news/20030425/03 on September 6, 2003: "Under existing policy, federal funds for HESC research are available only for a limited number of cell lines established before August 9, 2001. Of some 78 stem cell lines initially identified as meeting the eligibility criteria, only 11 lines are presently available for researchers, Specter noted. Many scientists and politicians have argued that this number inhibits meaningful research. And because the currently qualified stem cell lines have been grown using mouse feeder cells, there is the potential for mouse viruses and other contaminating proteins to be passed to human cells, making potential clinical trials risky and difficult to conduct." And, Kevin Davies, Bio-IT World Online, "Stem Cell Suicide," posted on July 16, 2003, and accessed at www.bioitworld.com/news/071603_report2919.html on October 6, 2003: "According to the NIH, only 11 of the federally sanctioned ES lines are currently available for distribution. More importantly, all of the existing ES lines were produced with mouse 'feeder' cells, rendering them unusable in any potential clinical context. Recent studies, however, have shown that human cells can substitute for the mouse feeder layer, leaving many researchers anxious to develop and characterize such lines."

44. For a few noteworthy examples, see Amy Coxon, Ph.D., from the Department of Health and Human Services, "Therapeutic Cloning: An Oxymoron," posted on the Center for Bioethics and Human Dignity website, 2002, accessed at www.cbhd.org/resources/cloning/coxon_2001-03-13_print.htm on August 30, 2003; United States Conference of Catholic Bishops, "What is Cloning?" copyright June 3, 2003, accessed at www.usccb.org/prolife/issues/bioethic/clonfact202.htm on October 6, 2003; Nigel M. de S. Cameron, Ph.D., "Human Cloning: The Necessity of a Comprehensive Ban," posted on the Comprehensive Christian World View website, accessed at www.ccwv.net/EssayDisplay.asp?recordID=283 on October 6, 2003; and Therese M. Lysaught, Ph.D., "The New Eugenics: Cloning and Beyond," posted on United States Conference of Catholic Bishops website, copyright June 3, 2003, accessed at www.usccb.org/prolife/issues/bioethic/clonfact202.htm on October 6, 2003. Also, for a comprehensive discussion of the overall cloning issue see Dr. Patrick Dixon, *The Genetic Revolution* (Kingsway, 1995), and available online at www.globalchange.com/books/Genesintro.htm.

45. See the President's Council on Bioethics official website, "Human Cloning and Human Dignity: An Ethical Inquiry," accessed at www.bioethics.gov/reports/cloningreport/index.html on October 6, 2003—see especially Chapter 3: On Terminology. Also see B. Vogelstein et al., "Please don't call it cloning!" *Science* 295 (2002): 1237, which has gotten a lot of play from the scientific/research side. And, see Dónal P. O'Mathúna's insightful commentary on this issue, "What to call human cloning: The technical terminology increasingly used in the cloning debate sidesteps the ethical questions raised," *EMBO Reports* 3, no. 6 (2002): 502–505. Or, Wesley J. Smith's pointed essay, "Closing in on Cloning—Don't expect an honest debate as the legislative fight heats up," *Weekly Standard,* January 14, 2002, accessed at www.health.thechurch.com.au/scr_001.html on October 6, 2003.

46. National Academy of Sciences, *Scientific and Medical Aspects of Human Reproductive Cloning* (Washington, D.C.: National Academy Press, 2002), p. E-4.

47. The President's Council on Bioethics' website, accessed at www.bioethics.gov/reports/cloningreport/terminology.html#note2 on October 6, 2003.

48. For a simplified, but accurate, overview of these procedures, see Craig C. Freudenrich, Ph.D., "How Cloning Works," on howstuffworks.com, accessed at http://science.howstuffworks.com/cloning1.htm on September 6, 2003. Also see the University of Utah's Genetic Science Learning Center, "What is Cloning?," accessed at http://gslc.genetics.utah.edu/units/cloning/whatiscloning/ on October 6, 2003, and the Cloning Webliography maintained by Susan K. Kendall, Ph.D., health sciences librarian at Michigan State University, accessed at www.lib.msu.

edu/skendall/cloning/ on September 6, 2003—both provide helpful resources for the non-scientist.

49. Hans Spemann, *Embryonic Development and Induction* (New Haven, CT: Yale University Press, 1938). Also see the discussion of cloning techniques on Stanford University's website, "Human Cloning," accessed at www.stanford.edu/~eclipse9/sts129/cloning/methods.html#scnt on August 30, 2003, and the Kayotic Development website for an explanation of Spemann's early contributions to the process of SCNT, accessed at www.abc.lv/thinkquest/tq-entries/24355/data/details/profiles/spemann.html on August 30, 2003.

50. For the original published reports of their research and methods, see I. Wilmut et al., "Sheep cloned by nuclear transfer from a cultured cell line," *Nature* 380 (1996): 64–66, and I. Wilmut et al., "Viable offspring derived from fetal and adult mammalian cells," *Nature* 385 (1997): 810–13. The Roslin Institute actually has two patents on its technique: PCT/GB96/02099, entitled "Quiescent cell populations for nuclear transfer," and PCT/GB96/02098, entitled "Unactivated oocytes as cytoplast recipients for nuclear transfer." See the discussion of cloning techniques on Stanford University's website, and on the Kayotic Development website, accessed at www.abc.lv/thinkquest/tq-entries/24355/data/details/techniques/roslin.html on August 30, 2003.

51. For the original published reports of their research and methods, see T. Wakayama et al., "Full-term development of mice from enucleated oocytes injected with cumulus cell nuclei," *Nature* 394 (July 23, 1998): 369–74. This technique is also included in the discussion of cloning on Stanford University's website and the Kayotic Development website, accessed at www.abc.lv/thinkquest/tq-entries/24355/data/details/techniques/honolulu.html on August 30, 2003. Or, see the story posted by Kristin Leutwyler on ScientificAmerican.com on July 27, 1998, "Send in the Clones: Using a new technique, scientists have cloned clones from clones," accessed at www.sciam.com/article.cfm?articleID=000186A6-697C-1CE2-95FB809EC588EF21 on August 30, 2003.

52. For early research on this method, see J. L. Hall et al., "Experimental Cloning of Human Polypoid Embryos Using an Artificial Zona Pellucida," the American Fertility Society conjointly with the Canadian Fertility and Andrology Society: 1993 Abstracts of the Scientific Oral and Poster Sessions; October 11–14, 1993: S1. Also see H. W. Jones et al., "On attempts at cloning in the human," *Fertility and Sterility* 61 (1994): 423–26; and J. Cohen and G. Tomkins, "The science, fiction and reality of embryo cloning," *Kennedy Institute of Ethics Journal* 4 (1994): 193–294. More recently, A. W. Chan et al., "Clonal propagation of primate offspring by embryo splitting," *Science* 287 (January 14, 2000): 317–19; and World Book, "Early scientific attempts at cloning," copyright 2002, accessed at www2.worldbook.com/features/features.asp?feature=cloning&page=html/attempts.html&direct=yes on August 30, 2003.

53. See the position statement of the American Medical Association regarding the use of artificial twinning for fertility purposes, *E-2.145 Pre-Embryo-Splitting*, posted on the AMA website on July 22, 2002, accessed at www.ama-assn.org/ama/pub/category/8443.html on October 6, 2003. This is also the process by which one could have twins or triplets who are born several years apart. The "clones" are kept in storage until the couple wants to have them implanted. And, of course, one of the reasons offered for this is to have a genetically identical "child" available in case one's born child needs an organ, a bone-marrow transfusion, etc.

54. See the article by Rhonda Rowland on CNN.com, "Embryo splitting caught in cloning controversy," 1997, accessed at www.cnn.com/HEALTH/9706/25/nfm.cloning/ on September 16, 2003.

55. See the published report by Jose B. Cibelli et al., "The First Human Cloned Embryo," *Scientific American* 286 (2002): 44–51.

56. See story by Dr. David Whitehouse, BBC News Online Science Editor, "Scientists use 'virgin birth' technique," posted on November 26, 2001, accessed at http://news.bbc.co.uk/1/hi/sci/tech/1676240.stm on September 6, 2003. Or, more recently: James Randerson on EurekaAlert.com, "Virgin birth method could found stem cells," posted on April 23, 2003, accessed at www.eurekalert.org/pub_releases/2003-04/ns-vbm042303.php on August 30, 2003;

CBSNews.com, "Scientists Eye 'Virgin Birth' Phenomenon," posted on May 5, 2003, accessed at www.cbsnews.com/stories/2003/05/05/tech/main552408.shtml on September 6, 2003; and Shaoni Bhattacharya, from the New Scientist Online News, "Dolly lab to create 'virgin birth' embryos," posted on June 10, 2003, accessed at www.newscientist.com/hottopics/cloning/cloning. jsp?id=ns99993815 on October 6, 2003.

57. See N. Rougier and Z. Werb, "Minireview: Parthenogenesis in mammal," *Molecular Reproduction and Development* 59 (2001): 468–74; J. B. Cibelli et al., "Somatic cell nuclear transfer in humans: Pronuclear and early embryonic development," *Journal of Regenerative Medicine* 2 (2001): 25–31; and J. B. Cibelli et al., "Parthenogenetic stem cells in nonhuman primates," *Science* 295 (2002): 819.

58. Sylvia Pagan Westphal, "'Virgin birth' method promises ethical stem cells," posted on NewScientist.com, April 28, 2003, and accessed at www.newscientist.com/news/news. jsp?id=ns99993654 on September 6, 2003. Also see H. Lin et al., "Multilineage Potential of Homozygous Stem Cells Derived from Metaphase II Oocytes," *Stem Cells* 21 (2003): 152–61; J. A. Byrne et al., "From intestine to muscle: Nuclear reprogramming through defective cloned embryos," *Proceedings of the National Academy of Sciences USA* 99 (2002): 6059–63; and Andy Coghlan, from New Scientist Online, "Cloning discovery may kill ethical objection," posted on April 22, 2002, accessed at www.newscientist.com/hottopics/cloning/cloning. jsp?id=ns99992196 on October 6, 2003.

59. For more on the issue of parthenogenesis, see Mark S. Latkovic, "The Science and Ethics of Parthenogenesis," *National Catholic Bioethics Quarterly* 2, no. 2 (Summer 2002): 245–55.

60. NIH, "Stem Cells: Scientific Progress and Future Research Directions," p. 17, accessed at http://stemcells.nih.gov/stemcell/pdfs/chapter3.pdf on August 30, 2003.

61. American Medical Association, Report 5 of the Council on Scientific Affairs, (A-03, adopted policy from the 2003 meeting): "The AMA: (1) supports biomedical research on multipotent stem cells (including adult and cord blood stem cells); (2) supports the use of somatic cell nuclear transfer technology in biomedical research (therapeutic cloning); (3) opposes the use of somatic cell nuclear transfer technology for the specific purpose of producing a human child (reproductive cloning); (4) encourages strong public support of federal funding for research involving human pluripotent stem cells; and (5) will continue to monitor developments in stem cell research and the use of somatic cell nuclear transfer technology. (Policy)" posted on the AMA website, accessed at www.ama-assn.org/ama/pub/article/2036-7819.html on October 6, 2003. Also see the AMA's official policy *E-2.147: Human Cloning (2-A-99),* issued in December 1999, posted on their website at www.ama-assn.org/apps/pf_online/pf_online?f_n=browse&doc=policyfiles/CEJA/E-2.147.HTM&&s_t=&st_p=&nth=1&prev_pol=policyfiles/CEJA/E-1.02.HTM&nxt_pol=policyfiles/CEJA/E-2.01.HTM&, accessed on October 6, 2003; George Q. Daley, M.D., Ph.D., "Cloning and Stem Cells: Handicapping the Political and Scientific Debates," *New England Journal of Medicine* 349 (July 17, 2003): 211–12; Konrad Hochedlinger, Ph.D., and Rudolf Jaenisch, M.D., "Nuclear Transplantation, Embryonic Stem Cells, and the Potential for Cell Therapy," *New England Journal of Medicine* 349 (July 17, 2003): 275–86; Art Caplan, Ph.D., "Cloning ethics: Separating the science from the fiction," posted on MSNBC.com on August 14, 2003 and updated on December 14, 2003, accessed at www.msnbc.com/id/3076920 on October 6, 2003; and the joint article by Timothy Caulfield, Abdullah Daar, Bartha Knoppers, Peter A. Singer, David Castle, and Ron Forbes in *The Hill Times,* "Not All Cloning Is Alike: MPs must not let outrageous claims of Raelians drive national policy development," February 24, 2003, posted on the Genome Prairie website, accessed at www.genomeprairie.ca/media/caulfield0203.htm on August 15, 2003.

62. For an excellent source of information on successes in adult stem cell research, visit the website of Do No Harm—The Coalition of Americans for Research Ethics at www.stemcellresearch.org.

63. Ibid., "News," accessed at www.stemcellresearch.org/news/index.html on October 6, 2003.

64. M. Lévesque and T. Neuman, "Autologous transplantation of adult human neural stem

cells and differentiated dopaminergic neurons for Parkinson disease: 1-year postoperative clinical and functional metabolic result," American Association of Neurological Surgeons annual meeting, Abstract #702, April 8, 2002.

65. M. Moran, "For cell transplants, is one brain better than two?," *American Medical News,* May 3, 1999, p. 29. For more information related to this story, see "Adult Stem Cells Used to Repair Damage from Parkinson's Disease," posted on the Multi-sclerosis.org website on April 9, 2002, accessed at www.multi-sclerosis.org/news/Apr2002/StemCellsRepairDamageInParkinsons.html on August 30, 2003; "Cell transplants treat Parkinson's," posted on BBCNews.com on April 9, 2002, accessed at http://news.bbc.co.uk/1/hi/health/1918347.stm on August 30, 2003; "First Case of Auto-Grafting of Neural Stem Cells into a Patient with PD," from Parkinson's Update, Issue 128, 2002, posted on the National Parkinson Foundation, Inc., website, accessed at www.parkinson.org/autografting.htm on September 6, 2003.

66. M. Moran, "For cell transplants, is one brain better than two?" *American Medical News,* May 3, 1999, p. 29.

67. See the story by Emma Young posted on NewScientist.com regarding a research study being conducted at Emory University on Parkinson's, "Retinal cell implants improve Parkinson's," posted on April 18, 2002, accessed at www.newscientist.com/news/news.jsp?id=ns99992182 on October 6, 2003. Also see the Do No Harm website, "Stem Cell Report," Spring 2002, accessed at www.stemcellresearch.org/stemcellreport/scr-2002-spring.htm on October 6, 2003.

68. S. S. Gill et al., "Direct brain infusion of glial cell line–derived neurotrophic factor in Parkinson disease," *Nature Medicine* 9 (May 2003): 589–95. Also see the story by Helen Pearson on Nature.com, "Triple hope for Parkinson's," posted online on March 31, 2003, and accessed at www.nature.com/nsu/030324/030324-12.html on October 6, 2003. Or see the story by Tudor P. Toma on The-Scientist.com, "Precise targeting in Parkinson's," posted on March 31, 2003, accessed at www.biomedcentral.com/news/20030331/03/ on October 6, 2003.

69. Nathan Salley, testimony before the House Government Reform Subcommittee on Criminal Justice, Drug Policy and Human Resources, July 17, 2002, posted on the Do No Harm website, accessed at www.stemcellresearch.org/testimony/salley.htm on August 15, 2003.

70. Ibid.

71. Department of Health and Human Services, Food and Drug Administration, Unrelated Allogeneic Cord Blood Banking and Transplant Forum, co-sponsored by the Center for Biologics Evaluation and Research, FDA, and National Heart, Lung and Blood Institute, NIH, Tuesday, August 15, 2000; written transcript accessed at www.fda.gov/cber/minutes/forum0815p2.htm on October 6, 2003. Also see Dr. Laughlin's published results, M. J. Laughlin et al., "Hematopoietic engraftment and survival in adult recipients of umbilical-cord blood from unrelated donors," *New England Journal of Medicine* 344 (June 14, 2001): 1815–22.

72. For more information on the specifics of umbilical cord blood as a source of stem cells, see L. Gore et al., "Successful cord blood transplantation for sickle cell anemia from a sibling who is human leukocyte antigen-identical: implications for comprehensive care," *Journal of Pediatric Hematology and Oncology* 22 (September–October 2000): 437–40; V. Rocha et al., "Graft-versus-host disease in children who have received a cord blood or bone marrow transplant from an HLA-identical sibling," *New England Journal of Medicine* 342 (June 22, 2000): 1846–54; E. Rainsford and D. J. Reen, "Interleukin 10, produced in abundance by human newborn T cells, may be the regulator of increased tolerance associated with cord blood stem cell transplantation," *British Journal of Haematology* 116 (March 2002): 702–709; and Cord Blood Donor Foundation at www.cordblooddonor.org.

73. See K. Ohnuma et al., "Cord blood transplantation from HLA-mismatched unrelated donors as a treatment for children with haematological malignancies," *British Journal of Haematology* 112 (March 2001): 981–87. Also see the story by James Meek, science correspondent for *The Guardian,* "Baby cord cells offer leukeamia breakthrough," posted online on July 9, 2002, accessed at www.guardian.co.uk/uk_news/story/0,3604,751956,00.html on October 6, 2003. Meek reports on the case of Stephen Knox, who at the age of thirty-one was given a transplant using umbilical cord blood stem cells to treat his leukemia: "It has been known for

some time that blood from newborn babies' umbilical cords, normally discarded at birth, contains stem cells which could be an alternative to bone marrow. A handful of British children have been treated in this way but it had been thought that adults could not. Even if matching cells could be found from one cord, they would not be enough to repopulate the entire marrow. Then Stephen Proctor, a consultant and leukaemia researcher at Newcastle University, heard by chance of operations in Canada where doctors had mixed matching and non-matching batches of cord cells together with remarkable success. On February 22, at Newcastle's Royal Victoria Infirmary, Professor Proctor's team injected a mixture of stem cells from the umbilical cords of seven babies into Mr. Knox, from Middleton-St-George, near Darlington, Co Durham. Mr. Knox had been given a few months to live after chemotherapy had failed. One of the cords was a perfect match: the other six were not. But instead of the body rejecting the unmatched cells, they appeared to act as boosters for the tiny number of matched ones, and Mr. Knox began to recover. The amount of blood which can be taken from an umbilical cord is about enough to fill a wine glass. But of that, only a tiny fraction—a few hundred out of billions of cells—will be the kind of stem cells needed to replace some six pounds of destroyed bone marrow. To the astonishment of Prof Proctor, Mr. Knox's white blood cell level was up to adequate levels by five weeks. 'I wouldn't have believed that was possible,' Prof Proctor said. 'Stephen is progressing much better than we thought he would and the transplant has worked much better and more quickly than we expected. It's a really exciting development and opens up huge possibilities. It has been carried out 23 times in the UK on children but never with an adult.'"

74. Beaumont Hospital's press release, "Teen 1st in world to get experimental stem cell heart treatment," copyright 2003, accessed at www.beaumonthospitals.com/pls/portal30/cportal30.story_page1?l_recent=265 on October 12, 2003.

75. Ibid.

76. Beaumont Hospital's press release, "Teen stem cell transplant patient shows improvement," copyright 2003, accessed at www.beaumonthospitals.com/pls/portal30/cportal30.story_page1?l_recent=302 on October 12, 2003.

77. See the story by Antonio Regalado, staff writer for the *Wall Street Journal,* "FDA Holds Up Work on Transplanted Stem Cells," posted on able2know.com on June 12, 2003, accessed at www.able2know.com/forums/viewtopic.php?t=8214&view=previous on October 6, 2003. Also see the story from Reuters Health, "Michigan teen gets stem cell transplant to heart," posted on Bioexchange on May 3, 2003, accessed at www.bioexchange.com/news/news_page.cfm?id=16475 on September 15, 2003. Or the report by Kristen Philipkoski posted on Wired News, "Stem Cells Heal a Broken Heart," posted on March 7, 2003, accessed at www.wired.com/news/medtech/0,1286,57944,00.html on October 12, 2003.

78. B. E. Strauer et al., "Myocardial regeneration after intracoronary transplantation of human autologous stem cells following acute myocardial infarction," *Deutsche Medizinische Wochenschrift* 126 (August 24, 2001): 932–38.

79. R. M. El Oakley et al., "Myocyte transplantation for cardiac repair: A few good cells can mend a broken heart," *Annals of Thoracic Surgery* 71 (2001): 1724–33.

80. See the story posted on Bioheart Inc.'s official website, "Injecting some hope: Cell therapy could lead to new treatments for congestive heart failure, whose sufferers now have few options," originally published on August 11, 2003, accessed at www.bioheartinc.com/news.php#75 on October 12, 2003. Also see Otesa Middleton and Johanna Bennett, "A Patient's Thigh Cells Seen Reviving a Damaged Heart," Dow Jones News Service, November 13, 2001, also on Bioheart Inc., accessed at www.bioheartinc.com/news.php#75 on October 12, 2003.

81. E. C. Perin et al., "Transendocardial, autologous bone marrow cell transplantation for severe, chronic ischemic heart failure," *Circulation* 107 (May 13, 2003): 2294–2302; Epub April 21, 2003, accessed at www.ncbi.nlm.nih.gov/entrez/query.fcgi?cmd=Retrieve&db=PubMed&list_uids=12707230&dopt=Abstract on October 6, 2003.

82. Marie-Louise Labat et al., "Small Facts About Stem Cells," abstract, World Federation of the Catholic Medical Associations, accessed at http://perso.club-internetfr/frblin/fiamc/03events/0209seoul/texts3/08labat/labat.htm on August 30, 2003.

83. Wesley J. Smith, "Spinning Stem Cells," in the National Review Online, posted April 23, 2002, accessed at www.nationalreview.com/comment/comment-smith042302.asp on August 30, 2003.

84. Maureen L. Condic, "The Basics About Stem Cells," *First Things* 119 (January 2002): 30–34, accessed from FirstThings.com at www.firstthings.com/ftissues/ft0201/articles/condic.html on August 30, 2003.

85. Anton-Lewis Usala, M.D., "The Case against Funding Human Embryonic Stem Cell Research," 2001, posted on the United States Conference of Catholic Bishops' website and accessed at www.usccb.org/prolife/programs/rlp/01usal.htm on Sept. 6, 2003.

86. Transcript, "Stem Cells: Moving Research from the Bench towards the Bedside: The Role of NIH and FDA," Thursday, September 4, 2003, accessed at www.bioethics.gov/transcripts/sep03/session3.html on October 6, 2003.

87. Ibid.

88. Ibid.

89. Ibid.

90. Charles Jennings, quoted by Kristen Philipkoski in "Cell Switch Stems Stem Cell Snit?" posted on Wired.com, March 1, 2001, and accessed at www.wired.com/news/technology/0,1282,42093-2,00.html on August 30, 2003.

91. George Q. Daley, M.D., Ph.D., "Cloning and Stem Cells—Handicapping the Political and Scientific Debates," *New England Journal of Medicine* 349 (July 17, 2003): 211–12, accessed at http://content.nejm.org/cgi/content/full/349/3/211 on September 5, 2003.

92. From the Editors, "Save Embryonic Stem Cell Research," posted on ScientificAmerican.com on May 2001, and accessed at www.sciam.com/article.cfm?articleID=00037C21-1829-1C70-84A9809EC588EF21&catID=2 on August 30, 2003.

93. NIH, "Stem Cell Information," Frequently Asked Questions, accessed at http://stemcells.nih.gov/faqs.asp#20 on August 30, 2003.

94. National Bioethics Advisory Commission, *Ethical Issues in Human Stem Cell Research,* vol. 1: *Report and Recommendations of the National Bioethics Advisory Board,* September 1999, accessed at www.georgetown.edu/research/nrcbl/nbac/stemcell.pdf on Sept. 6, 2003.

95. Immanuel Kant, *Grounding for the Metaphysics of Morals,* trans. James W. Ellington (Indianapolis: Hackett, 1981).

96. John Stuart Mill, *Utilitarianism* (Indianapolis: Hackett, 1979).

97. For an excellent contemporary account of *personalism,* see John Kavanaugh, S.J., *Who Count as Persons?* (Washington, DC: Georgetown University Press, 2001).

98. Jacques Maritain, *The Person and the Common Good* (Notre Dame, IN: University of Notre Dame Press, 1966), p. 47.

99. Ibid., p. 48.

100. Ibid., pp. 49–50.

101. Ibid., p. 55.

102. These dates are based upon fetal development information from www.infinet.com/~life/develop/doh.htm.

103. Sidney Callahan, "Abortion and the Sexual Agenda: A Case for Pro-Life Feminism," *Commonweal* 113 (April 25, 1986): 232–38.

104. For a fuller account of the principle of respect for persons, see Gregory R. Beabout and Daryl J. Wennemann's *Applied Professional Ethics* (New York: University Press of America, 1994), especially chapter 4, "Moral Principles."

105. The argument that somehow a fertilized ovum is not fully, or only potentially, human life rests upon the mistaken notion that human development goes through distinct stages—stages that carry "ontological" significance (that is, stages in which the being is actually changed when it passes through). Quite often terms like zygote, blastocyst, pre-embryo, embryo, and fetus are used in a manner suggesting that these are real distinctions during gestation, when they are actually arbitrary scientific labels placed upon what is acknowledged to be a fluid and dynamic process of development. Embryologists point out that while these terms

have become convenient for discussing the progress of development, they do not refer to what could be called actual stages of development except in an artificial sense. Our growing knowledge of genetics, fostered by the Human Genome Project, affirms that human development is a continuum—not a series of stages. Also see the helpful discussion by human embryologist C. Ward Kischer, Ph.D., "When does human life begin? The final answer," posted on the official website of the American Bioethics Advisory Commission, a division of the American Life League, accessed at www.all.org/abac/cwk004.htm on October 12, 2003.

106. For more on this issue see Dianne N. Irving, M.A., Ph.D., "When Do Human Beings Begin? 'Scientific' Myths and Scientific Facts," *International Journal of Sociology and Social Rights* 19 (1999): 22–47; Lee Silver, *Remaking Eden: Cloning and Beyond in a Brave New World* (New York: Avon Books, 1997); R. O'Rahilly and F. Muller, *Human Embryology & Teratology,* 3rd ed. (New York: Wiley-Liss, 2001); T. W. Sadler, *Langman's Medical Embryology,* 6th ed. (Baltimore: Williams & Wilkins, 1990), p. 30; K. L. Moore, *Before We Are Born* (Philadelphia: Saunders, 1983); L. Nilsson et al., *A Child is Born* (London: Faber & Faber, 1977); and R. Yanagimachi, "Mammalian Fertilization," in *The Physiology of Reproduction,* ed. E. Knobil, J. D. Neill, et al. (New York: Raven Press, 1988), p. 135.

107. Judge John T. Noonan, "An Almost Absolute Value in History," in *Contemporary Issues in Bioethics,* ed. Tom L. Beauchamp and LeRoy Walters, 4th ed. (Belmont, CA: Wadsworth Publishing Company, 1994), p. 280.

108. The case of developing a clone for the purposes of reproduction might, at first glance, seem a more difficult problem—why ban a life-giving procedure? The first and most obvious argument to this is that at this point the technology of cloning is fraught with problems. At best, the procedure has to be described as inefficient. As such, the process of cloning will not improve and become more efficient without further research. But that means creating clones for the sole purpose of doing research upon them, which I just argued was unethical. The hope of some future good does not make an unethical action good, nor even acceptable. But what if the technology becomes perfected, perhaps by other countries that do not ban its development? At that point, would cloning become ethical and acceptable? First, I would say that if a human clone is developed, since it is a unique individual human life, it must be allowed to develop fully. A clone would not be responsible for how it was developed. But at that point, if it ever comes, where technology perfects the cloning process, the decision to allow cloning in the United States would not be automatic. The reason is that we would still have to question the motive of anyone wishing to develop a clone. As many others have pointed out in testimonies regarding cloning, there will inevitably be social, psychological, economic, legal, and spiritual difficulties. All of these would have to be considered. I would presume that some reasons would be immediately ruled out—cloning a deceased loved one would be unethical because the new being would not be desired for itself. Even using cloning to provide a family for a couple that cannot naturally conceive a child would raise serious ethical questions, since children are not property that can be ordered and purchased. In short, there would be new ethical questions that would have to be addressed first—questions that we can only speculate about now. And so, further ethical analysis would be required. However, let me add that I concur with many others who simply find no acceptable reason to develop a clone. None of the arguments offered to support cloning seem to stand up under ethical scrutiny. Thus, a total ban on cloning is the only appropriate recourse at this time in our history. For a more detailed discussion of my views on cloning in general, see my article, "Cloning and Human Dignity," *Ethics & Medics* 29, no. 2 (February 2004): 1–2.

109. See M. Young et al., "Neural Progenitor Cells Lack Immunogenicity and Resist Destruction as Allografts," *Stem Cells* 21 (2003): 405–16, accessed at http://stemcells.alphamed-press.org/cgi/content/abstract/21/4/405?maxtoshow=&HITS=10&hits=10&RESULTFORMAT=&author1=young+&searchid=1066237563088_645&stored_search=&FIRSTINDEX=0&sortspec=relevance&volume=21&firstpage=405&journalcode=stemcells on October 12, 2003. Also see the recent testimony of William Pursley, president and CEO, Osiris Therapeutics, Inc., before the President's Council on Bioethics, session 4: "Stem Cells: Moving Research from the

Bench Toward the Bedside: The Role of Nongovernmental Activity," on September 4, 2003. Mr. Pursley speaks about the research his private company is doing using mesenchymal stem cells: "The safety of these cells in the universal application has been proven now. Allogenic MSCs have been given to 56 human beings. Thousands of various animal models have been used, rats, mice, goats, dogs, pigs, and baboons. This has been done in conjunction with the NIH, Hopkins, Cedars-Sinai, Texas Heart, et cetera. And at this point, over several years now, there has been no possibly or probably related serious adverse events associated with MSCs. This includes no infusion or direct administrative toxicity. There's no ectopic tissue formation. In other words, they aren't differentiating in cartilage in the heart, on the knee, et cetera, and there is no tumor formation at this time. And, in fact, we have two lead programs in Phase 2, which by definition from the agency standards, the FDA, means we have met their safety standards for biologic in order to move into Phase 2. So we are very happy to report we see and now the agency sees these cells as safe, allowing us to move into Phase 2." Specifically regarding the issue of immune rejection, Mr. Pursley notes later that: "As far as approaches to overcome immune reaction, we don't have any. We have found that there is no immune reaction against these cells, and not only that. We have found them to be immune suppressive selectively in appropriate situations." Posted on the President's Council on Bioethics' official website, accessed at http://bioethics.gov/transcripts/sep03/session4.html on October 6, 2003. Or, see the story posted on BBCNews.com, "Stem cell transplant boost," December 12, 2001, accessed at http://news.bbc.co.uk/1/hi/health/1706305.stm on October 15, 2003.

110. David A. Prentice, Ph.D., "Adult Stem Cells," presented to the President's Council on Bioethics, July 2003, draft, accessed at http://bioethics.gov/background/prentice_paper.html on August 30, 2003.

SELECTED BIBLIOGRAPHY ON GENETICS, STEM CELLS, AND CLONING

Branick, Vincent, and M. Therese Lysaught. "Stem Cell Research: Licit or Complicit?" *Health Progress* 80, no. 5 (1999).

Burns, Thaddeus J., and George P. Smith II. "Genetic Determinism or Genetic Discrimination?" *Journal of Contemporary Health and Law Policy* 11, no. 1 (1994): 23–61.

Cahill, Lisa Sowle, and Maureen Junker-Kenny, eds. *The Ethics of Genetic Engineering.* Maryknoll, NY: Orbis Books, 1998.

Cahill, Lisa Sowle, Gilbert Meilaender, and Albert Moraczewski, O.P. "Religion-Based Perspectives on Cloning of Humans." *Ethics and Medicine* 14, no. 1 (1998): 8–25.

Cataldo, Peter J., and Albert Moraczewski, O.P. *The Fetal Tissue Issue: Medical and Ethical Aspects.* Braintree, MA: Pope John XXIII Center, 1994.

Cole-Turner, Ronald, and Brent Waters, eds. *God and the Embryo: Religious Voices on Stem Cells and Cloning.* Washington, DC: Georgetown University Press, 2003.

Flaman, Paul. *Genetic Engineering: Christian Values and Catholic Teaching.* Boston: Paulist Press, 2002.

Guinan, Patrick. *Genetics: A Catholic Ethical Perspective.* Bloomington, IN: 1st Books Library, 2001.

Human Genome, Human Person, and the Society of the Future: Proceedings of the Fourth Assembly of the Pontifical Academy for Life. Vatican City State: Libreria Editrice Vaticana, 1999.

Morris, John F. "Cloning and Human Dignity." *Ethics & Medics* 29, no. 2 (February 2004): 1–2.

Shannon, Thomas A. "Ethical Issues in Genetics." *Health Progress* 80, no. 5 (1999).

PART V

Health Care Reform

W HY ARE CATHOLICS concerned with health care? The Catholic concern flows out of the Gospel call to serve as Jesus served others, and in so doing to serve Jesus as well. This concern also flows out of the social mission of the Church to work for the common good. As explained in the *Catechism of the Catholic Church:*

Life and physical health are precious gifts entrusted to us by God. We must take reasonable care of them, taking into account the needs of others and the common good.

Concern for the health of its citizens requires that society help in the attainment of living-conditions that allow them to grow and reach maturity: food and clothing, housing, health care, basic education, employment, and social assistance.[1]

In this final part of the book, then, we will explore whether or not the current health care system in this country—including the Catholic facilities that help make it up—promotes the true common good and serves humanity as Jesus would. Another way to put this is: does our health care system meet the needs of people *and* is it just?

Regarding current conditions, some Catholic scholars raise doubts on both counts. Americans continue to spend more and more of the gross national product on health care—some would say, disproportionately so—yet indications are that millions of people in this country are still not receiving even basic care. We also continue to hear about the growing number of people who are uninsured or underinsured, or who simply do not have access to even the most basic forms of health care. It would seem that many needs are not being met. Further, when we hear that the majority of those whose basic health care needs are not being met are children and women, the lack of justice in our current system of care begins to come into focus.

We often hear it argued today that health care is a "business"—this seems an obvious assumption because of the vast amounts of money it generates. But there is danger lurking in the fact that American society has accepted the "market mentality" behind the development and delivery of health care today. In traditional economics, we are told that the market is a "morally free zone." The presumption is that business takes care of itself due to the mutual desires of all parties involved. Thus, according to this view, bringing "morality talk" into discussions about our health care system would be unnecessary. And on the surface of things, in a pluralistic society like ours, the market approach seems to be an efficient way to deal with each other and tolerate our differences.

However, does the current "market mentality" behind health care delivery provide an adequate foundation for understanding what really goes on in actual "health care"? Consider the following points. It is difficult to shop around for health care services. Many of us are limited to specific health care providers by insurance packages. We are given the names of providers we can see—but how do we determine who is a good doctor for our medical needs? The reality is that buying a new car is far easier than picking a doctor or therapist. Further, when it comes to specialists, many people need direct referrals from their primary physicians—thus, personal choice is constrained even more. Of course, for those in rural areas the limitations run even deeper due to the limited number of providers and practitioners willing to serve in rural communities.

The problem here is not merely a quibble over the difference between *limited* choice and *complete* freedom of choice. Rather, we must remember economists argue that for the market to function, there must be no force, no fraud, and no monopolies. But the way health care delivery works in practice exerts *some* "force" on consumers, and a single hospital serving a large rural area certainly *seems* like a "monopoly." In short, people and health care institutions are not really "free" in the manner that the theory of capitalism requires.

We are also told that a key rule of the market is "Buyer beware!" What is implied in this cliché is that consumers must examine and research the products they purchase. The responsibility of the "seller of goods" appears limited. Yet such an attitude is simply untenable in health care. Given the fact that the various health care professions require extensive education and training, non-medical personnel cannot be expected to gain enough knowledge to become savvy "consumers" of health care products. Even when some individuals or families do go out and research diseases and treatments, they must indirectly rely upon the health care professionals who made such information available. Also, too often we forget the tremendous strain that an individual or family is under when dealing with disease and illness—especially when life is on the line or someone is suffering tremendously. Under such stress, few of us are capable of maintaining clear and sound rationality. All of this raises serious concerns over the ability to "beware" when dealing with health care.

Finally, in what manner can we even talk about "health" and "health care" as *products* to be sold on the market? Certainly a lot of "things" get used in health care—scalpels, scopes, IV tubes, drugs, bed pans, needles, walkers, bandages, casts, etc. And, when you receive your medical bills, you can find all of these things itemized—*everything has a price!* However, your renewed health is not actually in the IV fluid you received, although that may have been what staved off dehydration. Nor does one actually "purchase" a heart when one has a heart transplant. Health is much broader than all of this. Indeed, patients may receive all kinds of things to assist in their treatment, yet never get better. From the medical side, an important dictum (stated in many professional codes of ethics) is that one cannot make *guarantees* in health care. If workers repairing my roof do a poor job, I call them back to fix it—and if they do not fix it properly, I have recourse to sue them. But I can sue health care professionals only for malpractice. Malpractice must clearly be demonstrated and include an obvious error, proven intent to do harm, or negligence in duty. One cannot sue a doctor or therapist just because one has not been restored to health or because one is not satisfied. Medicine makes use of many wonderful sciences and technological tools. Nevertheless, medicine itself is not an exact science—medicine is an art. The "work" of medicine is a healthy human being. Health and health care, then, do not seem to be *products* in the normal understanding of economics.

So, why have we accepted the "market" analogy for health care, given these obvious weaknesses? There are probably numerous reasons for this, but at least part of the market attitude comes from a fundamental disagreement about the nature of health and health care. Many people—including Catholics—consider health an essential human need. For the Church's part, this has been a growing theme since the Second Vatican Council. In part 1 of the *Ethical and Religious Directives for Catholic Health Care Services*, titled "The Social Responsibility of Catholic Health Care Services," the American bishops unequivocally assert this point: "Catholic health care ministry is rooted in a commitment to promote and defend human dignity; this is the foundation of its concern to respect the sacredness of every human life from the moment of conception until death. The first right of the human person, the right to life, entails a right to the means for the proper development of life such as adequate health care."[2] Unfortunately, this belief that health and health care are basic human rights is not universally accepted within American society. We are a country of few entitlements—health, and more specifically health care, have simply not made everyone's list, as much of our current political debate over health care reform reveals. Rather, many portions of our society still view health care as a privilege, and so it is pursued in the same manner all other privileges are pursued—on the open market. But such an attitude is fraught with danger given the problems regarding the market noted above. In his 1991 encyclical *On the Hundredth Anniversary of Rerum Novarum,* John Paul II had warned of this danger: "There are many human needs which find no place on the market. It is a strict duty of justice and truth not to allow fundamental human needs to remain unsatisfied, and not to allow those burdened by such needs to perish."[3] Health and health care would be some of the needs the pope was speaking about, and so they should not be bartered for in the marketplace.

In this light, the Catholic perspective on health care takes a different approach than the current trends in society. Rather than view health care as a business, the Catholic tradition views health care as a *ministry.* The term "ministry" for Catholics refers to an activity that is considered an extension of Christ's work while on earth. During his public life, Jesus performed many miracles—but of prominence in the Gospels were his acts of healing. Catholics carry on this powerful example of Christ by reaching out to both heal and comfort the sick. As the American bishops explained in their General Introduction to the *Ethical and Religious Directives:*

Created in God's image and likeness, the human family shares in the dominion that Christ manifested in his healing ministry. This sharing involves a stewardship over all material creation (Gn 1:26) that should neither abuse nor squander nature's resources. Through science the human race comes to understand God's wonderful work; and through technology it must conserve, protect and perfect nature in harmony with God's purposes. Health care professionals pursue a special vocation to share in carrying forth God's life-giving and healing work.[4]

Health, then, is a basic human good that we should help all human beings—our neighbors—attain to the highest degree possible. Reflected in the Catholic concern over health care are the reciprocal notions of respect for human life and promotion of the common good. Respect for others requires an active pursuit of what is good for them, which includes most fundamentally health. And, by extension, the promotion of health in individual members of society is also a promotion of the common good in which we all share.

The attitude of Catholics is therefore far from the current trend of considering health care a market commodity. For Catholics, health care is not a business, but a work of love and charity to which all of us are called as members of the human family. It is true that business *structures* dominate the delivery of contemporary health care. But that fact by itself does not mean that we must let business *attitudes* constrain the ministry of serving the sick and suffering. It may be the case that using business tools and methods is the most efficient way to deliver health care in society today, especially in terms of rationing resources. But, then again, it may actually be the case that the business approach is not adequate for meeting the demands of justice and for promoting the common good. The point to remember is that the business methods we have adopted for distributing care are only tools for reaching the end here, which is improved health.

What does all of this imply for health care reform? In sum, the Catholic concern for reform in American health care is *not* motivated by desires for increased profits through "strategies" that focus on saving money and resources, or that attempt to make the delivery of health care more efficient in the business sense. The Catholic perspective seeks out reform as a means of extending the respect owed to all human beings and of promoting the common good. Catholics hold health as a basic human good. And reason shows that healthy people add to, develop, and empower society as a whole. Perhaps the reforms we bring about will, in the long run, save money and resources—especially if we can turn greater attention toward preventative health care, and if we can adequately meet the needs of all those who are uninsured or underinsured, or who lack access to basic care. But the focus here is on *care*—not economics and profits. We also need to emphasize that the Catholic concern for reform extends beyond just Catholic health care institutions. Justice is required at every level of health care. Thus, an important task for Catholics today in their social roles is to lobby for health care advocacy at the political level. This advocacy role can be seen in the recent efforts of the American bishops to make health care reform a priority in American politics.[5]

Now some might assume from the issues raised here regarding our current health care system and its capitalistic structure that the only alternative is a socialized approach to medicine, especially with the focus on the common good—but that is not necessarily the case. It is true that a socialized health care system might achieve some aspects of the common good better than our current capitalistic approach. That is a reality that anyone interested in health care reform ought to carefully consider. But that does not mean that socialized medicine would be the *only* way to reach the common good. Further, a socialized health care system would be just as prone to abuses and injustices as our current system if it is not managed well. At this point, I believe that the method of delivery is less important than clarifying the true goal of health care and its connection to the common good. Part of getting society to accept and act upon the Catholic concern, then, is to get them to understand the basic issues of human dignity at stake when talking about health, and to recognize the respect that all human beings deserve, regardless of income or social status. Only through a genuine respect for all can the true common good be achieved.

To guide our reflections on this final topic, we have two thought-provoking essays. The first is "Health Care Reform: Justice and the Common Good," by Clarke E. Cochran. From the title, one can see that Cochran builds upon the themes that have been laid out in this introduction. In his essay, Cochran explains the fundamental principles of Catholic social teaching as they specifically relate to health care. The foundational concepts of justice and the common good are explored in light of the Catholic tradition's emphasis on the fundamental "option for the poor." As Cochran points out: ". . . to tell whether a society is fulfilling its responsibility for justice and the common good, the place to look is the working poor, the disabled and impaired, and families without sufficient resources of their own to enter fully into the life of the community, without sufficient resources to furnish their own health insurance." In building his argument for reform, Cochran recognizes the important and significant changes that would be necessary to move the American health care system toward universal access—nor is he naïve in terms of how difficult such changes would be. That is why Cochran offers a plan for incremental reform based on what he describes as a comprehensive insurance package built on the present employer-based system. In many ways, this is the real significance of Cochran's essay—that he offers concrete and realistic suggestions for moving from the ideal of health care reform to its realization. As such, his insights into the weaknesses of American health care and his guidelines for genuine reform merit careful consideration, and have much to offer the current debate over health care reform in this country. For his part, Cochran recognizes that his plan of incremental reform will not provide the final solution, but instead is just the first step. Yet, it is a first step that we could begin taking today!

The final essay in this collection is by Rev. Michael D. Place, S.T.D., "Health Care Reform and the 'Consistent Ethic.'" At the outset, Place notes that the inspiration for his reflections is drawn from the life and work of Cardinal Joseph Bernardin of Chicago and his articulation of "the consistent ethic of life." Thus, Place begins by exploring the basis of "the consistent ethic of life" within scripture and the Catholic tradition. He then goes on to argue that the "the consistent ethic" has the power to serve as an antidote to our "fragmented, individualistic, market-driven health care system." To those cynics who worry that the "problem" is simply too big or too complicated to bring about much in the way of positive change—especially when one considers how much *money* is involved—Place reminds readers of other great "changes" that have occurred in America's history, such as the ending of slavery and the enfranchisement of women, as well as current efforts to wipe out illiteracy and intolerance. In all of those cases, Americans finally took a stand for justice and equality. Place argues that it is time now to take the same stand against the lack of access to basic health care that so many Americans face. If indeed we take such a stand, and work to reform health care through the lens of "the consistent ethic of life," Place claims that we will be left with ". . . a sketch of a health care system that recognizes the need for limits, that acknowledges the inevitability of decline and death, that treats health care as a service, that upholds the dignity of every person, and that promotes the health of our whole society." For Catholics and non-Catholics alike, believers and non-believers, men, women, young, old, rich, or poor, creating such a system of genuine health "care" is certainly a goal worth striving for with our whole heart and our whole soul.

In the end, I conclude with the inspiring words of the late John Paul II in *The Gospel of Life,* which sum up the spirit of this book:

In a word, we can say that the cultural change which we are calling for demands from everyone the courage to adopt a new life-style, consisting in making practical choices—at the personal, family, social and international level—on the basis of a correct scale of values: the primacy of being over having, of the person over things. This renewed life-style involves a passing from indifference to concern for others, from rejection to acceptance of them. Other people are not rivals from whom we must defend ourselves, but brothers and sisters to be supported. They are to be loved for their own sakes, and they enrich us by their very presence.[6]

NOTES

1. *Catechism of the Catholic Church,* English Translation for the United States of America (New York: Catholic Book Publishing Company, 1994), #2288, p. 551.

2. United States Conference of Catholic Bishops, *Ethical and Religious Directives for Catholic Health Care Services,* 4th ed. (Washington, DC: USCCB, 2001), p. 8.

3. John Paul II, *Centesimus Annus,* no. 34.

4. *Ethical and Religious Directives,* p. 7.

5. For example, see "Faithful Citizenship: A Catholic Call to Political Responsibility," *Origins* 33, no. 20 (October 23, 2003): 321, 323–30.

6. John Paul II, *Evangelium Vitae,* no. 98.

CHAPTER 11

Health Care Reform
Justice and the Common Good

CLARKE E. COCHRAN

Fragmentation, wasted resources, high costs, and barriers to medical care plague the American health care system. Decades of reform efforts, failed (the Clinton plan in 1994) and successful (State Children's Health Insurance Program [SCHIP] in 1997), have alleviated some problems, but exacerbated others.

This chapter applies central Catholic principles of justice and common good to designing a new set of reforms to meet the health needs of all Americans. It first outlines the meaning of these principles in the context of the unique characteristics of health care delivery and finance in the United States. Then it considers how the system would have to change in order to provide universal access. It describes an incremental reform based on access to a comprehensive insurance package built on the present employer-based system. Despite the fact that the reforms advocated here would improve the system, insurance and insurance guarantees are inherently limited as means of insuring access to health care. Some persons will inevitably fall between the cracks in any insurance-based system of health care. Therefore, churches and church-based medical institutions will continue to have a vital role to play in a reformed system. Because health care policy involves healing, it touches the deepest principles of Christian faith and intersects with religious institutions formed after the healing example of Christ.

The argument of this chapter leaves out numerous important issues on the political and ethical agenda. Concentrating on insurance coverage, it does not discuss the equally important political issue of federal funding and regulation of biomedical research with profound ethical implications: embryo research, cloning, and new forms of reproduction. Nor does it consider laws regarding euthanasia or a "patients' bill of rights." Health care for the aged and permanently disabled presents an equally complex set of policy problems. The chapter does not address Medicare reform or providing long-term care insurance. Each of these issues evokes considerable political and moral controversy. However, to consider them would stretch the boundaries of this chapter beyond reasonable limits.

Moreover, this chapter concentrates on the middle range of public policy questions. It does not consider the long-term problems of the design of the entire medical system, nor does it focus on short-term policy questions, such as changes in Medicaid payment rates. Rather, attention is on the health care reform agenda of the early twenty-first century.

Catholic Social Doctrine and Health Care Reform

Health care reform has been prominent on the political agenda since the 1992 election, in which President Clinton's promise of universal health insurance was a major factor in his victory. Nevertheless, his 1993 Health Security Act provoked a firestorm of debate in which the numbers of children without health insurance, the difficulties of obtaining employment-based insurance, and the consequences of going without insurance were prominent topics.[1] The failure of that legislation lowered the visibility of these issues, but they did not disappear, instead generating an agenda of small-step reforms to extend insurance to more persons. The State Children's Health Insurance Program, created by the Balanced Budget Act of 1997, is the most prominent product. Despite these efforts, more than 15 percent of Americans are without health insurance at any given time, and the average spell without insurance lasts more than one year. Persons without insurance suffer severe financial and health consequences when they fall ill or are injured during a spell without insurance.[2]

Catholic theology has thought long and hard about the relationship of church and government to social questions, such as the lack of health insurance for millions of persons and the place of the elderly in society.[3] It has also developed a rich body of reflection about health care and medical ethics. Applied to the issues under consideration in this chapter, Catholic social doctrine's emphasis on justice and the common good emerge as the most pertinent. Justice is the moral principle that addresses most directly social inequalities. Among the many ways in which citizens are equal and unequal, which kinds of *equality* does justice demand (equality in the right to vote, for example), and which forms of *inequality* does justice either demand (different prizes for the order of finish in a competition, for example) or permit (different types of automobiles, for example)? Clearly, differences in ability to obtain health care have significant personal and social consequences. Catholic theology subjects these inequalities to analysis in terms of justice and fairness.

At the same time, differences in insurance have consequences for the ways in which the community integrates (or fails to integrate) the working poor without insurance into its fabric. Emphasis on the common good within the Catholic tradition signals the centrality of the social nature of the human person. Men and women find fulfillment in community—in marriage, friendship, voluntary associations, neighborhoods, and political society. The responsibility of government is the common good; that is, maintaining, repairing, or even enhancing the conditions that facilitate community among citizens. To be without adequate health care in contemporary American society is to be a marginal, second-class citizen, a loose thread in the social fabric. The common good requires access of all persons to the basic goods of life, goods sufficient to allow their participation in the rights and responsibilities of the community.

Other chapters in this volume describe justice and the common good more fully. What follows is the barest summary of the concepts, as well as discussion of the virtue of prudence so important in public policy making. These summaries set the stage for the major substantive contribution of the chapter, a Catholic social theory–inspired description of health care reform. Although no single principle can provide a complete orientation to health care reform, justice and the common good carry the analysis a long way.

Justice

Theories of justice judge the fairness or unfairness of the multiplicity of equalities and inequalities within every human society. Persons may be equal in the right to vote, unequal in income. Most theories of justice regard equality in the right to vote (with obvious exceptions for children, mentally deficient persons, prisoners) as a demand of justice. It is unfair to allow some adult citizens to participate in political decision making and to exclude others. On the other hand, theories of justice widely disagree about whether any or some degrees of income inequality violate fairness. The tradition of Catholic social theory that grounds this chapter regards health care as one of the fundamental rights of the human person; therefore, a society that arbitrarily excludes some persons from access to health care violates human rights and, therefore, creates an injustice. It violates justice as well to make access to health care unusually difficult or burdensome, as when inequalities in income or education, for example, become obstacles to receiving needed care.[4] Moreover, inequalities in people's *health status* count as unjust when they are avoidable, unnecessary, and rooted in characteristics unrelated to need for medical attention, such as race, age, education, or income.[5]

Additionally, the special responsibilities that human beings have to protect persons unusually vulnerable to injury or exploitation (children, the elderly, the disabled) create an obligation for society, in the form of government, to ensure that these vulnerabilities do not exclude persons from basic goods.[6] Persons who are ill or injured often are defenseless, unable to assert their own rights or provide for their own care. They may receive less care than they need, impairing ability to be effective contributors to society. Health access inequalities grounded in vulnerability are unfair; justice requires social systems to provide care based on need.

For these reasons, in modern nations such as the United States with well-developed systems of medical care and the means to pay for them, justice requires that all citizens have access to a level of health care that (1) allows them a reasonable chance to continue to or to return to function as normal members of the community and (2) does not impose unreasonable financial burdens on individuals or on society.

Common Good

The Catholic tradition regards care for the common good as the defining responsibility of government. Justice is one aspect of the common good, but the concept refers more inclusively to the sum total of political, social, and economic conditions that allow the social nature of the human person to find expression in full, active participation in the life of the community.[7] Illness and injury force a person inward; social ties become difficult to maintain emotionally and physically. Health care is a fundamental aspect of the common good because it makes it possible for persons to heal and, thereby, to emerge from their illness into solidarity with fellow members of the community or to maintain solidarity during a chronic illness.[8]

Access to health care is basic to the common good also because health care is a social creation. In modern society, medical knowledge and medical institutions cannot exist without vast webs of financial and social support from private persons, voluntary associations, and governments. Medical training, professional licensing and accountability, payment for medical services, and construction capital depend upon the entire community's resources. They are "common goods" and, therefore, must be available on reasonable bases to the common; that is, to the entire community. Society cannot regard them as private, commodity transactions between professionals who possess resources and patients with the ability to pay these professionals.[9]

Option for the Poor

The priority of the needs of the poor tempers the Catholic tradition's commitment to justice and the common good. This priority is not so much a modification of the idea of justice, since the formal principle of justice demands the same for all classes in society; that is, what they are "due." In the realm of health care, this means that all are due access to a comprehensive insurance package described below. What the option for the poor does mean, however, is twofold: first, in any incremental strategy for movement from the current, non-universal health insurance system to a future, universal system, the needs of the poor for adequate coverage must be attended to at the beginning. Second, the rough gauge for any health system's adequacy is the health status of those at the economic, social, and cultural bottom of society. In short, to tell whether a society is fulfilling its responsibility for justice and common good, the place to look is the working poor, the disabled and impaired, and families without sufficient resources of their own to enter fully into the life of the community, without sufficient resources to furnish their own health insurance.

Individual Responsibility?

It might be objected that this argument places too much responsibility on government for serving justice and the common good. Is not personal responsibility also part of the Catholic moral tradition? Do not individuals possess a major (even the prime) responsibility to provide for their health? The answer to these questions clearly is yes. Evidence that adhering to simple health rules (limit consumption of food and alcohol, get enough sleep, do not smoke, get regular exercise, and so forth) adds both quality and length to life reinforces this conclusion. These are matters largely within the control of the person.

Catholic social theory applied to health care includes this truth.[10] However, Catholic *social* theory directs attention to collective responsibility, without denying that health insurance reforms may well include individual contributions in the form of premiums proportional to income and reasonable co-payments for treatment. Nevertheless, the cost of advanced health care places it beyond the means of any but the most wealthy; therefore, both the common good and justice prefer risk pooling, spreading it throughout the community, instead of individualized bearing of financial risk. Moreover, the medical profession's own ethics require treatment of the sick regardless of ability to pay, even when they bear major responsibility for their own condition (addicts, for example). Therefore, social insurance pools to which all have contributed (the responsible and irresponsible alike) are the preferred method of reimbursing the medical profession for the care it must provide. In addition, guaranteed comprehensive health insurance should include inducements, encouragements, and payment for individual action that improves health such as weight reduction, smoking cessation, and so forth.

Prudence

These brief accounts of justice and the common good have appealed to "reasonableness." What is reasonable health care reform? What are reasonable inequalities in health status? Justice and the common good, because they bear upon law and politics, are among those principles most in need of the virtue of prudence. Unlike moral principles that are relatively simple of application and which apply in all circumstances (for example, the prohibition against killing innocent persons), justice and common good must adapt to constantly changing circumstances. In most instances, they do not issue clear and unambiguous demands. Instead, they set an agenda for practical reason to investigate the particulars of a social issue (uninsurance, for example) and to propose the response most compatible with the demands of morality and with the opportunities and limitations of present social reality. As the theologian Richard McCormick has argued, theological bioethics does not generate many concrete decisions; rather, it (1) highlights threats to basic goods, (2) incorporates faith into the basic dispositions of persons in respect to health care (benevolence, justice, relief of suffering), and (3) informs practical reason about the direction of solutions to political problems.[11]

In addition, principles of justice and the common good are the least distinctively "Catholic" principles within Catholic social doctrine. Other Christian, as well as other religious and secular ethical systems, can readily recognize the centrality to public life of fairness and community. In this regard, we might think of the Catholic tradition as a "carrier" or "reminder" of social principles open to broad consensus about government's responsibility for the health of its citizens.[12]

Health Insurance for All

This account of justice and common good in health care sets universal health insurance for all citizens as the ultimate goal. Such insurance must meet every person's need for good quality, comprehensive health care at a reasonable cost. Why health *insurance?* What might such comprehensive insurance look like? How fast must the United States move toward this goal? What is the role of nongovernmental institutions, especially churches and church-related health care, in meeting this goal? The present section addresses these questions.

Being without Insurance

Satisfying justice and common good does not demand a system of health insurance. The principles require only that all citizens have good access to comprehensive health care. They do not describe the means of achieving the goal. Indeed, those nations with national health services, most notably Great Britain, do not employ insurance. Few, however, recommend such a scheme for the United States, with its very different political, social, cultural, and medical system. In the American context, *health insurance,* overwhelmingly obtained through one's employer, is the principal means of access to meet medical needs in a way that financially overburdens no one in the insurance pool.

The consequences of being without insurance demonstrate its centrality to fair access to care. The number and percentage of persons without health insurance rose steadily until 1999, when they dipped slightly. In 1988, approximately 32 million persons (slightly over 13 percent of the population) lacked public or private health insurance. By 2004, the figure approached

46 million (15.7 percent). The average uninsured spell lasts nearly a year, and about 15 percent of such spells last two years or longer.[13] Lacking insurance does matter in direct consequences to the health and financial security of uninsured persons who need medical care. Moreover, it also matters *indirectly* for many others: families who struggle to find a way to get care for their loved one; employers who lose days of work; hospitals which have to provide treatment but incur bad debt; taxpayers who subsidize charity care in public hospitals; and insured persons whose premiums provide some cross subsidies for uninsured persons.

Numerous studies demonstrate that people without insurance postpone needed care, often to their physical detriment.[14] They enter hospitals sicker than insured persons, but are discharged more quickly and are more likely to die during a hospital stay. In addition, the uninsured (compared with insured persons with similar health needs) receive fewer knee replacements, coronary bypasses, and visits to physicians. They also tend to lack a regular source of medical care. They are more likely to suffer a ruptured appendix, to incur avoidable hospitalizations, and to have worse outcomes from a wide variety of health conditions. Financially, the uninsured have high rates of long-term medical debt and high rates of bankruptcy caused, in part, by medical bills. Because lack of insurance correlates with income, race, ethnicity, age, education, and place of residence, it is not possible to attribute all of these consequences to being without insurance; it is, however, fair to attribute considerable significance to its absence.

To inquire deeply into the causes of so many living without insurance would take us too far afield.[15] For workers (the majority of the uninsured), the cause is inability to afford steeply rising premiums or an employer that does not offer insurance. Moreover, the economy has shifted from high-benefit manufacturing jobs to low-benefit service, technical, contract, and part-time employment. Medicaid covers only about half of the poor at whom it is aimed, and it declined in enrollment briefly in the late 1990s as a result of 1996 welfare reform legislation;[16] SCHIP, enacted in 1997, covers only the children of the working poor, not adults with greater health care needs. Recent growth in Medicaid and SCHIP has not offset the decline in employment-based insurance. In addition, some citizens act irresponsibly; they fail to enroll their children in programs for which they are eligible; they spend available income on things less important than health insurance.

Regardless of the causes, the poor health outcomes and financial burdens attributable to being uninsured impose unfair penalties and inequities

on those lacking insurance and make it more difficult for them to participate fully in social life. They violate the demands of the common good by
diminishing community and by allowing common goods (medical facilities, professional knowledge, and curative skills) to be unfairly concentrated
toward ability to pay, rather than medical need.

Basic, Comprehensive, or Maximal Insurance?

Therefore, justice and the common good require that all citizens have
health insurance. This conclusion, however, tends to generate fear of health
care rationing. Moreover, what level of insurance coverage does justice require: basic only, comprehensive, or insurance for every possible beneficial
procedure?

Fear of rationing is not unreasonable, but it is misplaced. Every health
care system rations care, including the United States. Rationing mechanisms exist whenever there are goods that everyone might want, but that
not all can have (for example, a heart operation using the most advanced
techniques by the best cardiovascular surgeon in the nation). Markets are
devices for rationing goods. The American health care system uses them extensively (and often unfairly) to allocate health care resources toward those
with good insurance and away from those without it. Financial resources
count in a market system, but they are unrelated to the need for health care,
the principal criterion for rationing within a Catholic account of health care
justice. The American system also rations by waiting lines, limits on coverage under insurance policies, co-payments, managed care rules, and a
variety of other mechanisms. All of these recognize the reality of limits to
health care provision, but their recognition is distorted (and the rationing
misjudged) because they are read through the lens of income, education,
and insurance status, rather than through the lens of health care need.

Because limits require rationing, that is, public decisions about the level of access to care due to common citizenship, it is politically impossible
and morally unnecessary to attempt to provide every person with access to
the most complete range of highest quality care imaginable. Maximal insurance is financially impossible to provide to all; providing the best care
to everyone is physically impossible. Therefore, they are not morally obligatory. Even systems of universal insurance or national health care commonly
allow citizens to purchase from their discretionary funds medical services
beyond those covered by the comprehensive plan held by every citizen. As
long as insurance covers comprehensive and reasonable needs for all, there

should be no objection from Catholic social doctrine when some choose to spend their discretionary income on tummy tucks, while others choose high performance automobiles. However, payment for insurance premiums eventually should move toward a proportion of income, rather than the present mainly "flat rate" system.

But guaranteed universal insurance limited merely to basic, medically necessary acute care does not satisfy the standards of justice or common good. It is, in fact, equivalent to the present system in which anyone who becomes sick enough will receive emergency care! The only difference between the present system of inadequate care for the uninsured and a system of insurance for basic medical necessities would be a reduction of the financial burdens of acute care. Because symptoms and conditions less than acute would still be costly to the poor or near-poor, they would continue to postpone needed medical care until their conditions worsen enough to require hospitalization. Solidarity and equality of citizenship do not permit such burdens on citizens at the bottom of the social scale. The availability and affordability of health care should not depend on income, occupation, or other factors divorced from need for medical attention.

Therefore, social justice and the common good point to a health insurance system somewhere between basic care and "supercare"; that is, toward guaranteed coverage for the set of health care interventions that assures a statistically good chance over one's lifetime of avoiding premature death and disability.[17] Under such a system, everyone has insurance coverage for diagnosis and treatment of illnesses and conditions most likely to interfere with living a full, normal life span. It includes coverage for those treatments most likely to allow persons to function as fully and normally as possible for their place in the life cycle. The idea of a normal life span draws on the Catholic view that, although physical death is an evil connected to human sinfulness, it is not the ultimate evil, which is spiritual death. Moreover, Jesus' own death and resurrection has already conquered death. Therefore, morality does not demand from the political system research on and insurance coverage for technologies of indefinite life extension. The focus here is on the normal human life span (seventy-five to eighty years) and the opportunity to flourish at all stages in that span. What counts as human flourishing will vary with the normal processes of human growth, development, and decline, processes that constitute facts of the created world.

Because medical science over time will change the specific diagnoses and treatments entailed in the notion of decent, comprehensive health coverage, this account cannot specify detailed coverages. However, it can describe in general terms the kinds of interventions that would and would not qualify for coverage.[18] Such a system would not focus all of its attention on medicine. The common good demands public health spending to ensure the adequacy and safety of food; clean water; epidemic and vector control; health and wellness education; immunizations; and enforcement of safe and healthy work environments. Promoting justice might well require diverting funds from advanced genetic and medical technology research to environmental research and to public health initiatives that could contribute more to health improvement.

Health insurance itself should cover at least the following: medical care effective in providing palliation of pain and symptoms of illness (regardless of the stage of life and whether the condition is acute, chronic, or terminal); primary care delivered by physicians, dentists, nurses, and other health professionals; emergency care for any life-threatening or serious illness or injury; and curative treatments for conditions that most interfere with normal growth and development of children and adolescents, that most interfere with persons contributing to society in adulthood; and that are most likely to cause premature death or disability. Pharmaceuticals and preventive health measures compatible with these goals also should be part of the plan. Therefore, guaranteed, universal, comprehensive health insurance coverage includes such measures as prenatal and infant care; rehabilitation services designed to return persons as closely as possible to normal functioning; health promotion and disease prevention; generous comfort care for the elderly and dying. It does not cover such things as fertility treatments; genetic selection or enhancement; abortion or euthanasia; cosmetic surgery designed to enhance natural abilities (as opposed to repairing injuries or abnormal features); expensive screening tests; or high-tech rescue medicine for persons at the end of life.

Getting from Here to There

To specify a goal is difficult enough. The principle of prudence counsels an equally intensive look at the means to pursue the goal. The best is often enemy of the good; single-minded focus on immediate achievement of a lofty goal can destroy real possibilities for limited achievements. Yet settling for second best may put the brakes on movement toward fuller achievement of the ultimate goal. These are truisms; they do not get us very much farther than the admonition: Don't go too fast; don't go too slow! But how fast is too fast? How slow is too slow? The centrality of prudence in Catholic moral theology counsels two things: attention to the real possibilities inherent in any political situation, and willingness to compromise when necessary.[19]

The Demands of Justice: Incremental or Immediate?

The American Catholic bishops and the Catholic Health Association of the United States (CHA) have long pressed for universal health insurance. Their proposals have been consistent with the Christian principles described above, but also have tended to be more generous in coverage. During the 1993–94 health care reform debate, the CHA weighed in with a full proposal to address access, cost of health care, quality, and providing long-term care for an aging population. Their approach won the support of the U.S. bishops.[20] At a time when it seemed possible that the United States might enact immediate and comprehensive health reform, these sweeping proposals made good sense, though it was reasonable to question the details.

The present political climate, however, is not favorable to sweeping reform. The focus of Congress and the president in the late 1990s and early 2000s has been on Medicare, with most attention given to prescription drugs (the new Medicare Part D), Medicare long-term reform, and Medicare managed care. Congress also focused on patient privacy, health information technology, quality improvement, and cost control. Those without insurance, or fundamental restructurings of the system to move it toward justice and the common good, received scant attention. Washington and state capitals seldom saw the preferential option for the poor. In this political context, the Catholic Health Association advanced a slimmed-down proposal for comprehensive reform that acknowledged the advisability of an incremental, sequential strategy.[21]

Indeed, apart from the particular political climate of the present time, there are major impediments to immediate reform embedded in American politics. First, American political institutions are structured in such a way as to provide numerous blocking opportunities for groups opposed to major reform.[22] Indeed, with the current highly fragmented condition of American health care, there are numerous groups with contrasting stakes in the system. Putting together a coalition in support of systematic reform along the lines advocated above would be impossible. Second, American political culture is market-oriented and strongly affirms individual responsibility for health care.[23] Language of justice and common good, let alone preferential option for the poor, has difficulty finding traction in a culture in which each is supposed to take care of himself/herself. Not impossible; witness Social Security and free public education. Nevertheless, even those venerable institutions currently are under attack by more individualistic and market-oriented ideas. Third, major political and social reforms require broad and deep movements to generate the momentum to break public apathy and to sustain public attention over time.[24] Finally, "windows of opportunity," when public attention, legislative interests and structures, and presidential interests align, open rarely for sweeping social change.[25] Slightly open in 1993–1994, the window is firmly closed in the early years of the twenty-first century.

Prudential judgment, therefore, supports keeping the sweeping *goals* of universal insurance securely in sight, but suggests exploring ways to take achievable steps, even though modest, toward those goals. Prudence also counsels a strategy of alliance and compromise to build a coalition strong enough to support small steps in the right direction.[26] In addition, success at building alliances and the results of modest, but solid legislative achievements could be the foundation for more sweeping reform (though it also runs the danger of achieving the most appealing reforms and exhausting political will and momentum before achieving the goal). Given the American federal system, with responsibility for health care policy divided between federal and state governments, the strategy must be shared. The states currently have a role in implementing and paying for public insurance for poor and low-income persons (Medicaid and SCHIP), and they are the traditional regulators of the health insurance business. States, therefore, will be called upon to implement some of the reforms proposed below, but they have inherent financial limitations, and the nationalization and even globalization of the economy means that they must give way to the federal government on a wide range of policies.[27]

Employment-Based?

Because the arguments above counsel incremental reform, they advise building on the present employer-based insurance system. This is not to say that this system is without major flaws; rather, it is to say this is the system through which two-thirds of all Americans purchase insurance. Most (though certainly not all) policies purchased through employers achieve the principal goals. They spread financial risk among a large pool of individuals, protecting workers and many of their dependents from monetary disaster when illness or injury strike, and they assure coverage for a comprehensive range of medical treatments.[28]

Therefore, the first responsibility of public policy advocacy is to preserve and to extend employment-based health insurance for workers and their dependents. The federal tax system encourages such insurance by providing tax breaks for their purchase to employers and to employees. Although these also encourage too-generous policies for middle- and upper-income employees, their support for the present system is central; so, reform should retain them. Tax breaks to encourage the self-employed to purchase insurance should be more rapidly deployed than under current law.

The rising cost of health care means that employers will in the future seek ways to pass more of the cost directly to their workers, creating financial incentives for low-wage employees to decline coverage. Moreover, small employers find it very difficult to buy insurance at competitive rates, producing low rates of employer-based insurance in small businesses. There are two possible strategies for addressing these issues. The first is legislation to provide small businesses with access to larger purchasing pools, either through state-supported purchasing cooperatives or through opening up the Federal Employee Health Benefit Program (FEHBP) to small private companies. Doing these makes sense, although there are complicated technical issues and federal employees and their unions are understandably nervous about making changes in a successful program.

The second strategy is to provide federal tax credits to low-wage workers to assist with premiums on employer-based insurance or to purchase individual policies when their employer does not offer insurance. Because it is market-oriented, this strategy appeals to Republicans and to conservatives, and it was the centerpiece of President Bush's early health reform proposals. This proposal has important disadvantages, however. First, such a credit will not reach the workers it aims at unless it is refundable (meaning low-income workers who do not owe federal income tax would receive a check from the IRS for the value of the credit, as with the present Earned Income Tax Credit). However, refundable credits are more expensive than straight tax credits. Second, since the cost of a comprehensive, private market family health insurance policy is more than $6,000 per year, the tax credit would have to be set rather high for low-wage workers to find it attractive. President Bush's proposal was for a refundable credit of $2,000, far too low. Third, subsidized policies will appeal most to high-risk individuals, so their premiums will have to be set higher than present average premi-

ums. Fourth, and most significantly for the long run, encouraging individual policies makes the insurance system even more fragmented than at present, encouraging waste, inefficiency, and high administrative costs that add
no medical benefit. This is so because there are costs involved in designing a
wide variety of individual plans to appeal to individual needs, costs in marketing, selling, and underwriting each individual policy, and high "back office" costs in physician practices, clinics, and hospitals in filing insurance
claims with dozens of carriers whose multiple policies have different coverages and co-payment schemes.

Therefore, the strategy most prudent in the current political environment is to forge a compromise of the proponents of the tax credit and FE-
HBP strategies with the proponents of expanding *public programs* to cover
more low- and moderate-income persons. This strategy would accept small
group insurance market reform and tax credits aimed at low-income and
middle-income persons in return for support for expansion of Medicaid
and SCHIP.

Public Programs

Because employment strategies alone are insufficient, Medicaid and
SCHIP must be part of health care reform. These are the public programs
focused on no cost or low cost insurance for the poor and near-poor. Although each has unacceptable gaps and limitations in coverage and although eligibility and coverage vary by state, they provide at least minimum
insurance for those unable to afford private insurance. Congress established
Medicaid in 1965 as the counterpart to Medicare. It is a joint federal-state
program with coverage for the poorest persons. Most of its funding, however, provides care to the elderly and disabled. Poor children also have good
coverage under Medicaid, but it is very limited for non-disabled adults.
Congress created the State Children's Health Insurance Program in 1997 to
cover children above the income levels that qualify for Medicaid, but whose
parents have incomes too low to afford good private insurance. It covers
children only, leaving out low-wage, working adults.[29]

There are two major directions for expansion of Medicaid and SCHIP.
First, adults are more at health risk than children; therefore, an incremental strategy of insurance expansion would strongly favor current proposals
automatically to cover with Medicaid and SCHIP the *parents* of children already eligible. The advantage is that new programs and new bureaucratic
systems would not have to be devised to extend health insurance coverage

to low-wage, part-time, or seasonal working adults. The mechanisms are already in place; only funding is lacking. The second direction for expansion is simplified eligibility. Currently, Medicaid fails to enroll about half of all eligible children; millions eligible for SCHIP remain unenrolled. The reasons are many: lack of publicity, complex forms and qualification rules, parental irresponsibility, distrust of government, fear of deportation among illegal residents with legal children, and so forth. State and federal law could address some of these by radically streamlining qualification procedures and lengthening enrollment periods before re-qualification would be necessary.

Specific measures to implement these goals would include:

- Additional federal funding to pay for intensive outreach to children currently eligible for Medicaid and SCHIP, but not enrolled.
- Presumptive eligibility based on minimal financial information with simplified enrollment and documentation forms.
- Enrollment periods of at least one year before re-qualification (requiring more funding).
- Additional funding to make the parents of children who qualify for Medicaid and SCHIP automatically eligible.
- Extension of SCHIP to low-income pregnant women.
- Extension of Medicaid and SCHIP to low-income legal immigrant children and parents who arrived in the United States after August 22, 1996 (the cutoff date for eligibility under current law).

In short, an incremental strategy for justice and the common good in health care, while attending first to the health needs of the poor and near-poor, would build on the existing employment-based system, expand and simplify public programs, and pursue limited market-based insurance reforms and incentives.

The Limits of Incrementalism

Even with this feasible, but difficult legislative strategy, the maximum achievable (optimistic) estimate of additional coverage is half of the currently uninsured, leaving 20 million or more persons without coverage. Moreover, those most likely to take advantage of new opportunities for coverage are those who know that they have a high need for coverage, what insurance theory refers to as "adverse selection." Adverse selection puts pressure on spending, possibly raising private premiums and making them unaffordable for some persons and raising public spending beyond estimates, putting pressure on federal and state budgets. Moreover, the public strategy raises fears of "crowd out," which refers to the possibility that already insured persons will drop employment coverage to take advantage of newly expanded and cheaper public programs. The seriousness of these problems is a matter of some debate, but neither is avoidable in an incremental strategy. Only immediate, fundamental reform that required all employers to provide insurance or that required all persons to purchase private insurance (and subsidies to make that possible) could avoid adverse selection or crowd out. Such fundamental reform seems not politically possible in the near future.

Apart from these two problems, an incremental strategy must face other issues. Many barriers to good health are not a direct product of being uninsured. There are three significant barriers to health care access only partly related to income or insurance status. First, certain groups have unique obstacles to health care, particularly immigrants, both legal and illegal. Second, many of the poor engage in irresponsible behaviors that interfere with obtaining needed health care. Third, the structure of the health care system itself makes it difficult for persons without educational resources and social skills to find the care they need. There is an important role for Christians in overcoming all three barriers.

Religious Communities and Health Care

Persons in the United States illegally, usually working for very low wages and existing on the margins of society, cannot afford to pay for health care, and they are not entitled to coverage under federal or state programs, except emergency medical care for life-threatening conditions. Even when *some* family members are legal residents, or even *citizens*, they may decide *not* to apply for the benefits the law gives them, for fear of exposing other family members who are not legal.

Legal immigrants *do qualify* for some federal and state health care programs, and they may receive coverage through employment. However, recent changes in the law have tightened and restricted the kinds of benefits for which such persons qualify. Though nations and their governments must recognize the difference between citizens and strangers, *Christians must not.* It is incumbent upon the Christian community to find ways to meet their health care needs. Subsidiarity (attention to the division of responsibilities between government and non-governmental entities and among federal, state, and local governments) comes into play in health care reform.

Even when poor persons have Medicaid or some form of private insurance, they may not always use their access in appropriate ways.[30] This statement, of course, is not true of all the poor, and numerous middle-class families have similar responsibility issues. However, the circumstances of hardscrabble life make it difficult for poor persons to exercise responsible decision making for themselves and their children (or at least *responsible* from the perspective of more comfortable middle-class life). Addictions interfere with responsibility; shifting addresses and unreliable transportation and child care arrangements make it difficult to keep appointments with health care providers; poor education or limited intellectual and language skills upset compliance with directions about self-care or medications. Appointments are not kept, even at free clinics. Promises to stop smoking or to stop drinking fall away. Children do not receive vaccinations. Christians who wish to be healers in Jesus' footsteps can find or invent new ways to overcome these obstacles.

Responsibility issues interact with barriers in health care structures themselves. What looks like irresponsible behavior is sometimes simple lack of the intellectual, emotional, or social resources to negotiate one's way through large, bureaucratic institutions. Linguistic and cultural barriers on both sides—health professionals and clients—exacerbate noncompliance. Health care for the poor is often delivered in public hospitals largely staffed by foreign medical graduates, thus creating a double cultural barrier, or by young residents passing through toward more rewarding placements. Waiting rooms are crowded, appointments difficult to obtain, and transportation to health care facilities expensive or erratic. Public hospitals often lack sufficient funding and staff.

There are many examples of creative approaches to meeting the health needs of the poor and near-poor. This section can describe only a few, and even these very briefly: community health centers and other "safety net" institutions, traditional hospital-based community outreach, Christian ministries dedicated to the most wretched of the urban poor, comprehensive poverty medicine programs, and parish-based ministries focusing on health and well-being in addition to traditional curative health care.

Because community health centers (CHCs) often incorporate attention to outreach and follow-up, social services, and transportation, they can work on and encourage the kinds of compliance and personal responsibility that are impossible for public hospitals and large Medicaid managed care organizations. Finding ways for local churches and other religious organizations to work with CHCs is an important challenge of the next decade. One way might be to use parish centers or child care facilities as CHC satellite centers, especially for enrollment, outreach, and basic health education. This strategy, of course, does not absolve governments of their own responsibility to provide adequate funding for CHCs, for public hospitals, and other public services for the uninsured.

Church-Affiliated Health Care Institutions

Churches and religious organizations operate numerous health care facilities: hospitals, clinics, and nursing homes being the most prominent. Religious organizations, especially Catholic, operate approximately 15 percent of all community hospitals and 20 percent of all community hospital beds. These institutions have a legal and moral responsibility, as well as a responsibility to the faith that created them, to benefit the communities in which they are located. This benefit is not only in the form of medical care for the particular individuals that enter them. Responsibility extends to *community education and outreach programs,* special services made available to the community as a whole.[31]

For example, hospitals could fund, fully or partially, a variety of services that the uninsured need or that may not be included in the comprehensive insurance plan above. These could be offered on a free or on a sliding scale according to income:

- Community health centers (described above).
- A mobile mammography van, a mobile dentistry van, and a mobile clinic to travel inner cities or rural communities. These vans could also provide special services to seasonal workers when they are in the community.
- Prenatal and post-natal nurturing programs.
- Counseling centers for low-income persons with mental health needs.
- School-based neighborhood centers in low-income neighborhoods to provide health education, literacy training, parent-school cooperation, and other activities.

Urban Health Care Ministries

There are a wide variety of health care ministries specifically directed to the urban poor, particularly the *homeless* and the *addicted.* Parishes and congregations run some; others are freestanding. They share a commitment to place medicine in the gaps of the established health-care institutions. They provide free or minimal-cost physician services, nursing, and immunizations, and they do it at the doorsteps of those who need it.[32]

For example, Christ House, in Washington, D.C., is a medical recovery shelter for homeless, addicted men. It takes men too sick to be on the streets. The men live in the house, together with a community of physicians, staff persons, and their families. This Christian community fills the gap between conventional homeless shelters, which provide little or no health care and very limited in-patient recovery programs in the inner cities. In addition to providing treatment for addiction, Christ House becomes a Christian community for the men who live there.

Washington's Church of the Saviour founded Columbia Road Health Services and its affiliated clinics. They now include support and affiliations with other congregations in the Washington area. As of the early 1990s, Columbia Road was a complete family-practice clinic with over 15,000 patient visits a year, predominantly from the refugee Hispanic community. Without clinics like Columbia Road, they would have nowhere to turn for ordinary treatments for accidents and illnesses less than life- or limb-threatening. Of equal significance, these poorest of the poor have access to a community that loves them.

Parishes and Christian Health Professionals

New structures do not always need building outside of the local congregation and apart from the personal responsibilities of Christian health professionals. Many of the elderly and the poor belong to congregations. Congregations also are home to dentists, nurses, physicians, and other health professionals. There are three different, yet complementary, features of a creative congregational approach: care for individual health-impaired members of the congregation; a holistic concept of health; and, especially for congregations located in poor neighborhoods, outreach and advocacy for the uninsured in their localities.[33]

Congregations can set up home visitations to the elderly and the chronically ill, using parish volunteers. Such efforts can provide continuity and coordination of care, as well as encourage wellness at a personal level. Persons who already visit shut-ins for prayer and fellowship can be trained to make basic health assessments and to watch for warning signs of impending health crises. The parish nurse program is one model for congregational outreach. Such programs generally involve a congregation employing a registered nurse to serve as a resource for health and wellness in the parish.

Congregations can also assemble the health professionals who are already members of the congregation to plan health and wellness opportunities and to staff health education programs. Mentally ill persons, for example, may be enabled to function within the community by having a network of friends and support from the congregation to call upon when life seems to be spiraling out of control. Congregations can be places that connect and coordinate multiple community resources for those members (and their neighbors) who lack the resources to do their own coordination.

One example of a religious foundation encouraging such local initiatives is Wheat Ridge Ministries, in Itasca, Illinois, which makes grants focusing on holistic medicine, parish nurse programs, and seed money for local "health and hope" ministries. Another is the Lutheran Charities Foundation in St. Louis, which supports such ministries as Our Little Haven, a nonprofit organization that facilitates foster-care placements for HIV-positive children, and a community summer sports program at Ebenezer Lutheran Church. In San Francisco, the Vesper Society makes grants that forge collaboration between health institutions and faith communities.[34] Suburban partner churches of inner city churches can help with costs of printing information materials, funding transportation, and other logistic support.

Conclusions

The same principles and policy conclusions that govern health care reform for the non-elderly characterize, *mutatis mutandis,* health care for elderly persons. They too require insurance for standard, comprehensive health care at a cost to them that does not exceed a reasonable proportion of their means. Justice as meeting need is a particularly strong principle when applied to the elderly, since the need for medical attention increases with age beyond sixty-five. Moreover, as persons age, they run the increasing risk of becoming marginal to the community, not only because they are no longer in the workforce, but also because illness and disability limit their ability to interact with other citizens.

Persons over sixty-five in the United States already have the kind of comprehensive insurance described above (or an approximation of it) in Medicare. Therefore, health care reform as it touches the aged means Medicare reform. In addition, the special circumstances of most of the aged mean that the details of financing and delivering needed health care must be adapted. In general, the elderly have a greater need for medical services but limited flexibility in generating income sufficient to pay for these services. Therefore, Medicare's financing must be different from ordinary health insurance. Second, many of the elderly have an ensemble of chronic and acute conditions requiring extensive coordination among many health care providers and numerous social services. However, the conditions of aging in many of these same persons limit their own ability to coordinate complex systems of care. Therefore, health care reform must pay attention to ensuring a *continuum of care.* Third, as people age, their likelihood of needing formal long-term care increases. Therefore, health care reform should take financing and delivery of long-term care into consideration. All of these are the stuff of Medicare reform debates in Washington and are well beyond the scope of this chapter.

The present chapter has briefly described the principles of justice, common good, and preferential option for the poor and applied them to extending insurance coverage to all persons in the United States. It advocates an incremental reform, building on the current system of employment-based insurance, providing some subsidies for purchase of individual policies, and extending Medicaid and SCHIP to additional persons. The danger of incremental reform is that the compromises necessary to achieve some progress toward the demand in Catholic social doctrine for universal coverage will sap energy for achieving the full goal. If Congress were to adopt the reforms advocated above, it would at best cut the uninsurance rate in half (to about 20 million persons, or 7 percent of the population). However, these would be those less likely to generate sympathy for greater progress— moderate-income working adults, the long-term unemployed, the homeless, illegal immigrants, and the like. Some of these persons should receive free care through the community and church resources described above. Leaving some in second-class status continues to offend justice, common good, and option for the poor. Moreover, these reforms will leave the American health care system plagued with fragmentation, inefficiencies, and high administrative costs.

For all these reasons the next steps in health care reform beyond those above will be extraordinarily difficult. These steps can be mentioned briefly, but the political will to take them cannot be predicted. The steps are:

1. A legal mandate for all persons to purchase health insurance.

2. Automatic enrollment of all employed persons in employer-based insurance with a premium proportional to income deducted from their paychecks (and from employers) to pay for the insurance.

3. Subsidies or tax benefits to employers with large numbers of part-time or low-wage workers to help to finance this insurance.

4. Expansion of Medicaid and SCHIP to all legal, permanent residents of the United States who do not have employer-based insurance.

5. Insurance plan simplification—a limited number of employment-based insurance options with standard benefits, similar to the limited number of "Medigap" options under Medicare.

Catholic social doctrine dreams big in the health care arena. The question is whether this dream can inspire Catholics and other citizens to the kinds of political action necessary to realize the vision. Incremental reform is the first step.

NOTES

1. Mark E. Rushefsky and Kant Patel, *Politics, Power, and Policy Making: The Case of Health Care Reform in the 1990s* (Armonk, NY: M. E. Sharpe, 1998); Nicholas Lanham, *A Lost Cause: Bill Clinton's Campaign for National Health Insurance* (Westport, CT: Greenwood, 1996); Pauline Vaillancourt Rosenau, ed., *Health Care Reform in the Nineties* (Thousand Oaks, CA: Sage, 1994); Theda Skocpol, *Boomerang: Clinton's Health Security Effort and the Turn against Government in U.S. Politics* (New York: Norton, 1996); and Jacob S. Hacker, *The Road to Nowhere: The Genesis of President Clinton's Plan for Health Security* (Princeton, NJ: Princeton University Press, 1997).

2. "Income, Poverty, and Health Insurance Coverage in the United States, 2004," Report P60-229 (www.census.gov/prod/2005pubs/p60-229.pdf; accessed July 17, 2006); Kaiser Family Foundation, "The Uninsured and Their Access to Health Care" (www.kff.org; accessed July 17, 2006).

3. Good introductions to Catholic social doctrine are Marvin L. Krier Mich, *Catholic Social Teaching and Movements* (Mystic, CT: Twenty-Third Publications, 1998); Thomas Massaro, S.J., *Living Justice: Catholic Social Teaching in Action* (Franklin, WI: Sheed & Ward, 2000); Clarke E. Cochran and David Carroll Cochran, *Catholics, Politics, and Public Policy: Beyond Left and Right* (Maryknoll, NY: Orbis, 2003); Rodger Charles, S.J., *An Introduction to Catholic Social Teaching* (San Francisco: Ignatius, 1999). For basic materials in Catholic medical ethics, see Kevin D. O'Rourke, O.P., and Philip Boyle, eds., *Medical Ethics: Sources of Catholic Teachings*, 2nd ed. (Washington, DC: Georgetown University Press, 1993), and Benedict M. Ashley, O.P., and Kevin D. O'Rourke, O.P., *Health Care Ethics: A Theological Analysis*, 4th ed. (Washington, DC: Georgetown University Press, 1997).

4. See Pope John XXIII's declaration in the encyclical *Pacem in Terris*, no. 11; also Michael Walzer, *Spheres of Justice: A Defense of Pluralism and Equality* (New York: Basic Books, 1983), chapter 3; Charles J. Dougherty, *Back to Reform: Values, Markets, and the Health Care System* (New York: Oxford University Press, 1996), especially chapters 3 and 5; and Philip S. Keane,

S.S., *Catholicism and Health-Care Justice: Problems, Potential, and Solutions* (New York: Paulist Press, 2002).

5. Norman Daniels, Bruce Kennedy, and Ichiro Kawachi, *Is Inequality Bad for Our Health?* (Boston: Beacon Press, 2000), pp. 14–15.

6. See Robert E. Goodin, "Vulnerabilities and Responsibilities: An Ethical Defense of the Welfare State," *American Political Science Review* 79 (September 1985): 775–87.

7. Joseph Cardinal Bernardin, *Celebrating the Ministry of Healing* (St. Louis, MO: Catholic Health Association of the United States, 1999), p. 95; Clarke E. Cochran, "Yves R. Simon and 'the Common Good': A Note on the Concept," *Ethics* 88 (April 1978): 229–39; Dougherty, *Back to Reform*, chapter 6; David Hollenbach, S.J., *The Common Good and Christian Ethics* (New York: Cambridge University Press, 2002).

8. On solidarity as the virtue of the common good, see Judith A. Dwyer, ed., *The New Dictionary of Catholic Social Thought* (Collegeville, MN: Michael Glazier, 1994): 908–12; Joseph Cardinal Ratzinger, *The Meaning of Christian Brotherhood* (San Francisco: Ignatius Press, 1993 [1960]); and Catholic Health Association of the United States, *With Justice for All: The Ethics of Healthcare Rationing* (St. Louis, MO: Catholic Health Association of the United States, 1991), p. 16.

9. Clarke E. Cochran, "The Common Good and Health Care Policy: Three Meanings," *Health Progress* 80 (May/June 1999): 41–44, 47.

10. For example, the Catholic Health Association's principles for health care reform emphasize that care for health and delivery of health is a *shared* responsibility of individuals, family, employers, voluntary agencies, and government. *Continuing the Commitment: A Pathway to Health Care Reform* (St. Louis, MO: CHA, 2000), p. 10.

11. Richard A. McCormick, S.J., *Corrective Vision: Explorations in Moral Theology* (Kansas City, MO: Sheed & Ward, 1994), pp. 141–48.

12. Michael J. Himes and Kenneth R. Himes, *Fullness of Faith: The Public Significance of Theology* (Mahwah, NJ: Paulist, 1993), pp. 33ff., and Thomas Massaro, S.J., *Catholic Social Teaching and United States Welfare Reform* (Collegeville, MN: Liturgical Press, 1998), p. 249.

13. See note 2 above and Katherine Swartz, "Dynamics of People without Insurance: Don't Let the Numbers Fool You," *Journal of the American Medical Association* 271 (January 15, 1994): 64–66.

14. See, among many, John Z. Ayanian et al., "Unmet Health Needs of Uninsured Adults in the United States," *Journal of the American Medical Association* 284 (October 25, 2000): 2061–69.

15. A convenient summary is Robert Kuttner, "The American Health Care System: Health Insurance Coverage," *New England Journal of Medicine* 340 (January 14, 1999): 163–68.

16. Karl Kronebusch, "Medicaid for Children: Federal Mandates, Welfare Reform, and Policy Backsliding," *Health Affairs* 20 (January–February 2001): 97–111.

17. The description of this insurance scheme draws on Daniel Callahan's idea of "sustainable medicine" in *False Hopes: Overcoming the Obstacles to a Sustainable, Affordable Medicine* (New Brunswick, NJ: Rutgers University Press, 1999). It is indebted as well to Norman Daniels, *Just Health Care* (New York: Cambridge University Press, 1985). See also Cardinal Bernardin's *Celebrating the Ministry of Healing*, pp. 70–82, and CHA, *Continuing the Commitment*.

18. Callahan, *False Hopes*, pp. 252–74.

19. This refers to political, not moral compromise. The former preserves and adheres to fundamental principles, but recognizes that in difficult circumstances their realization often must take a circuitous route with many pauses along the way. Moral compromise, on the other hand, means abandoning some principles in order to achieve progress on others.

20. CHA, *Setting Relationships Right: A Proposal for Systematic Healthcare Reform* (St. Louis: MO: CHA, 1993), and National Conference of Catholic Bishops, "Resolution on Health Care Reform," *Origins* 23 (July 1, 1993): 97, 99–102. See earlier CHA discussions of these issues in CHA, *No Room in the Marketplace: The Health Care of the Poor* (St. Louis, MO: CHA, 1986), and CHA, *With Justice for All?*

21. Most notably in CHA, *Continuing the Commitment.* See also www.chausa.org/Pub/MainNav/whatwedo/coveringanation; accessed July 17, 2006.

22. Sven Steinmo and Jon Watts, "It's the Institutions, Stupid! Why Comprehensive National Health Insurance Always Fails in America," *Journal of Health Politics, Policy, and Law* 20 (Summer 1995): 329–72.

23. For example, Donald W. Light, "The Restructuring of the American Health Care System," and James A. Morone, "Gridlock and Breakthrough in American Health Politics," both in *Health Politics and Policy,* 3rd ed., ed. Theodore J. Litman and Leonard S. Robbins (Albany, NY: Delmar Publishers, 1997), pp. 46–74.

24. Jacob S. Hacker and Theda Skocpol, "The New Politics of U.S. Health Policy," *Journal of Health Politics, Policy, and Law* 22 (April 1997): 315–38.

25. John Kingdon, *Agendas, Alternatives, and Public Policies,* 2nd ed. (New York: Harper-Collins, 1995).

26. For example, see the Cover the Uninsured alliance (http://covertheuninsured.org/partners; accessed July 17, 2006).

27. Marsha R. Gold et al., "Health Insurance Expansion through States in a Pluralistic System," *Journal of Health Politics, Policy, and Law* 26 (June 2001): 581–615. Recently enacted universal coverage mandates in Maine and Massachusetts are likely to fail for these reasons.

28. Although many present policies are more generous than the decent, comprehensive package advocated above, some are less generous. Moreover, the wide variety of policies available contributes to the high administrative costs and inefficiencies of American health care. Discussing these issues here, however, would take us too far afield. Moreover, recommending legislation to standardize private health insurance policies is not feasible in the present political climate.

29. For a summary of these programs, see for example, Kant Patel and Mark E. Rushefsky, *Health Care Politics and Policy in America,* 3rd ed. (Armonk, NY: M. E. Sharpe, 2006), chapter 3.

30. It is important not to be glib in holding the poor responsible. For many, mere daily survival is heroic. See David Hilfiker, *Not All of Us Are Saints: A Doctor's Journey with the Poor* (New York: Hill & Wang, 1994). Recent research indicates that "irresponsible" smoking or drinking or other bad health habits account for only a small percentage of the difference in death rates between the poor and non-poor. In fact, alcohol consumption increases with income. See Paula M. Lantz et al., "Socioeconomic Factors, Health Behaviors, and Mortality: Results from a Nationally Representative Prospective Study of U.S. Adults," *Journal of the American Medical Association* 279 (June 3, 1998): 1703–8.

31. On community benefit definition and requirements, see www.chausa.org/Pub/MainNav/ourcommitments/communitybenefits; accessed July 17, 2006).

32. David Hilfiker's *Not All of Us Are Saints* describes two ministries in Washington, DC, with which he has been affiliated: Christ House and a network of clinics that includes Columbia Road Health Services, Community of Hope Health Services, and a clinic at the So Others May Eat soup kitchen.

33. The following ideas and examples draw substantially upon *Strong Partners: Realigning Religious Health Assets for Community Health* (Atlanta, GA: The Carter Center, 1998). The Christian Community Health Fellowship (CCHF) is approximately two decades old. It is a national network of Christian health professionals and others concerned about the health-care needs of impoverished communities in the United States (www.cchf.org; accessed July 17, 2006).

34. *Strong Partners* provides a number of examples of such foundations and the issues that they face. The Catholic Health Association of the United States' journal, *Health Progress,* also regularly features examples of these kinds of efforts.

CHAPTER 12

Health Care Reform and the "Consistent Ethic"

MICHAEL D. PLACE

The truth is, of course, that each life is of infinite value. Protecting and promoting life, caring for it and defending it is a complex task in social and policy terms. I have struggled with the specifics often and have sensed the limits of reason in the struggle to know the good and do the right. My final hope is that my efforts have been faithful to the truth of the gospel of life and that you and others like you will find in this gospel the vision and strength needed to promote and nurture the great gift of life God has shared with us.
— Cardinal Joseph Bernardin[1]

In his living, and especially in his dying, Cardinal Joseph Bernardin embraced the innate dignity of every human being as God's creation. He was compassionately connected to others, especially, at the end of his life, to those who also suffered from cancer. These personal qualities gave testimony to three core themes of the Catholic moral vision:

- The sacredness of our human life.
- Our call to be responsible stewards of that life.
- The interwoven social fabric of our human existence.[2]

This article originally appeared in *Health Progress* (March–April 2000): 49–55. Copyright © 2000 by the Catholic Health Association. Reprinted with permission.

Cardinal Bernardin's life was based on Catholic belief and practice. The articulation of a simple phrase—"the consistent ethic of life"—was one of his great contributions, drawing together as it does the richness of the scriptures, our Catholic tradition, our experience of ministry, and human reason. Within the Catholic community, the *consistent* ethic has allowed believers to embrace both the pro-life and the pro-justice efforts of the Church. Although the media sometimes seem to take great delight in reporting disagreements among various groups within the U.S. Catholic Church, the consistent ethic of life acts as a counter to that phenomenon. The consistent ethic binds us together in a way that enhances the Catholic community. Equally important, it enables us to be a stronger witness of Gospel values to the wider public. It calls us to a deeper concern for all people, particularly for the weak and vulnerable, whose dignity is threatened and whose potential is blocked by unjust conditions.

Consistent Ethic of Life: Sources and Meaning

To understand the consistent ethic of life, I begin with Pope John Paul II's *Evangelium Vitae*.[3] This encyclical proclaimed the "gospel of life" as central to Jesus' message. It called on the community of faith to mobilize a new culture to counter the moral decline that allows so many kinds of violence—war, abortion, and capital punishment, among them—to threaten life. John Paul II called on "people of life" to share the good news of the gospel of life. I believe that employing the consistent ethic as an intellectual and moral framework—inspired as it is by scripture, rooted in church tradition, born out in experience, and known through reason—is one way to share that good news.

Scripture

Throughout scripture, there is an undeniable affirmation of the sacred nature of human life, our duty to steward it wisely, and our obligation to protect and nurture the lives of others, particularly the weak and vulnerable. In Genesis, we read that humankind was created in the image of God. "God saw everything that he had made, and indeed, it was very good" (Gn 1:31). At the end of his long life, Moses exhorted the Israelites to "choose life" (Dt 30:19).

Not only are we called to life; we are called also, through Christ, to "have life, and have it abundantly" (Jn 10:10). We are to treasure our life and, as in the parable of the talents, to be trustworthy servants who use our gifts wisely (Mt 25:14–30)

As a way of recognizing life's sanctity and our own potential, we are also called to protect and nurture the lives of others. St. Paul exemplified this when he wrote to the Thessalonians, "So deeply do we care for you that we are determined to share with you not only the gospel of God but also our own selves" (1 Thes 2:8). At the end of time, all people, indeed all nations, will be judged by how well each gave to the least among them.

Tradition

These scriptural themes are a consistent thread woven through the theological tradition and teachings of the Catholic Church. We can turn to the *Catechism of the Catholic Church* and find there the Church's teaching in favor of human solidarity, love for the poor, a just social order, and charity. In those same pages, the Church's condemnation of homicide, abortion, euthanasia, and the use of the death penalty is explicit. All these teachings are linked by the central affirmation of the dignity of every human being and are given special attention in Church teachings such as *Gaudium et Spes, Pacem in Terris,* and, more recently, *Evangelium Vitae.*

Experience

The Church's experience in the healing, teaching, and serving ministries also shapes and reflects these commitments to life's sacredness and our obligation to nurture and protect the lives of others, especially the poor. Through the healing ministries, we are reminded how precious and fragile life is. It becomes clear that for any one person to preserve his or her life and live it responsibly, a certain dependence on the goodwill and care of others is necessary.

Reason

Within the Catholic tradition, reason and faith are not contradictory but mutually supportive. By virtue of reason, we have the ability to distinguish between good and evil. In *Veritatis Splendor,* John Paul II noted that "it is in the light of the dignity of the human person—a dignity which must be affirmed for its own sake—that reason grasps the specific moral value of certain goods toward which the person is naturally inclined."[4] The light of reason enabled Aquinas to posit that there is a natural essence to every being.[5] Every human being possesses a built-in dynamism that moves him or her toward fullness. This human trait marks what it means to be human and is deserving of deep respect.

The respect due every individual life because of our innate human dignity is a concept embraced by ancient philosophers, articulated by enlightened thinkers, and immortalized in our Declaration of Independence. Plato, Aristotle, and Kant all saw the human person as a creature imbued with intrinsic value, intended for a meaningful purpose, and understood in the context of relationships.

That the consistent ethic is consonant with reason—as well as with scripture, tradition, and experience—is important. It enables adherents to speak to those outside the Catholic tradition and share with them a coherent, persuasive rationale for the defense of life.

Value of Consistent Ethic in Public Debate

I believe the consistent ethic of life echoes certain American values. It is consonant with—and can enrich our understanding of—such quintessential American concepts as liberty, equality, the pursuit of happiness, civic duty, and the "American dream" of success and achievement. As Abraham Lincoln said in the Gettysburg Address, this country was "conceived in liberty and dedicated to the proposition that all men are created equal." Implicit in the Declaration of Independence and the Constitution is recognition of the essential dignity of every human being. By virtue of being human, all people are endowed with certain inalienable rights. But also deeply embedded in our national heritage is the premise that we are not disconnected individuals pursuing our own interests. In the words of our Constitution, we are "a people" attempting to form a "more perfect union" intended "to establish justice, insure domestic tranquillity, provide for the common defense, promote the general welfare, and secure the blessings of liberty to ourselves and our posterity."

Throughout our history, Americans have differed over the interpretation of American values and what it means to be "a people." One need only look at our current conservative and liberal strains in politics. Conservatives tend to wax poetic about their interest in liberty when it comes to economics, but are far less libertarian when it comes to social values. Liberals, by contrast, seek to restrain freedom in the sphere of economic activity but hold that freedom should reign in such areas as abortion and euthanasia. The consistent ethic of life reinforces the ideas of freedom, greatness, and equality of opportunity, but always with an underlying awareness of the relational nature of being human. Our nation's founders did not view the pursuit of happiness as a selfish chase after whatever happened to please us, but rather as the seeking of a worthy and virtuous life. The consistent ethic of life brings us back to that original meaning of *life* as precious, of *liberty* as the condition for pursuing a happy—meaning worthy and virtuous—life, and finally of *equality* as requiring an atmosphere in which disparate people might flourish.

Our Contemporary Context

At this point in our nation's history, we are in great need of the consistent ethic as a kind of corrective lens through which we can take a fresh look at traditional American values. How might the ethic counter the fragmentation, individualism, and commercial orientation that mark our culture?

Fragmentation

As we begin a new century, John Courtney Murray's insights in *We Hold These Truths* gain a deeper significance.[6] When he wrote in 1960, he called attention to the common values operative in our country. "The whole premise of public argument," he wrote, "if it is to be civilized and civilizing is that the consensus is real, that among the people everything is not in doubt, but that there is a core of agreement, accord, concurrence, acquiescence. We hold certain truths; therefore we can argue about them."

It was that very premise that enabled Martin Luther King Jr. to be so persuasive and effective in the civil rights struggle. The founding fathers' underlying assumptions about human dignity and liberty—coupled with the religious vision of a society in which all could flourish—gave shape and purpose to King's leadership. The dramatic progress made in the 1960s to ensure the civil rights of blacks in America was due in large part to that common heritage.

But it may not be immediately obvious, a generation later, that we still "hold certain truths." Recent decades have been marked by a decided lack of common ground. Commentators offer diverse reasons for the fragmentation that pervades our culture. Some say it has emerged from the "specialization" of politics, an ironic byproduct of the civil rights movement, with groups devoted exclusively to one or two specific agendas or issues. Others blame (or credit) the proliferation of information through such media as the Internet and cable television. This results in a bewildering multitude of voices and at times hampers common conversation. Still others claim it is enthrallment to the media themselves—in particular, to the TV sets before which so many of us spend so many hours—that increasingly dissuades people from joining social and community groups.[7]

Individualism

Another dimension of this fragmentation can be seen in the way "morality" has come to be viewed as personal and individual. People refer to "your morals" versus "my morals," as if there were no moral principles that bind together all people. A central principle—the dignity and rights of every individual—seems to have been skewed into something almost unrecognizable as a valid moral starting point. In *Evangelium Vitae,* John Paul II identifies this disintegration as "postmodern relativism."[8] In *Veritatis Splendor,* he insists that "the primordial moral requirement of loving and respecting the person as an end and never as a mere means also implies, by its very nature, respect for certain fundamental goods, without which one would fall into relativism and arbitrariness."[9]

In our culture, we have so emphasized the status of individual freedom and independence as to have seemingly forgotten the underlying beliefs that guard human dignity and human rights: that each life is precious, that each life is meant to flourish, and that each of us has a responsibility to ensure that all people have the opportunity to find fulfillment. When these convictions are neglected, the individual is elevated—but there is emptiness below. The moral terrain becomes barren and dry.

Market Values

A third force meriting attention is our culture's insistence on effectiveness as judged in the market. In the technological revolution of the past century, it became tempting to measure a person's worth by his or her usefulness. Now, in the twenty-first century, we struggle to uphold the true dignity of each individual as a person, a unique and special reality, not a commodity or utensil.

Contemporary Signs of Hope

But these three facets of contemporary life, as discouraging as they may seem, may actually be helping to create fertile ground for the cultivation of the consistent ethic of life in the public square.

Spiritual Yearning

Perhaps as a reaction to the pace of modern life, with its emphasis on utility and function, a popular yearning for great personal spirituality has emerged. Today's spiritual gurus encourage their followers to seek spiritual fulfillment not only in personal well-being, but in serving others as well. John Paul II, in *Evangelium Vitae,* said that the gospel of life is not for believers alone, but for everyone and for "every human conscience which seeks the truth and which cares about the future of humanity."[10]

For all those who seek answers to the question of life's meaning, the consistent ethic of life has this to say: Every life is valuable and meaningful. Each person's life is meant to be lived as fully as possible. We are all meant to be in relationships and to work together to create conditions that promote human flourishing. By reiterating this truth, the consistent ethic of life can help answer the spiritual and moral yearnings even of those not rooted in the Catholic tradition.

Dissatisfaction with Autonomy

On one hand, the individual enjoys an elevated place in our culture. On the other, people are increasingly dissatisfied with autonomy as the guiding light in moral analysis. Bruce Jennings, a moral philosopher at the Hastings Center in New York, describes the triumph of autonomy as "the terrible singularity, the chilling aloofness of the sovereign moral will."[11] The "good" cannot be judged solely by its ability to satisfy an individual's choice, because there are good and bad choices.

Ethicists and philosophers are beginning to question our culture's emphasis on autonomy and are calling to mind other values that affect moral virtue. The consistent ethic of life recognizes the innate value of the individual and the need for that individual to flourish—but to flourish always in the context of the social fabric of life and his or her obligation to help others flourish as well.[12]

Power of the Media

Images possess undeniable power in our media-saturated society. The images of a little girl being rescued after having fallen in a well, of a woman being pulled from earthquake wreckage, of a small boat carrying a man to safety in a flood—all have something in common. They have the power to bring people together, to communicate values, and to trace connections between people and events. Because we belong to a society fascinated with images, it may be possible for us who believe in the gospel of life to employ such symbols to express some of our nation's fundamental values. Allow me to present a few examples.

When Mother Teresa died, the media showed powerful images of her reaching out to the most physically vulnerable, the poorest of the poor. Her life, as seen in these images, was a witness to the moral impulse to address the most basic human needs of others. Her caring for others captures and expresses the respect due to every person.

Another strong image was that of American rescue workers helping to pull trapped people out of the wreckage of the earthquake in Turkey. This was a clear example of people who, having developed their own potential, were using it in the service of others. In living color, we witnessed a powerful moral drama unfold.

Such images convey an alternative to the dramas involving polarization and individualism we normally see on TV. They reveal that what is best in the human person is the impulse to use our gifts and talents to benefit others, not just ourselves.

There is a noble purpose in being human, an inexorable pull toward realizing our dignity, our potential, and our connection to others. The consistent ethic of life celebrates life as a gift, liberty as the freedom to develop one's potential for greatness, happiness as a reward for pursuing that greatness, and the common good as the condition that promotes the true dignity and potential of all people.

American Health Care Reform

Our fragmented, individualistic, and market-driven health care system—marked by many of the same traits that define our broader culture—could benefit from the consistent ethic of life. Cardinal Bernardin began some of this work, particularly in his last years. For example, he reflected on the link between the consistent ethic and health care reform in a speech at the National Press Club in Washington, D.C., in 1994.[13]

Fragmentation

One symptom of our diseased health care system, like the larger society, is fragmentation in *all* its facets—health insurance, health care delivery, and health policy. Let us start with health insurance.

As we know, the American insurance system is a combination of public and private payers and providers. There is nothing inherently wrong with a system as diverse as ours, but in practice it leaves many gaps. The most glaring is that at the moment there are some 44 million people in this country, or about 16.3 percent of our population, not covered by any of those options. Our health insurance system is based on the presumption that employers will provide the insurance. But many small businesses are unable to afford the high cost of doing so.

Looking at our health insurance system, one gets the feeling that it is patched together—but without glue. A patchwork system like ours might work if it had some explicit underlying principles consonant with a consistent ethic of life and American ideals. But, as it is, our system is built on values that, although they seem distinctly American, actually conflict with the values we hold true.

One serious consequence of this fragmentation is that many who lack health insurance delay seeking medical attention and use emergency room care when it can no longer be avoided. Hospitals end up, when they can, shifting the cost of uncompensated care to the insured, thereby increasing the cost of insurance—putting it even further out of reach for those who lack it. Or hospitals accept bad debt, thus limiting the resources they might use in other areas of health care delivery. Health care delivery is also fragmented in the sense that health insurance is tied to employment, so that a change in health plans or a loss of insurance inevitably accompanies any job change.

Finally, our nation has no coherent health care policy. The current system provides outstanding episodic rescue care but lacks the coordination needed for treatment for chronic illness, despite the fact that chronic illness is much more prevalent. Similarly, care for a presenting illness often does not address its root cause, especially when these roots are such social ills as poverty, inadequate housing, or a polluted environment. A good example of this fragmentation is the absence of a coherent federal policy regarding the long-term care needs—including affordable housing, home care, assisted living, or nursing home care—of our rapidly increasing elderly population.

Because we have no coherent health care policy, we are forced to change the system bit by bit, here and there, with little overarching strategy or agreed-on principles to guide those changes. Even those changes are made difficult by special interests, such as those of insurance companies, doctors, hospitals, and patient groups defined by specific diseases. And these groups, when lobbying on proposed legislation, tend not to have the larger picture of the health care system in mind.

Individualism

Individualism also significantly affects our health policy. This is most evident in the difficulty we have had in sparking public interest in reforming the system. Most insured people probably view their own health insurance and health care as being adequate. Losing one's insurance and being unable to find coverage is seen as an individual problem, rather than a systemic one. As long as *I* am healthy and happy, I'm not worried about the health care system.

But we should consider the possibility that those who are without health insurance may be too busy battling illness while trying to make ends meet to bring their problems before the public. They may, for those reasons, be voiceless. It may be those who benefit from the current system, or are at least reasonably well served by it, who have the responsibility for ensuring that *everyone* shares in it. Unfortunately, those who benefit have been all too silent.

Market Values

Historically, health care delivery—or more correctly, acute care delivery and later insurance coverage such as Blue Cross—was carried on in the voluntary or not-for-profit sector of our society. I would argue, as Cardinal Bernardin did quite forcefully in his Harvard Business School Club of Chicago address, that this is the preferred focus because of the nature of health care as a social good.[14]

In recent years, however, the delivery and financing of health care have increasingly been seen as belonging to the investor-owned, publicly traded sector of our society, with health care often offered as a commodity like any other in the market. As a result, those who provide health care are too often seen as business owners, rather than service providers. Patients are seen as consumers, rather than as vulnerable people needing help or as citizens seeking to improve their community's health status.

This transition from a local service industry to a huge, multibillion-dollar and multinational corporate endeavor has happened so quietly and gradually that we have failed to take adequate note of it. For many people, the logic of a market-based system must inevitably be the market's efficiency, cost control, and profit margins. As long as health care is viewed primarily in economic terms, it will be difficult to galvanize support for changes beyond market reform.

The Need to Take a Stand

The consistent ethic of life comes into play as an antidote to the fragmented, individualistic, and market-based nature of our health care system. A system based on the consistent ethic would rectify the fragmentation of our current system, in which some are served very well and others not at all. As a framework for evaluating any policy, the consistent ethic would insist that all life be valued. Any practice, any law would have to institutionalize that value. Ensuring that every person has access to health care would be more than a policy objective; it would be viewed as a moral imperative.

But can this happen? Are not the forces just noted too strong, the trend irreversible? I think not. The language of the consistent ethic can further the growing search for meaning, ease increasing dissatisfaction with unbridled autonomy, and employ images and symbols in a way that can invite profound change.

Inviting and nurturing such a sea change would not be something new in the American experiment. In this country, we have been able to free slaves; enfranchise women; guarantee all a public education; and protect civil rights based on the fundamental principles of dignity, freedom, and the equal right of each person to pursue happiness.

As a nation, however, we have yet to take the same stand against lack of care for the uninsured ill that we have taken against illiteracy and intolerance. I believe we must take a stand. In a lecture delivered in April 1999, I proposed a national dialogue that, if carried on well, would result in a consensus that access to basic health care is an "essential building block" for our free society.[15] I suggested that the foundational themes of the consistent ethic of life—human dignity, stewardship, and the common good—could deepen some of our society's core values in a way that changes our perspective on health care. From that new perspective, we will regard ill health as a threat to the pursuit of a fulfilling and purposeful life. We will not allow access to our health care system to depend on individual circumstances—the good fortune of working for an employer who provides adequate insurance, for example, or of qualifying for Medicaid or Medicare. No. *Accessible and affordable health care for all will be a central tenet of our health care system.* That system will guarantee an adequate level of care to all people and will do three things to ensure that all people are able to develop their potential to live a fulfilling and purposeful life. It will:

- Seek to prevent illness.
- Promote the well-being of those who are ill.
- Protect the health of the entire community.

Certainly we have made great strides in preventing and combating illness. Yet, just as a healthy delivery system will strive to prevent and cure sickness to ensure the full participation of all in the pursuit of happiness, it will also recognize the frailty of human life and the inevitability of sickness and death. It will recognize what all humanity holds in common: our mortality. It will recognize our responsibility in the face of that mortality to create a system that cares for the chronically and hopelessly ill in a way that promotes their wholeness and upholds their humanity.

Promoting the well-being of the ill is a dimension of health care that obviously cannot be quantified. This is another reason why health care cannot be left to the vagaries of the marketplace. Health care cannot be shaped the way other industries are shaped, because it is different in kind. It goes to the heart of the conditions necessary to sustain a common good in which every person can flourish.

A responsive health care system that takes account of human solidarity will also be needed if we are to identify and forestall threats to the health of the community, including environmental hazards, gun violence, and suicide. The wholeness, or health, of the community depends on the existence of healthy and safe environments in which people can live.

Our consistent ethic of life, then, challenges the fragmented nature of our health care system. It deplores the notion that individuals must struggle alone to find a way into the health care system. And it counters the notion that health care is purely a commodity to be bought and sold, rather than a precondition for pursuing happiness.

Allocation of Health Care Resources

One other foundational category related to the common good is responsible stewardship of resources. How can the common good, as a dimension of the consistent ethic of life, assist us in determining how to allocate our health care resources? Obviously, this is a complex issue. Currently 15.5 percent ($1.1 trillion) of our domestic national product (DNP) is spent on the various aspects of health care. Just eighteen years ago, it was 8.9 percent of DNP. Such an increase raises the question: Should there be any limit on these expenditures and, if so, how as a nation should we make such a determination?

For example, should how much we spend on health care be determined simply by market forces or by federal mandate, or in some other way? What would be the criteria guiding such a decision-making process? Is national defense, for example, more important than the nation's health? If so, by how much?

As if those questions were not complex enough, there is also the parallel issue of how we allocate the existing resources—that $1.1 trillion—in a just and equitable manner . . . . Such a conversation will not come easily. Allocation is often taken as being the same as "rationing," and the concept of rationing does not sit well given America's dedication to a certain understanding of liberty.

But one could argue that rationing is being done now, although that word is never used to describe it. For example, health plans (or the employers who purchase them) decide which health problems they will or will not cover—they ration coverage. And our nation's failure to institute universal coverage ensures that many of the 44 million uninsured get only that care available in emergency rooms and free clinics. This, too, is a form of rationing.

In recent years, there have been various proposals to develop more explicit criteria for allocating health care resources. Oregon, for example, received a federal waiver to develop for citizens on Medicaid a statewide health system with a guaranteed "basic benefit package" set by state policy.

As we begin to think about resource allocation, we will again find the consistent ethic of life helpful. Our understanding of human dignity, for example, will require any allocation decisions to be applied equitably and without discrimination. Similarly, because access to adequate health care is a fundamental human right, there must be a baseline of services not subject to political trade-offs. That same inalienable dignity would require an open and participative process involving all those affected by allocation decisions. And any allocation must have an ethical priority ensuring that resources are provided to the disadvantaged. Good stewardship also requires monitoring the social and economic effects of allocation decisions to make sure that the consequences of those decisions were the ones intended.

Finally, an integral understanding of the common good will provide an important framework for decision making. It will insist that allocation decisions focus not just on individuals but also on the health status of communities and those social forces which can better enhance personal and communal health. A rich understanding of the common good challenges a notion of "liberty" that says individuals should be able to receive whatever health services they desire even if, medically speaking, those services are considered futile.

When we view health care reform through the lens of the consistent ethic of life, we are left with the certainty that life is indeed precious and full of possibilities, that together we must establish the conditions that allow all to share in those possibilities. We are left with a sketch of a health care system that recognizes the need for limits, that acknowledges the inevitability of decline and death, that treats health care as a service, that upholds the dignity of every person, and that promotes the health of our whole society.

I believe we can have such a system, and I believe this system could be crafted entirely in the private sector, or entirely in the public sector, or as a mix between the two. What it must *not* be is the fragmented, individualistic, and market-driven system we have now. What it cannot be is a system with no design, without the underlying values that embrace life and seek justice. It must be a health care system that is consistent. It must have an ethical foundation. And it must be a system that celebrates life in its fullest sense—a system that promotes human purposes and ends, even in the midst of sickness and death. In utilizing the consistent ethic in this way, we will be acting as the cardinal often asked us to act. We "will have the courage to move beyond the past and the creativity to address the future."[16]

NOTES

1. Joseph Bernardin, "Remaining a Vigorous Voice for Life in Society," *Origins* 26 (September 26, 1996): 242.

2. See J. Bryan Hehir, "Identity and Institutions," *Health Progress* 76, no. 8 (1995): 17–23.

3. John Paul II, *Evangelium Vitae*, reprinted in *Origins* 24, no. 42 (April 6, 1995).

4. *Veritatis Splendor,* no. 48, reprinted in *Origins* 23, no. 18 (October 14, 1993): 312.

5. See Thomas Aquinas, *The Summa Contra Gentiles,* Bk. III, Ch. III, in *Introduction to Saint Thomas Aquinas,* ed. Anton G. Pegis (New York: Modern Library, 1948).

6. John Courtney Murray, *We Hold These Truths: Catholic Reflections on the American Proposition* (New York: Sheed and Ward, 1960).

7. See Robert D. Putnam, "Bowling Alone: America's Declining Social Capital," *Journal of Democracy* 6, no. 1 (1995): 65–78. Putnam argues in his now famous article that Americans are today much less apt than formerly to build "social capital" by joining civic and social organizations. "The most obvious and probably the most powerful instrument of this revolution is television."

8. *Evangelium Vitae,* no. 20, p. 697.

9. *Veritatis Splendor,* no. 48, p. 313.

10. *Evangelium Vitae,* no. 101, p. 724.

11. Bruce Jennings, "Active Euthanasia and Forgoing Life-Sustaining Treatment: Can We Hold the Line?" *Journal of Pain and Symptom Management* 2, no. 1 (1991): 316.

12. *Veritatis Splendor,* no. 32, p. 308.

13. Joseph Bernardin, "The Consistent Ethic of Life and Healthcare Reform," in *Celebrating the Ministry of Healing: Joseph Cardinal Bernardin's Reflections on Healthcare* (St. Louis, MO: Catholic Health Association of the United States, 1999), pp. 70–82.

14. Bernardin, "Making the Case for Not-for-Profit Healthcare," in *Celebrating the Ministry of Healing,* pp. 83–93.

15. Michael D. Place, "Healthcare: Essential Building Block for a Free Society," Joseph B. Brennan Lecture, Georgetown University, April 20, 1999.

16. Joseph Bernardin, "A Sign of Hope," Archdiocese of Chicago, 1995, p. 11.

SELECTED BIBLIOGRAPHY ON
HEALTH CARE REFORM

Arbuckle, Gerald A. *Healthcare Ministry: Refounding the Mission in Tumultuous Times.* Collegeville, MN: Liturgical Press, 2000.

Bernardin, Joseph. *Selected Works of Joseph Cardinal Bernardin: Church and Society,* vol. 2. Edited by Alphonse P. Spilly. Chicago, IL: Liturgical Press, 2000.

Bouchard, Charles E., O.P. "Catholic Healthcare and the Common Good." *Health Progress* 80, no. 3 (1999).

Brodeur, Dennis. "Guidance for a Failing System: Catholic Social Teachings Provide the Needed Principles." *Health Progress* 76, no. 7 (1995): 30–35.

DeBlois, Jean, C.S.J. "The American Health Care System and the Pursuit of Health." In *Values and Public Life,* edited by G. Magill, 199–224. Lanham, MD: University Press of America, 1995.

———. "The Mission Imperative: Our Foundation and Market Advantage." *Health Progress* 78, no. 2 (1997).

Dillon, Mary Ann, R.S.M. "A Dynamic Force for Change: The Common Good Provides the Rationale for a Healthcare System for All." *Health Progress* 78, no. 2 (1997): 31–33.

Glaser, Brian B., and John W. Glaser. "Systemic Reform Is Vital to Our Ministry." *Health Progress* 83, no. 3 (2002).

Kaveny, Kathy, and James Keenan. "Ethical Issues in Health Care Restructuring." *Theological Studies* 5, no. 6 (1995): 136–50.

Keane, Phillip S. *Catholicism and Health-Care Justice: Problems, Potential, and Solutions.* Boston: Paulist Press, 2002.

———. *Health Care Reform: A Catholic View.* Mahwah, NJ: Paulist Press, 1993.

Langan, John. "Catholic Social Teaching and the Allocation of Scarce Resources." *Kennedy Institute of Ethics Journal* 6, no. 4 (1996): 401–5.

Lavastida, Jose I. *Health Care and the Common Good: A Catholic Theory of Justice.* Lanham, MD: University Press of America, 1999.

O'Rourke, Kevin D., O.P. "Catholic Healthcare as 'Leaven.'" *Health Progress* 78, no. 2 (1997).

General Bibliography

Arbuckle, Gerald A. *Healthcare Ministry: Refounding the Mission in Tumultuous Times.* Collegeville, MN: Liturgical Press, 2000.

Ashley, Benedict, O.P., and Albert Moraczewski, O.P. "Cloning, Aquinas, and the Embryonic Person." *National Catholic Bioethics Quarterly* 1, no. 2 (Summer 2001): 189–202.

———. *Living the Truth in Love: A Biblical Introduction to Moral Theology.* New York: Alba House, 1996.

———. *Theologies of the Body: Humanist and Christian.* Boston: National Catholic Bioethics Center, 1995.

Ashley, Benedict, O.P., and Kevin D. O'Rourke, O.P. *Health Care Ethics: A Theological Analysis.* 4th ed. Washington, DC: Georgetown University Press, 1997.

Beabout, Gregory R., and Daryl J. Wennemann. *Applied Professional Ethics.* New York: University Press of America, 1994.

Bernardin, Joseph Louis. *Celebrating the Ministry of Healing: Joseph Cardinal Bernardin's Reflections on Healthcare.* St. Louis, MO: Catholic Health Association of the United States, 1999.

———. *Joseph Cardinal Bernardin: A Moral Vision for America.* Washington, DC: Georgetown University Press, 1998.

———. "Remaining a Vigorous Voice for Life in Society." *Origins* 26 (September 26, 1996): 237–42.

Bohr, David. *Catholic Moral Tradition.* Huntington, IN: Our Sunday Visitor, 1999.

Bouchard, Charles E., O.P. "Catholic Healthcare and the Common Good." *Health Progress* 80, no. 3 (1999).

Boyle, Philip, and Kevin D. O'Rourke, O.P. "Medical Ethics: Sources of Catholic Teachings." *Health Progress* 81, no. 3 (2000).

Branick, Vincent, and M. Therese Lysaught. "Stem Cell Research: Licit or Complicit?" *Health Progress* 80, no. 5 (1999).

Brodeur, Dennis. "Catholic Health Care: Rationale for Ministry." *Christian Bioethics* 5, no. 1 (April 1999): 5–25.

———. "Guidance for a Failing System: Catholic Social Teachings Provide the Needed Principles." *Health Progress* 76, no. 7 (1995): 30–35.

Callahan, Sidney. "Abortion and the Sexual Agenda: A Case for Pro-Life Feminism." *Commonweal* 113 (April 25, 1986): 232–38.

———. "The Moral Case against Euthanasia." *Health Progress* 76, no. 1 (1995).

Cataldo, Peter J. "Pope John Paul II on Nutrition and Hydration: A Change of Catholic Teaching?" *National Catholic Bioethics Quarterly* 4, no. 3 (Autumn 2004): 513–36.

———. "Reproductive Technologies." *Ethics & Medics* 21 (1996): 1–3.

Cataldo, Peter J., and Albert S. Moraczewski, O.P. *Catholic Healthcare Ethics: A Manual for Ethics Committees.* Boston: National Catholic Bioethics Center, 2002.

———. *The Fetal Tissue Issue: Medical and Ethical Aspects*. Braintree, MA: Pope John XXIII Center, 1994.

Catechism of the Catholic Church. English Translation for the United States of America. New York: Catholic Book Publishing Company, 1994.

Catholic Health Association of the United States. *Care of the Dying: A Catholic Perspective*. Part 3. St. Louis, MO, 1993.

———. *Continuing the Commitment: A Pathway to Health Care Reform*. St. Louis, MO, 2000.

Cessario, Romanus. *Introduction to Moral Theology*. Washington, DC: Catholic University of America Press, 2001.

Charles, Rodger, S.J. *An Introduction to Catholic Social Teaching*. San Francisco: Ignatius, 1999.

Cioffi, Alfred. *Fetus as Medical Patient: Moral Dilemmas in Prenatal Diagnosis*. Lanham, MD: University Press of America, 1995.

Cochran, Clarke E. "The Common Good and Health Care Policy: Three Meanings." *Health Progress* 80 (May/June 1999): 41–44, 47.

Cochran, Clarke E., and David C. Cochran. *Catholics, Politics, and Public Policy: Beyond Left and Right*. Maryknoll, NY: Orbis Books, 2003.

Cole-Turner, Ronald, and Brent Waters, eds. *God and the Embryo: Religious Voices on Stem Cells and Cloning*. Washington, DC: Georgetown University Press, 2003.

Condic, Maureen L. "The Basics about Stem Cells." *First Things* 119 (January 2002): 30–34.

Congregation for the Doctrine of the Faith. *Declaration on Euthanasia*. Washington, DC: United States Catholic Conference, 1980.

———. *Donum Vitae* (*The Gift of Life*, February 22, 1987). Boston: Pauline Books (media edition), 2003.

DeBlois, Jean, C.S.J., Patrick Norris, O.P., and Kevin D. O'Rourke, O.P. *A Primer for Healthcare Ethics: Essays for a Pluralistic Society*. Washington, DC: Georgetown University Press, 2000.

DeBlois, Jean, C.S.J., and Kevin D. O'Rourke, O.P. "Introducing the Revised Directives." *Health Progress* 76, no. 3 (1995).

Dillon, Mary Ann, R.S.M. "A Dynamic Force for Change: The Common Good Provides the Rationale for a Healthcare System for All." *Health Progress* 78, no. 2 (1997): 31–33.

Doerflinger, Richard. "Destructive Stem Cell Research on Human Embryos." *Origins* 28 (April 29, 1999): 769–73.

Dort, Veronica M., and Edward J. Furton. *Ethical Principle in Catholic Health Care*. Boston: National Catholic Bioethics Center, 1999.

Dougherty, Charles J. *Back to Reform: Values, Markets, and the Health Care System*. New York: Oxford University Press, 1996.

Finnis, John. "Personal Integrity, Sexual Morality, and Responsible Parenthood." *Anthropos* (now *Anthropotes*): *Rivista di Studi sulla Persona e la Famiglia* 1, no. 1 (1985): 46.

Flaman, Paul. *Genetic Engineering: Christian Values and Catholic Teaching*. Boston: Paulist Press, 2002.

Furton, Edward J., ed. *What Is a Man, O Lord? The Human Person in a Biotech Age*. Boston: National Catholic Bioethics Center, 2002.

Gaudium et Spes (*Joy and Hope, Pastoral Constitution on the Church in the Modern World*). Boston: Pauline Books (media edition), 1965.

George, Robert P. *Clash of Orthodoxies: Law, Religion, and Morality in Crisis*. Wilmington, DE: ISI Books, 2001.

———. "The Ethics of Embryonic Stem Cell Research and Human Cloning." In *Building a Culture of Life 30 Years after Roe v. Wade*, edited by William L. Saunders and Brian C. Robertson, pp. 23–31. Washington, DC: Family Research Council, 2002.

Gilham, Charles, and Peter Leibold. "A Voice against Physician-Assisted Suicide." *Health Progress* 78, no. 3 (1997): 44–47.

Gomez-Lobo, Alfonso. *Morality and the Human Goods: An Introduction to Natural Law Ethics.* Washington, DC: Georgetown University Press, 2002.

Gormally, Luke, ed. *Culture of Life, Culture of Death.* Chicago: St. Augustine Press, 2001.

———, ed. *Euthanasia, Clinical Practice, and the Law.* London: St. Augustine Press, 1994.

———, ed. *Issues for a Catholic Bioethic.* Chicago: University of Chicago Press, 2001.

———, ed. *Moral Truth and Moral Tradition: Essays in Honour of Peter Geach and Elizabeth Anscombe.* Dublin and Portland, OR: Four Courts Press, 1994.

Goyette, John, Mark S. Latkovic, and Richard S. Myers, eds. *St. Thomas Aquinas and the Natural Law Tradition: Contemporary Perspectives.* Washington, DC: Catholic University of America Press, 2004.

Griese, Orville N. *Catholic Identity in Health Care: Principles and Practice.* Braintree, MA: Pope John XXIII Center, 1987.

Grisez, Germain. *Difficult Moral Questions.* Vol. 3 of *The Way of the Lord Jesus.* Quincy, IL: Franciscan Press, 1997.

Grisez, Germain, John Finnis, Joseph Boyle, and William E. May. "'Every Marital Act Ought to Be Open to New Life': Toward a Clearer Understanding." *The Thomist* 52 (1988): 365–426.

Guinan, Patrick. *Genetics: A Catholic Ethical Perspective.* Bloomington, IN: 1st Books Library, 2001.

Gula, Richard M. *Euthanasia: Moral and Pastoral Perspectives.* Boston: Paulist Press, 1995.

Haas, John M. *Crisis of Conscience.* New York: Crossroad/Herder and Herder, 1996.

Hahn, Kimberly Kirk. *Life Giving Love: Embracing God's Beautiful Design for Marriage.* Ann Arbor, MI: Servant Publications, 2002.

Heaney, Stephen J., ed. *Abortion: A New Generation of Catholic Responses.* Boston: National Catholic Bioethics Center, 1992.

Hilgers, Thomas W. "The Natural Methods for the Regulation of Fertility: The Authentic Alternative." *Linacre Quarterly* 62 (1995): 52–59.

Hollenbach, David, S.J. "Virtue, the Common Good, and Democracy." In *New Communitarian Thinking: Persons, Virtues, Institutions, and Communities,* edited by Amitai Etzioni. Charlottesville: University of Virginia Press, 1995.

Irving, Dianne N. "When Do Human Beings Begin? 'Scientific' Myths and Scientific Facts." *International Journal of Sociology and Social Rights* 19 (1999): 22–47.

Jeffreys, Derek S. "Euthanasia and John Paul II's 'Silent Language of Profound Sharing of Affection': Why Christians Should Care about Peter Singer." *Christian Bioethics* 7, no. 3 (2001): 359–78.

Kass, Leon, M.D. *Life, Liberty, and the Defense of Dignity: The Challenge for Bioethics.* San Francisco: Encounter Books, 2002.

———. *Toward a More Natural Science: Biology and Human Affairs.* New York: Free Press, 1985.

Kass, Leon, M.D., and James Q. Wilson. *The Ethics of Human Cloning.* Washington, DC: American Enterprise Institute Press, 1998.

Kavanaugh, John, S.J. *Who Count as Persons? Human Identity and the Ethics of Killing.* Washington, DC: Georgetown University Press, 2001.

Kaveny, Kathy, and James Keenan. "Ethical Issues in Health Care Restructuring." *Theological Studies* 5, no. 6 (1995): 136–50.

Keane, Phillip S. *Catholicism and Health-Care Justice: Problems, Potential, and Solutions.* Boston: Paulist Press, 2002.

———. *Health Care Reform: A Catholic View.* Mahwah, NJ: Paulist Press, 1993.

Keown, John. *Euthanasia and Public Policy: An Argument against Legalization.* Cambridge: Cambridge University Press, 2002.

Kilner, John F., Arlene B. Miller, and Edmund D. Pellegrino, eds. *Dignity and Dying: A Christian Appeal.* Grand Rapids, MI: Eerdmans Publishing, 1996.

Latkovic, Mark S. "The Science and Ethics of Parthenogenesis." *National Catholic Bioethics Quarterly* 2, no. 2 (Summer 2002): 245–55.

Lavastida, Jose I. *Health Care and the Common Good: A Catholic Theory of Justice.* Lanham, MD: University Press of America, 1999.

Lee, Patrick. *Abortion and Unborn Human Life.* Washington, DC: Catholic University of America Press, 1996.

Llano, Alejandro. "The Catholic Physician and the Teachings of Roman Catholicism." *Journal of Medicine and Philosophy* 21, no. 6 (1996): 639–49.

McInerny, Ralph M. *The Question of Christian Ethics.* Washington, DC: Catholic University of America Press, 1993.

Maestri, William F. *Do Not Lose Hope: Healing the Wounded Heart of Women Who Have Had Abortions.* New York: Alba House, 2000.

———. *What the Church Teaches: A Guide for the Study of Evangelium Vitae.* Boston: Daughters of St. Paul Press, 1996.

———. *What the Church Teaches: A Guide for the Study of Veritatis Splendor.* Boston: Daughters of St. Paul Press, 1994.

Massaro, Thomas, S.J. *Living Justice: Catholic Social Teaching in Action.* Franklin, WI: Sheed & Ward, 2000.

Mastroeni, Anthony J., ed. *Is a Culture of Life Still Possible in the U.S.?* Chicago: St. Augustine Press, 1999.

May, William E. *Catholic Bioethics and the Gift of Human Life.* Huntington, IN: Our Sunday Visitor, 2000.

———. *An Introduction to Moral Theology.* Rev. ed. Huntington, IN: Our Sunday Visitor, 1994.

———. "Tube Feeding and the 'Vegetative' State." *Ethics & Medics* 23, no. 12 (December 1998): 1–2.

Morris, John F. "Cloning and Human Dignity." *Ethics & Medics* 29, no. 2 (February 2004): 1–2.

Nairn, Thomas A. "Reclaiming our Moral Tradition." *Health Progress* 78, no. 6 (1997): 36–39.

National Catholic Bioethics Center. *A Catholic Guide to End-of-Life Decisions.* Boston: National Catholic Bioethics Center, 1997.

———. *Reproductive Technologies, Marriage and the Church.* Braintree, MA: Pope John XXIII Center, 1988.

National Conference of Catholic Bishops. *Economic Justice for All.* Washington, DC: NCCB, 1986.

Noonan, John T., Jr. "An Almost Absolute Value in History." In *The Morality of Abortion,* edited by John T. Noonan, Jr., pp. 1–59. Cambridge, MA: Harvard University Press, 1970.

———, ed. *The Morality of Abortion.* Cambridge, MA: Harvard University Press, 1970.

O'Donnell, Thomas J. *Medicine and Christian Morality,* 3rd rev. ed. New York: Alba House, 1996.

O'Rourke, Kevin, O.P. "On the Care of 'Vegetative' Patients: A Response to William E. May's 'Tube Feeding and the "Vegetative" State.'" *Ethics & Medics* 24, no. 4 (April 1999): 3–4.

———. "Pain Relief: The Perspective of the Catholic Tradition." *Journal of Pain and Symptom Management* 7, no. 8 (1992): 485–91.

Overberg, Kenneth R., S.J. *Creating a Culture of Life.* Allen, TX: Thomas More Publishing, 2002.

Pellegrino, Edmund D., M.D. "Decisions to Withdraw Life-Sustaining Treatment: A

Moral Algorithm." *Journal of the American Medical Association* 283, no. 8 (February 23, 2000): 1065–67.

——. "The Internal Morality of Clinical Medicine: A Paradigm for the Ethics of the Helping and Healing Professions." *Journal of Medicine and Philosophy* 26, no. 6 (December 2001): 559–79.

Pellegrino, Edmund D., M.D., and David C. Thomasma. *The Virtues in Medical Practice.* New York: Oxford University Press, 1993.

Pinckaers, Servais, O.P. *Morality: The Catholic View.* Chicago: Saint Augustine's Press, 2001.

——. *The Sources of Christian Ethics.* Washington, DC: Catholic University of America Press, 1995.

Pontifical Academy for Life. *The Dignity of the Dying Person: Proceedings of the Fifth Assembly of the Pontifical Academy for Life.* Vatican City: Libreria Editrice Vaticana, 2000.

——. *Human Genome, Human Person, and the Society of the Future: Proceedings of the Fourth Assembly of the Pontifical Academy for Life.* Vatican City: Libreria Editrice Vaticana, 1999.

——. *Reflections on Human Cloning.* Vatican City: Libreria Editrice Vaticana, 1997.

Pope John XXIII. *Pacem in Terris (Peace on Earth,* April 11, 1963). Boston: Pauline Books, 1982.

Pope John Paul II. *Evangelium Vitae (The Gospel of Life).* Boston: Pauline Books (media edition), 1995.

——. *Fides et Ratio (Faith and Reason).* Boston: Pauline Books (media edition), 2003.

——. *Salvifici Doloris (On the Meaning of Human Suffering).* Washington, DC: U.S. Catholic Conference, 1984.

——. *The Theology of the Body: Human Love in the Divine Plan.* Boston: Pauline Books and Media, 1997.

——. *Veritatis Splendor (The Splendor of Truth).* Boston: Pauline Books (media edition), 1993.

Pope Paul VI. *Humanae Vitae (On Human Life).* Boston: Pauline Books (media edition), 1968.

Schockenhoff, Eberhard. *Natural Law and Human Dignity: Universal Ethics in an Historical World.* Translated by Brian McNeil. Washington, DC: Catholic University of America Press, 2003.

Seifert, Josef. "Substitution of the Conjugal Act or Assistance to It? IVF, GIFT and Some Other Medical Interventions. Philosophical Reflections on the Vatican Declaration 'Donum Vitae.'" *Anthropotes: Rivista di Studi sulla Persona e Famiglia* 2 (1988): 273–86.

Shannon, Thomas A. "Ethical Issues in Genetics." *Health Progress* 80, no. 5 (1999).

——. "Prenatal Genetic Testing: The Potential Loss of Human Dignity Will Demand a Consistent Ethical Response from Catholic Health Care." *Health Progress* 82, no. 2 (2001): 33–35.

Silver, Lee. *Remaking Eden: Cloning and Beyond in a Brave New World.* New York: Avon Books, 1997.

Smith, Janet. *Humanae Vitae: A Generation Later.* Washington, DC: Catholic University of America Press, 1991.

——, ed. *Why Humanae Vitae Was Right: A Reader.* San Francisco: Ignatius Press, 1993.

Smith, Russell E., ed. *Conserving Human Life.* Braintree, MA: Pope John XXIII Center, 1989.

——. *The Gospel of Life and the Vision of Health Care.* Braintree, MA: Pope John XXIII Center, 1996.

——, ed. *The Splendor of Truth and Health Care.* Boston: National Catholic Bioethics Center, 1995.

Spiritual Journeys. Edited by Sr. Stanislaus Kennedy, R.S.C. Dublin, Ireland: Veritas Publications, 1997.

Sulmasy, Daniel P., O.F.M., M.D., and Edmund Pellegrino, M.D. "The Rule of Double Effect: Clearing Up the Double Talk." *Archives of Internal Medicine* 159, no. 6 (March 22, 1999): 545–50.

Talone, Patricia A. *Feeding the Dying: Religion and End-of-Life Decisions.* New York: Peter Lang Publishing, 1996.

Taylor, Charles. *Sources of the Self.* Cambridge, MA: Harvard University Press, 1989.

Torchia, Joseph, O.P. "Artificial Hydration and Nutrition for the PVS Patient: Ordinary Care or Extraordinary Intervention." *National Catholic Bioethics Quarterly* 3, no. 4 (Winter 2003): 719–30.

Tropman, John E. *The Catholic Ethic and the Spirit of the Community.* Washington, DC: Georgetown University Press, 2002.

Tuohey, John F. "Mercy: An Insufficient Motive for Euthanasia." *Health Progress* 74, no. 8 (1993): 51–53.

U.S. Conference of Catholic Bishops. *Ethical and Religious Directives for Catholic Health Care Services.* 4th ed. Washington, DC: USCCB, 2001.

Wildes, Kevin Wm., S.J., ed. *Infertility: A Crossroad of Faith, Medicine, and Technology.* Norwell, MA: Kluwer Academic Publishers, 1997.

Willems, Elizabeth L. *Understanding Catholic Morality.* New York: Crossroad/Herder and Herder, 1997.

Zimbelman, Joel. "A Blessing in Disguise? Empowering Catholic Health Care Institutions in the Current Health Care Environment." *Christian Bioethics* 6, no. 3 (2000): 281–94.

Contributors

BENEDICT ASHLEY, O.P., is emeritus professor of moral theology at Aquinas Institute of Theology. He received the medal *Pro Ecclesia et Pontifice* from Pope John Paul II. He is co-author with Kevin O'Rourke, O.P., of *Health Care Ethics: A Catholic Theological Approach,* and the author of numerous other books including *Living the Truth in Love: A Biblical Introduction to Moral Theology* and *Theologies of the Body: Humanist and Christian.*

GREGORY R. BEABOUT is associate professor of philosophy at Saint Louis University. His research and teaching are in the areas of ethics and social philosophy, and he has particular interest in personalism and Catholic social thought, as well as the writings of Kierkegaard and Pope John Paul II.

JOHN BERKMAN is associate professor of philosophy and theology at the Dominican School of Philosophy and Theology/Graduate Theological Union. He is editor of *The Hauerwas Reader* and *The Pinckaers Reader.* He writes and lectures extensively on moral theology and medical ethics, especially on end-of-life issues in the Catholic tradition.

CLARKE E. COCHRAN is a professor of political science and an adjunct professor in the Department of Health Organization Management at Texas Tech University. He is the author of several books and numerous articles and reviews. His most recent book, written with David Carroll Cochran, is *Catholics, Politics, and Public Policy: Beyond Left and Right.*

CATHERINE GREEN teaches philosophy at Rockhurst University and lectures in the nursing schools at the University of Kansas and the Research College of Nursing. She has published essays in political philosophy, the philosophy of knowledge, and ethics. Her current area of research is the philosophy of nursing.

JOHN KAVANAUGH, S.J., is a professor of philosophy and director of Ethics across the Curriculum at Saint Louis University. He is the "Ethics Notebook" columnist for *America* magazine. His most recent book is *Who Count as Persons? Human Identity and the Ethics of Killing.*

WILLIAM E. MAY is Michael J. McGivney Professor of Moral Theology at the John Paul II Institute for Studies on Marriage and Family at the Catholic University of America. He is author of more than a dozen books, including *An Introduction to Moral Theology, Marriage: The Rock on Which the Family Is Built,* and, most recently, *Catholic Bioethics and the Gift of Human Life.*

JOHN F. MORRIS is an associate professor of philosophy at Rockhurst University. His specialty is contemporary medical/bioethics. He has published a number of articles on ethics and medical ethics, including "Is It Possible to Be Ethical?" in *OT Practice,* and "Cloning and Human Dignity" in *Ethics & Medics.*

MICHAEL D. PLACE, a priest of the archdiocese of Chicago, is vice president for ministry development for Resurrection Health Care. He is chair of the International Federation of Catholic Health Care Institutions and from 1998 to 2005 was president of the Catholic Health Association of the United States.

KEVIN D. O'ROURKE. O.P., is the founder of the Center for Health Care Ethics at Saint Louis University and professor of bioethics at the Neiswanger Institute of Bioethics and Public Policy, Stritch School of Medicine, Loyola University, in Chicago. He has written several articles and books on bioethics and is co-author with Benedict Ashley, O.P., of *Health Care Ethics: A Theological Analysis,* now in the 5th edition.

JEANNE HEFFERNAN SCHINDLER is a member of the Department of Humanities and Augustinian Traditions at Villanova University and an affiliate professor in the Villanova Law School. Her primary research field is political theory. She has lectured and published articles on Christian political thought, democratic theory, and faith and learning.

BRENDAN SWEETMAN is a professor of philosophy at Rockhurst University. He is author or editor of many books, as well as author of more than fifty articles and reviews. His most recent books are *Why Politics Needs Religion: The Place of Religious Arguments in the Public Square* and, edited with Curtis Hancock, *Faith and the Life of the Intellect.*

Index

abortion, 3, 4, 20, 28, 46, 51–53, 56, 107–24, 215; direct, 46, 112, 113, 217; view of in the early Christian church, 110–13, 119, 122n18; and health of the mother, 114, 124n41; legal aspects of, 31, 51–53, 114–15, 117, 123n28, 124n42, 124n45, *see also Akron v. Akron Center for Reproductive Health, Inc., Doe v. Bolton, Planned Parenthood v. Casey, Roe v. Wade, Stenberg v. Carhart, Webster v. Reproductive Health Services*; moral case against, 113–19; pro-choice arguments for, 51–53, 114–18

Accreditation Council for Graduate Medical Education (ACGME), 107, 108, 120n2, 120n4

acquired immune deficiency syndrome (AIDS), 5, 23, 225

"Address of Reanimation" (Pius XII, 1957), 133

adult stem cell research, 205, 208, 209, 254, 257, 266–71, 272, 282, 283; current human therapeutic applications with, 266–71, 293n62

adult stem cells, 205, 216, 257–60, 261, 267–71, 274–75, 283, 285–86n22, 286n26, 287n29, 288n38; plasticity/potency of, 258–60, 274–75, 286n26, 287n29; proliferation of, 285–86n22, 286n26; sources of, 257, 258

Advanced Cell Technology (ACT), 264

AIDS. *See* acquired immune deficiency syndrome

Akron v. Akron Center for Reproductive Health, Inc. (1983), 123n28

allowing to die, 4, 135–37

American Association of Neurological Surgeons, 267

American bishops, 1, 8, 34, 130, 132, 152, 304, 306. *See also* Pennsylvania bishops; Texas bishops

American Fertility Society, 292n52

American Life League, American Bioethics Advisory Commission, 297n105

American Medical Association, 184, 266, 267, 292n53, 293n61; statement of support for somatic cell nuclear transfer, 293n61

American Medical News, 267

amniocentesis: and abortion, 215, 229

animal viruses: fear of transferring to humans in research, 263, 290n42, 290–91n43

Anthrogenesis Corporation, 284n12

Aquinas, Saint Thomas. *See* Saint Thomas Aquinas

Aristotle, 87n33, 105n5, 105n6, 106n10, 109, 252, 277, 337

artificial fertilization, 60–64, 65–69, 73–78; Catholic teaching on, 65–69, 77–78, 85; ethical evaluation of, 69–77; heterologous, 60, 61, 62–63, 66, 67, 69, 73–74, 76, 87n38; homologous (AIH), 60, 62, 63, 66, 67, 68, 69, 73–75, 76, 77, 85n1. *See also* artificial insemination; gamete intrafallopian tube transfer (GIFT); in vitro fertilization; pronuclear-stage tubal transfer (PROST); sperm intrafallopian tube transfer (SIFT); tubal ovum transfer with sperm (TOTS); zygote intrafallopian tube transfer (ZIFT)

artificial insemination, 60–61, 65–66, 68; Catholic teaching on, 65–66, 68–69, 77–78; ethical evaluation of, 69–77; heterologous (by a donor, AID), 61, 65, 69, 86n14; homologous (AIH), 60, 65, 68, 69, 73, 74, 76–77, 85n1, 86n14. *See also* artificial

artificial insemination (cont.)
fertilization; gamete intrafallopian tube transfer (GIFT); sperm intrafallopian tube transfer (SIFT); tubal ovum transfer with sperm (TOTS)
artificial nutrition and hydration. See medically assisted nutrition and hydration (MANH)
artificial twinning, 264, 292n52, 292n53
Ashley, Benedict, O.P., 57n10, 75–76, 84, 106n8, 190n2, 331n3
assisted reproduction: Catholic teaching on, 78–85. See also gamete intrafallopian tube transfer (GIFT); low tubal ovum transfer (LTOT); tubal ovum transfer with sperm (TOTS)
Athenagoras, 122n18
Augustine, Saint. See St. Augustine
autonomy, 9, 19, 29–42, 87n44, 132, 153, 159, 168, 191–92n23, 202, 246, 276, 277, 340, 344, see also choice; free will; self-determination; ordered, 29, 30–33, 35, 40–41, 42; radical, 29, 30–31, 32–33, 35–39, 42, 276; and respect for persons, 29–42

Balanced Budget Act (1997), 310
basic care, 136, 144, 219, 301–2, 305, 318, 344
Battin, Margaret, 180, 189, 191n18, 191–92n23
Beaumont Hospital, Royal Oak, Michigan, 269–70
Beethoven, 198
Bernardin, Cardinal Joseph, 334, 335, 341–42, 343, 347. See also consistent ethic of life
Berry, Wendell, 165
Beyond Prejudice: The Moral Significance of Human and Non-Human Animals (Evelyn Pluhar), 16
bioethics, 2, 3, 5, 7, 8, 9, 10, 11, 33, 34, 134, 203, 314; Catholic approach to, 2, 7, 8, 9, 10, 11, 33, 34, 203
Bioheart Inc., 295n80
biological diversity, 92, 226, 236–37, 246
Birth Control Commission, 104n2
Blackmun, Justice Harry, 144
blastocoel, 256
blastocyst, 204, 255, 256, 265, 266, 278, 279, 280, 282, 296n105
blastomere separation. See artificial twinning
Blue Cross, 343
bone marrow transplants, 205, 257, 258, 268, 271

Bonhoeffer, Dietrich, 122n21
Bonnville, Dimitri, 269–70
Booth, William, 168
Bordo, Susan, 244
Brock, Daniel, 189, 191–92n23, 242
Brody, Baruch, 53
Brown, Louise, 61, 85n5
Buck, Carrie, 249n5
Budziszewski, Jay, 116, 118, 123n37, 123–24n39

Cahill, Lisa Sowle, 74, 87n38
Callahan, Daniel, 22–23, 171n37, 332n17
Callahan, Sidney, 279
Campbell, K. H. S., 64
Canadian Fertility and Andrology Society, 292n52
canon law. See Code of Canon Law
Caplan, Arthur L., 227, 228–29
Carlson, John W., 83
Case Western Reserve University, 269
Cassidy, Shelia, 23–24
Cataldo, Peter, 83, 88n58
Catechism of the Catholic Church, 34, 45, 65, 106n8, 112, 122n22, 122n24, 136–37, 195–96, 197, 200, 301, 336
Catholic Bishops of England, 73
Catholic Church: pro-life stance, 45–46, 109–13, 119, 154, 335; social teaching of, 301, 304, 310–15, 318, 330, 331
Catholic Health Association of the United States (CHA), 15–16, 320, 332n20
Catholic health care ministry, 1, 24, 201, 219, 304–5, 336
Catholic Medical Association, 120–21n4
Catholic scholarship, 2, 7, 8, 9–11, 12, 55, 134, 135, 301; role of philosophy in, 7, 9, 10–11, 12–13n9
Catholic tradition, 8, 9, 10, 11, 12, 33–35, 48, 55, 87n44, 104–5n2, 127, 128, 130, 132, 133, 135, 150, 153, 172n41, 195, 197, 200, 204, 209, 217, 304, 311, 312, 313, 315, 335, 336
Cedars-Sinai Medical Center, Los Angeles, California, 267
Center for Bioethics and Human Dignity, 291n44
Center for Biologics Evaluation and Research (of the FDA), 294n71
Centesimus Annus, On the Hundredth Anniversary of Rerum Novarum (John Paul II, 1991), 304
chastity: virtue of, 99

children: natural desire for, 50–51, 74, 98; not property/objects, 50, 51, 68, 70, 73, 76, 85, 297n108; without health insurance, 310, 316, 323, 324

Children of Choice (John A. Robertson), 227

choice: personal/private, 2, 9, 39, 40, 52, 71, 90, 159, 202, 227, 229, 235, 238, 239, 240, 302, 340; and rational deliberation, 91, 234, 246; self-determining, 9, 12, 19, 29, 30–31, 32, 36–38, 39, 40–41, 42, 72. *See also* autonomy; free will; self-determination

Christ House, Washington, D.C., 328, 333n32

Christian Community Health Fellowship (CCHP), 333n33

Christian: duty to preserve life, 130, 132, 134, 144, 150–57, 170n19; love, 2, 34, 102–3, 106n10, 111, 339; temporal mission of, 7, 10, 11

civil rights, 54, 338, 344

Clement of Alexandria, 122n18

Clever, Dr. Henry, 108

clone: definition of, 263–64

cloning, 64, 76, 86n12, 93, 115–16, 196, 197, 204, 206, 253, 262–66, 276, 293n61, 297n108; arguments against doing with humans, 69, 275–83; techniques, 64, 115–16, 262–66. *See also* artificial twinning; parthenogenesis; reproduction, agametic, asexual; reproductive cloning; somatic cell nuclear transfer (SCNT); therapeutic cloning

Cloning-for-Biomedical-Research. *See* therapeutic cloning

Cloning-to-Produce-Children. *See* reproductive cloning

Cloning Webliography (Michigan State University), 291–92n48

Coats, Senator Dan (R-IN), 120n2

Code of Canon Law, 111, 112, 122n18, 122n19, 122n20, 122n22

Collins, Francis S., M.D., 212

Columbia Road Health Services, 328

common good, 5, 45–46, 96, 106n11, 187, 206, 254, 277–78, 281–82, 301, 305–6, 309–31, 332n8, 341, 345, 346, 347; and health care reform, 301, 309–33, 346, 347; promotion of, 278, 301, 305; true mark of, 278

community, 9, 15, 18, 94, 96, 103, 106n9, 130, 167, 170n19, 197, 239, 247, 276, 277, 311, 312–13, 315, 325, 327, 328, 329, 345; human, 12, 15, 16, 94, 95, 99, 101, 197, 203, 206, 209, 223, 239, 278, 281, 282, 312; medical, 120–21n4, 145, 157, 207, 219, 224, 244; scientific, 10, 197, 253, 254, 259

Community of Hope Health Services, 333n32

conception, 48, 61, 63, 64, 79–80, 81, 82, 83, 111–12, 114, 116, 118–19; view that life begins at, 3–4, 46–47, 48, 49, 50, 51, 52, 53–54, 115, 206, 209, 304

Condic, Maureen, 272

Congregation for the Doctrine of the Faith (CDF), 46, 47, 50, 65, 106n14, 130–31, 134, 190n4, 197, 209

Congressional Research Service, Domestic Social Policy Division, 290–91n43

conjugal act, 66, 67, 69, 79–80; assisting, 67, 78–84; unitive and procreative meaning of, 68, 69, 71, 78. *See also* marital act; sexual intercourse

Connery, John, S.J., 110, 111–12, 121n8, 121n12, 121–22n17, 122n18

conscience, 46, 50, 89, 101, 103, 175, 340

consequentialism, 91, 277. *See also* utilitarian ethics

Considine, Douglas, 57n7

consistent ethic of life, 334–38; consonant with traditional American values, 341, 342, 345. *See also* Bernardin, Cardinal Joseph

Constitution of the United States of America, 52, 337

contraception, 54, 89–106; as intrinsically evil, 90–92, 104–5n2, 105n4

cooperation: formal, 217–18; immediate, 217–18; material, 217–18; mediate, 217–18; proximate material, 217–18

Copernicus, 212

Cord Blood Donor Foundation, 294n72

Council of Ancyra (314), 122n18

Council of Elvira (305), 122n18

Council of Nicea (325), 78

Cover the Uninsured, 333n26

Cruzan, Nancy, 143, 153

culture of death, 129

culture of life, 120

Daley, George Q., M.D., Ph.D., 274, 287n29

Day, Dorothy, 168

death and dying, 15, 17, 20, 22, 23, 25, 49, 127–41, 148, 152, 153, 157, 163–64, 166, 175; Catholic response to, 2, 127, 128, 130–31, 132, 136–37, 140–41, 154, 165, 168, 219, 318; fear of, 22–23, 128, 234, 236–37, 345, 347

Death of Ivan Ilyich, The (Leo Tolstoy), 22
Death with Dignity Act (Oregon, 1997), 173
Decalogue, 112. *See also* Ten Commandments
Declaration of Independence, 31, 337
Declaration on Euthanasia (Congregation for the Doctrine of the Faith, 1980), 130–31, 134, 190n4
Declaration on Procured Abortion, The (Congregation for the Doctrine of the Faith, 1974), 46
Decretum (Gratian, 1140), 122n19
DeMarco, Donald T., 84, 121n8, 122n19
denucleated oocyte. *See* oocyte, denucleated
deontological ethics, 275–77
Department of Health and Human Services (of the FDA), 269
determinism, 93, 198, 199
Didache, 110, 121n12, 121–22n17
"Diet America" (Patrick McCormick), 165, 166, 167–68
dignity: of a dying person, 18, 130–31, 136–37, 140; fear of losing, 128, 135, 191n20; human, 7, 10, 11, 18, 29, 33–35, 42n11, 45–46, 79, 94, 128, 129, 130, 138, 195–96, 197, 201, 204, 210n1, 254, 304, 306, 334, 336–37, 339, 341, 346, 347
Discovery Institute, 260
Dixon, Dr. Patrick, 291n44
DNA, 21, 197, 198, 200, 222, 248, 263, 265, 289n40, 290–91n43
Do No Harm—The Coalition of Americans for Research Ethics, 259, 283, 293n62
Doe v. Bolton (1973), 114
Doerfler, John, 79–80, 81, 82, 83, 84
Dolentium Hominum (John Paul II, 1985), 12n1
Dolly (the cloned sheep) 64, 69, 196, 264
Donovan, J. P., 143, 151
Donum Vitae, The Gift of Life (Congregation for the Doctrine of the Faith, 1987), 47, 65, 66–69, 70, 71, 72, 79, 87n44, 210n1
duty ethics. *See* deontological ethics
Dworkin, Ronald, 116, 118, 189, 191–92n23

eating practices: communal and social elements of, 166–67; Eucharistic significance of, 146, 164–65, 168, 172n46. *See also* feeding
Edwards, Robert, 61
egg cell, 54, 61–62, 64, 68, 74, 83, 115, 240, 263, 264–65; enucleated, 264. *See also* oocyte; ova/ovum

Einstein, Albert, 253
Elders, Joycelyn, 20
Eli Lilly, 222
embryo, 47, 48, 53, 60, 61, 62, 63, 64, 66, 111, 115–16, 196, 197, 204, 206, 213, 217, 229, 256–57, 263, 264, 265, 272, 275, 278, 280, 281, 282; destruction/killing of, 48, 62, 73, 122n21, 196, 197, 204–5, 206, 216, 253, 257, 265, 266, 269, 281–82, 283; freezing of, 51, 62; moral status of, 116, 197, 272, 280–81; respect for, 51, 66–67, 196, 204–5, 281
embryo splitting. *See* artificial twinning
embryo transfer, 60, 61–63, 73, 75. *See also* in vitro fertilization
embryology, 47–48, 51, 54, 95, 116, 280, 281, 296–97n105; and the question of ensoulment, 47, 48, 106n8, 111
embryonic stem cell research, 204, 216, 254, 260–66, 271–83; connection to cloning, 253, 262–66, 274, 276; destruction of embryos for, 196, 204, 206, 216, 253, 256–57; ethical arguments against, 275–83; fear of transferring animal viruses to humans in, 263, 290n42, 290–91n43; lack of success, 205, 260–62, 271–74; and "proof of concept," 261, 273–74, 290n42
embryonic stem cells, 204, 209, 216, 217, 253, 256–57, 258–59, 260–262, 265, 271–75, 283, 284n7, 286n26, 288n38, 288–89n39, 289n40, 289–90n41, 290n42, 290–91n43; harvesting of, 216, 218, 275, 204, 255, 256–57, 265; human (hESCs), 256, 260–62, 271, 272, 284n7, 288–89n39, 290n42, 290–91n43; immune rejection problems with, 262, 272, 283, 289n40; plasticity/potency of, 258–59, 286n26, 288n38; tumor formation with, 261–62, 272; unstable genetic expression in, 262
Emory University, 268
Encyclopedia of Bioethics (ed. by Warren T. Reich), 85n1
end-of-life, 18, 132–33, 134, 174, 319; and demands for futile care, 132–133. *See also* death and dying
endowments: of human nature, 19–20, 30, 31, 34, 35, 39, 42, 48, 76, 120, 129, 141n2, 200, 210n1, 337
ensoulment, 46–47, 48, 51, 94–95, 100, 106n8, 111–12, 122n20, 210. *See also* embryology, and the question of ensoulment
enucleated egg cell. *See* egg cell, enucleated

Epistle of Barnabas, 110–11

ES cells. *See* embryonic stem cells

Essentials of Human Embryology (Keith L. Moore), 47

Establishment Clause, 3, 5

Ethical and Religious Directives for Catholic Health Care Services (USCCB), 1, 8, 33, 42n11, 130, 132, 141n11, 152, 170n19, 217, 303–4

Ethical Issues in Human Stem Cell Research (National Bioethics Advisory Commission), 275

ethical personalism. *See* personalism

ethics, 11, 18, 19, 35, 93, 104, 105n4, 105n5, 150, 162, 181, 195, 196, 201, 218, 252, 254, 275–78, 279–80, 281. *See also* bioethics; health care ethics

ethics of complicity (Margaret Olivia Little), 243–44

eugenics, 223, 229

euthanasia, 23, 32, 130, 131, 134, 135–38, 152, 159, 173–92; active (by commission), 135, 136–37, 174, 190n4; arguments for, 177–78, 179 -81, 186–87, 188–89, 191n14, 191n22, 191–92n23; Catholic view of, 33, 130–31, 134, 136–37, 190n12, 336; difference from allowing to die, 135–37, 150, 174–75; "in principle" argument against, 176–81, 187–88; involuntary, 174, 185, 190–91n13; passive (by omission), 135, 137–38, 159, 174, 190n4; practical argument against, 181–88, 191n19; voluntary, 173–74, 185. *See also* physician-assisted suicide; suicide

Evangelium Vitae, The Gospel of Life (John Paul II, 1995), 7, 12, 45–46, 48, 50, 54, 113, 127, 129, 175, 204, 307–8, 335, 336, 339, 340

evil, 35, 75, 87n38, 90–91, 100, 104–5n2, 105n3, 105n4, 136, 141, 150, 206, 217, 218, 318, 336; intrinsic, 90–91, 100, 104–5n2, 105n4, 218

evolution, 92, 93, 94, 95, 97, 102, 236–37

extraordinary means of prolonging life. *See* prolonging life, extraordinary means of; withdrawing/withholding medical treatment

faith and reason, 7–10, 12, 48, 50, 102–4, 131–32, 336–37

Federal Employee Health Benefit Program (FEHBP), 322, 323

feeding: Eucharistic significance of, 164–68. *See also* eating practices

fertilization, 47–48, 49, 50, 54, 60–64, 65–69, 73–81, 83–84, 85n1, 86n14, 95, 264, 280, 296–97n105. *See also* artificial fertilization; artificial insemination; assisted reproduction; in vitro fertilization

fetal tissue research, 216, 217

fetus, 16, 17, 19, 22, 25, 51, 52–53, 54, 109, 111–12, 115, 116, 117, 119, 121n8, 122n19, 124n42, 124n45, 204–5, 215, 216, 217, 218, 224, 228, 229, 260, 268, 296–97n105; formed and unformed distinction of, 109, 111–12, 121n8, 122n19; as an object of experimentation, 204–5, 229

Fifth Commandment, 112

Fides et Ratio, Faith and Reason (John Paul II, 2003), 7, 9, 10–11, 12–13n9

Finnis, John, 71

First Amendment, 3

First Things, 272

Flavius, Josephus, 121n10

Food and Drug Administration (FDA). *See* United States Food and Drug Administration

Ford, John, S.J., 104–5n2, 105n4

Frankfurt, Harry, 36, 38

free will, 34, 35, 75, 94, 95, 198. *See also* autonomy; choice; self-determination

freedom, 30, 31, 32, 33, 36–37, 38, 39, 41, 71, 72, 93, 94, 102, 177, 179, 189, 196, 198, 202, 212, 223, 227–28, 230, 231, 234, 235, 240–48, 250n41, 302, 337, 339, 341, 344; negative, 36, 37; positive, 36, 37, 38; and responsibility, 31, 32, 37, 38, 41, 196, 198, 228, 234

Frontline (PBS), 21

Fukyama, Francis, 250n36

futility: in medicine, 132–33, 135–36, 150, 158

Galileo, 253

gamete intrafallopian tube transfer (GIFT), 60, 64; Catholic debate over, 83–84, 88n58

gametic cells, 60, 61, 62, 63, 69, 73, 77, 87n38, 115, 280

Gaudium et Spes, Joy and Hope (Second Vatican Council, *1965*), 336

Gearhart, John, 284n7

gene pool, 196, 200, 204

genetic code, 53, 115, 128, 264, 265

genetic counseling, 215–16

genetic defects, 61, 211, 212, 213, 215, 230, 281

genetic disease, 159, 199–200, 201, 202, 211, 212, 213, 214–15, 223, 225–26, 243, 247 genetic enhancement, 200, 202–3, 222–51

genetic information, 196–99; and determinism, 198; and reductionism, 197–98; and social norms, 242–44, 247

genetic intervention, 199–228

genetic manipulation, 196, 222, 223, 224, 225, 227, 228, 229, 240, 247, 248

genetic marker, 199

genetic research, 196, 198, 199, 200, 202, 212, 216, 235; attitude of fatalism in, 198–99; treatment/enhancement distinction, 199–200, 223, 224–27, 247

Genetic Revolution, The (Patrick Dixon), 291n44

genetic screening, 199, 213–16. *See also* amniocentesis; prenatal diagnosis

George, Robert, 115–16, 118

germ-line, 200, 201, 202, 204

Geron Corporation, 260, 288–89n39, 290n42

Gettysburg Address (Abraham Lincoln), 31, 337

GIFT. *See* gamete intrafallopian tube transfer

Gilbert, Walter, 243

Gill, Steven, 261

Glendon, Mary Ann, 114

God, 10, 25, 34, 45, 46, 49, 59, 64, 68, 71, 78, 94, 97, 99, 104, 110, 131–32, 141, 164, 165, 200, 210n1, 301; as Creator, 45, 77, 100, 102, 111, 112, 119, 120, 122n21, 127, 128, 196, 334; friendship with, 45, 219; our dependence upon for existence, 49–50

grace, 12, 45, 102, 106n10, 112, 132, 164

Gratian, 122n19

grave burden, 4, 133, 134–35, 136; and prolonging life, 4, 136; as a subjective judgment, 134–35. *See also* prolonging life, and grave burden; withdrawing/withholding medical treatment, excessive burden argument for

Green, Ronald M., 228

Griese, Orville, 83, 88n56

Grines, Cindy, M.D., 270

Grisez, Germain, 84, 88n57, 105n4

Gustafson, James, 159

happiness, 90–91, 92–93, 94, 95, 96, 99, 100–101, 102, 105n4, 106n11, 179, 201, 223, 232, 233–40, 337–38, 341, 344, 345

harm principle (John Stuart Mill), 189

Harvard Business School Club of Chicago, 343

Hastings Center, New York, 340

Hays, Richard, 110, 121n11, 121n12, 122n21

health, 37–38, 132, 133, 134, 172n41, 214–15, 224–27, 243, 247–48, 301, 303–4, 305, 306, 312, 313, 345

health care: access to, 301, 305, 309, 312, 313, 315, 317, 325, 344–45, 346–47; as a market commodity, 302–5, 313, 317, 341, 343–44, 345; right of the human person to, 304, 346; socialized approach to, 306; and the working poor, 311, 313, 316

health care ethics: Catholic approach to, 1–13

Health Care Ethics: A Theological Analysis (Benedict Ashley, O.P. and Kevin O'Rourke, O.P.), 46–47, 57n10

health care professionals, 28, 33, 132, 149, 150, 170n15, 214, 215–16, 219, 224, 303, 304, 313, 326, 328–29

health care resources: allocating, 219, 305, 317, 346–47; fear of rationing, 305, 317, 346

health care reform: and American politics, 306, 309, 310, 320–21, 337–38; Catholic concern for, 301–8; and Catholic social doctrine, 310–15, 317–18, 330, 331; and the common good, 301, 305–6, 309, 311, 312–21, 324, 330; incremental versus immediate, 320–21; and justice, 302, 304, 305, 309, 311, 313–21, 324; through comprehensive health insurance, 309, 313, 314, 315, 317–19, 329

health care system: fragmentation of, 309, 320, 323, 330, 341, 342–43, 344, 345

Health Progress, 333n34

Health Quarterly, The, 23

Health Security Act (1993), 310

Hebrew law: formed and unformed fetus distinction in, 109, 111, 121n8

Hess, Julius, 169n9

HGP. *See* Human Genome Project

Hippocrates, 132, 146

Hitler, Adolf, 223

HIV. *See* human immunodeficiency virus

Hoekstra, Representative Peter (R-MI), 120n2

Holmes, Justice Oliver Wendell, 249n5

Holy Spirit, 103, 104

House Government Reform Subcommittee on Criminal Justice, Drug Policy and Human Resources, 294n69

human action: components of, 35–37; doing versus making, 72–74; and ends, 75–76,

89–90, 92, 99, 105n4, 112–13, 136–37, 244, 339; and intention, 4, 15, 65, 75, 83, 84, 87n38, 87n44, 89–90, 100, 101, 110, 114, 122n24, 135–38, 139, 173, 174, 175, 179, 184, 196, 217–18, 231, 242, 303; and means, 35, 60, 66, 67, 75, 76, 77, 79, 80, 82, 85, 89–91, 100, 101, 112–13, 122n24, 132, 133–34, 136–37, 145, 146, 150–51, 153–54, 159–60, 170n18, 170n19, 174–175, 190n4, 196, 207, 208, 227, 228, 234, 244, 304, 312, 319, 339; and motive, 20, 135, 160, 182, 196, 197, 206, 297n108

human being: animality of, 16, 20, 21, 22, 23, 93, 95, 233; created in the image of God, 34, 35, 42n11, 45, 51, 77, 128, 198, 304, 335; frailty of, 20, 22–24, 25, 117, 129, 345; material dimension of, 8, 49, 93, 94, 96, 98, 99, 111, 118, 132, 197, 198, 233, 235, 237; spiritual dimension of, 8, 21, 47, 93, 94–95, 99, 102, 197, 209, 210n1. *See also* human person

human development, 20, 28, 47–48, 49, 51, 73, 95, 109, 111, 112, 114, 115–16, 118–19, 122n20, 129, 196, 204, 205, 233, 256, 259, 264, 277, 280–81, 296–97n105, 318, 319

human embodiment, 8, 18, 19, 20, 21, 25, 99, 166, 171–72n38, 212

Human Embryology & Teratology (Ronan O'Rahilly and Fabiola Muller), 47–48

human embryonic stem cells (hESCs). *See* embryonic stem cells, human

human fulfillment, 19, 95, 96, 98, 100, 311, 339, 345

Human Genome Project (HGP), 10, 53, 197, 211–12, 219, 222, 225, 243, 296–97n105

human immunodeficiency virus (HIV), 5, 225, 329

human life: duty to preserve, 130, 132, 134, 144, 145, 150–57, 170n19, *see also* Christian duty to preserve life; as a free gift from God, 49, 72, 110, 128, 130, 198, 334; sanctity of, 12, 50, 120, 176, 304, 334, 335, 336

human nature, 8, 10, 11, 25, 90, 99, 102, 128–29, 180, 223, 233–40, 277, 280–82

human person: dignity of, 7, 10, 11, 18, 33–35, 72, 74, 78, 85, 94, 131, 138, 195, 197, 204, 210n1, 336–37, 307, 339, 341, 347; material dimension of, 18, 19, 20, 21, 23, 25, 93–95, 99, 197–98, 209, 233, 248; rational nature of, 12, 34, 35, 93, 94, 95, 200, 201, 212, 233–34, 237, 246, 248, 336–37; respect for, 9, 28–30, 33–35, 39, 40–42, 45–46, 47, 48, 50,

94, 156, 198, 200, 201, 206, 209, 210n1, 280, 336–37; as sexual, 91, 92–95, 98, 102; as social, 201, 246, 277–78, 311, 312; spiritual dimension of, 21, 93–95, 99, 102, 197–98, 209, 210n1. *See also* human being

human rights, 31, 34, 45–46, 47, 54, 94, 95, 112, 113, 176, 180, 189, 197, 200, 209, 230–32, 243, 247, 304, 312, 337, 339

Humanae Vitae, On Human Life (Paul VI, 1968), 85n5, 89–90, 99, 100, 103, 104–5n2, 105n4

Humanae Vitae: A Generation Later (Janet E. Smith), 105n4

illness, 129, 130, 150, 159, 185–86, 191n17, 191–92n23, 211, 215, 226, 255, 303, 312–13, 318, 319, 322, 328, 329, 342, 343, 345

in vitro fertilization (IVF), 51, 60, 61–63; Catholic teaching on, 65–66, 68, 69, 77–78, 85, 86n14, 204–5; ethical evaluation of, 69–77; and stem cell research, 213, 216. *See also* artificial fertilization; pronuclear-stage tubal transfer (PROST); zygote intrafallopian tube transfer (ZIFT)

individualism, 30–31, 338, 339, 341, 343

infanticide, 16, 112, 121n8, 121n10, 121–22n17123–124n39

infertility, 50, 61, 62, 63, 78, 80, 82, 100, 110; Catholic response to, 50, 78

Institute of Neurosciences, Bristol, England, 268

integrity, 71, 133, 244–45

"Interim Pastoral Statement on Artificial Nutrition and Hydration" (Texas bishops, 1990), 153–57

International Congress of Catholic Doctors, 66

IVF. *See* in vitro fertilization

Jennings, Bruce, 340

Jennings, Charles, 274

Jerome Lejeune Foundation, 271

Jesus Christ, 1–2, 12, 25–26, 42n11, 77–78, 85, 87n45, 93, 102–3, 104, 112, 113, 122n22, 127, 131–32, 140–41, 166, 202, 301, 304, 309, 318, 326, 335–36; healing ministry of, 1–2, 25–26, 202, 304, 309, 326; redemptive power of his passion, death, and resurrection, 42n11, 127, 131–32, 140–41, 318

Jobes, Nancy Ellen, 143, 168–69n1

John XXIII, 34, 331n4

John Paul II, 1, 7, 9, 10–11, 12, 12–13n9, 34, 45–46, 48, 50, 54, 67, 68, 75, 78, 86n27, 87n39, 87n44, 104–5n2, 113, 120, 127, 129, 131, 134, 140–41, 175, 204–5, 210n4, 304, 307–8, 335, 336, 339, 340

John Paul II Institute for Studies on Marriage and Family, 88n48

Jonas, Hans, 236–37, 239

Joy, Bill, 21

Judeo-Christian tradition, 18, 131

Juengst, Eric, 242–43

justice, 5–6, 7, 46, 95–96, 102, 103, 244, 278, 279, 301–2, 304, 305, 306, 309–33, 335, 336, 337, 346, 347; and health care reform, 309–33

Juvenile Diabetes Research Foundation International, 284n6, 286n26

Kant, Immanuel, 87n44, 276, 337

Kass, Leon, M.D., 25, 27n18, 219, 273

Kavanaugh, John, S.J., 28, 48, 53, 141n2, 191–92n23, 296n97

Keller, Evelyn Fox, 225, 227, 228, 243

Keller, Helen, 19–20, 198

Kelly, Gerald, S.J., 143, 144, 150–52, 153–54, 158, 159, 170n18, 170n20, 171n26

killing, 16, 48, 112–13, 119, 120–21n4, 151, 181, 217, 314, 336; intentional, 18, 114, 122n24, 173–74, 205; in just war, 181; in self-defense, 181. *See also* euthanasia; physician assisted-suicide; suicide

King, Dr. Martin Luther, Jr., 338

Kitcher, Philip, 229, 230

Knox, Stephen, 294–95n73

Kramer, Peter, 244–45, 248

Kuhse, Helga, 189, 191–92n23

Labat, Marie-Louise, 271

Lactantius, 122n18

Langman, Jan, 47

"language of the body" (John Paul II), 68, 71. *See also* "theology of the body, the"

Laughlin, Dr. Mary J., 269

law of unintended consequences, 226, 248

Lee, Patrick, 113–14, 118, 123n35, 123n36, 124n45

Leibrecht, Bishop John, 168–69n1

Levesque, Dr. Michel, 267–68

Listening to Prozac (Peter Kramer), 244–45

Little, Margaret Olivia, 243–44

low tubal ovum transfer (LTOT), 80–81, 84

LTOT. *See* low tubal ovum transfer

Lutheran Charities Foundation, St. Louis, Missouri, 329

Magisterium, 48, 59, 65, 69, 78, 84, 210n1

Maguire, Daniel, 191n19

Manganaro, Sr. Ann, S.L., M.D., 25–26

MANH. *See* medically assisted nutrition and hydration

Maritain, Jacques, 277–78

marital act, 70–71, 77–78, 99–101

marriage, 50, 67, 69, 70–71, 76, 77, 90, 96–97, 98, 99, 100–101; as a sacrament, 102–3; sexual union in, 65, 66, 69, 76

McAfee, Larry James, 168–69n1

McCabe, Herbert, 167

McCarthy, Donald, 83

McClellan, Mark B., M.D., 273–74

McCormick, Patrick, 165–68

McCormick, Richard A., S.J., 74, 75, 76, 314

McFadden, Charles, 150, 151–52, 153–54, 158, 159, 170n18

McGee, Glenn, 288n38

McMahon, James, 123–24n39

Medicaid, 149, 310, 316, 321, 323–24, 326, 330, 331, 345, 346

Medical Embryology (Jan Langman), 47

Medical Ethics (Charles McFadden), 150

Medical Training Nondiscrimination Act (1995), 120n2

medically assisted nutrition and hydration (MANH), 134, 143–72, 175, *see also* withdrawing/withholding medical treatment; changing medical practice in regard to, 162–64; development of Catholic teaching on, 150–57, *see also* Pennsylvania bishops; Texas bishops; excessive burden argument for withdrawing/withholding, 154, 156, 159–60, 175; fatal pathology argument for withdrawing/withholding, 154–55, 157–58; medical history of, 146–49; quality of life argument for withdrawing/withholding, 160–61; spiritual purpose of life argument for withdrawing/withholding, 158–59

Medicare, 310, 320, 323, 329–30, 331, 345

medicine: as an art, 303; not an exact science, 185, 303; regenerative, 209, 282

Medico-Moral Problems (Gerald Kelly, S.J.), 150

Medigap options, 331
Meilaender, Gilbert, 171–72n38
Michigan State University, 291–92n48
Mill, John Stuart, 189, 276
Missouri Legislature, 3
Monsanto, 222
Moore, Keith L., 47
Mosaic law: legal personhood under, 109–10
Moses, 104, 335
Muller, Fabiola, 47–48
Multi-Society Task Force on PVS, 171n31
Murray, John Courtney, 338
Murray, Robert F., 225
Murrell, Dr. Kevin J., 120–21n4

NARAL Pro-Choice America, 119
National Academy of Sciences, 263
National Bioethics Advisory Commission, 86n12, 275
National Catholic Bioethics Center, 2
National Center for Human Genome Research, 220n1
National Conference of Catholic Bishops (now the USCCB), 33, 42n11, 154. See also United States Conference of Catholic Bishops (USCCB)
National Federation of Catholic Physicians Guild, 120–21n4
National Heart, Lung and Blood Institute (of the NIH), 294n71
National Institutes of Health (NIH), 216, 224, 255–62, 266, 273, 275, 288n35, 288n38, 289n40, 290n42, 290–91n43, 297–98n109
National Marrow Donor Program, 285n21
National Parkinson Foundation, Inc., 294n65
National Press Club, Washington, D.C., 342
National Review Online, 260, 271–72
Natural Family Planning (NFP), 55, 89, 99, 102
natural law ethics, 12, 35, 197, 277–79. See also personalism
naturalism, 25, 210n4
Nature, 64, 287n29
Nature Medicine, 268
Nature Neuroscience, 274
Nazi/Nazism, 179, 202, 218; hypothermia research, 218
Netherlands: abuse of legalized euthanasia in, 183–84, 190n11, 190–91n13, 191n17. See also Remmelink study

Neupogen, 270
New England Journal of Medicine, 4, 108, 274
New Testament, 109, 110, 121–22n17
Newcastle University, 294–95n73
Newsweek, 255
Newton, Isaac, 240
Nicodemus, 140–41
Nicomachean Ethics (Aristotle), 105–6n6, 106n10
Nietzsche, Friedrich, 17, 24
NIH. See National Institutes of Health
Noonan, John T., 53–54, 104–5n2, 106n15, 108, 121n12, 281
nuclear transfer technology. See somatic cell nuclear transfer
nutrition and hydration. See medically assisted nutrition and hydration
"Nutrition and Hydration: Moral Considerations" (Pennsylvania bishops, 1992), 153–57, 171n31

O'Connor, Justice Sandra Day, 124n42
O'Neill, William, M.D., 270
O'Rahilly, Ronan, 47–48
O'Rourke, Kevin, O.P., 46–47, 84, 169n2, 331n3
objective moral order, 31–33, 38, 39, 40, 42, 91, 178, 206
obligation to respect human life, 128, 130, 196, 335, 336. See also human life, sanctity of
Office of Technology Assessment, 229
Old Testament, 109. See also Decalogue; Septuagint; Torah
On Being and Essence (De Ente et Essentia, Saint Thomas Aquinas), 49
oocyte, 47, 62, 64, 264, 265, 266; denucleated, 64, 264. See also egg cell; ova/ovum
option for the poor, 313, 320–21, 330
ordinary means of prolonging life. See prolonging life, ordinary means of; withdrawing/withholding medical treatment
Osiris Therapeutics, Inc., 297–98n109
Ottaviani, Cardinal Alfredo, 104–5n2
Our Little Haven, 329
ova/ovum, 21, 47–48, 49, 60, 61, 62, 63, 64, 73, 75, 79, 80–82, 83, 84, 95, 100, 115, 264, 280, 296–97n105. See also egg cell; oocyte

Pacem in Terris, Peace on Earth (Pope John XXIII, 1963), 331–32n4, 336

pain management, 130, 136, 151–52, 319
Palmer, Julie Gage, 227
Pareira, Morton, 147–48, 162, 170n14
Parens, Erik, 227
parthenogenesis, 263, 264–65, 293n59
partial birth abortion, 16, 114
Paul VI, 71, 85n5, 104–5n2, 105n4
Pellegrino, Edmund, M.D., 6, 133, 191n15
Pennsylvania bishops: statements on the use
    of medically assisted nutrition and hydra-
    tion, 144, 153–57, 159, 160, 171n31
Person and the Common Good, The (Jacques
    Maritain), 277–78
personalism, 252, 254, 277–81, 282–83,
    296n97
personhood: Catholic view of, 34, 118–19,
    199, 212; critiques of the functional-
    ist approach to, 19, 20, 118–19, 124n45,
    171–72n38, 278–82; functionalist approach
    to, 16, 28, 116–18, 158–59, 171n37, 279; pro-
    choice positions on, 116–18; pro-life posi-
    tion on, 118–19
"personhood argument": weaknesses of,
    278–82
Philo, 121n8
philosophy: role in Catholic scholarship. *See*
    Catholic scholarship, role of philosophy in
physician-assisted suicide, 4, 18, 174. *See also*
    euthanasia; suicide
Pius IX, 122n19
Pius XII, 65–66, 67, 68, 106n8, 133, 158
Planned Parenthood, 119
Planned Parenthood v. Casey (1992), 31
Plato, 238, 337
Pluhar, Evelyn, 16, 20
pluralism: and arguments for euthanasia,
    177–78, 188; in society, 5, 281, 302
Pontifical Academy for Life, 64, 65, 69
Pontifical Commission for the Apostolate of
    Health Care Workers (1985), 1
Porter, Jean, 74, 87n44, 105n5
Potts, Stephen, 187, 191n21
prenatal diagnosis: and abortion, 20. *See also*
    amniocentesis; genetic screening
Prentice, David, Ph.D., 259, 283, 287n29
President Abraham Lincoln, 31, 337
President George W. Bush, 260, 263, 268, 322
President James A. Garfield, 146
President William J., Clinton, 309, 310
President's Council on Bioethics, 259, 263,
    273, 283, 297–98n109

Princeton University, 15
principle of double-effect 4, 6, 184, 190n4, 218
pro-choice, 51–52, 53, 114, 116–18, 119, 124n45
procreation, 50, 59, 65, 67–69, 70–71, 90,
    95–98, 99–101; versus reproduction, 72–77
Proctor, Robert N., 228
Proctor, Stephen, 294–95n73
pro-life, 3, 45–46, 109, 110–20, 279, 335
prolonging life: extraordinary means of,
    133–34, 150–54, 159–60, 170n18, 170n19,
    174–75, 190n4; and futile medical treat-
    ment, 4, 132–33, 135–36; and grave burden,
    4, 136; ordinary means of, 133–34, 136–37,
    150–54, 155, 159–60, 170n18, 170n19, 174–
    75, 190n4; proportionate versus dispro-
    portionate means of, 134,136, 170n19, 175.
    See also withdrawing/withholding medi-
    cal treatment
pronuclear-stage tubal transfer (PROST), 63
proportionalism, 75, 87n38; repudiated by
    John Paul II, 75, 87n39, 104–5n2
PROST. *See* pronuclear-stage tubal transfer
Public Broadcasting Service (PBS), 21, 23
Pugwash movement, 253

quality of life, 128, 145, 160–61, 162, 171n37,
    186, 188–90, 190n12, 191–92n23, 202, 230.
    See also withdrawing/withholding medi-
    cal treatment, quality of life argument for
Quill, Timothy E., M.D., 4, 6
Quinlan, Karen Ann, 143, 153

Rachels, James, 189, 190n8, 191n22, 191–92n23
Reflections on Cloning (Pontifical Academy
    for Life, 1997), 65, 69
Republic (Plato), 238
Reich, Warren T., 85n1
Reiman, Jeffrey, 118
Reinhardt, Judge Stephen, 17, 18
relativism, 177–78, 189–90, 232, 277, 339
religious voice: marginalization of, 3–6
Remmelink study, 190–91n13
reproduction, 45–57, 95–96; agamic, 60, 64;
    asexual, 64, 92–93, 115, 263; versus procre-
    ation, 72–77. *See also* cloning; reproduc-
    tive cloning; sex; sexual intercourse
reproductive cloning, 64, 69, 76, 92–93, 115,
    263, 293n61, 297n108. *See also* cloning;
    somatic cell nuclear transfer
Reproductive Health Services, 4, 52
reproductive technologies, 59–88; and sur-

rogacy, 61, 63, 76, 87n38. *See also* artificial fertilization; artificial insemination; assisted reproduction; cloning; gamete intrafallopian tube transfer (GIFT); in vitro fertilization; low tubal ovum transfer (LTOT); pronuclear-stage tubal transfer (PROST); reproduction, agametic, asexual; reproductive cloning; sperm intrafallopian tube transfer (SIFT); tubal ovum transfer with sperm (TOTS); zygote intrafallopian tube transfer (ZIFT)

respect for persons, 28–42, 45–46; in the Catholic tradition, 33–35

Rethinking Life and Death (Peter Singer), 15

Reuters Health, 270

right to life, 7, 45–46, 54, 120, 122n21, 176, 181, 210n1, 304

Robertson, John A., 227, 229, 230

Roe v. Wade (1973), 3, 53, 114, 117; trimester framework in, 114, 123n28, 124n42

Roslin Institute, Edinburgh, Scotland, 64, 264, 292n50

"Rule of Double Effect: Clearing Up the Double Talk, The" (Edmund Pellegrino, M.D. and, Daniel P. Sulmasy, O.F.M., M.D.), 6

Russell, Bertrand, 253

Saint Augustine, 87n30

Saint Cyprian, 122n18

Saint Luke's Episcopal Hospital, Houston, Texas, 271

Saint Paul, 35, 46, 104, 121n12, 336

Saint Peter, 113

Saint Thomas (the Apostle), 26

Saint Thomas Aquinas, 2, 35, 49, 87n33, 105n4, 105–6n6, 106n9, 106n11, 158, 244, 252, 277, 336

Saint Vincent DePaul, 168

Salley, Nathan, 268–69

Salvifici Doloris, On the Christian Meaning of Human Suffering (John Paul II, 1984), 131, 140–41

Scalia, Justice Antonin, 52

Schiavo, Terri, 171, 180

SCHIP. *See* State Children's Health Insurance Program

SCIDS. *See* severe combined immune deficiency syndrome

Science, 260

Scientific American, 275

scientific research: Catholic attitude towards, 195–96, 200, 210n1; limits of, 196, 253–54; materialistic reductionism in, 102, 197

SCNT. *See* somatic cell nuclear transfer

Second Vatican Council, 34, 112, 303

secular culture/society, 3, 5, 33, 196, 207

secular humanism, 2, 10, 177, 315

Seifert, Josef, 79, 82, 84

self-awareness, 116, 118, 279

self-determination, 29, 30, 31, 32, 35, 36–37, 38–39, 40–41, 42, 72, 87n44, 153, 180. *See also* autonomy; choice; free will

self-development, 48, 54, 280–81

Septuagint, 109, 111, 121n8

severe combined immune deficiency syndrome (SCIDS), 241

sex: extramarital, 99, 105n3; marital, 71, 76, 97, 98, 99, 101; teleology of, 54, 71, 91, 92–93, 96, 97, 98, 99, 101, 102

sexual intercourse, 89, 92, 93, 95, 97; inseparability of the unitive and procreative meanings of, 65, 68, 70, 71, 85n5, 90, 99–101; procreative meaning of, 59, 65, 67, 68, 69, 71, 72–78, 95–96, 100, 106n14; unitive meaning of, 65, 66, 67, 69, 71, 72, 73, 76, 77, 79, 93, 96–98, 100, 101, 106n13

Shannon, Thomas A., 74, 87n38

Shettles, Dr. Landrum, 117–18

SIFT. *See* sperm intrafallopian tube transfer

Simon of Cyrene, 85

Simon, Yves R., 223, 234–35, 237, 238–39, 245–46, 249n6, 250n41

Singer, Peter, 15–16, 18, 19, 20, 25, 118, 279

Smith, Dr. Pamela, 121n4

Smith, Janet E., 105n4

Smith, Wesley J., 260, 271–72

Social Security, 321

Sokolowski, Robert, 231

somatic cell, 64, 115, 199, 241, 264, 266

somatic cell nuclear transfer (SCNT), 64, 86n12, 115–16, 264–66, 274, 292n49, 293n61; basic technique, 264, 292n49; Honolulu technique, 264; Roslin technique, 264. *See also* cloning; reproductive cloning; therapeutic cloning

soul: Catholic view of, 46–47, 94–95, 100, 106n8, 197, 210n1. *See also* embryology, and the question of ensoulment; ensoulment

Spemann, Hans, 264, 292n49

sperm: collecting through masturbation, 60, 62, 64, 73, 83, 84

sperm donor/vendor, 61, 63
sperm intrafallopian tube transfer (SIFT), 63
Star Link corn, 241–42
State Children's Health Insurance Program
    (SCHIP), 309, 310, 316, 321, 323–24, 330, 331
stem cell line: embryonic, 257, 262–63, 275,
    290–91n43
stem cell research. See adult stem cell re-
    search; embryonic stem cell research
stem cells, 196, 205, 213–14, 216–18, 255–56,
    258–60, 283; multipotent, 259, 288n39,
    293n61; pluripotent, 213, 216, 257, 258,
    259–60, 262, 288n38, 293n61; sources of,
    213–14, 256–58; totipotent, 258–59. See also
    adult stem cells; embryonic stem cells
Stenbegr v. Carhart, 123n30
Steptoe, Patrick, 61
Stevens, Justice John Paul, 3–4
stewardship of scarce resources, 219, 346, 347
suffering: Catholic response to, 1, 127, 130–32,
    140–41, 168, 305; emotional aspects of, 129,
    137, 189, 303; as justification for euthanasia/
    suicide, 128, 135, 173–74, 180–81, 184, 185,
    191n17, 191n22; salvific nature of, 2, 131–32,
    140–41; transformative nature of, 131
suicide, 176, 179–80, 189, 191–92n23; at
    the end-of-life, 130, 174, 180, 186, 188,
    190–91n13. See also euthanasia; physician-
    assisted suicide
Sullivan, Annie, 20
Sullivan, Joseph, 151
Sulmasy, Daniel P., O.F.M., M.D., 6
Summa Theologiae (Saint Thomas Aquinas),
    87n33, 105–6n6, 106n10
Sun Microsystems, 21
Susman, Frank, 52–53, 54
Switzer, Sara Marie, 117

Talmud: legal personhood under, 109–10
Tamika, 26
Tarnier, Stephane, 169n9
Taylor, Charles, 25, 38
Teachings of the Apostles, 110
Ten Commandments, 46. See also Decalogue
Teresa, Mother, 25, 341
Texas bishops: statements on the use of
    medically assisted nutrition and hydra-
    tion, 144, 153–57
"theology of the body, the" (John Paul II),
    86n27. See also "language of the body"

therapeutic cloning: for harvesting embry-
    onic stem cells, 197, 204, 206, 262–66,
    293n61; misnomer, 263, 283; as unethical,
    204–5, 275–82. See also cloning; somatic
    cell nuclear transfer
Third Reich, 223
Thompson, Judith Jarvis, 118
Thomson, Dr. James, 260, 284n7
Time, 255
Torah, 110
Tolstoy, Leo, 22
Tonti-Filippini, Nicholas, 84, 88n57
totipotent cell, 116, 213, 258–59. See also stem
    cells, totipotent
TOTS. See tubal ovum transfer with sperm
trophoblast, 256, 257
"troubled dream of life" (Daniel Callahan),
    22–23
tubal ovum transfer with sperm (TOTS), 84
tube feeding: medical history of, 146–49.
    See also medically assisted nutrition and
    hydration
Turner, Dennis, 267
Twilight of the Gods (Friedrich Nietzsche), 17

umbilical cord blood stem cells, 205, 206,
    257, 268–69, 293n61, 294n72, 294–95n73
unborn human beings: moral status of, 3, 7,
    16–17, 51–53, 54, 110–20, 124n41
undifferentiated cells, 116, 255–56. See also
    stem cells; unspecialized cells
Unified Parkinson's Disease Rating Scale, 267
uninsured, 301, 305, 316–17, 318, 324–25, 327,
    328, 344, 346
United States Conference of Catholic Bish-
    ops (USCCB), 272. See also National Con-
    ference of Catholic Bishops
United States Congress, 20, 229, 320, 323, 330
United States Food and Drug Administra-
    tion (FDA), 203, 268, 269, 270, 273,
    290–91n43, 297–98n109
United States Supreme Court, 3, 27n6, 31, 52,
    114, 117–18, 123n28, 184, 249n5
unity of truth, 8, 9
universal health insurance, 310, 315–19, 320,
    321, 330, 346
University of Hawaii, 264
University of Pennsylvania, 169n7, 288n38
University of Utah, 272, 291–92n48
University of Wisconsin, 260

unspecialized cells, 255. *See also* stem cells;
    undifferentiated cells
Usala, Dr. Anton-Lewis, 272
utilitarian ethics, 181, 183, 191n14, 254, 275–77.
    See also consequentialism

value of life, 176–77, 179–81, 186, 188–90
Van Nostrand's Scientific Encyclopedia (ed. by
    Douglas Considine), 47
Vanier, Jean, 25
Vatican II. *See* Second Vatican Council
Veritatis Splendor, The Splendor of Truth
    (John Paul II, 2003), 75, 87n39, 104–5n2,
    210n4, 336, 339
Vesper Society, San Francisco, California, 329
viability, 51, 114, 116, 117–18, 124n41, 124n42;
    as contingent on technology, 117–18,
    124n42, 279
vice, 91, 99, 101
Vilmut, Jan (*also* Ian Wilmut), 64, 69, 292n50
"virgin birth" method of cloning. *See* parthe-
    nogenesis
Virgin Mary, 110
virtue, 91, 95, 96, 98, 101, 338, 340
virtue ethics, 105n5, 276
Vitoria, Francisco de, 2

Wadlington, Walter, 61
Wall Street Journal, 261
Walters, Leroy, 227
Warren, Mary Ann, 16, 118, 123–24n39

Watson, James, 222
We Hold These Truths (John Courtney Mur-
    ray), 338
Webster v. Reproductive Health Services
    (1989), 3, 51–52
Wheat Ridge Ministries, Itasca, Illinois, 329
White, Justice Byron, 124n45
Williams, William, 164–65
Wired, 21
withdrawing/withholding medical treat-
    ment, 2, 18, 133, 135–36, 137–38, 145, 150–61,
    168, 171n37, 174, 175; excessive burden ar-
    gument for, 4, 130, 132, 133–37, 138, 154, 156,
    159–60, 170n19, 174–75; fatal pathology
    argument for, 135, 136–37, 154–55, 157–58;
    quality of life argument for, 160–61; spiri-
    tual purpose of life argument for, 158–59
womb: artificial, 93, 117
World Federation of the Catholic Medical
    Associations, 271
World Health Organization (WHO), 224–25

xenotransplantation: fear of transferring
    animal viruses into humans, 290n42

Zerhouni, Elias A., M.D., 273
ZIFT. *See* zygote intrafallopian tube transfer
zygote, 47–48, 62, 63, 73, 205, 209, 233,
    258–59, 278–81, 282, 296–97n105; respect
    for, 47, 205, 209, 282
zygote intrafallopian tube transfer (ZIFT), 63

Medicine, Health Care, & Ethics: Catholic Voices was designed and typeset in Minion by Kachergis Book Design of Pittsboro, North Carolina. It was printed on 60-pound Natural Offset and bound by McNaughton & Gunn of Saline, Michigan.